The king runs

Shaking off his shadows,
His armor clanking,
Scattering bones,
Tasting flesh and blood,
Crushing groaning hearts,

Stepping in alone
To a distant beyond.

BLEACH 32 HOWLING

STARS AND

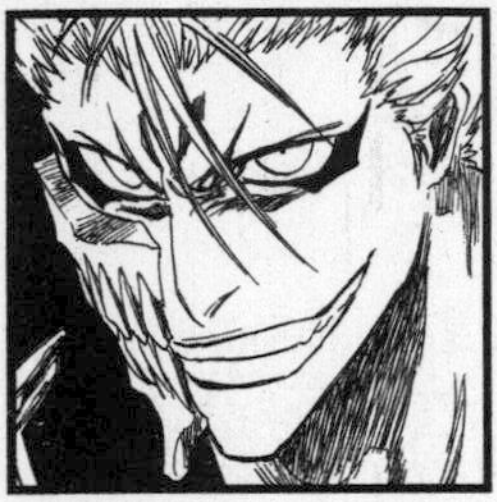

黒崎一護
Ichigo Kurosaki

Grimmjow
グリムジョー

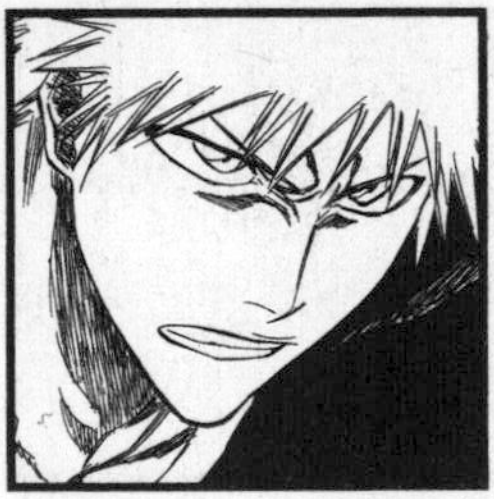

plot

When high school student Ichigo Kurosaki meets Soul Reaper Rukia Kuchiki his life is changed forever. Soon Ichigo is a soul-cleansing Soul Reaper too, and he finds himself having adventures, as well as problems, that he never would have imagined. Now Ichigo and his friends must stop renegade Soul Reaper Aizen and his army of Arrancars from destroying the Soul Society and wiping out KarakuraTown as well.

When Orihime disappears into Hueco Mundo, Ichigo infiltrates Aizen's stronghold Las Noches with his friends to rescue her, but some harrowing battles with the Espadas leave them defeated. As Ichigo lies seriously injured, Grimmjow appears with Orihime and orders her to heal Ichigo so the two can fight a fair battle.

BLEACH ALL

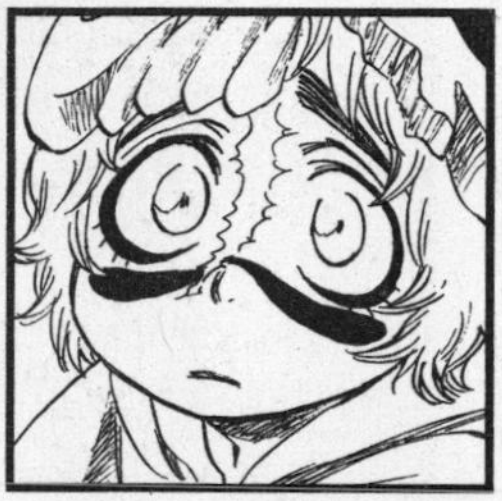

井上織姫

Orihime Inoue

Nel

ネル

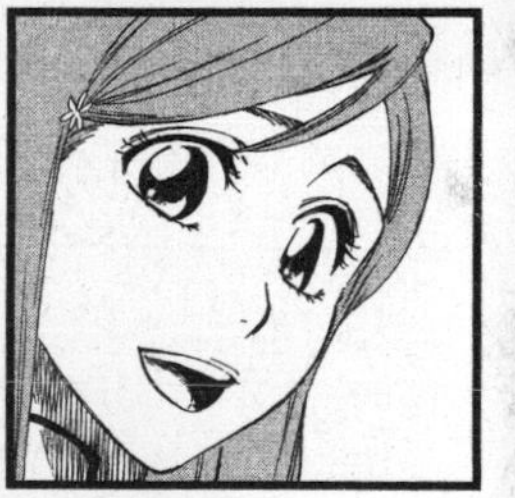

STORIES

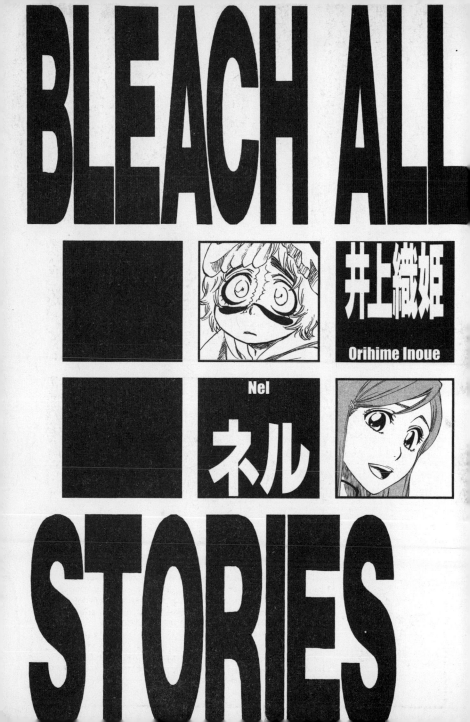

BLEACH 32

HOWLING

Contents

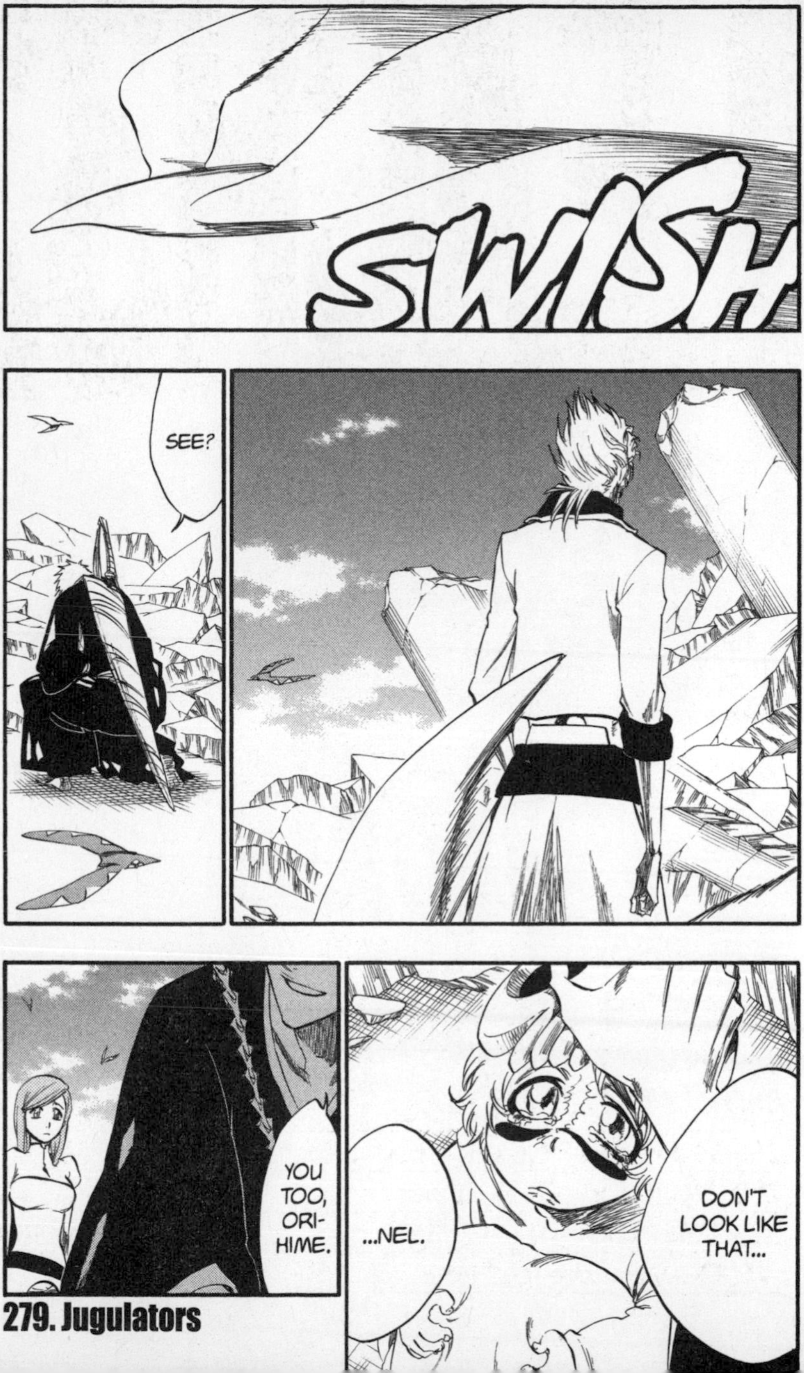
SWISH
SEE?
DON'T LOOK LIKE THAT...
...NEL.
YOU TOO, ORI-HIME.

279. Jugulators

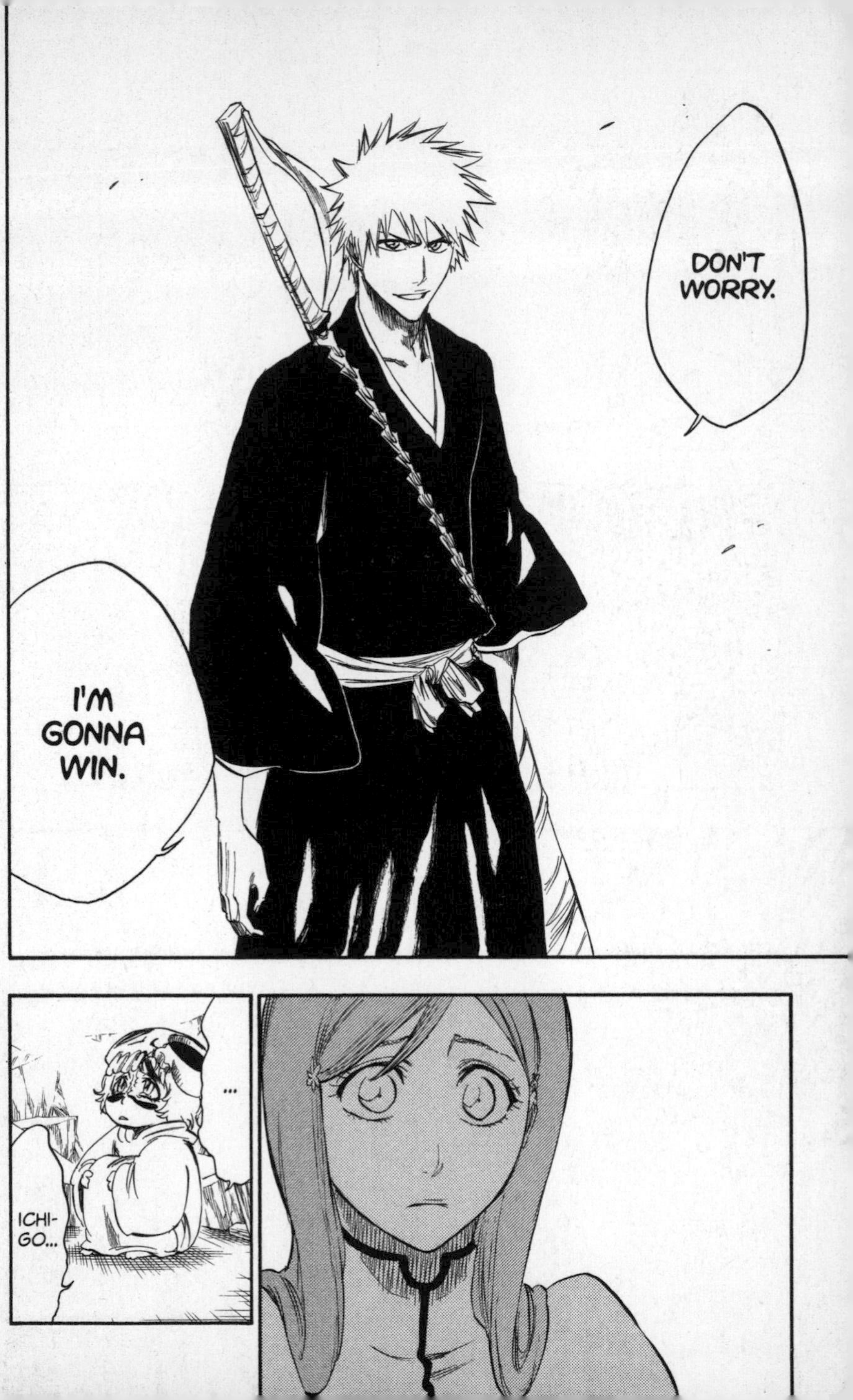
DON'T WORRY.
I'M GONNA WIN.
...
ICHI-GO...

READ THIS WAY

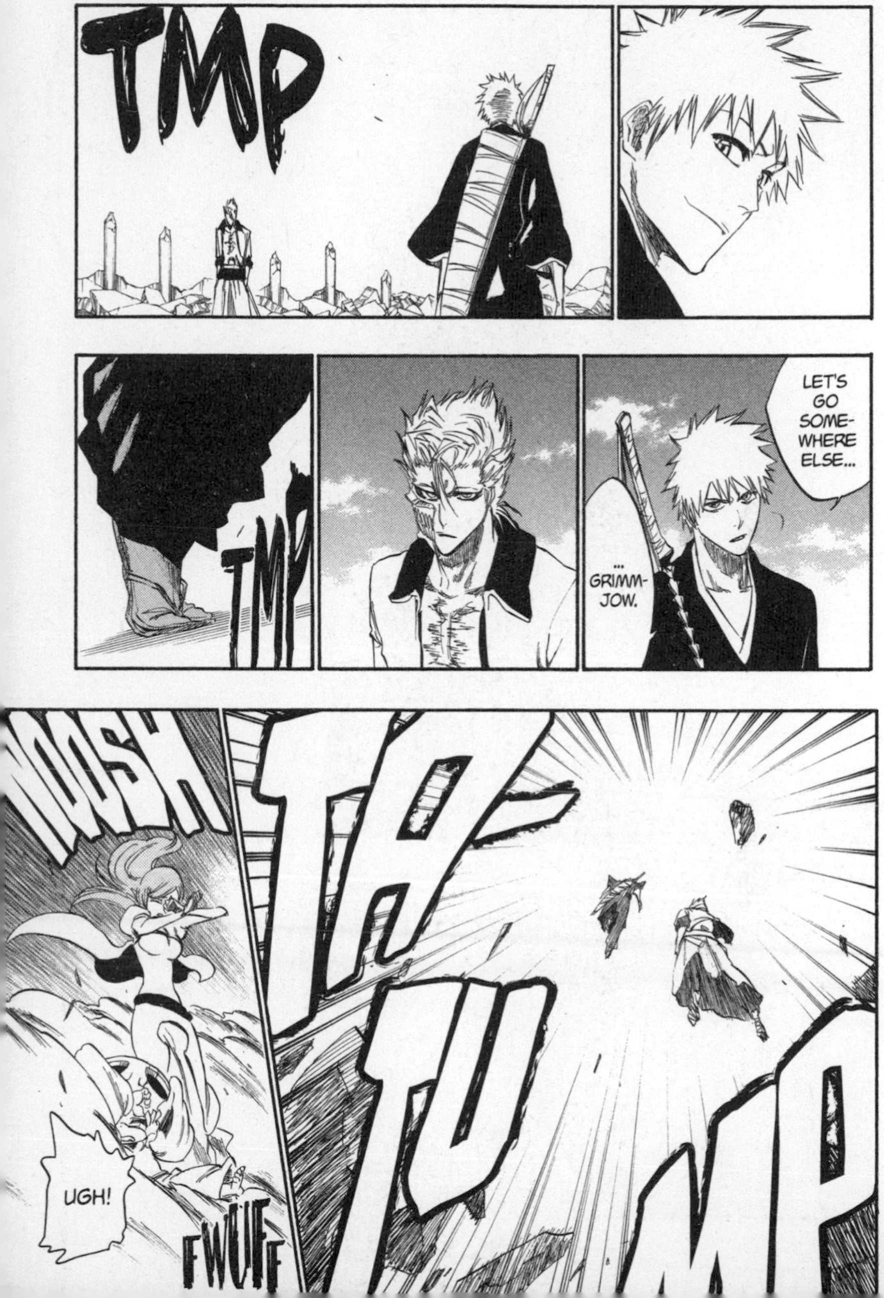
TMP
LET'S GO SOMEWHERE ELSE...
... GRIMMJOW.
TMP
TA-TUMP
UGH!
FWUFF

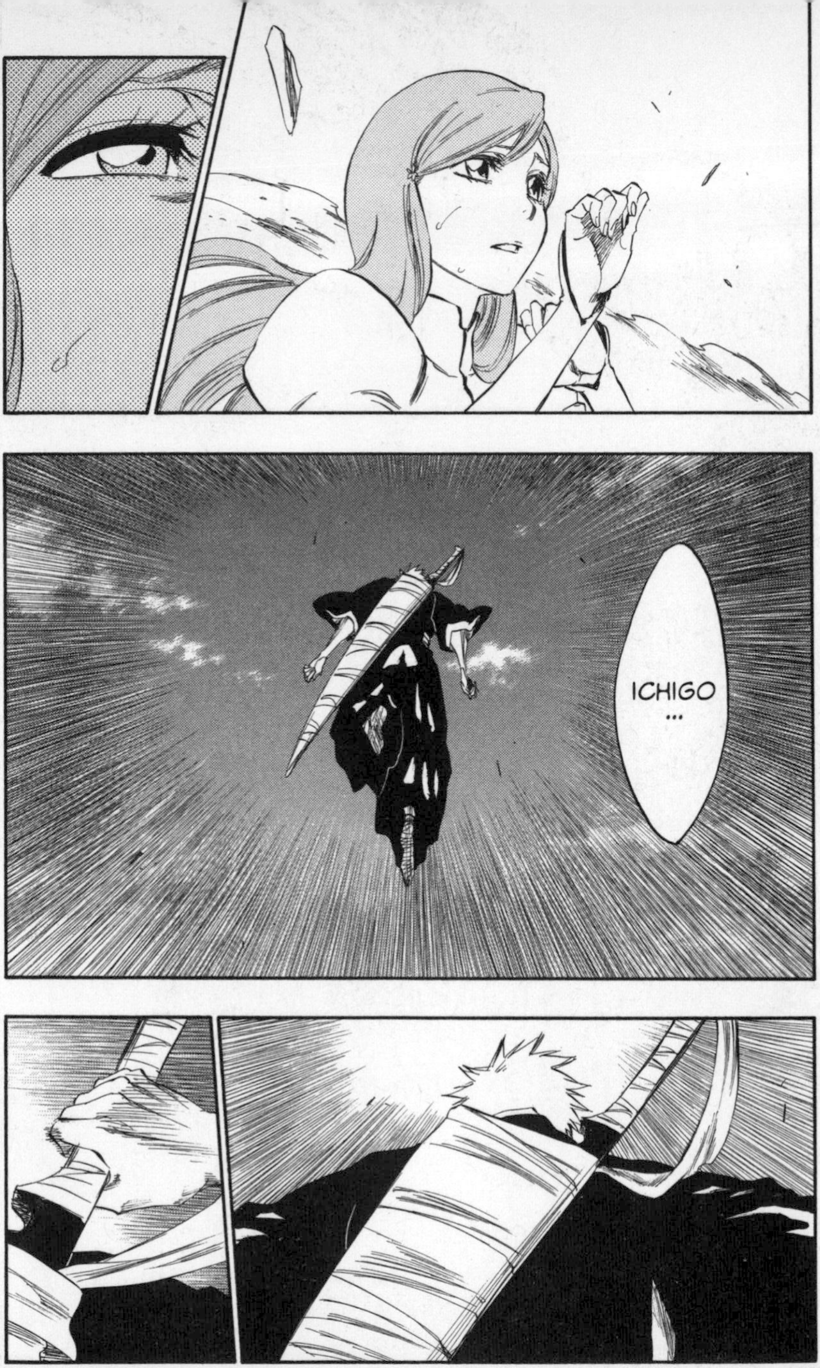
ICHIGO
...

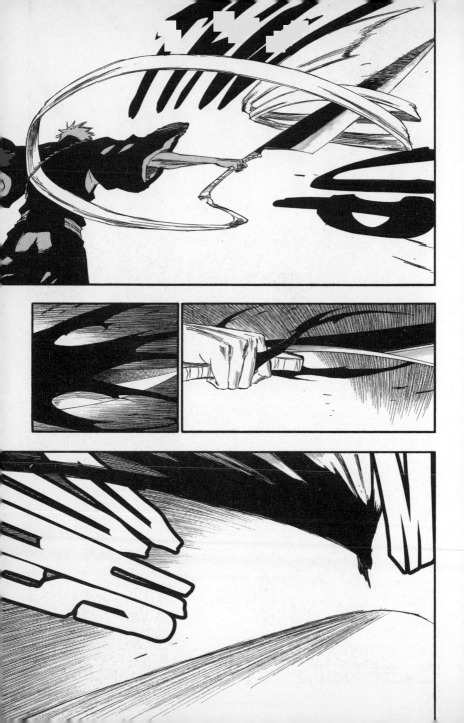

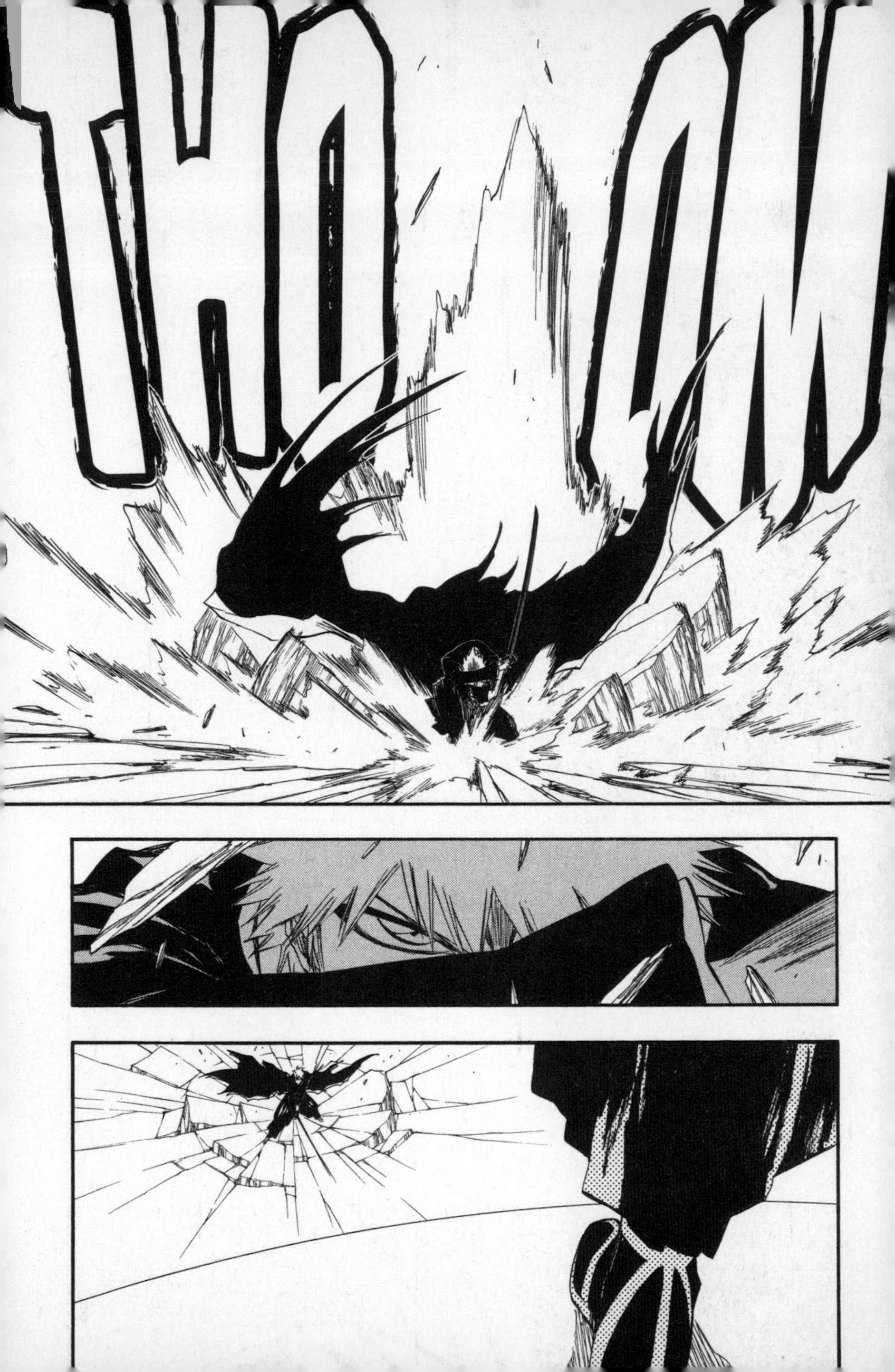
THOOM

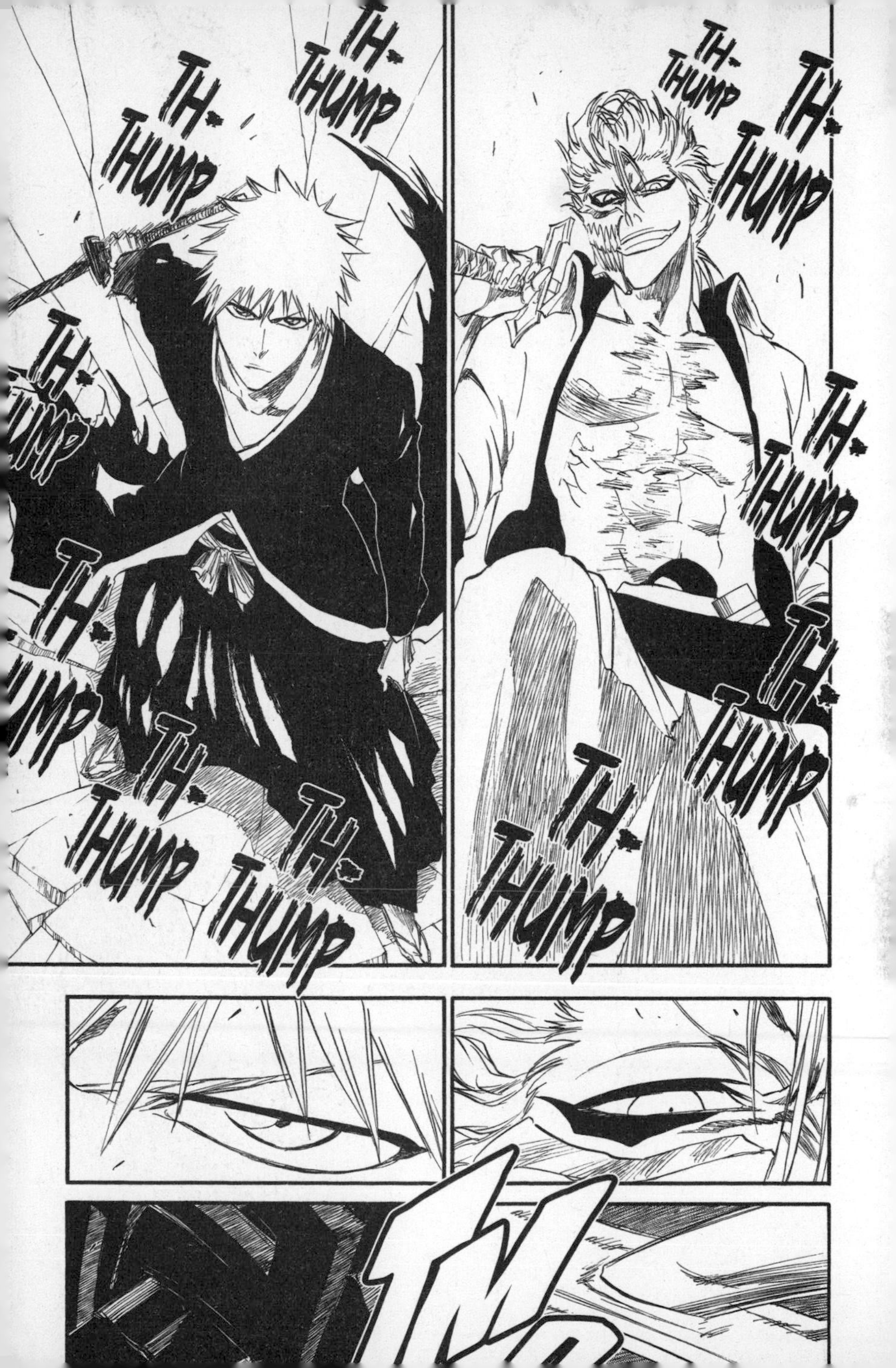

TH-THUMP
TH-THUMP
TH-THUMP
TH-THUMP
TH-THUMP
TH-THUMP
TH-THUMP
TH-THUMP
TH-THUMP
TH-THUMP
TH-THUMP

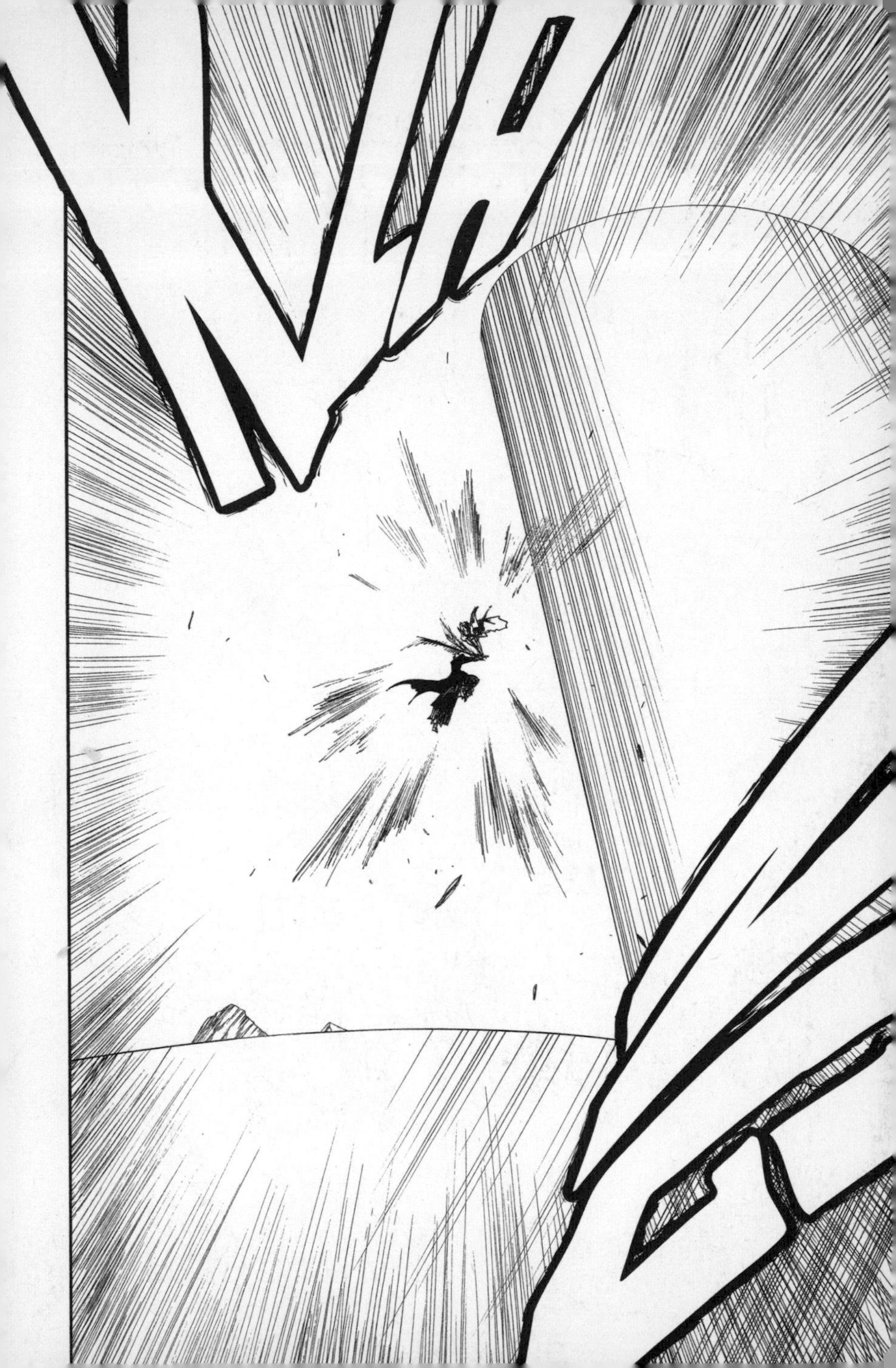

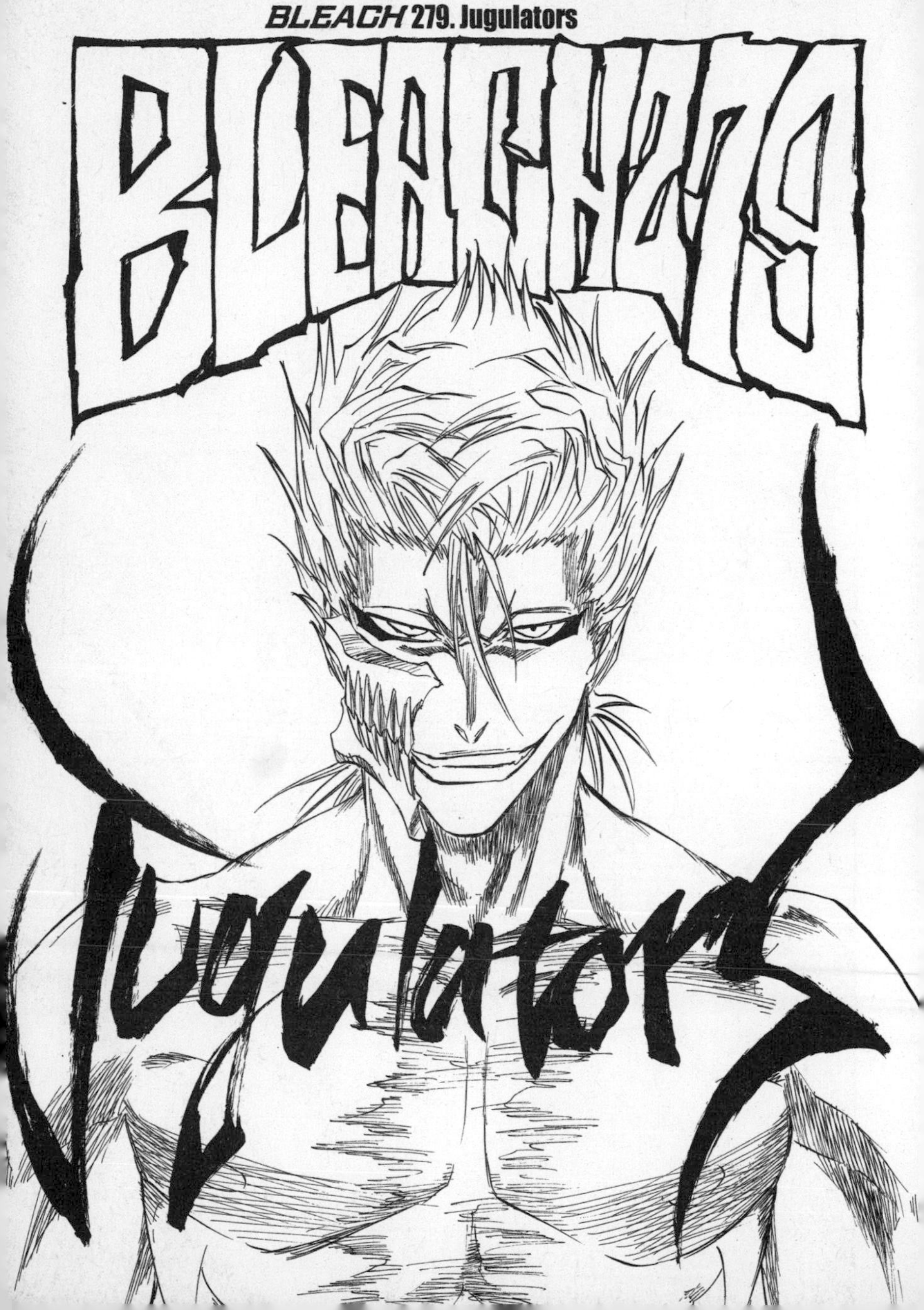
BLEACH 279. Jugulators
BLEACH 279
Jugulators

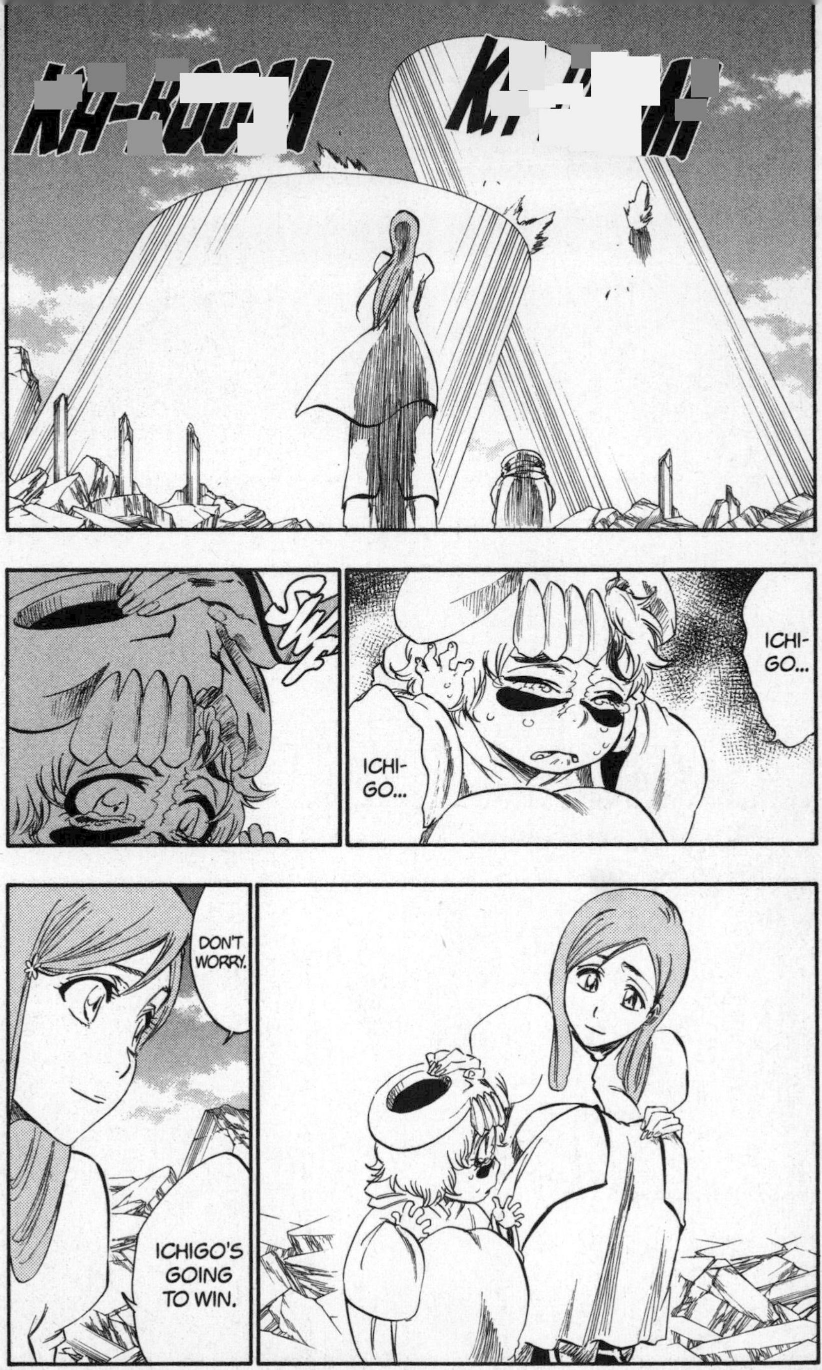
ICHI-GO...
ICHI-GO...
DON'T WORRY.
ICHIGO'S GOING TO WIN.

READ THIS WAY

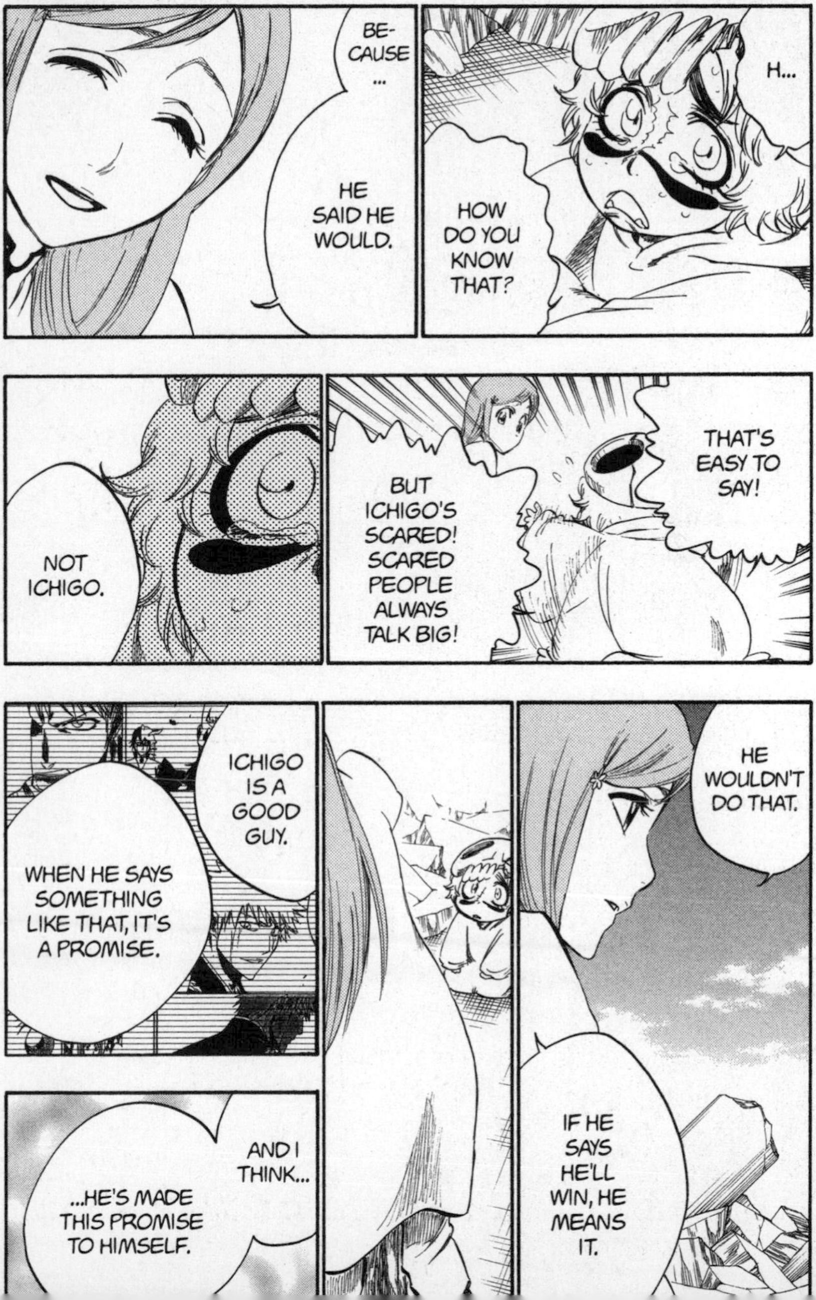
H...
HOW DO YOU KNOW THAT?
BE-CAUSE...
HE SAID HE WOULD.
THAT'S EASY TO SAY!
BUT ICHIGO'S SCARED! SCARED PEOPLE ALWAYS TALK BIG!
NOT ICHIGO.
HE WOULDN'T DO THAT.
IF HE SAYS HE'LL WIN, HE MEANS IT.
ICHIGO IS A GOOD GUY.
WHEN HE SAYS SOMETHING LIKE THAT, IT'S A PROMISE.
AND I THINK...
...HE'S MADE THIS PROMISE TO HIMSELF.

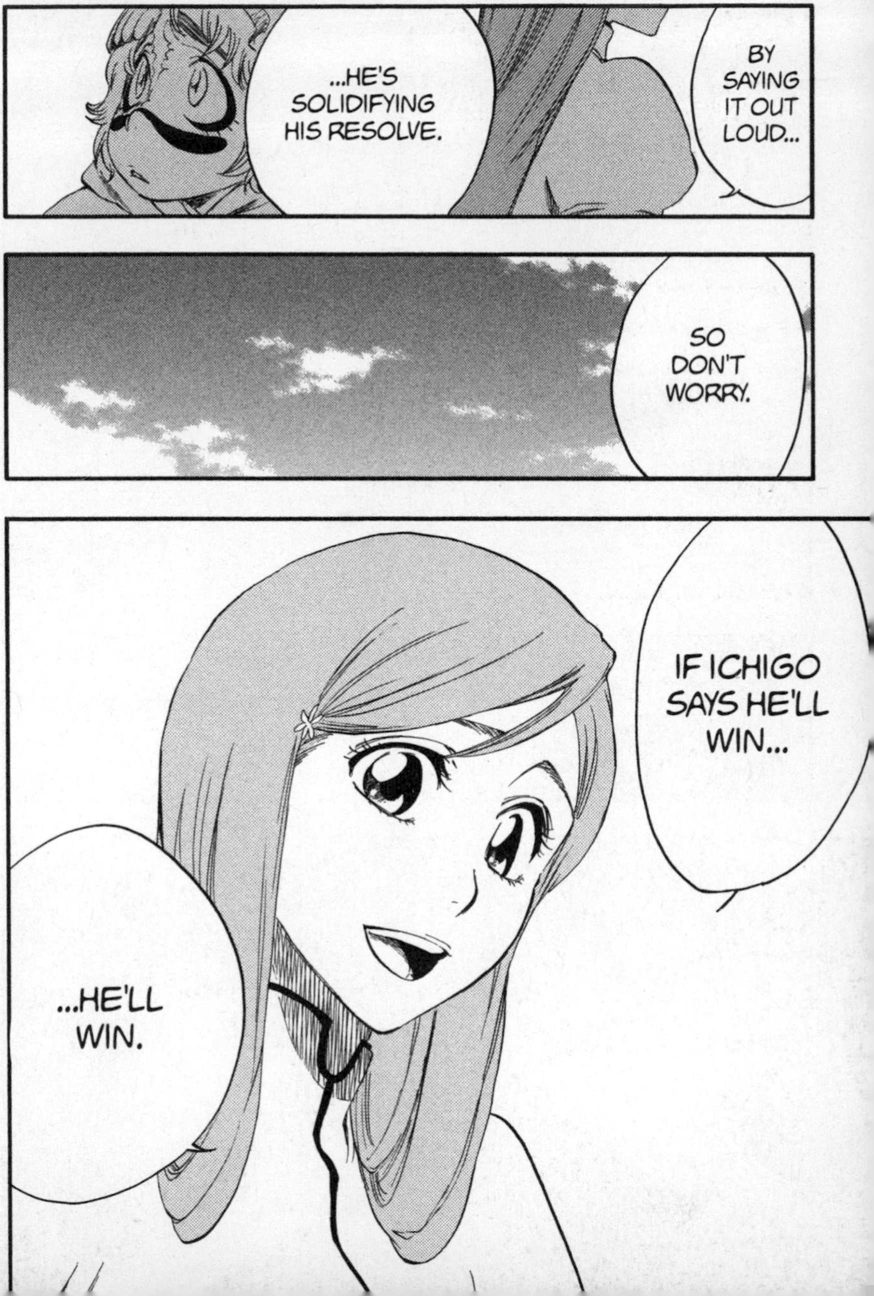
BY SAYING IT OUT LOUD...
...HE'S SOLIDIFYING HIS RESOLVE.
SO DON'T WORRY.
IF ICHIGO SAYS HE'LL WIN...
...HE'LL WIN.

NOW...

...AND WAIT.

...LET'S HAVE FAITH IN HIM...

KRK

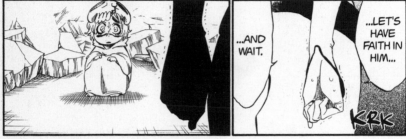

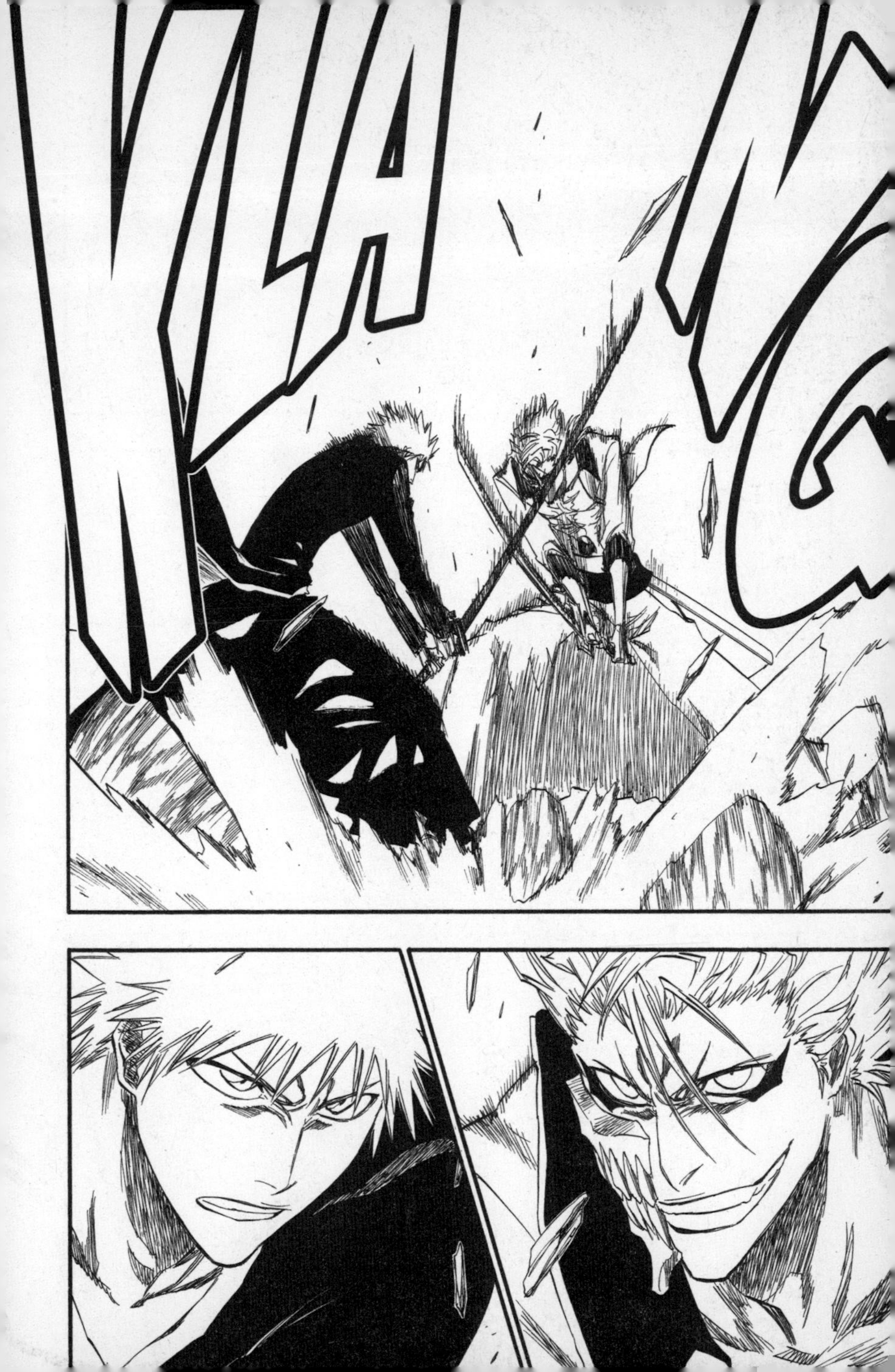
VLA

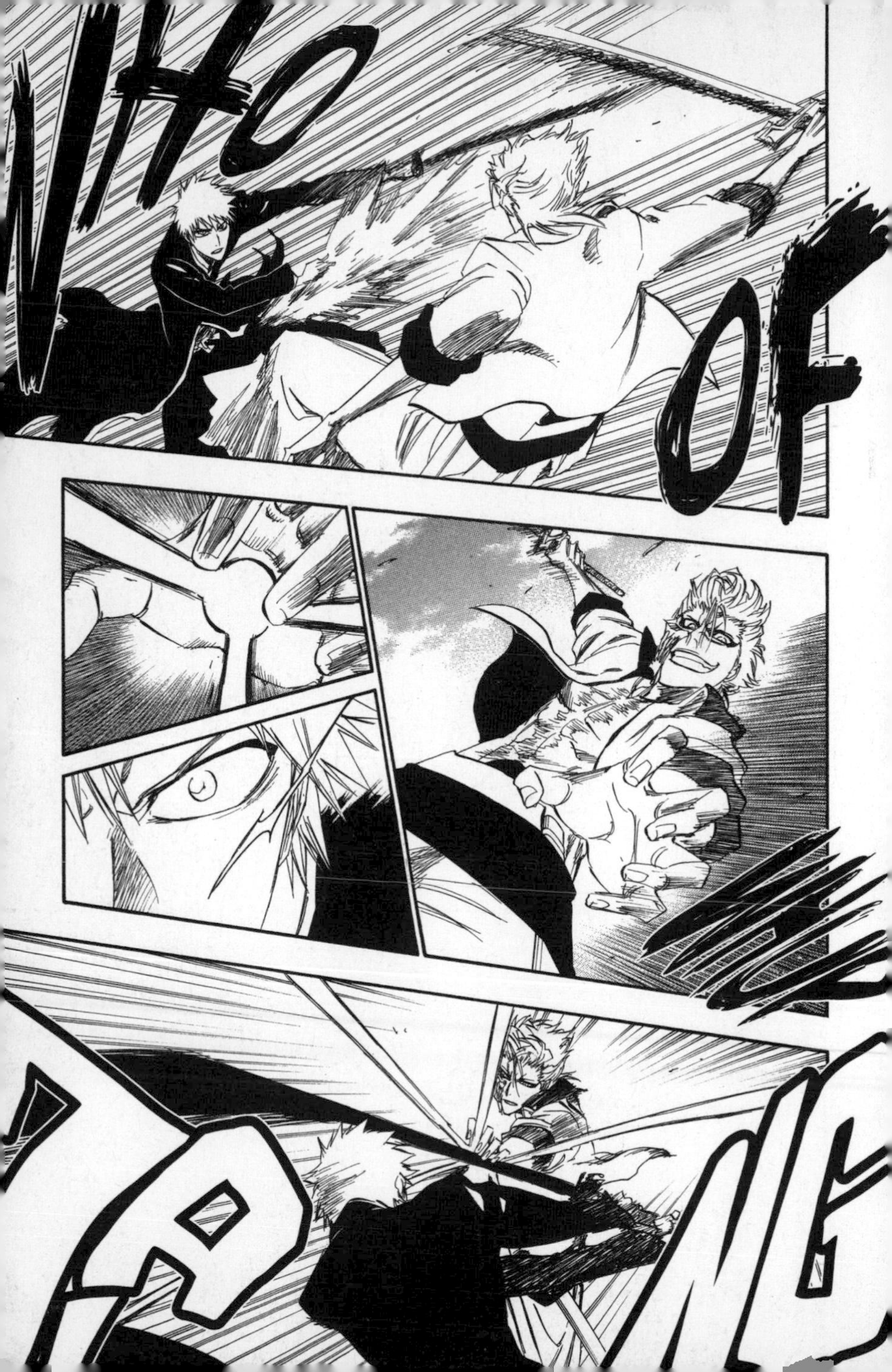

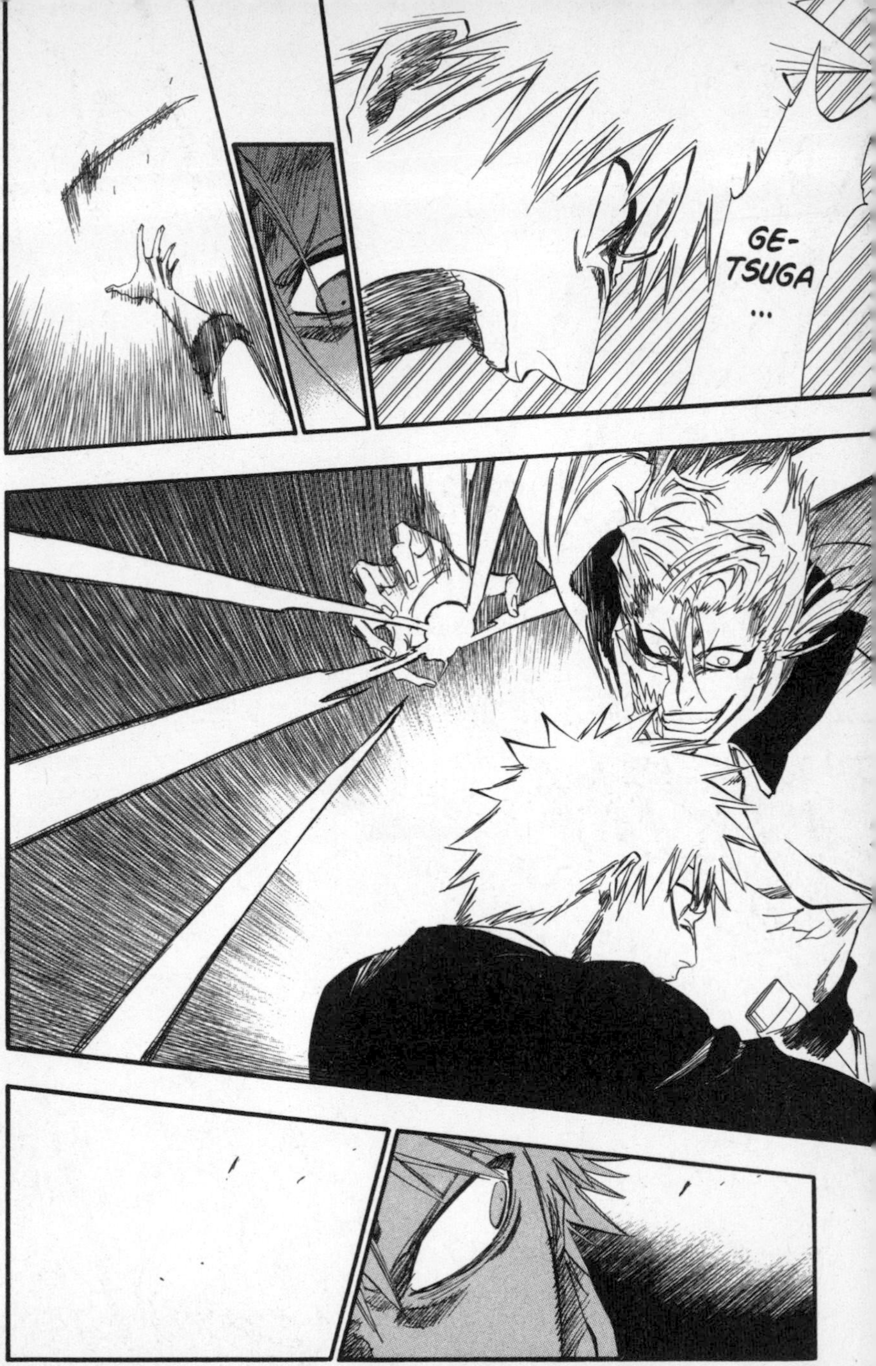
GE-
TSUGA
...

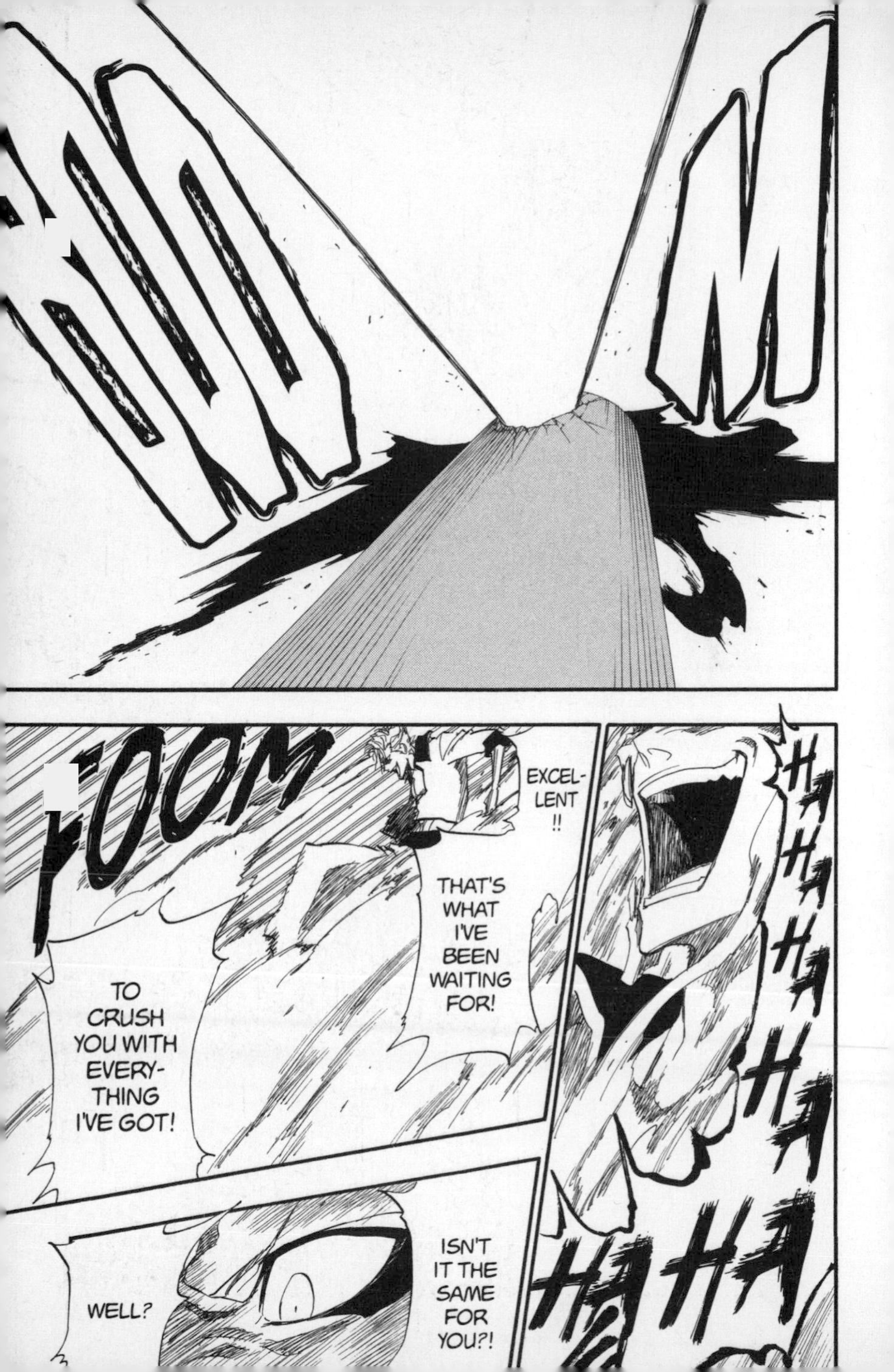
HAHAHAHAHAHAHA
EXCEL-LENT!!
THAT'S WHAT I'VE BEEN WAITING FOR!
TO CRUSH YOU WITH EVERY-THING I'VE GOT!
ISN'T IT THE SAME FOR YOU?!
WELL?

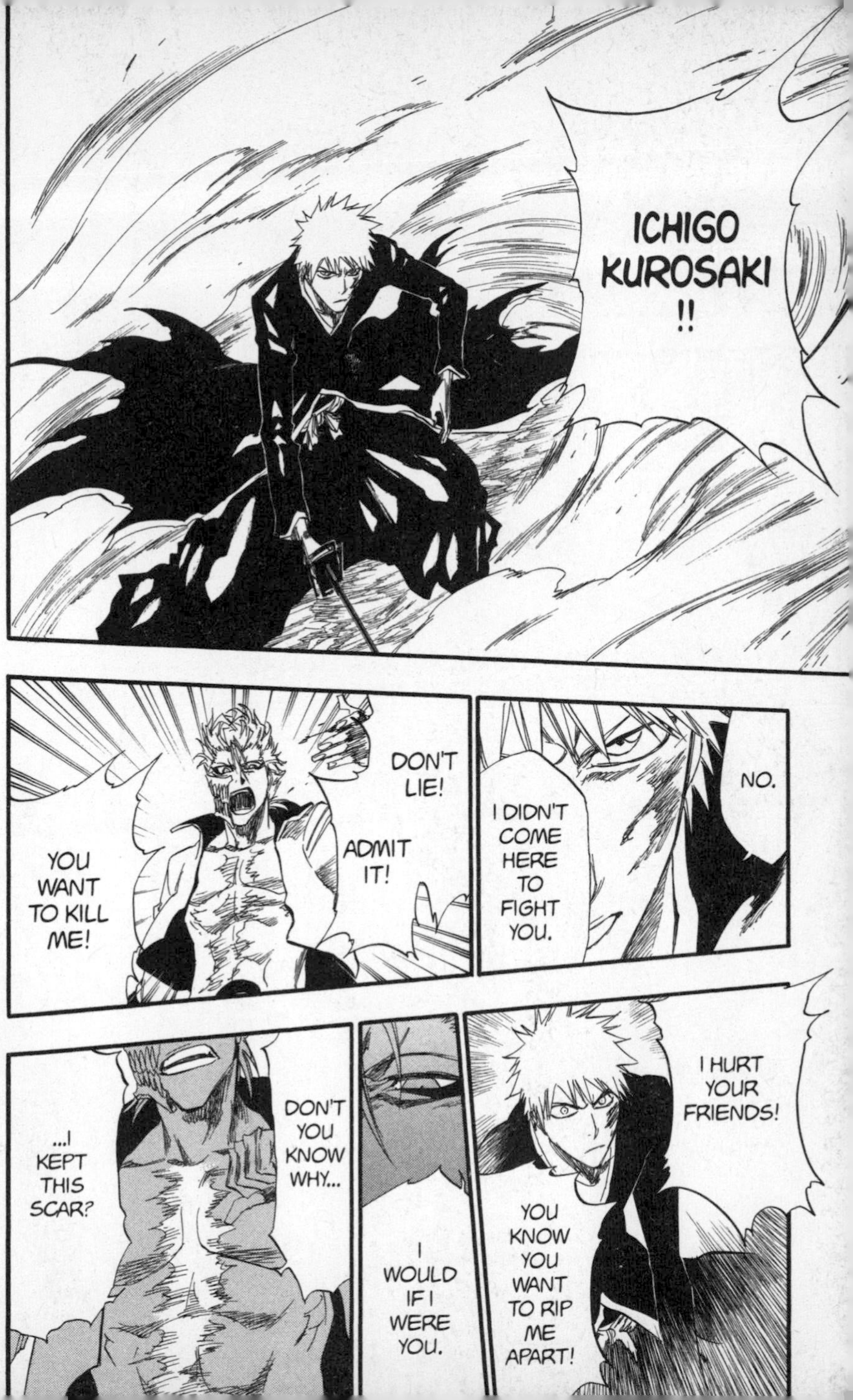
ICHIGO KUROSAKI !!
NO.
I DIDN'T COME HERE TO FIGHT YOU.
DON'T LIE!
ADMIT IT!
YOU WANT TO KILL ME!
I HURT YOUR FRIENDS!
YOU KNOW YOU WANT TO RIP ME APART!
I WOULD IF I WERE YOU.
DON'T YOU KNOW WHY...
...I KEPT THIS SCAR?

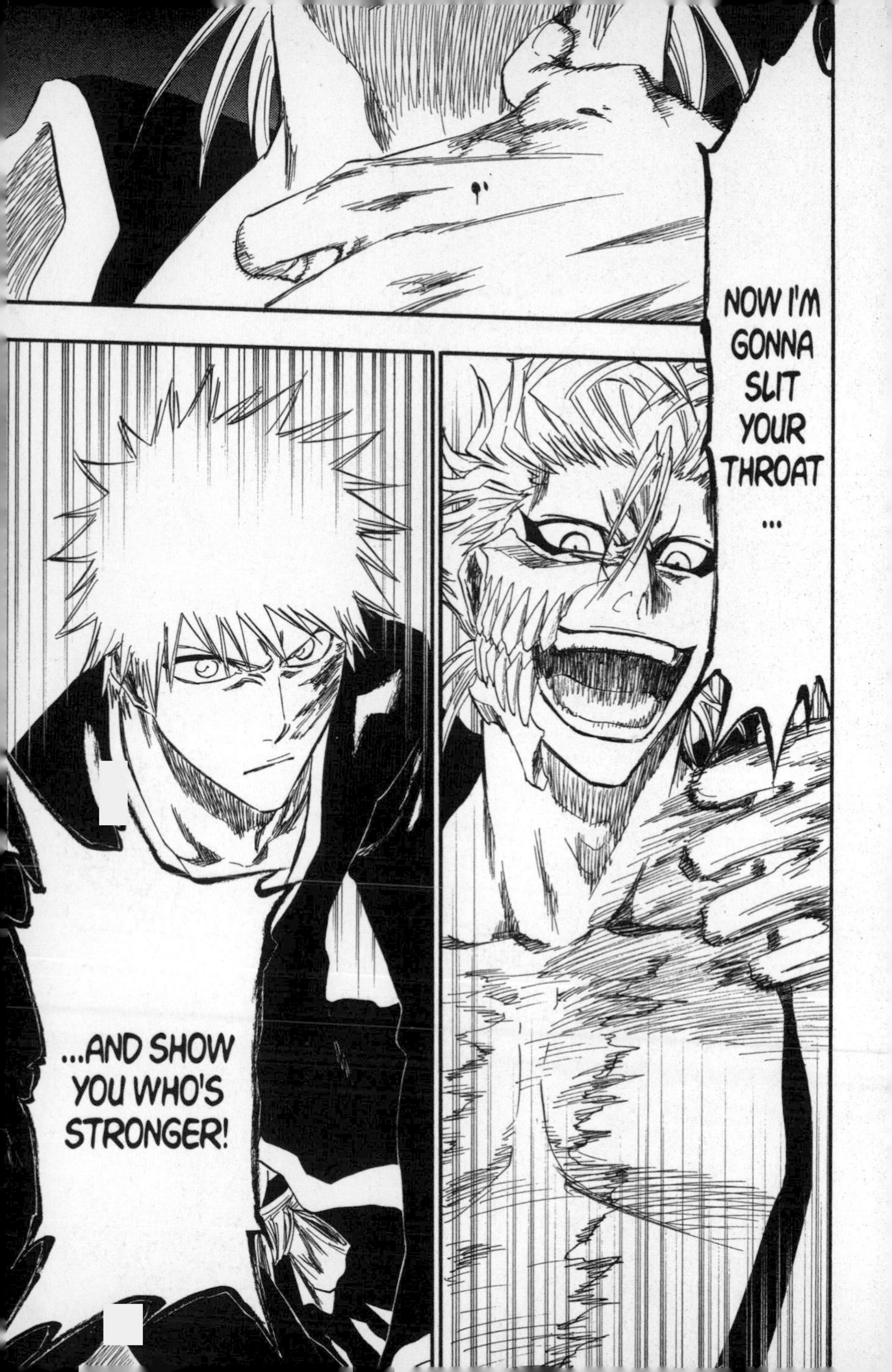
NOW I'M GONNA SLIT YOUR THROAT ...
...AND SHOW YOU WHO'S STRONGER!

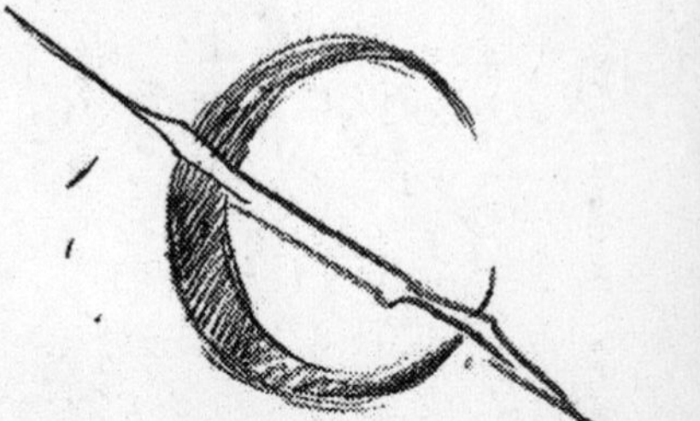

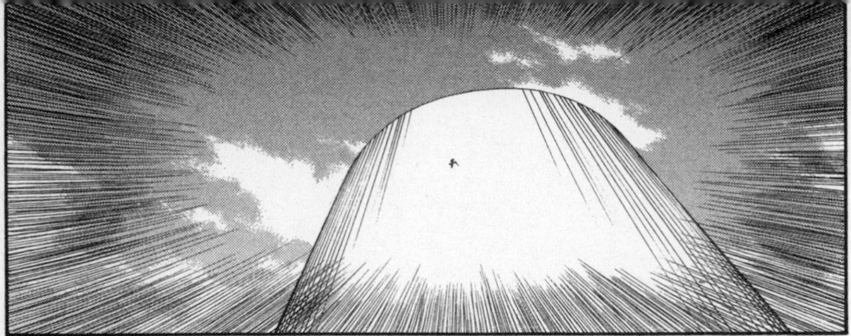

280. Jugulators 2

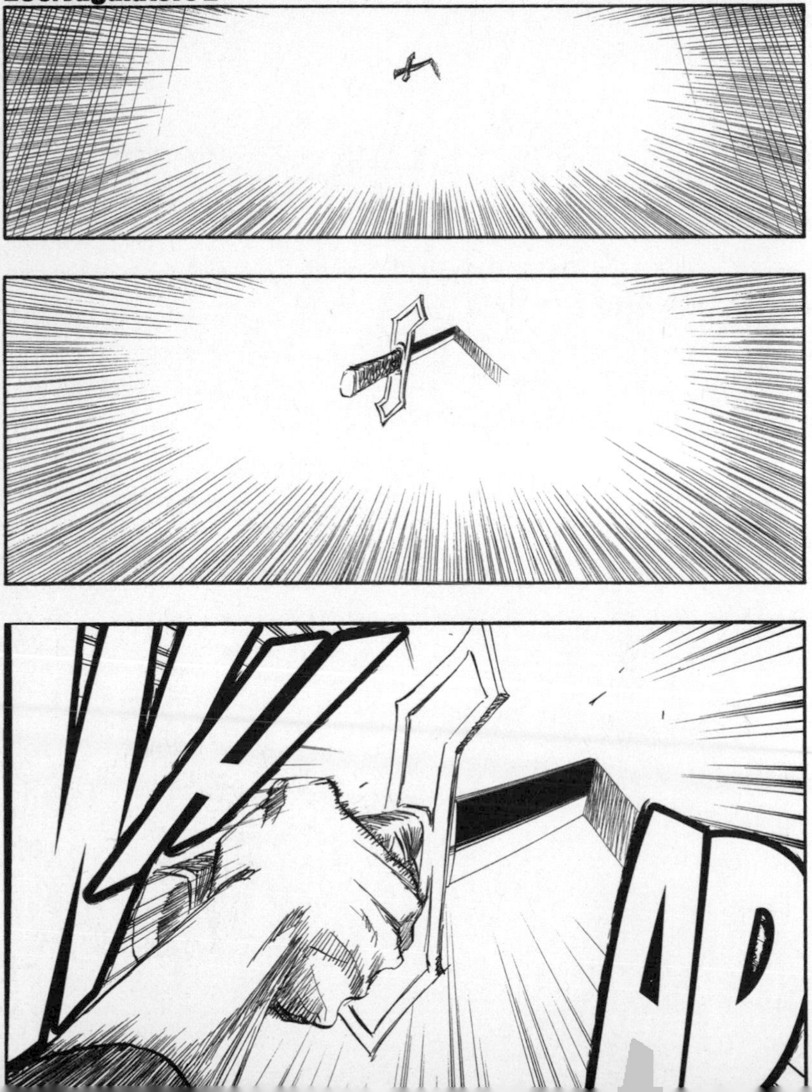
WHAD

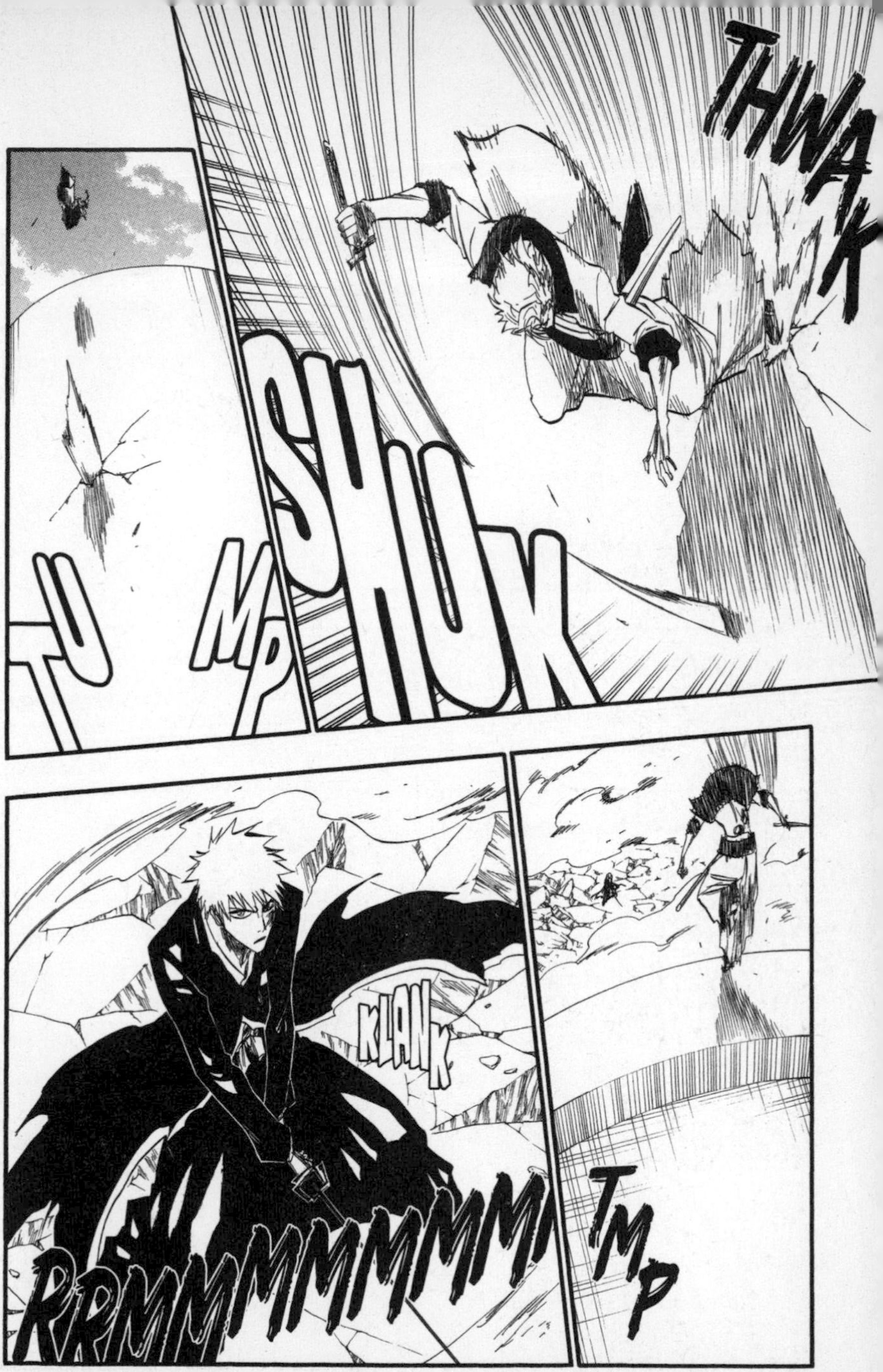
THWAK
SHUK
TUMP
KLANK
RRMMMMMMMMMM
TMP

READ THIS WAY

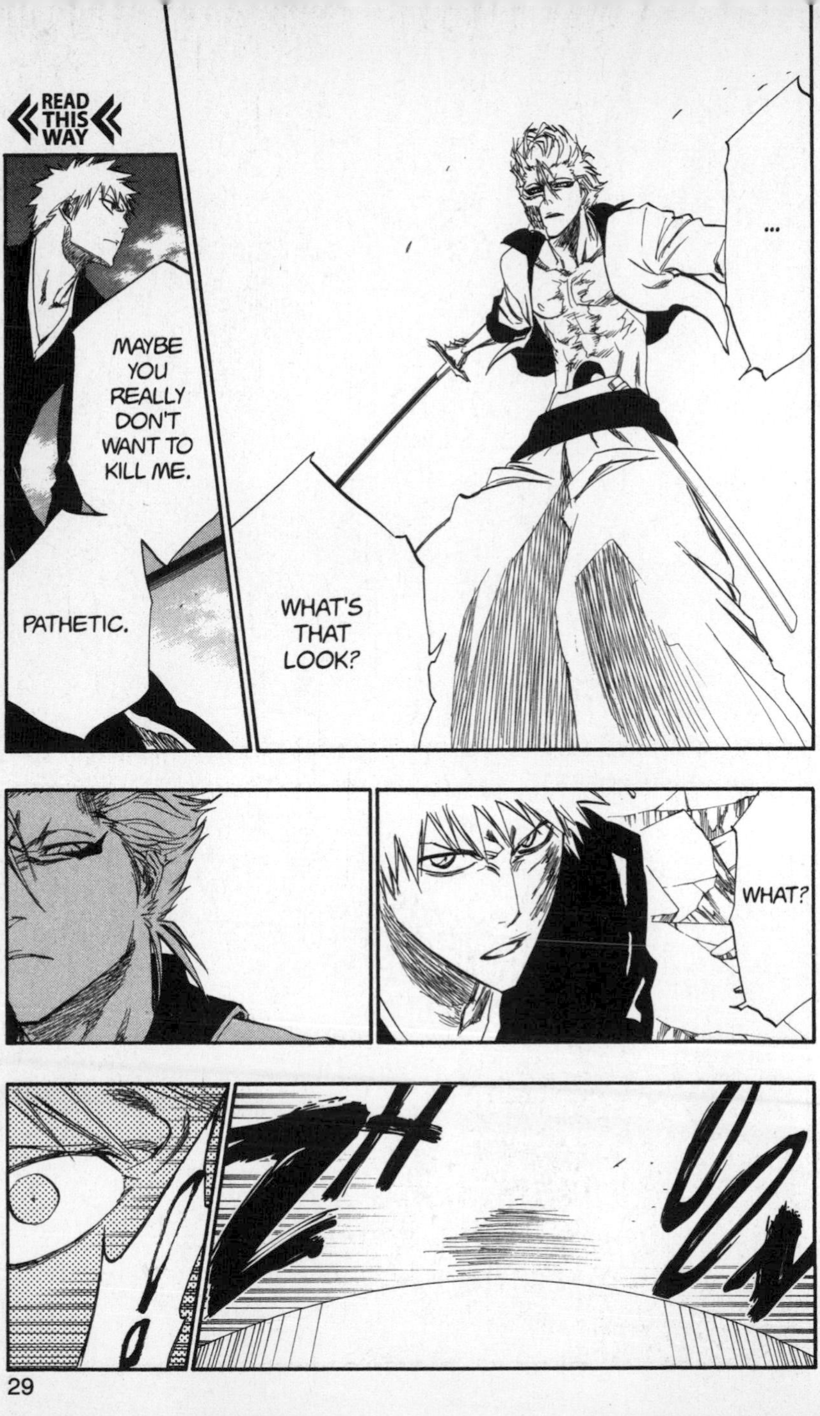

...
WHAT'S THAT LOOK?
MAYBE YOU REALLY DON'T WANT TO KILL ME.
PATHETIC.
WHAT?

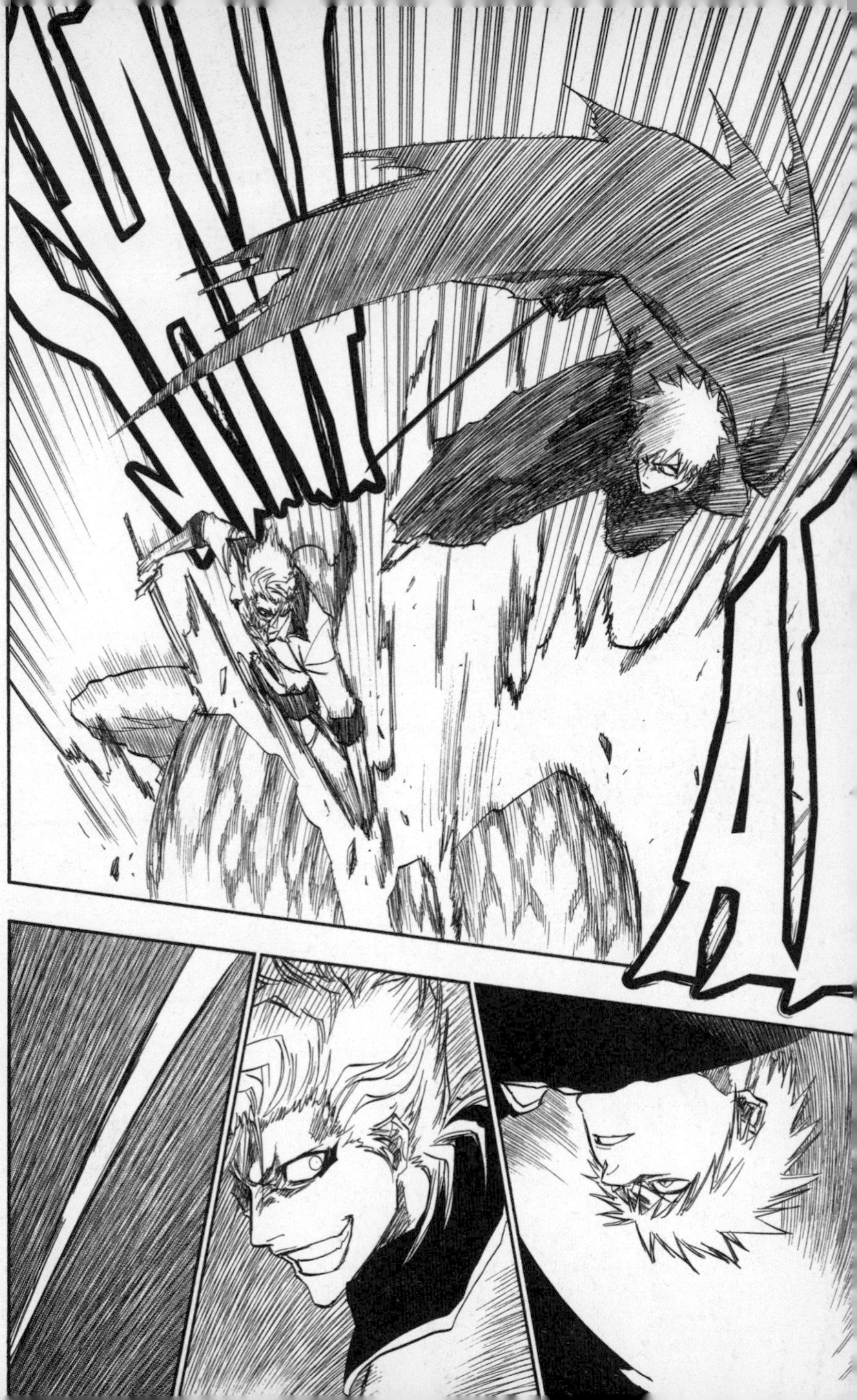

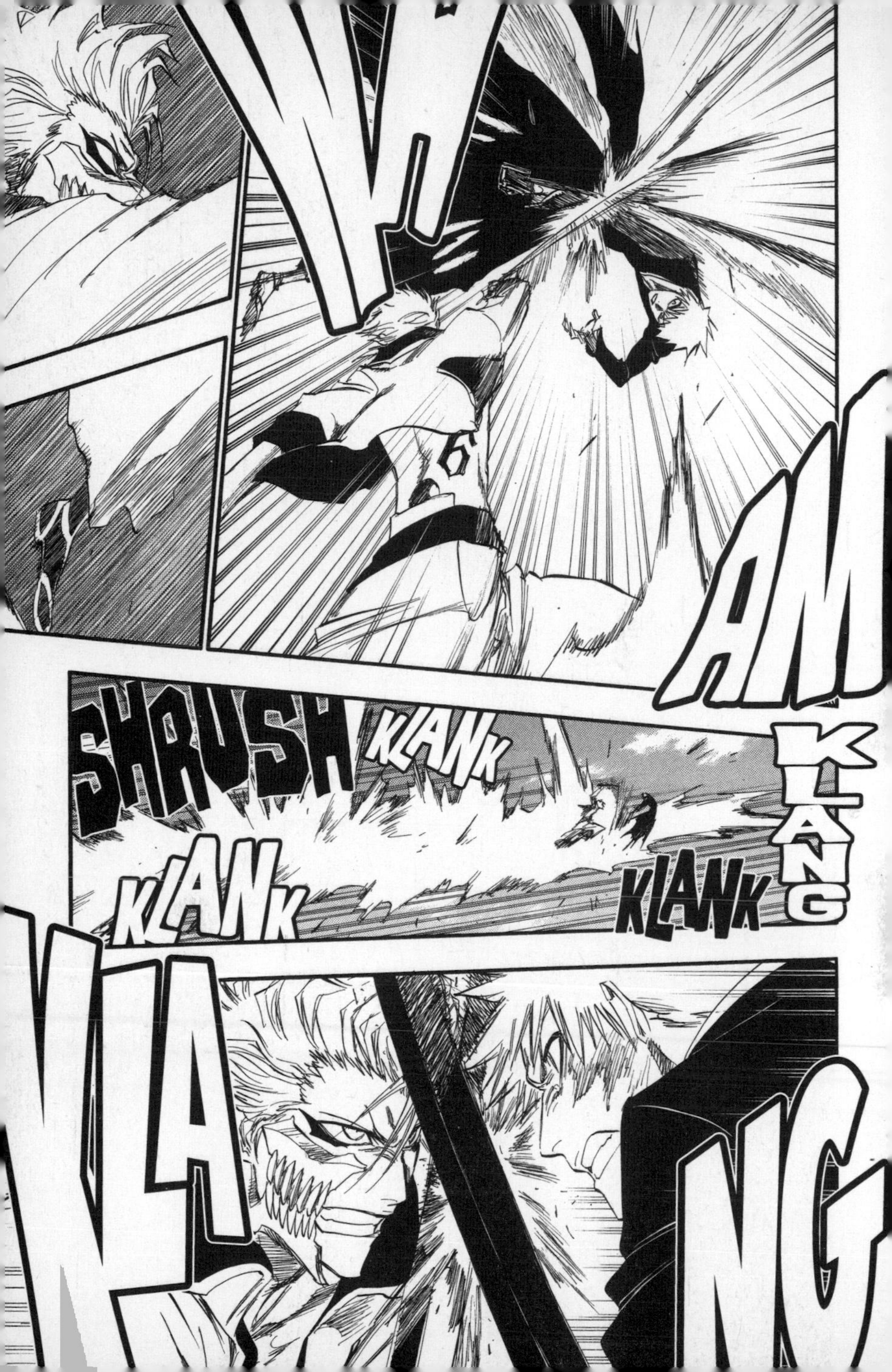
AM
KLANG
KLANK
KLANK
SHRUSH
KLANK
LA
NG

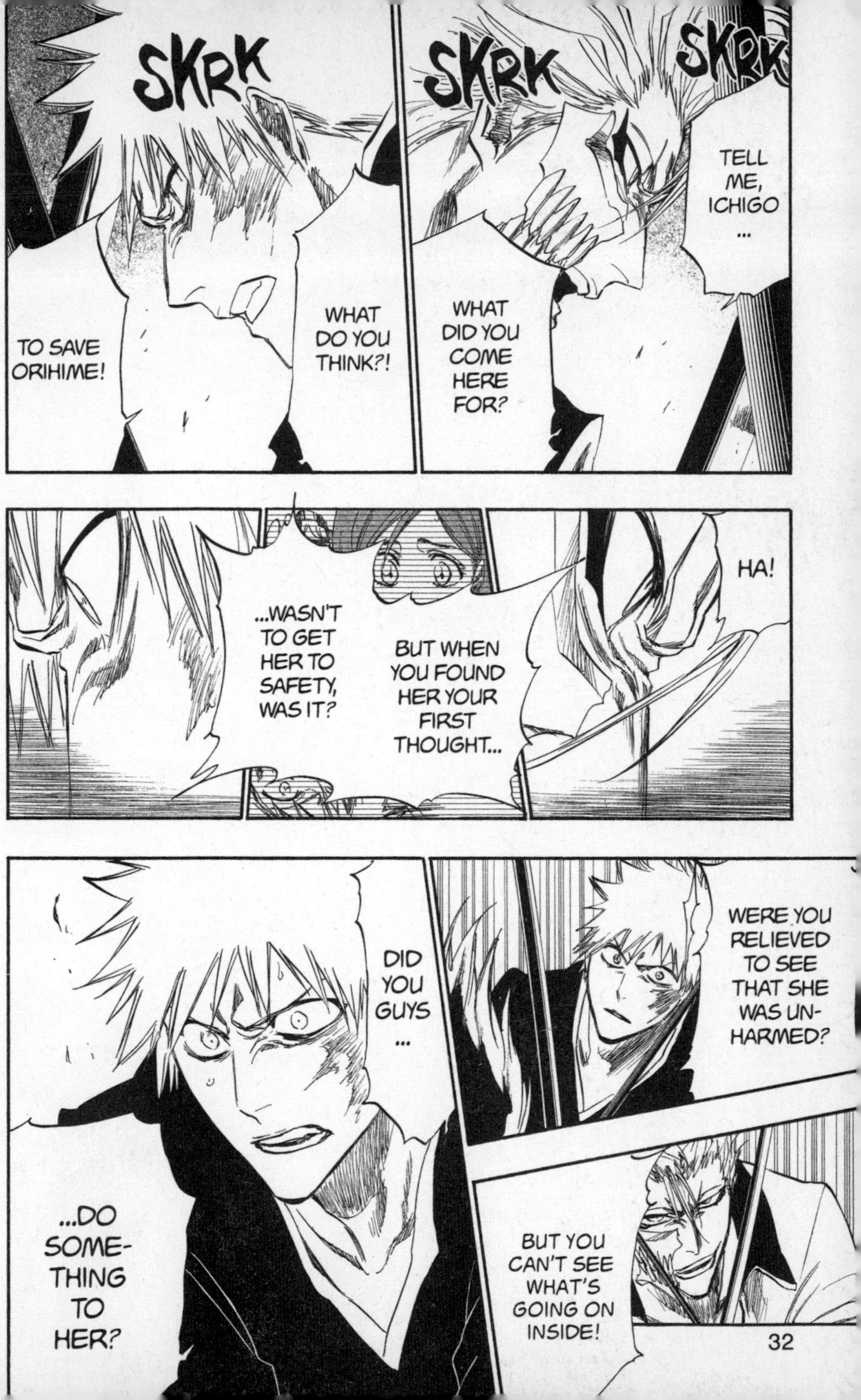
SKRK
SKRK
TELL ME, ICHIGO ...
WHAT DID YOU COME HERE FOR?
SKRK
WHAT DO YOU THINK?!
TO SAVE ORIHIME!
HA!
BUT WHEN YOU FOUND HER YOUR FIRST THOUGHT...
...WASN'T TO GET HER TO SAFETY, WAS IT?
WERE YOU RELIEVED TO SEE THAT SHE WAS UN-HARMED?
BUT YOU CAN'T SEE WHAT'S GOING ON INSIDE!
DID YOU GUYS ...
...DO SOME-THING TO HER?

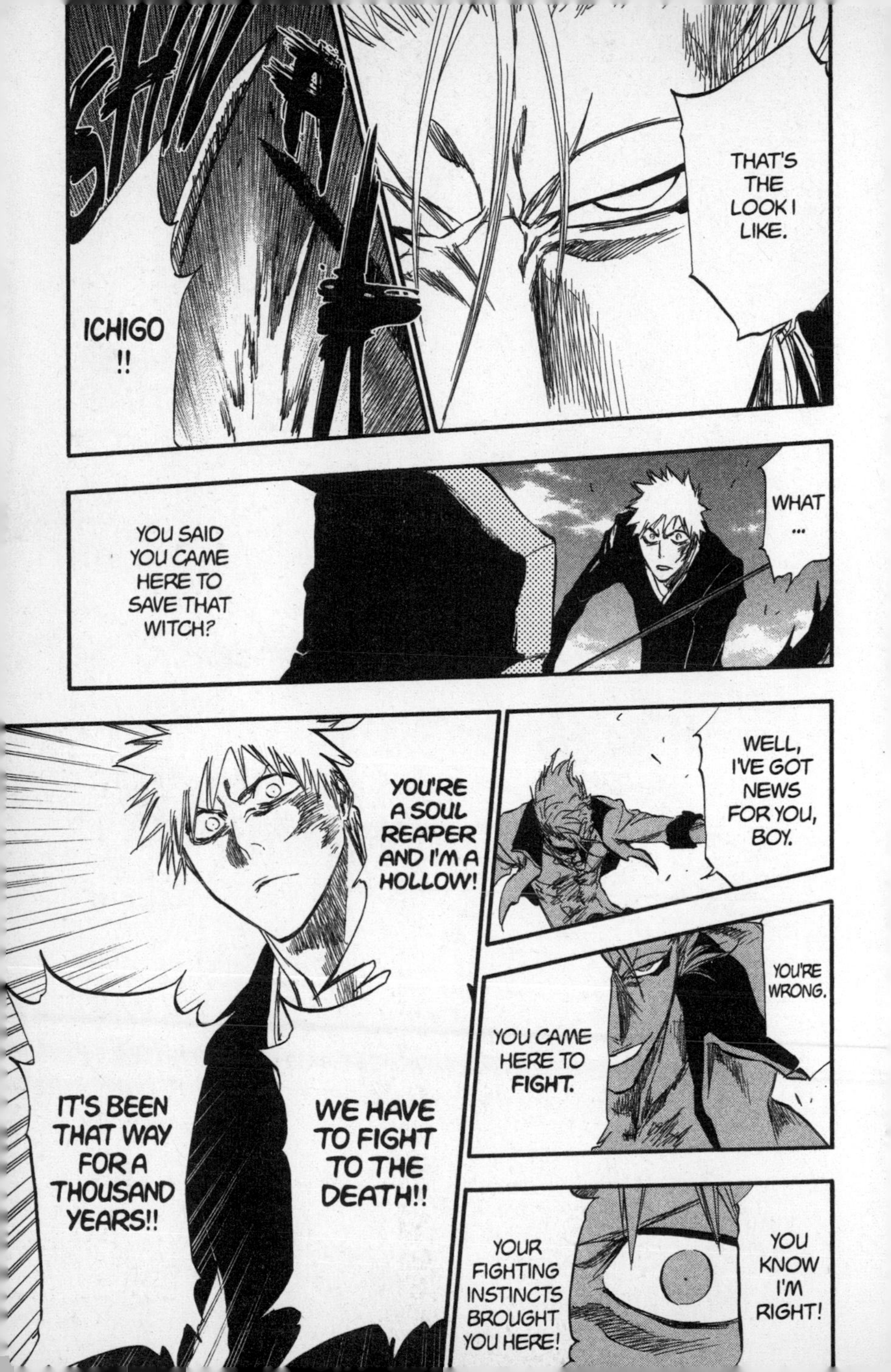

THAT'S THE LOOK I LIKE.
ICHIGO !!
WHAT ...
YOU SAID YOU CAME HERE TO SAVE THAT WITCH?
WELL, I'VE GOT NEWS FOR YOU, BOY.
YOU'RE WRONG.
YOU CAME HERE TO FIGHT.
YOU KNOW I'M RIGHT!
YOUR FIGHTING INSTINCTS BROUGHT YOU HERE!
YOU'RE A SOUL REAPER AND I'M A HOLLOW!
WE HAVE TO FIGHT TO THE DEATH!!
IT'S BEEN THAT WAY FOR A THOUSAND YEARS!!

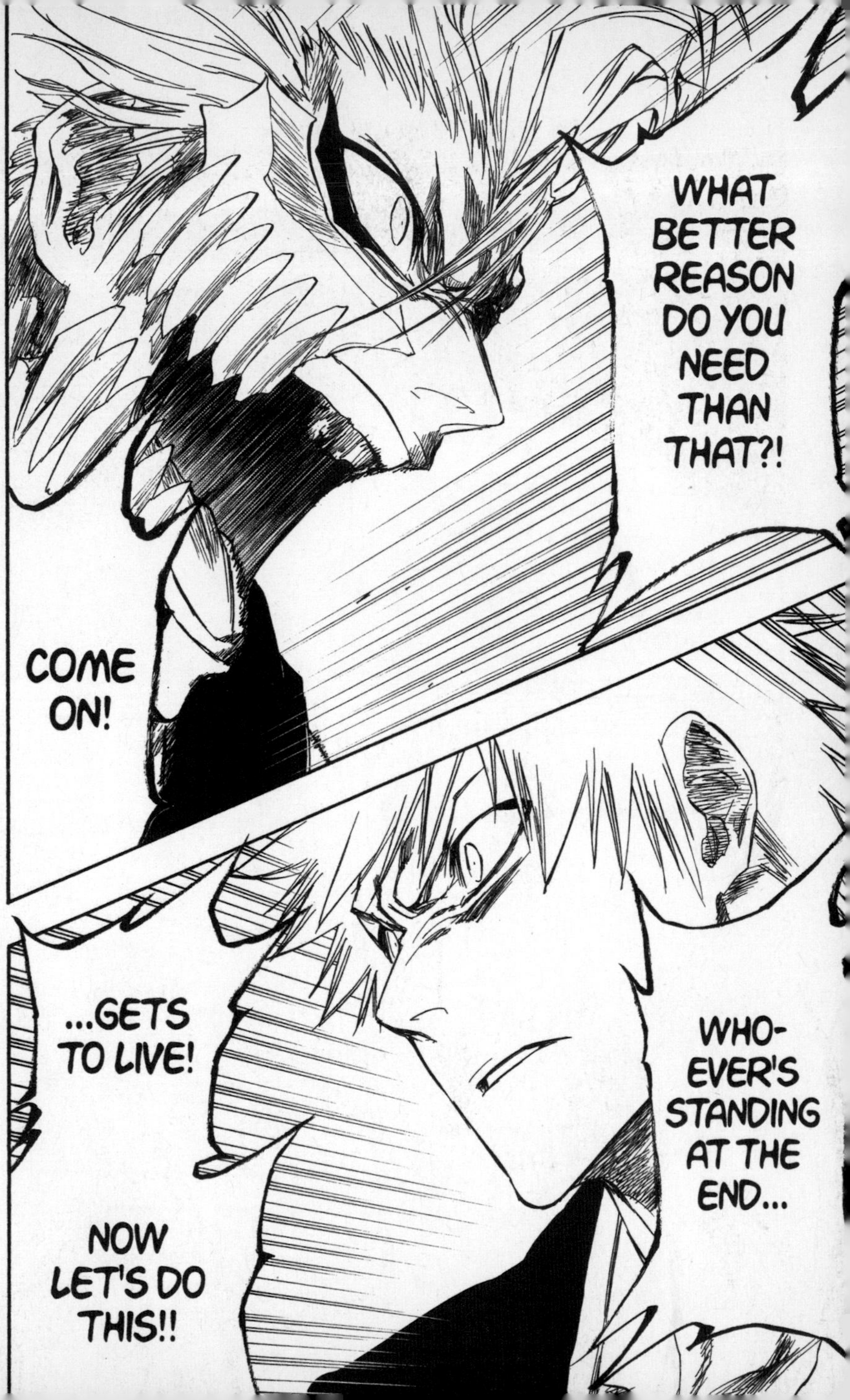
WHAT BETTER REASON DO YOU NEED THAN THAT?!
COME ON!
WHO-EVER'S STANDING AT THE END...
...GETS TO LIVE!
NOW LET'S DO THIS!!

BLEACH 280. Jugulators 2

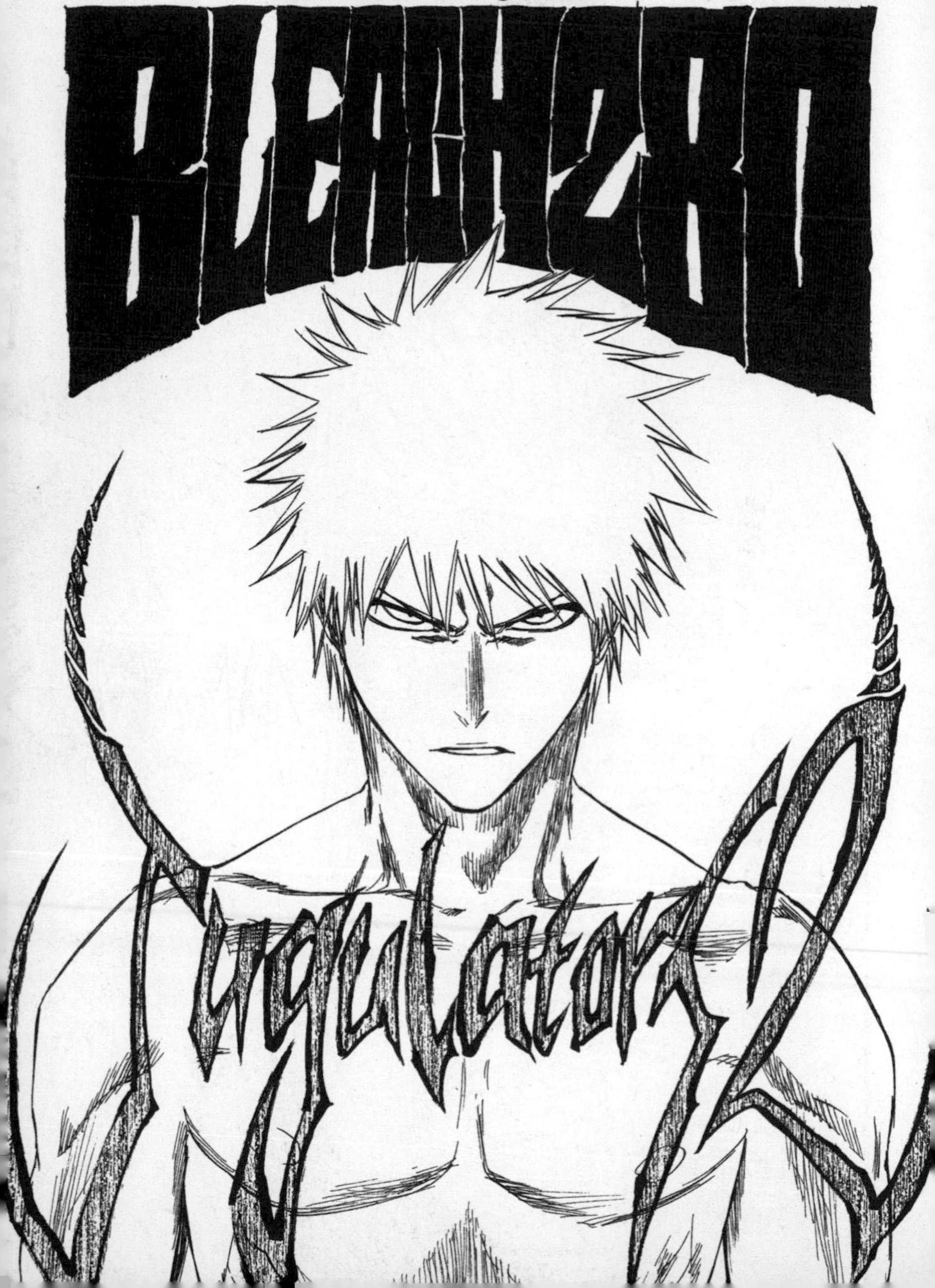
Jugulators 2

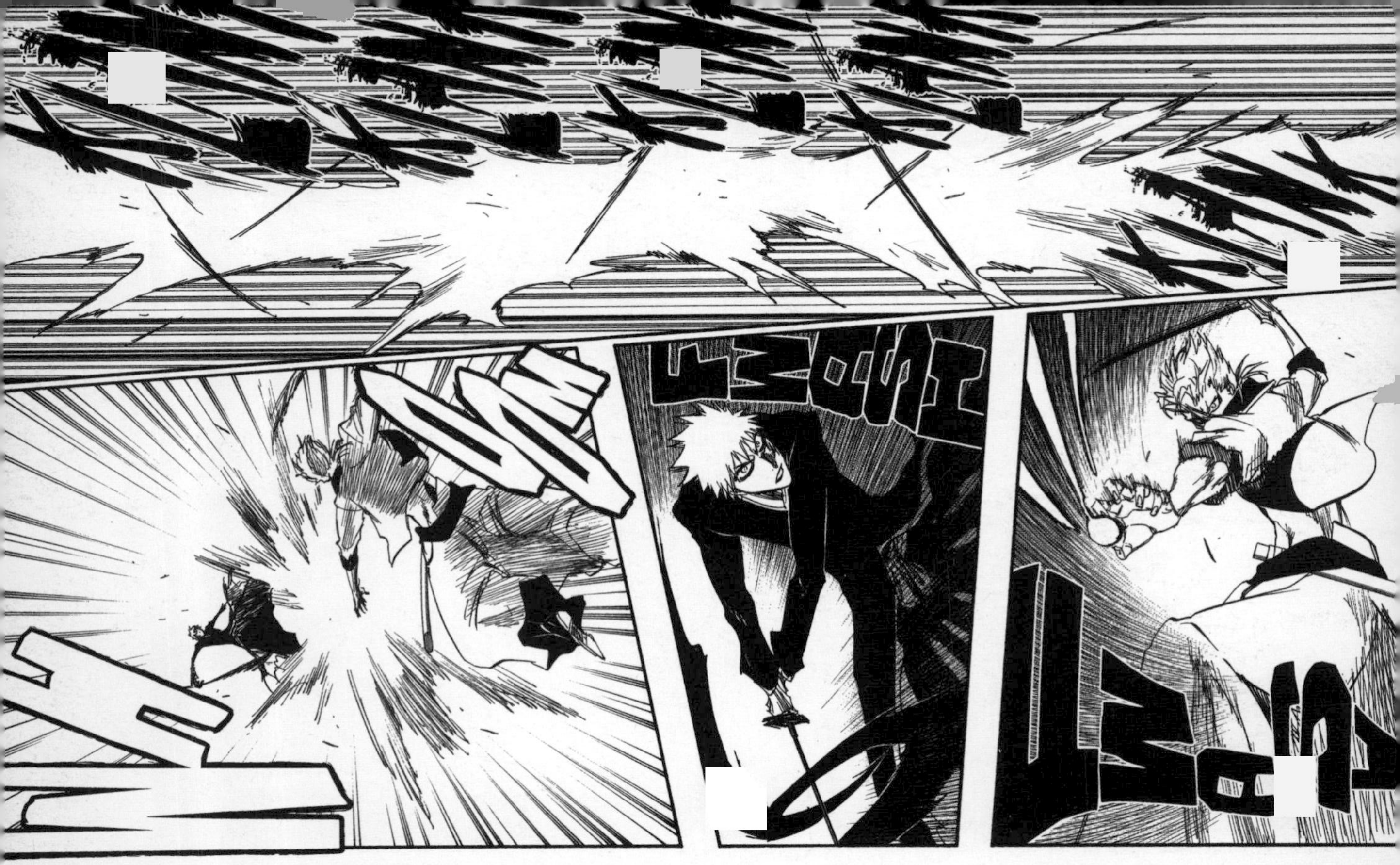
FWASH
FWASH

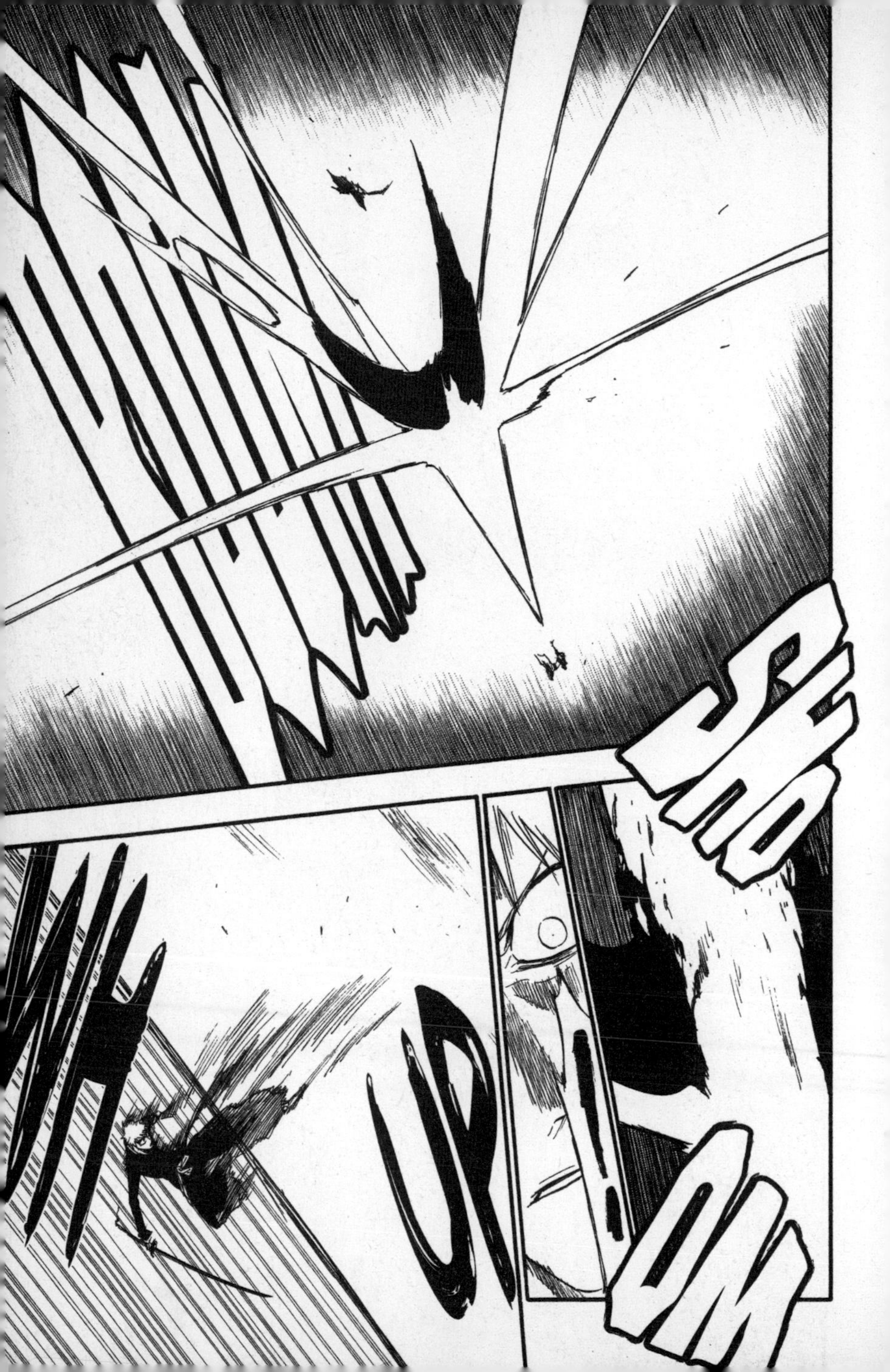
SHOOM

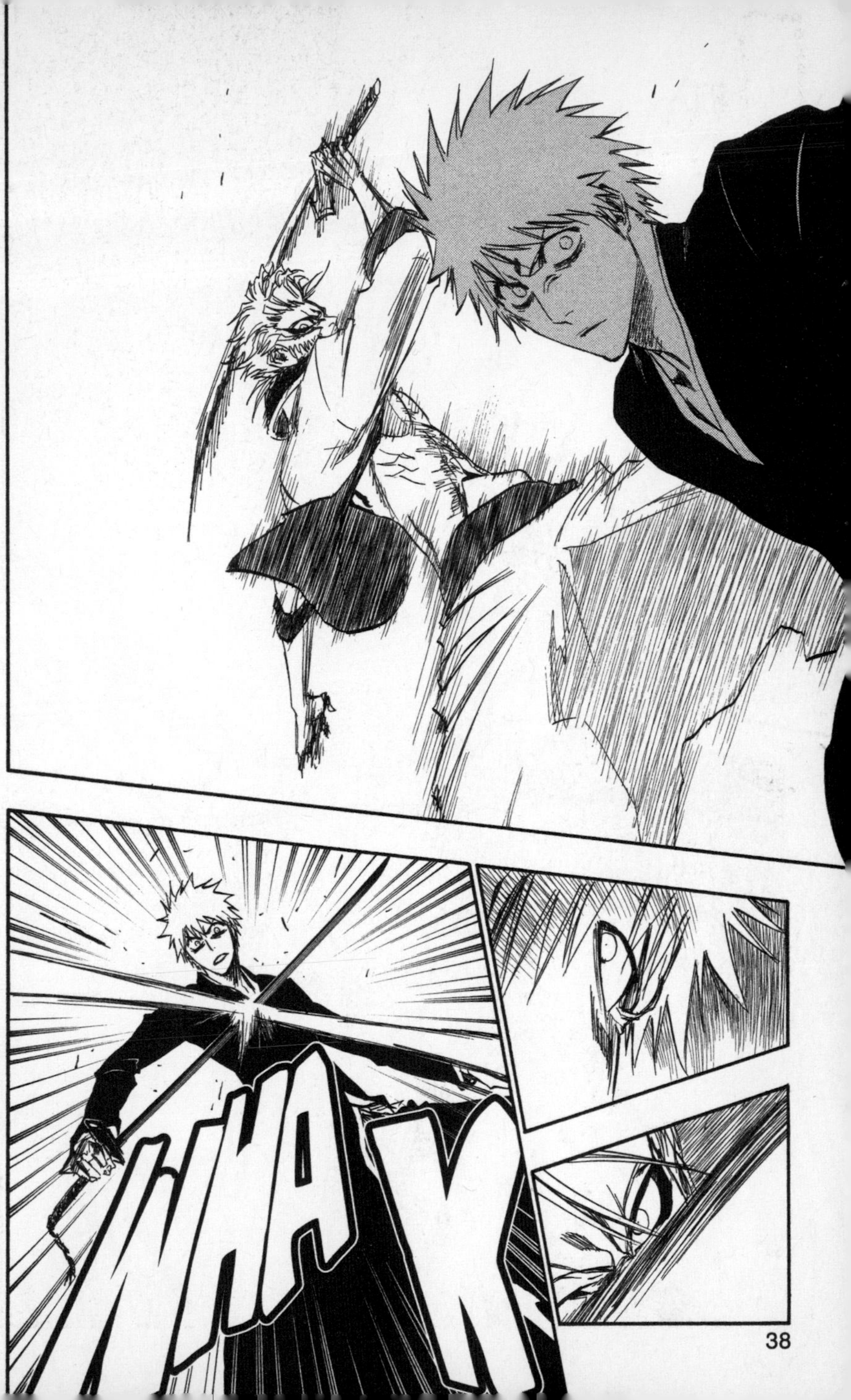
WHAK

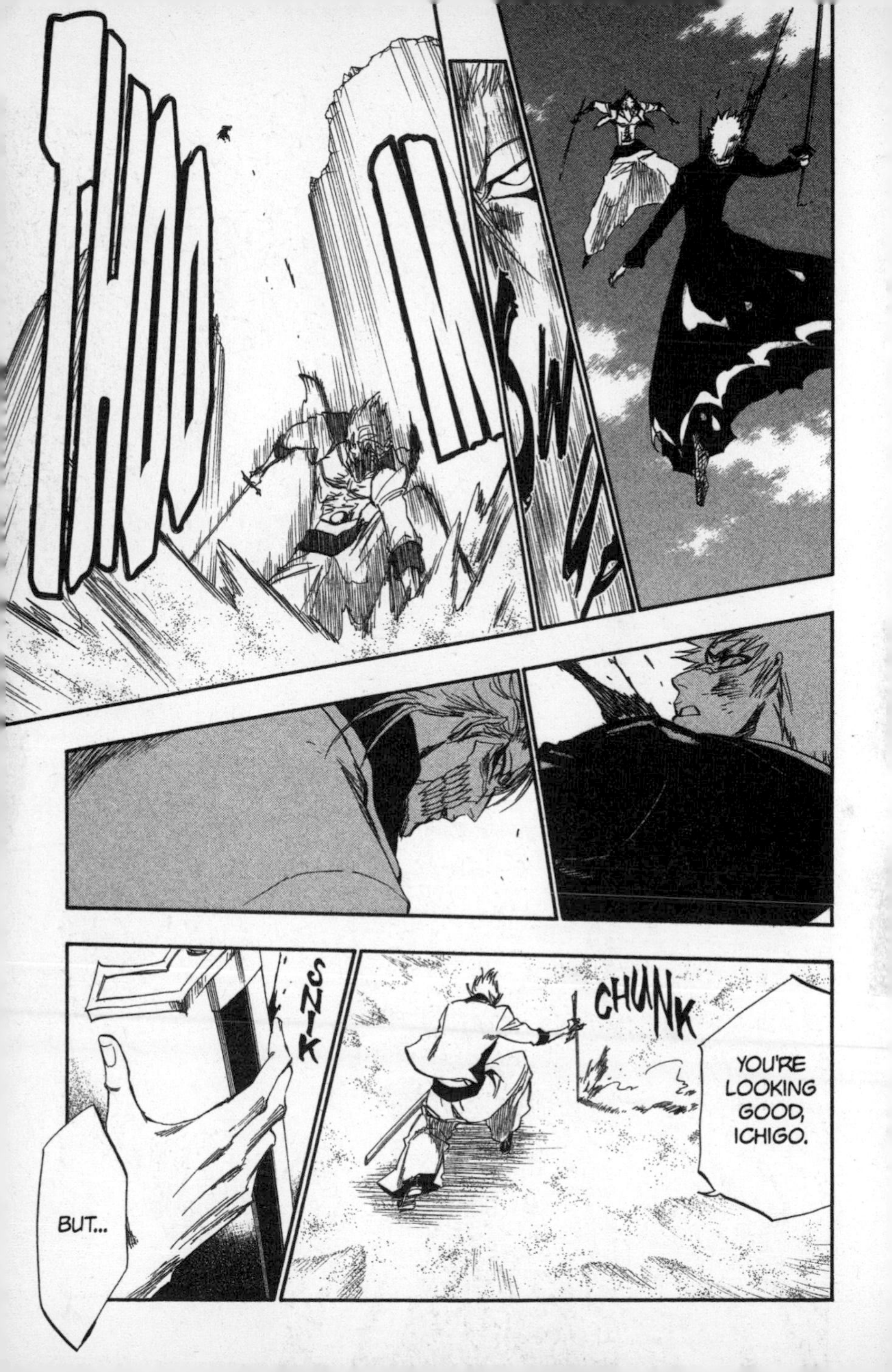
SWISH
THUD
CHUNK
YOU'RE LOOKING GOOD, ICHIGO.
SNIK
BUT...

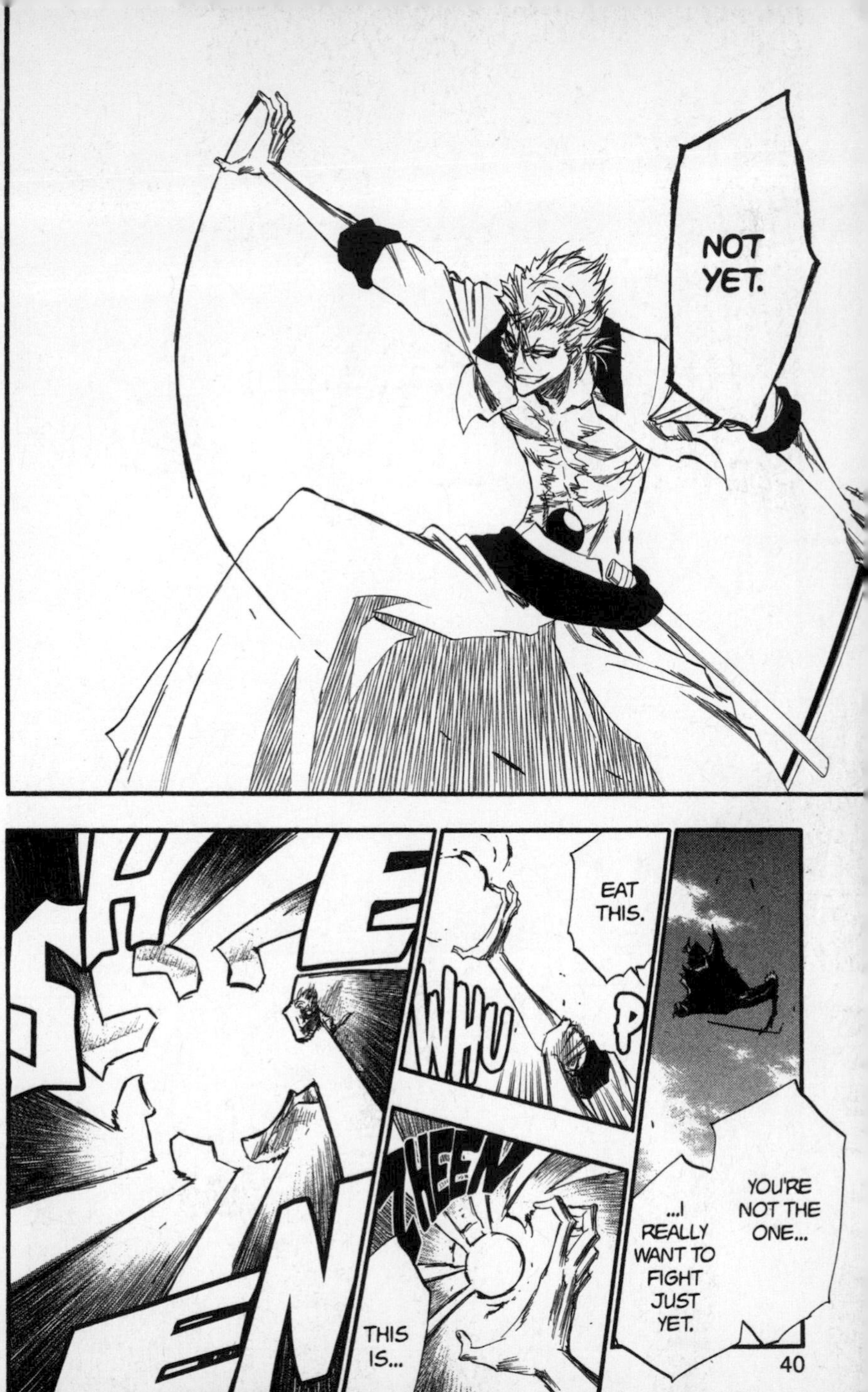
NOT YET.
YOU'RE NOT THE ONE...
...I REALLY WANT TO FIGHT JUST YET.
EAT THIS.
WHUP
THIS IS...

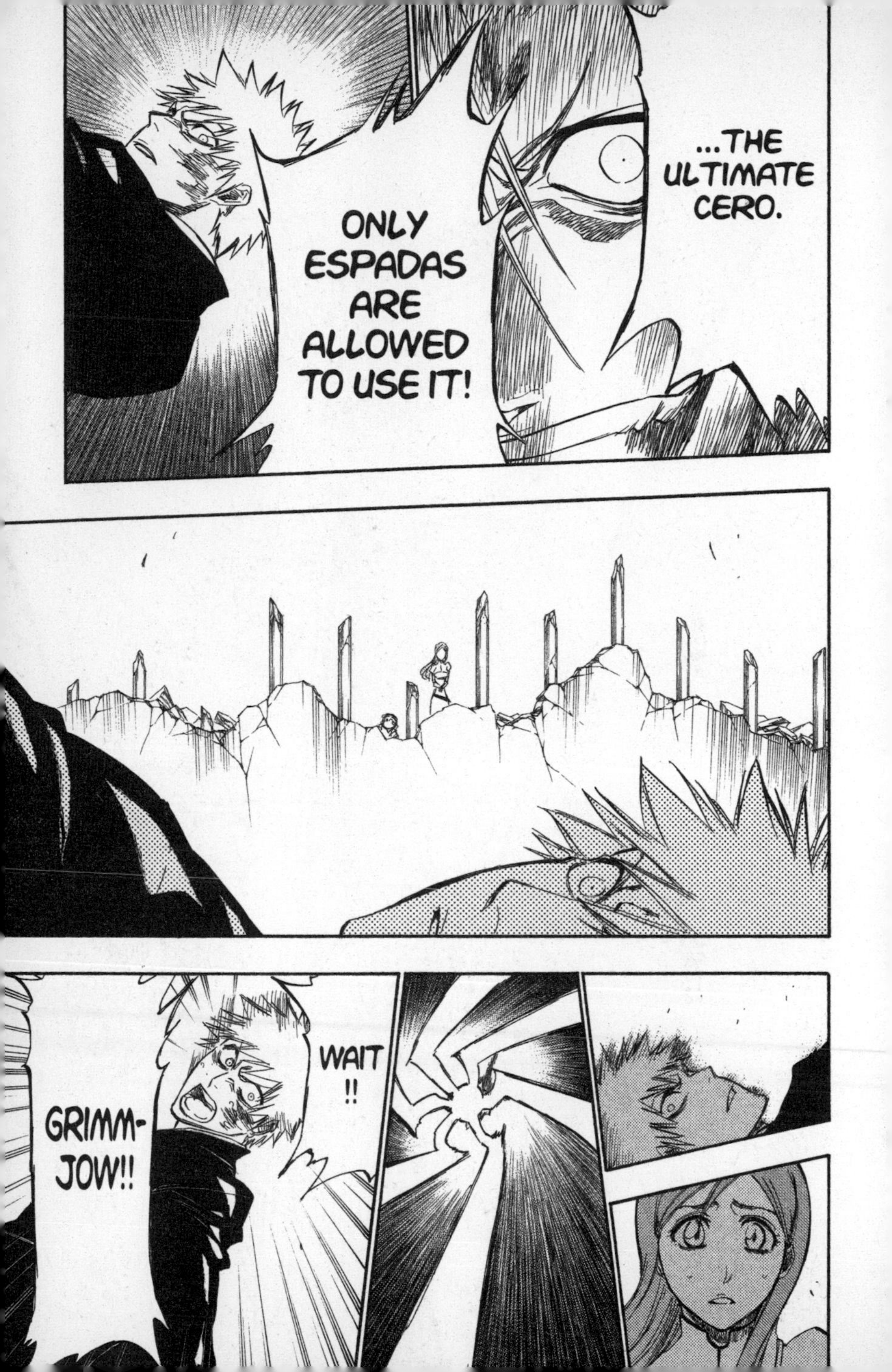
...THE ULTIMATE CERO.
ONLY ESPADAS ARE ALLOWED TO USE IT!
WAIT !!
GRIMM-JOW!!

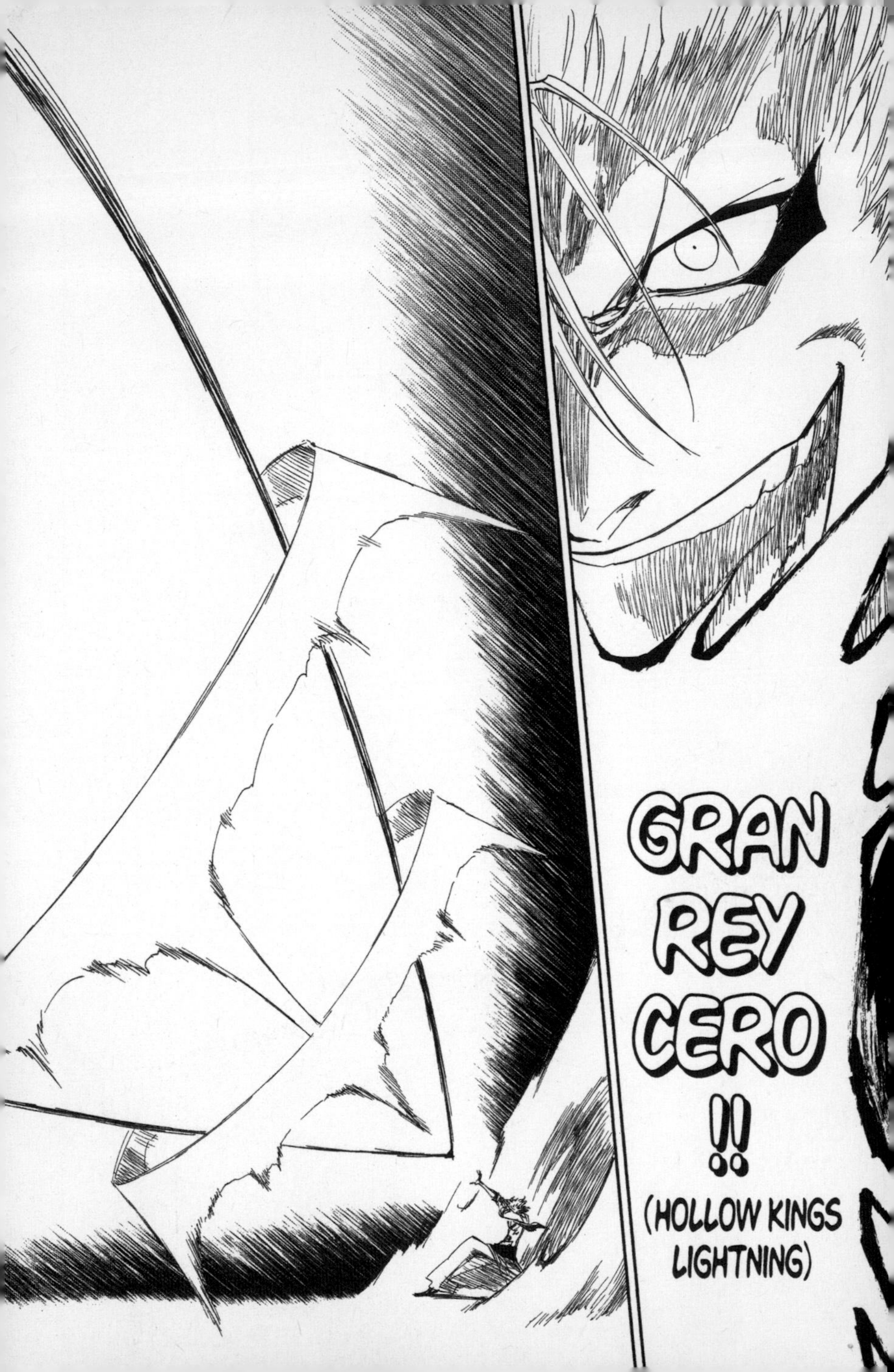
GRAN REY CERO!!
(HOLLOW KINGS LIGHTNING)

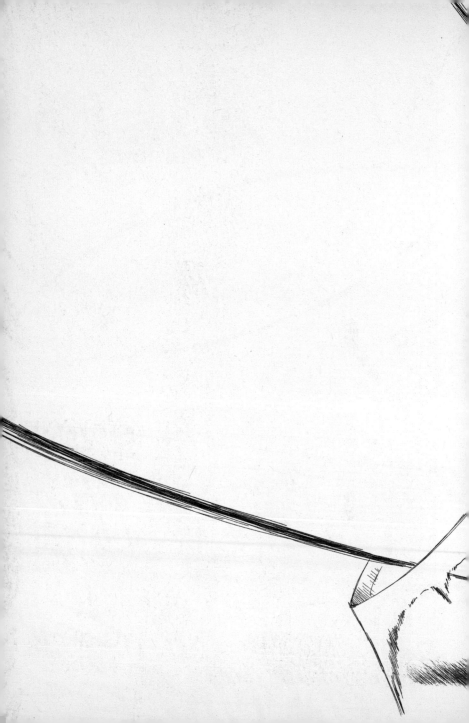

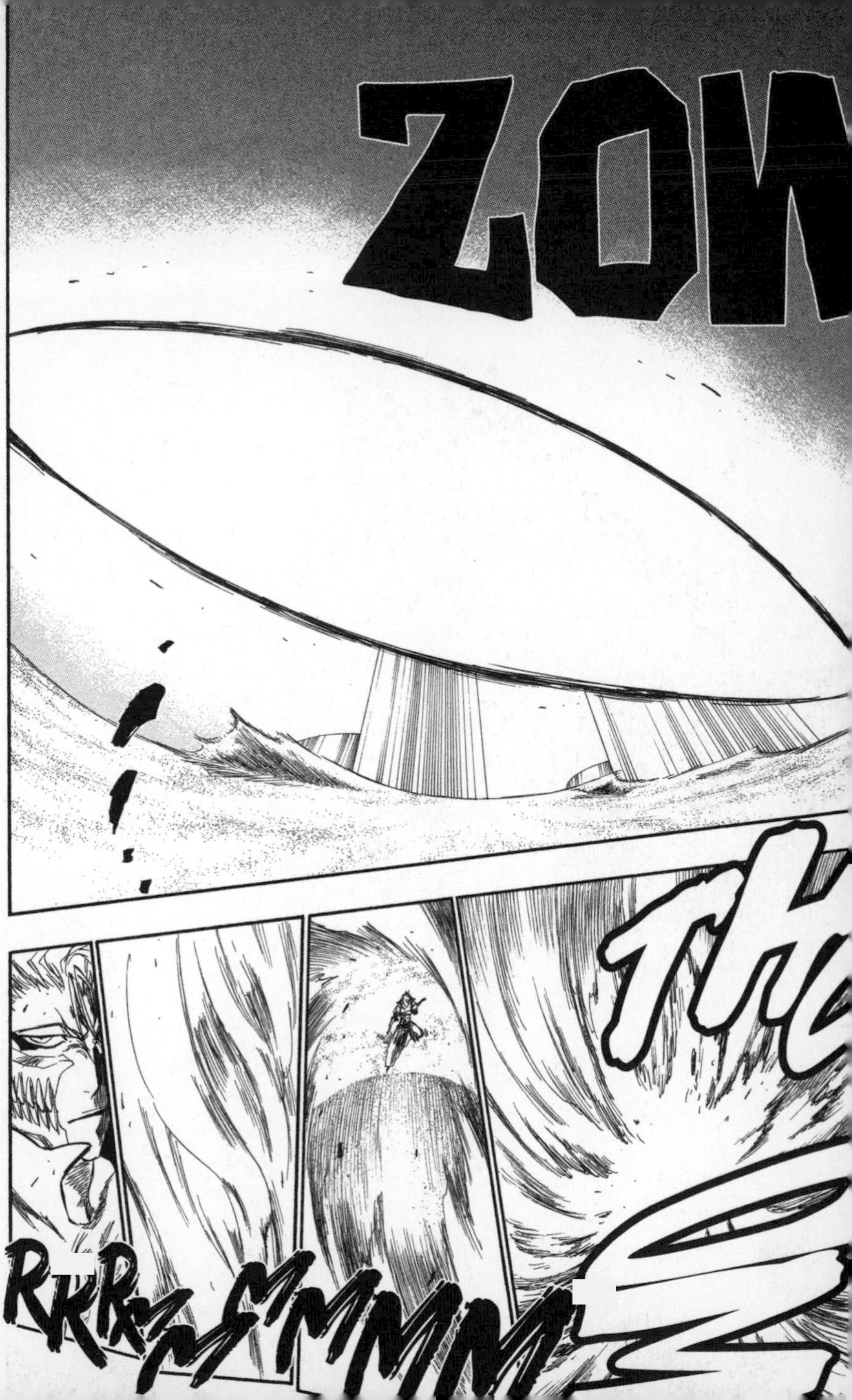
ZOW

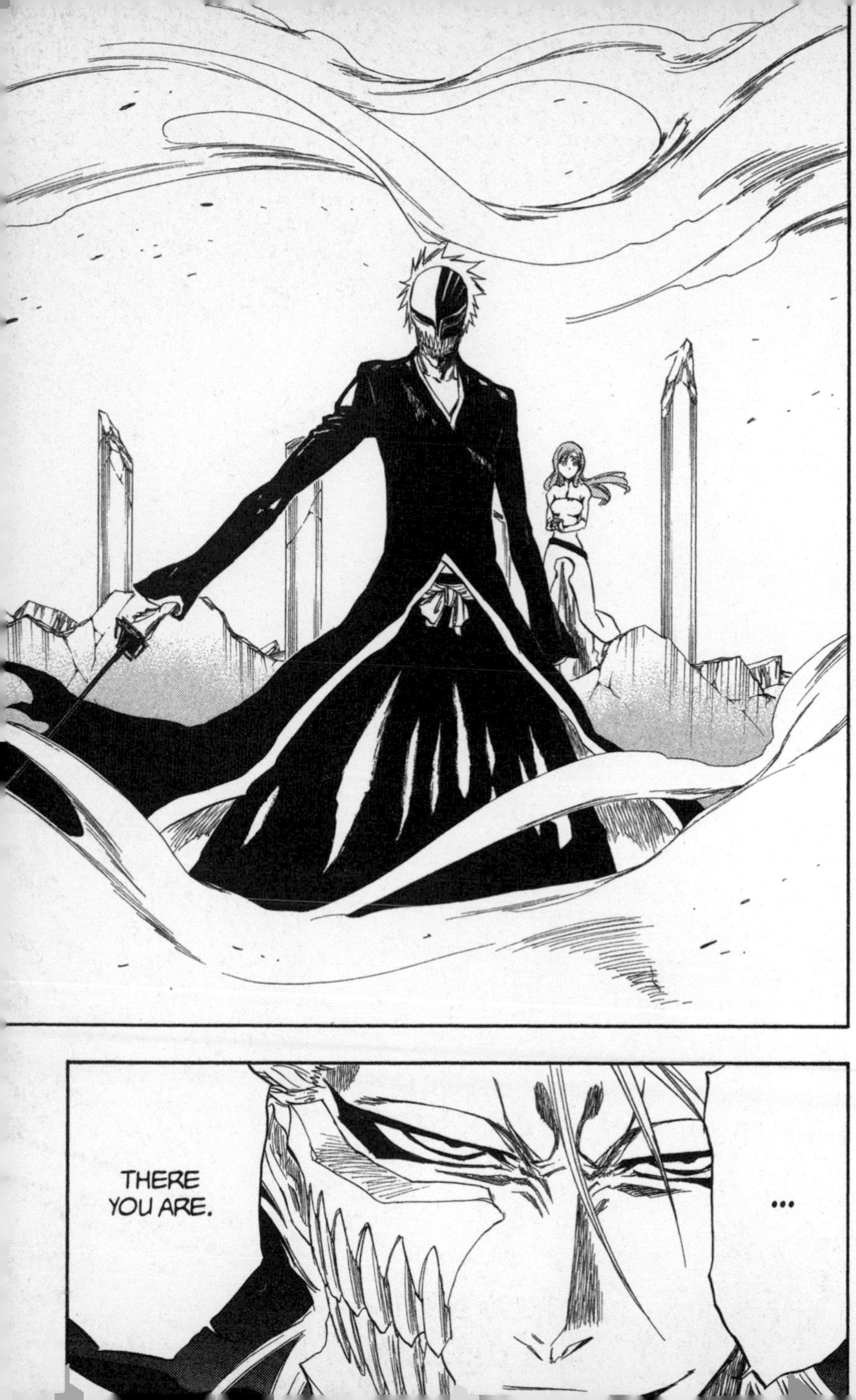
THERE YOU ARE.
...

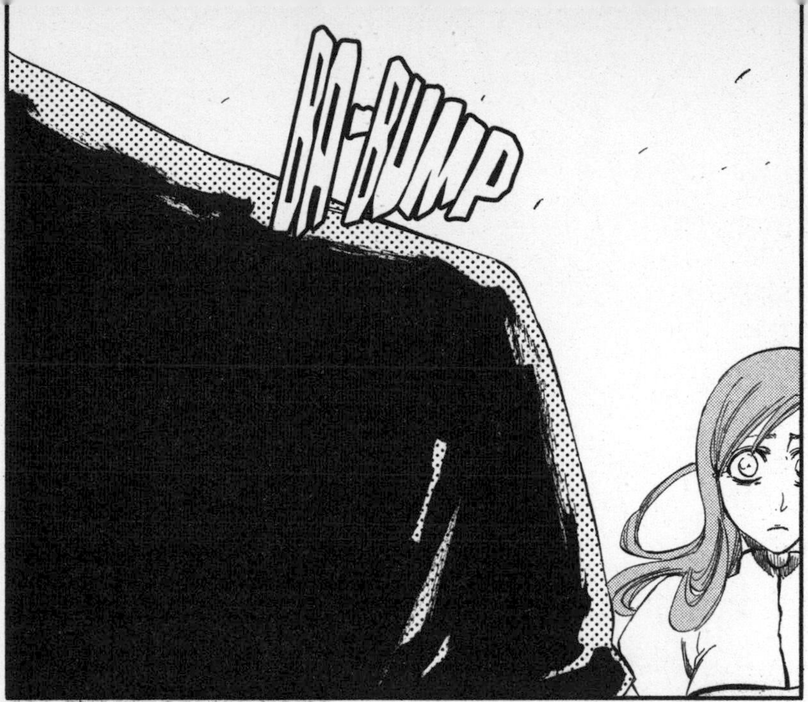
BA-BUMP

281. THE VULGARIAN NOISE

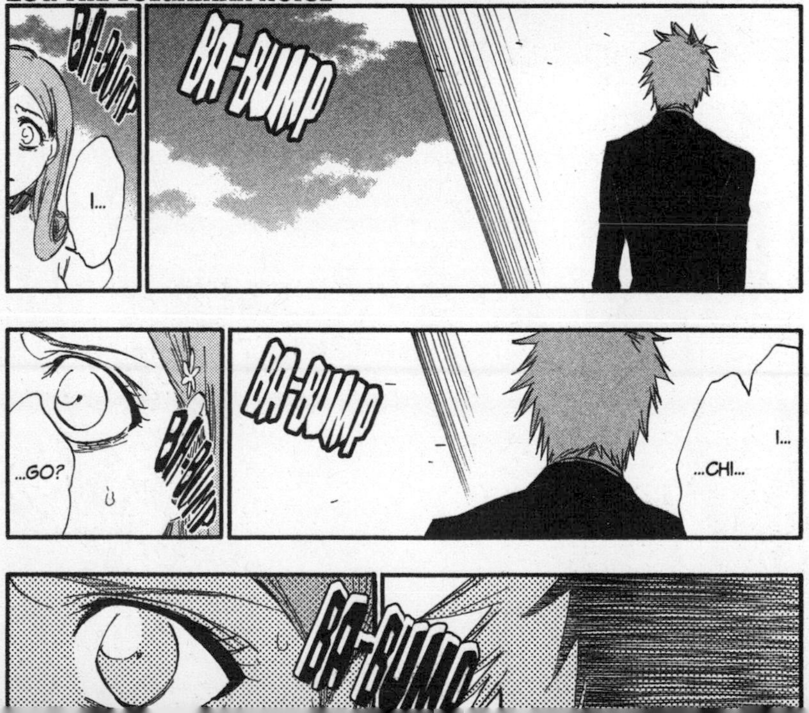
BA-BUMP
BA-BUMP
I...
I...
...CHI...
BA-BUMP
BA-BUMP
...GO?
BA-BUMP

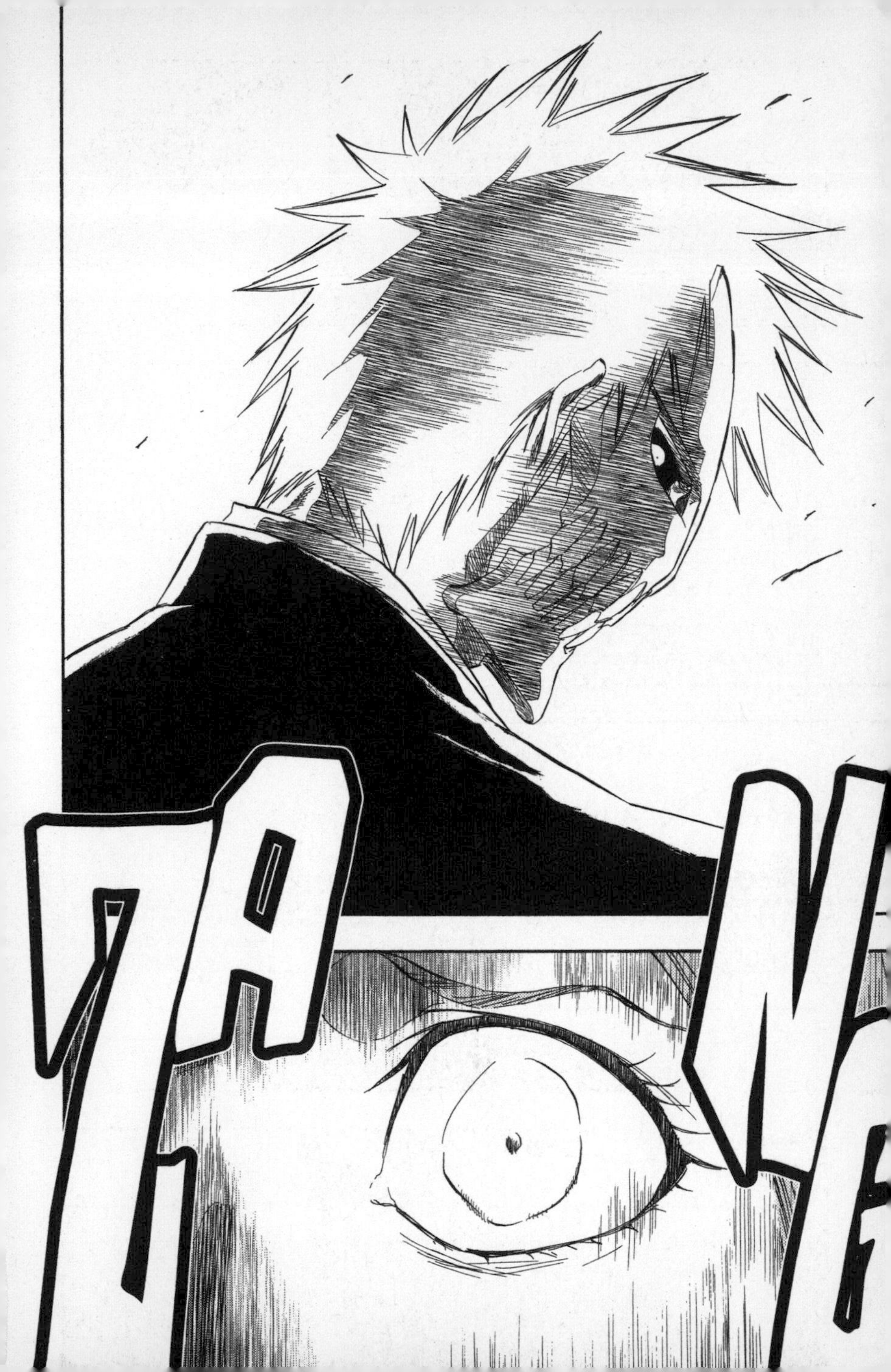
ZA

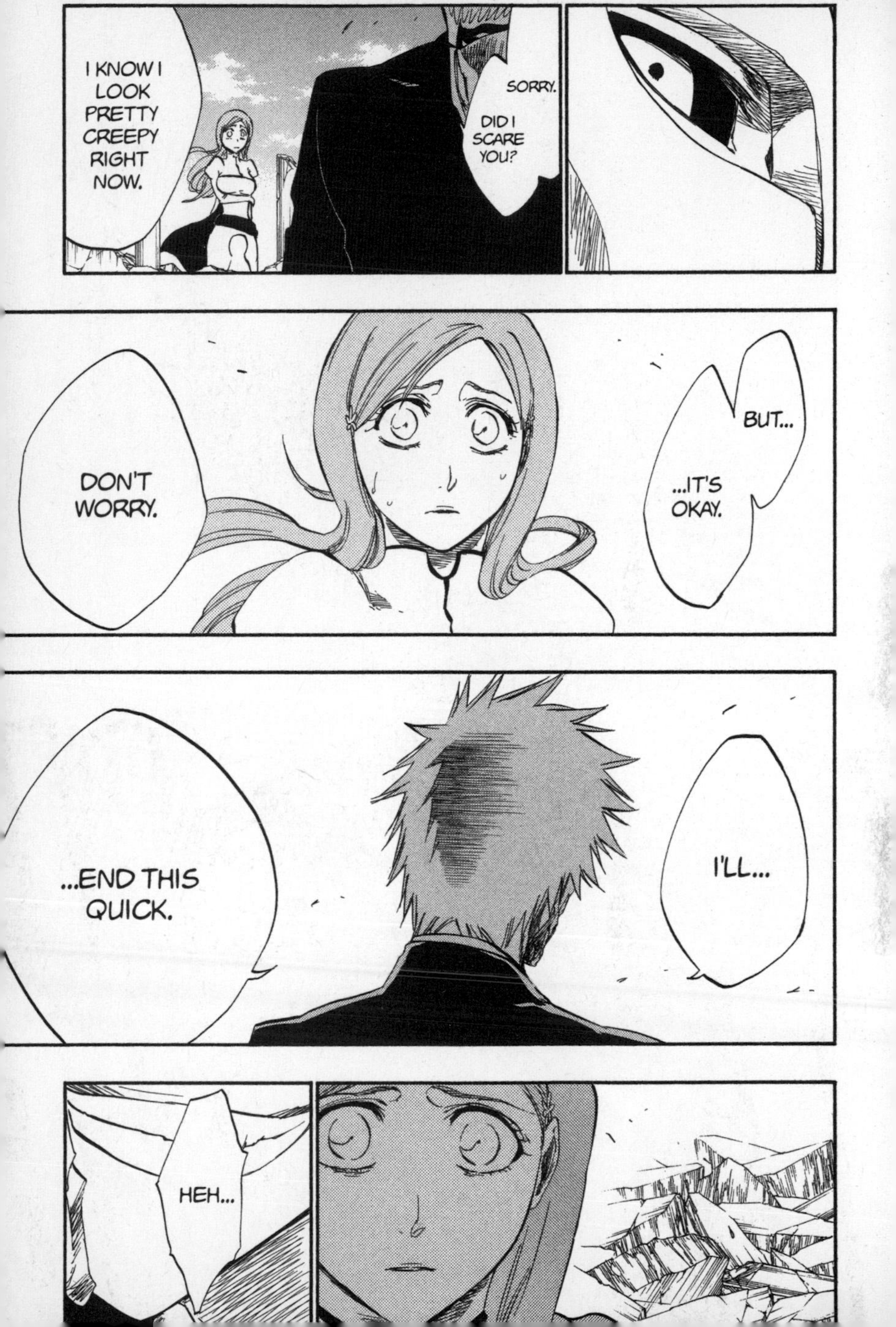
SORRY.
DID I SCARE YOU?
I KNOW I LOOK PRETTY CREEPY RIGHT NOW.
BUT...
...IT'S OKAY.
DON'T WORRY.
I'LL...
...END THIS QUICK.
HEH...

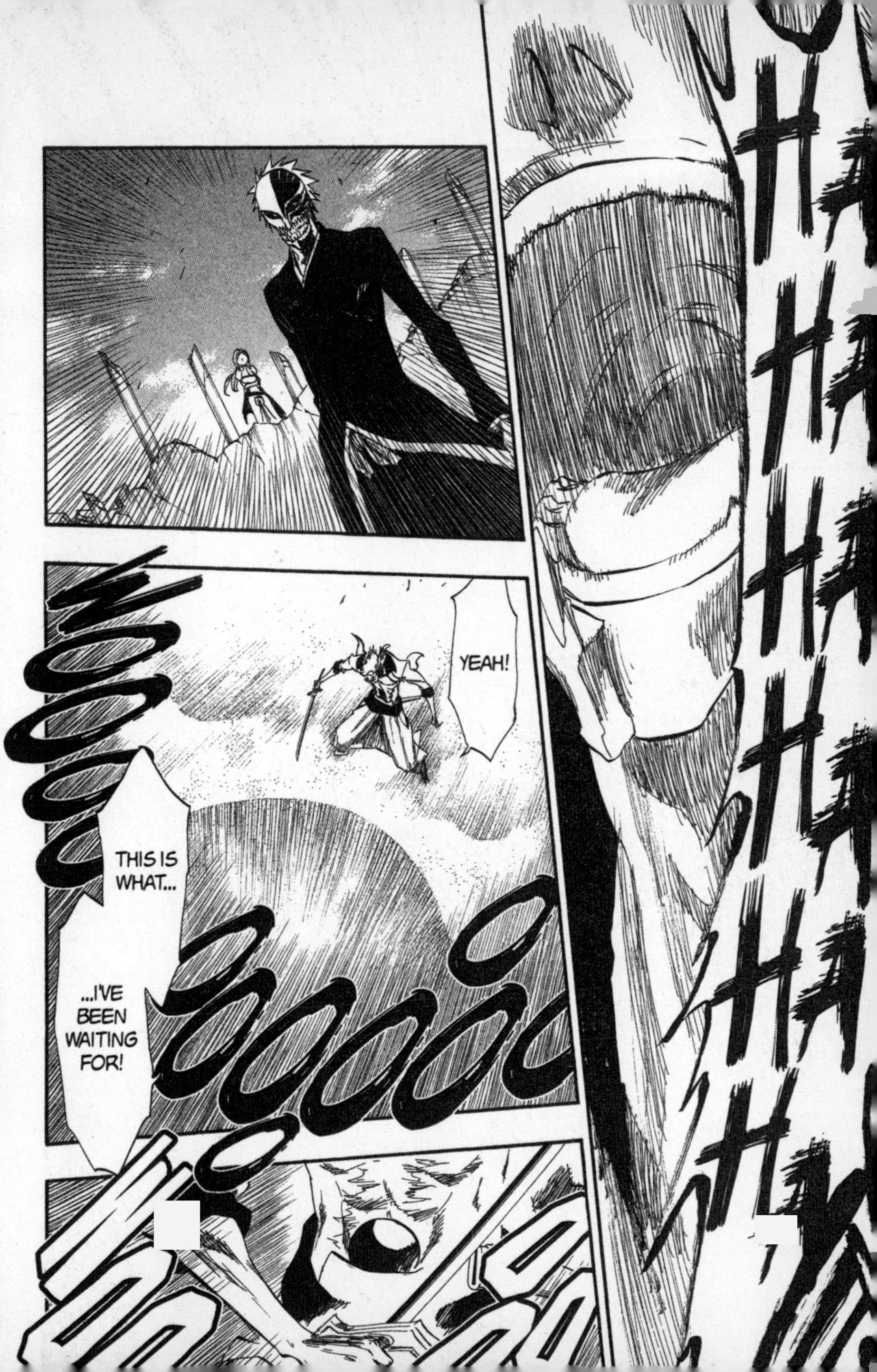
YEAH!
THIS IS WHAT...
...I'VE BEEN WAITING FOR!
HA HA HA HA HA HA HA

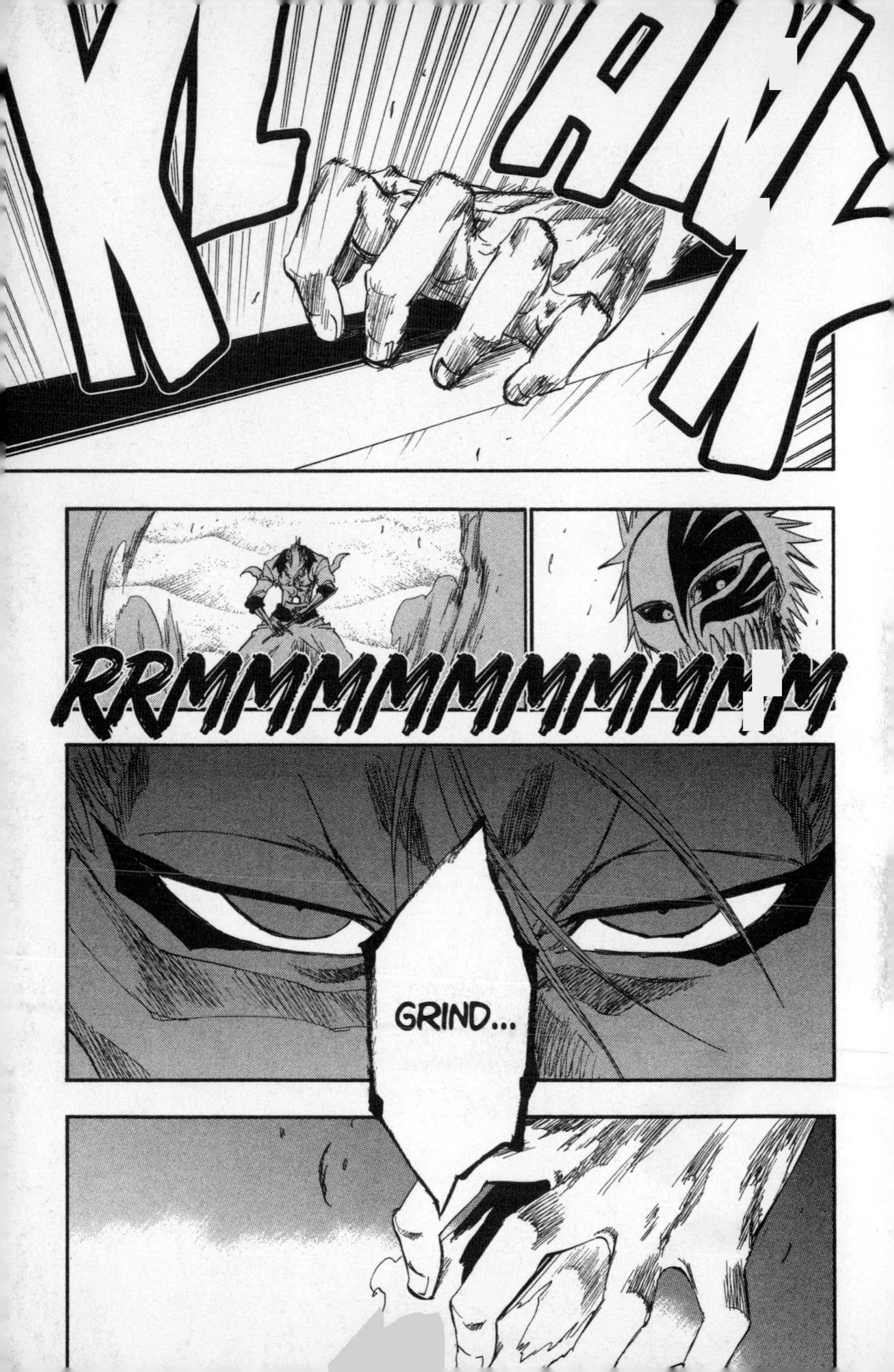
KLANK
RRMMMMMMMMMMMM
GRIND...

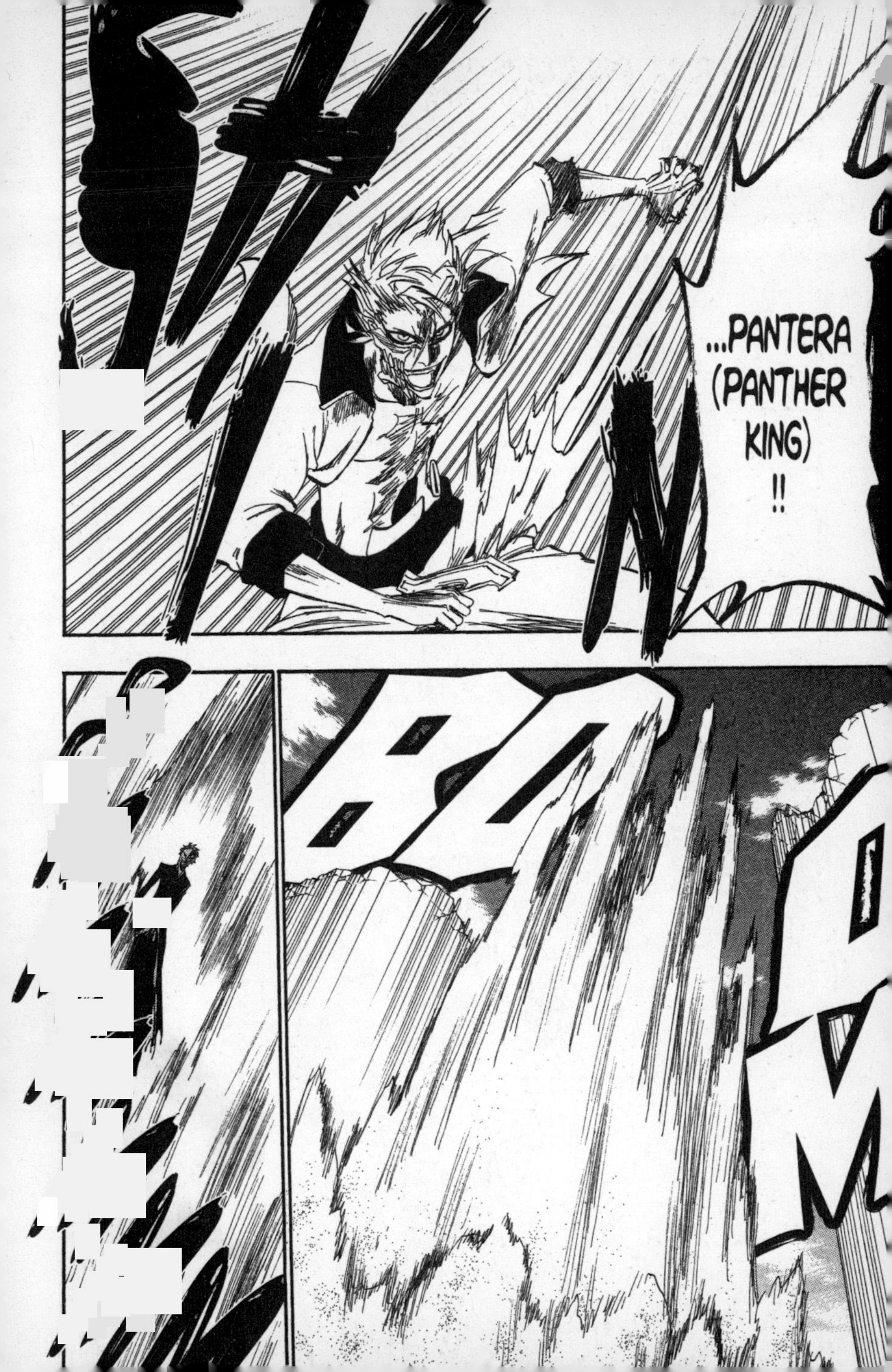
...PANTERA (PANTHER KING) !!

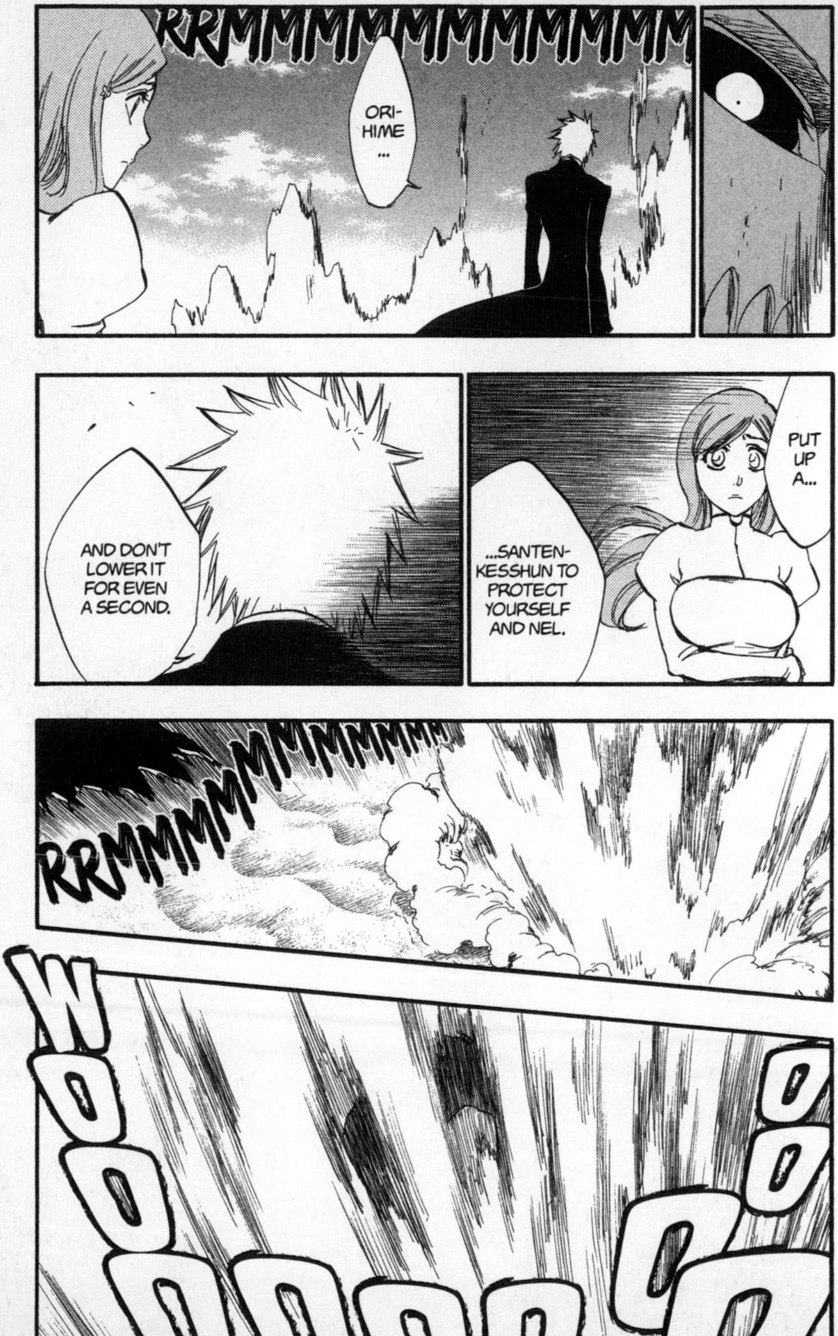
RRMMMMMMMMMMMMMMM
ORI-HIME...
PUT UP A...
...SANTEN-KESSHUN TO PROTECT YOURSELF AND NEL.
AND DON'T LOWER IT FOR EVEN A SECOND.
RRMMMMMMMMMMMMM
WOOOOOOOOOOOOO

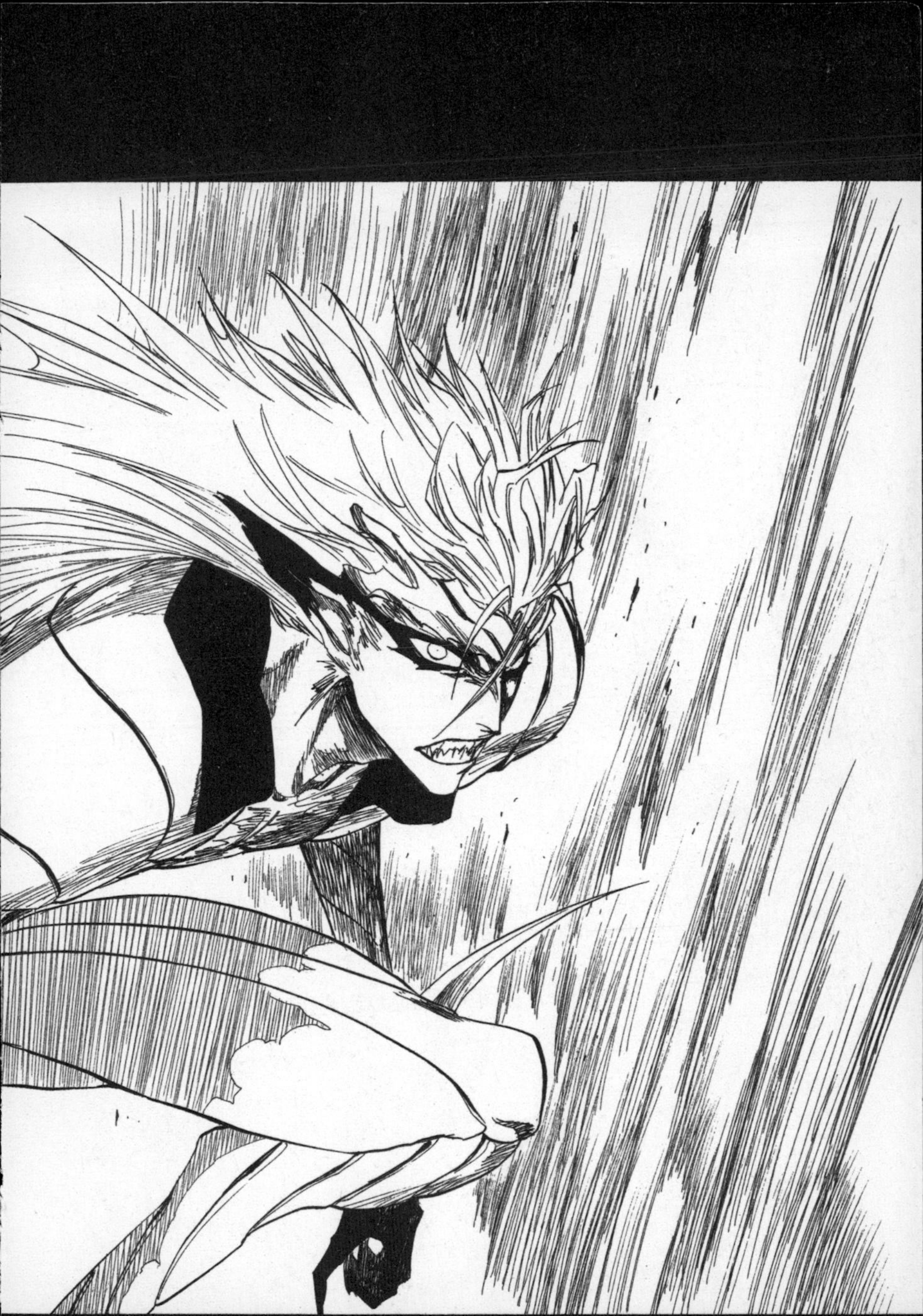

BLEACH281.

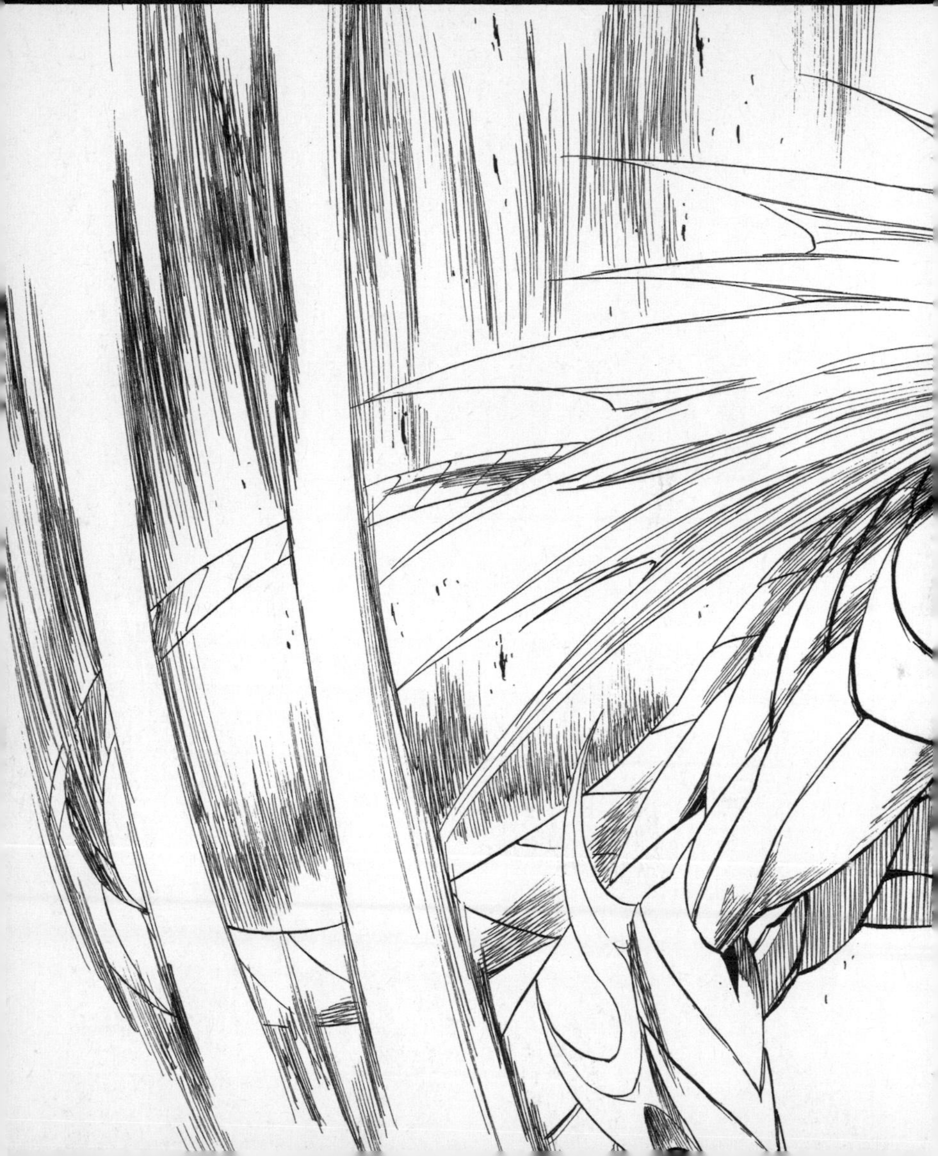

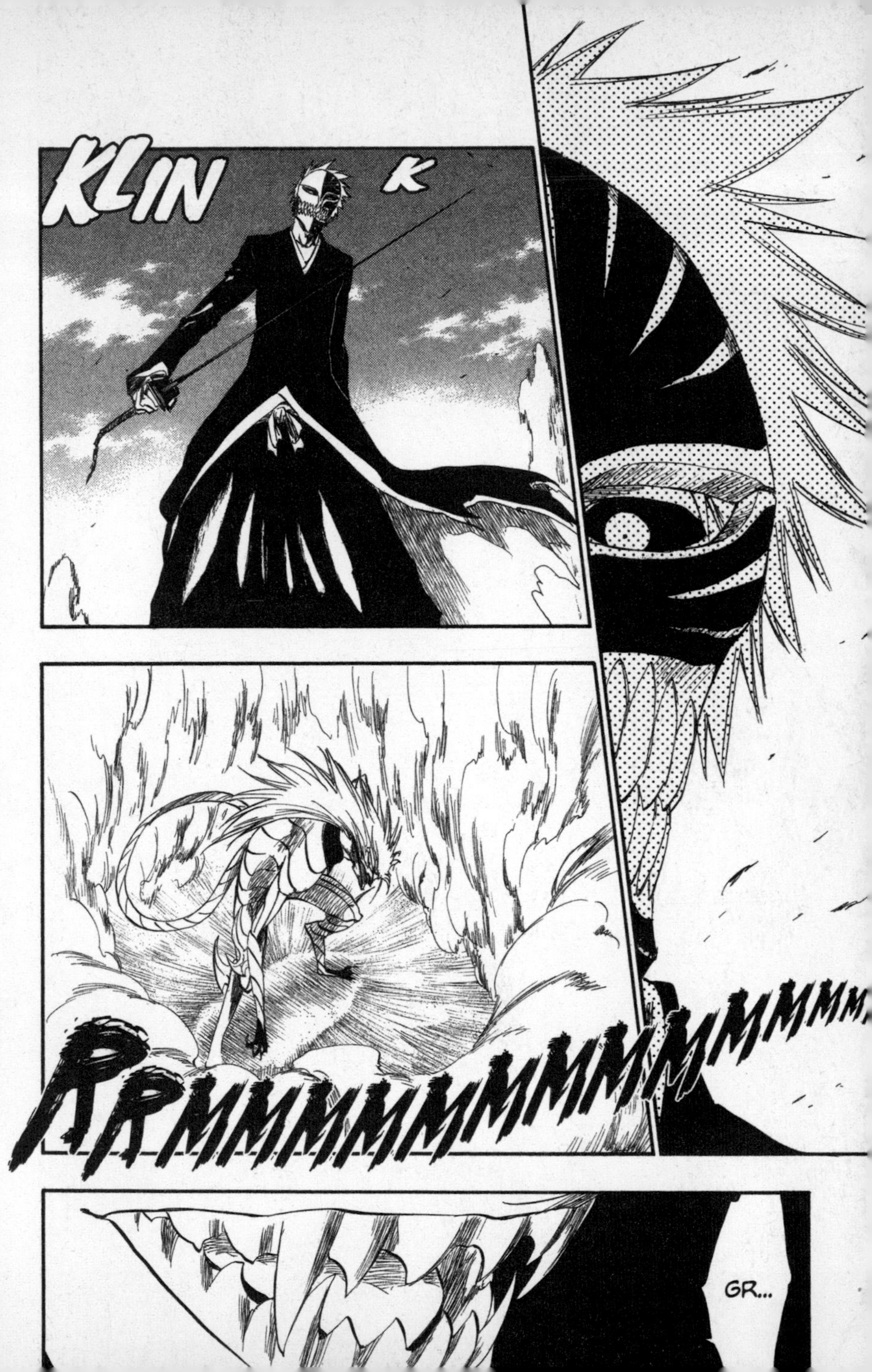
KLIN K
RRMMMMMMMMMMMMMMMMMMMMM
GR...

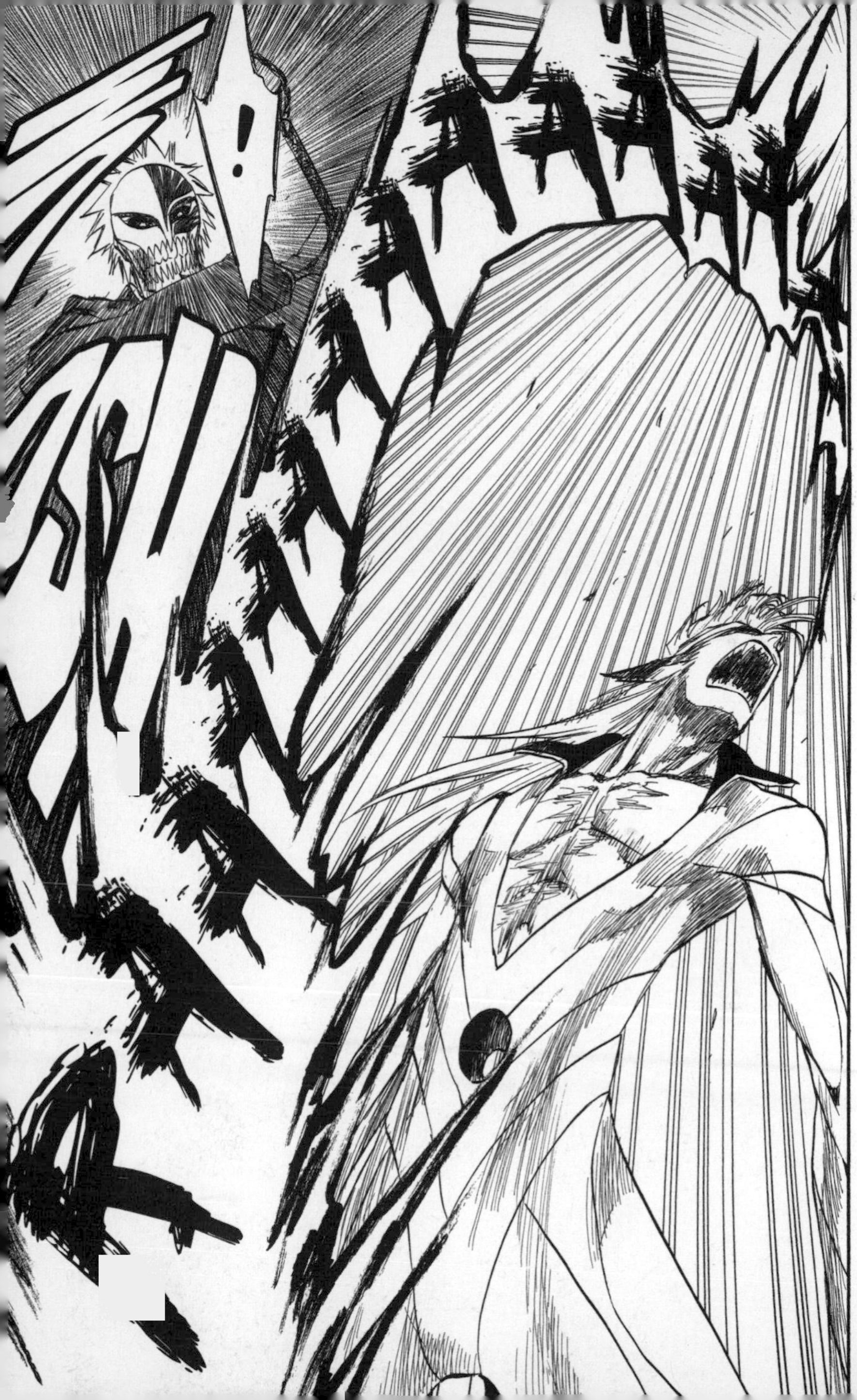
!

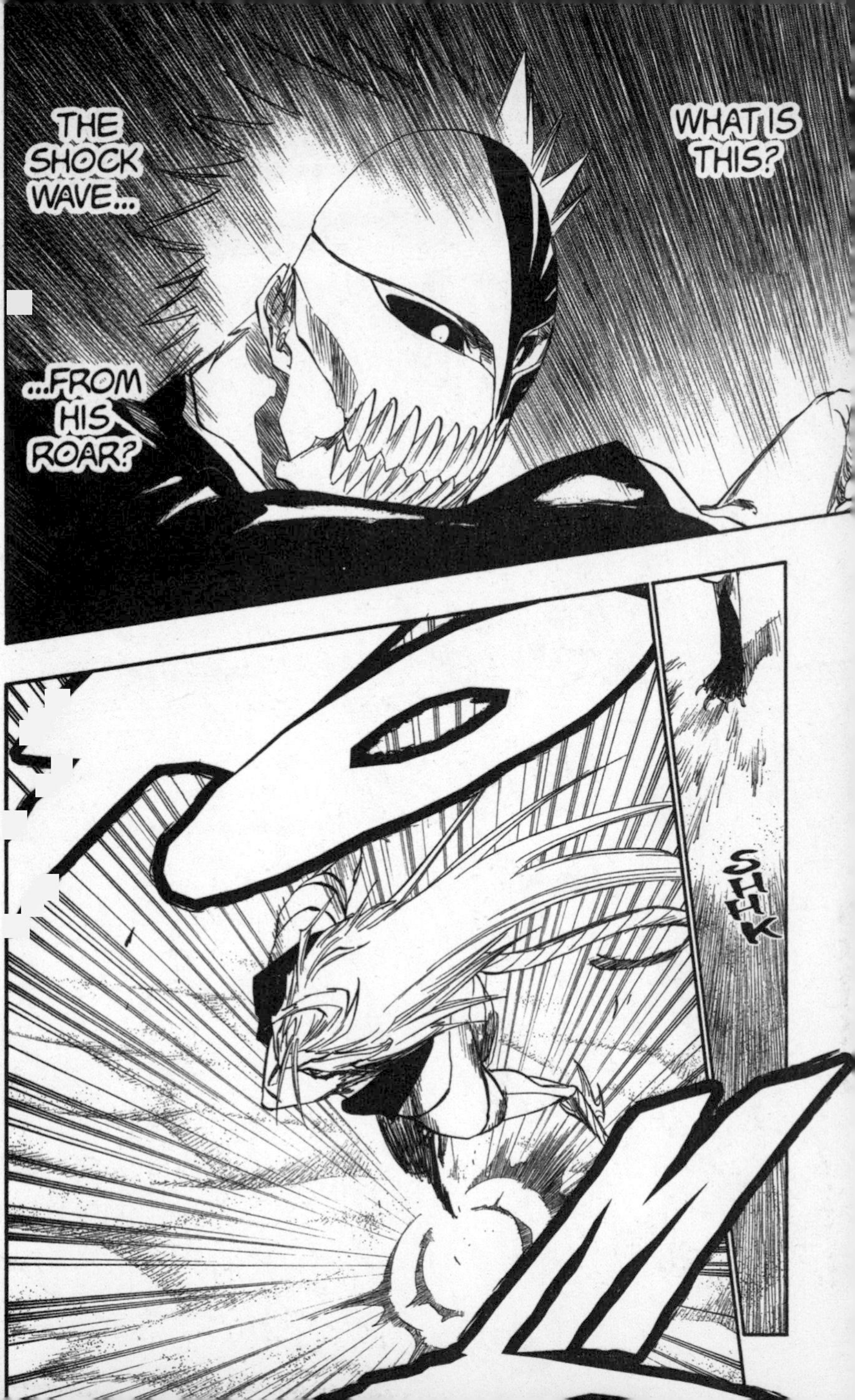
WHAT IS THIS?
THE SHOCK WAVE...
...FROM HIS ROAR?
SHHK

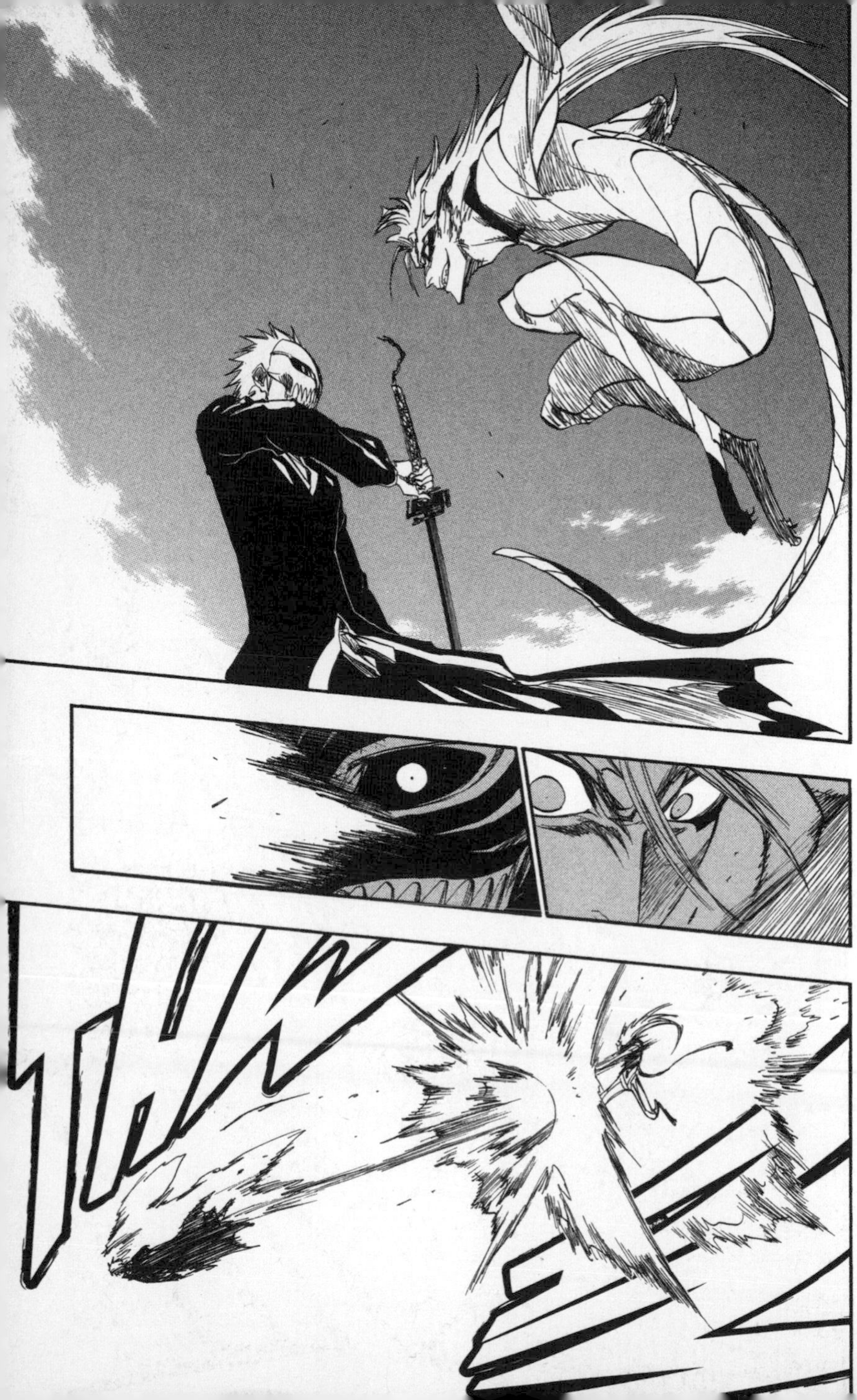

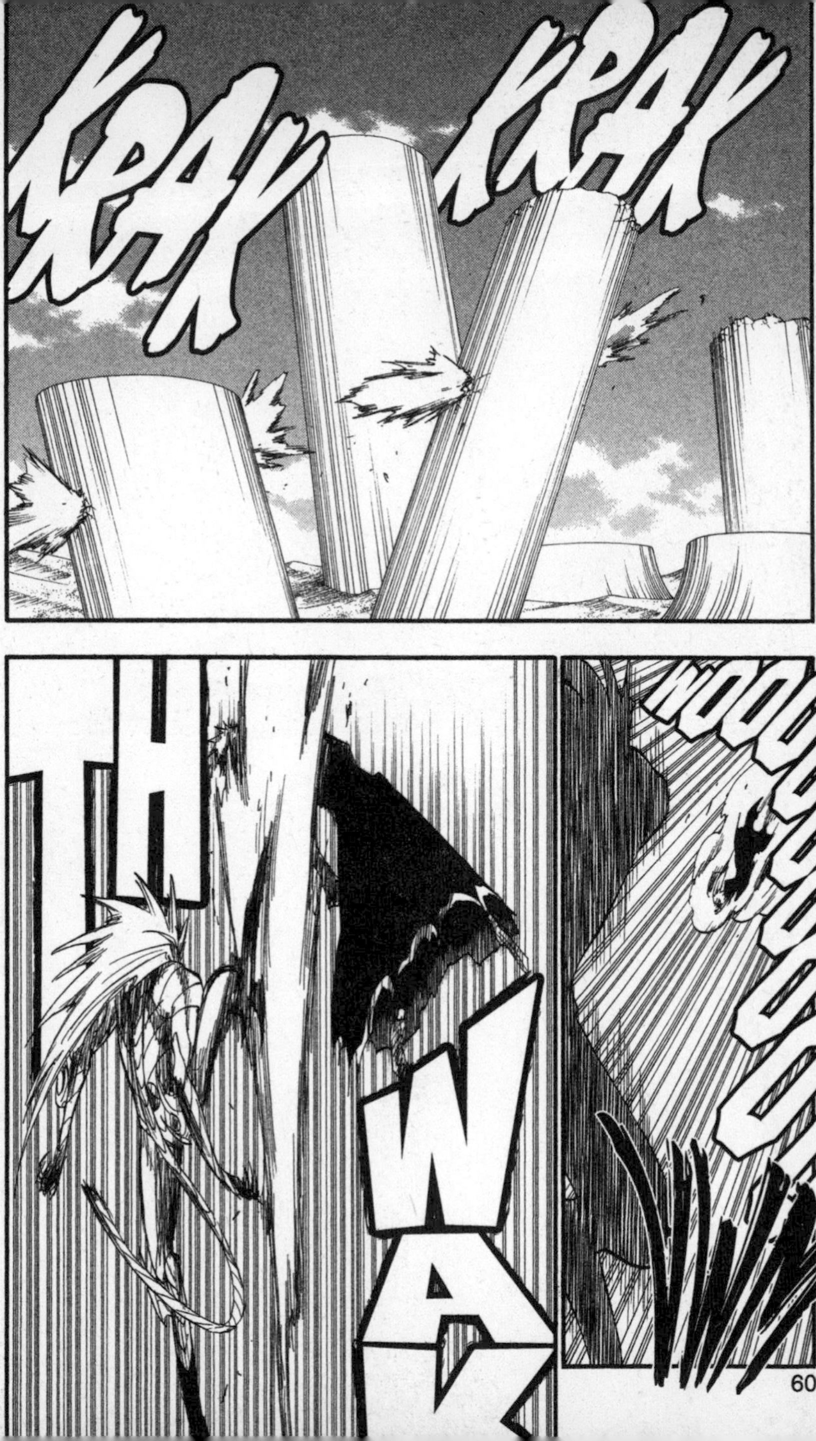
KRAK
KRAK
THWAK

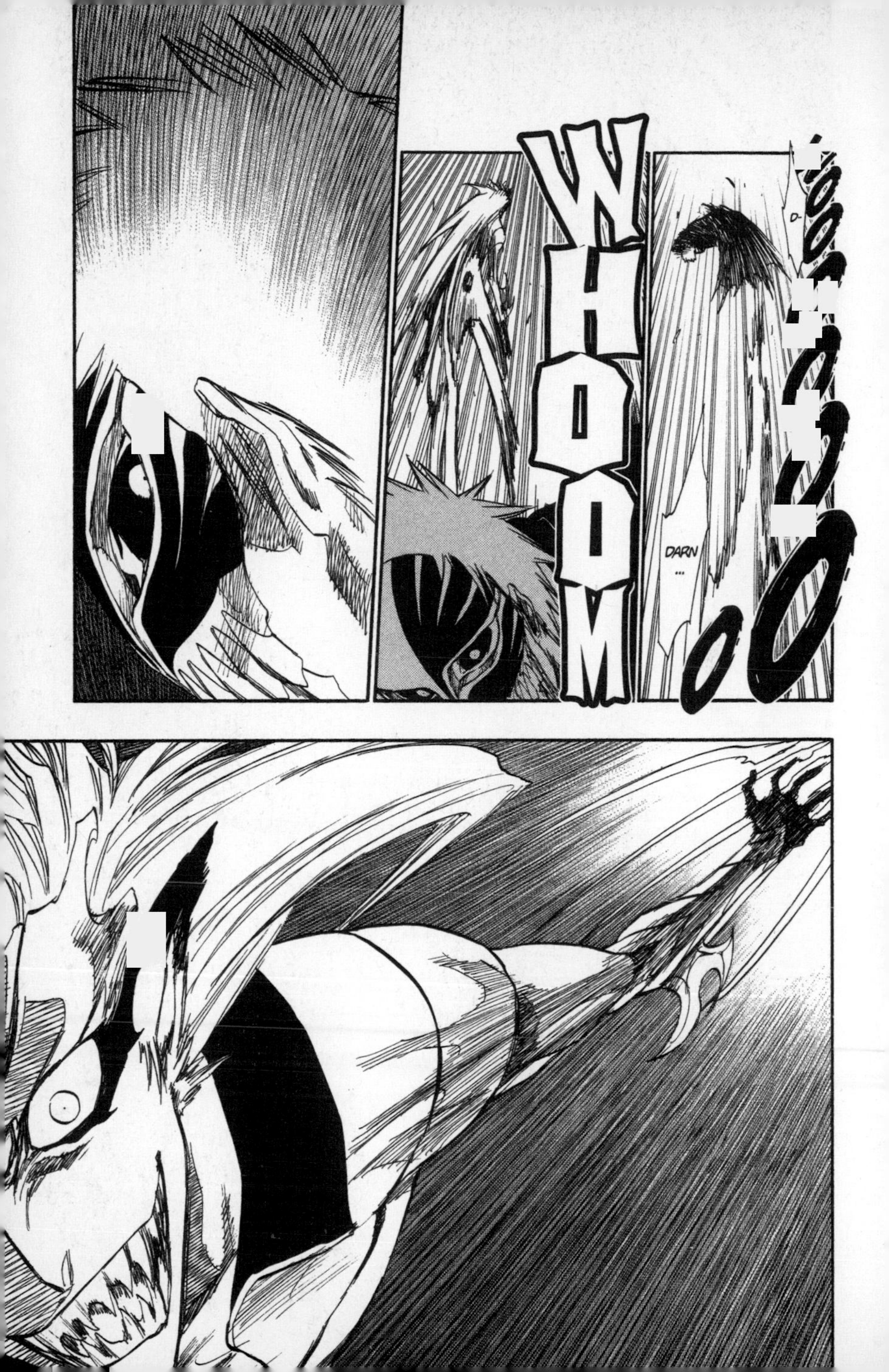
DARN ...
WHOOM

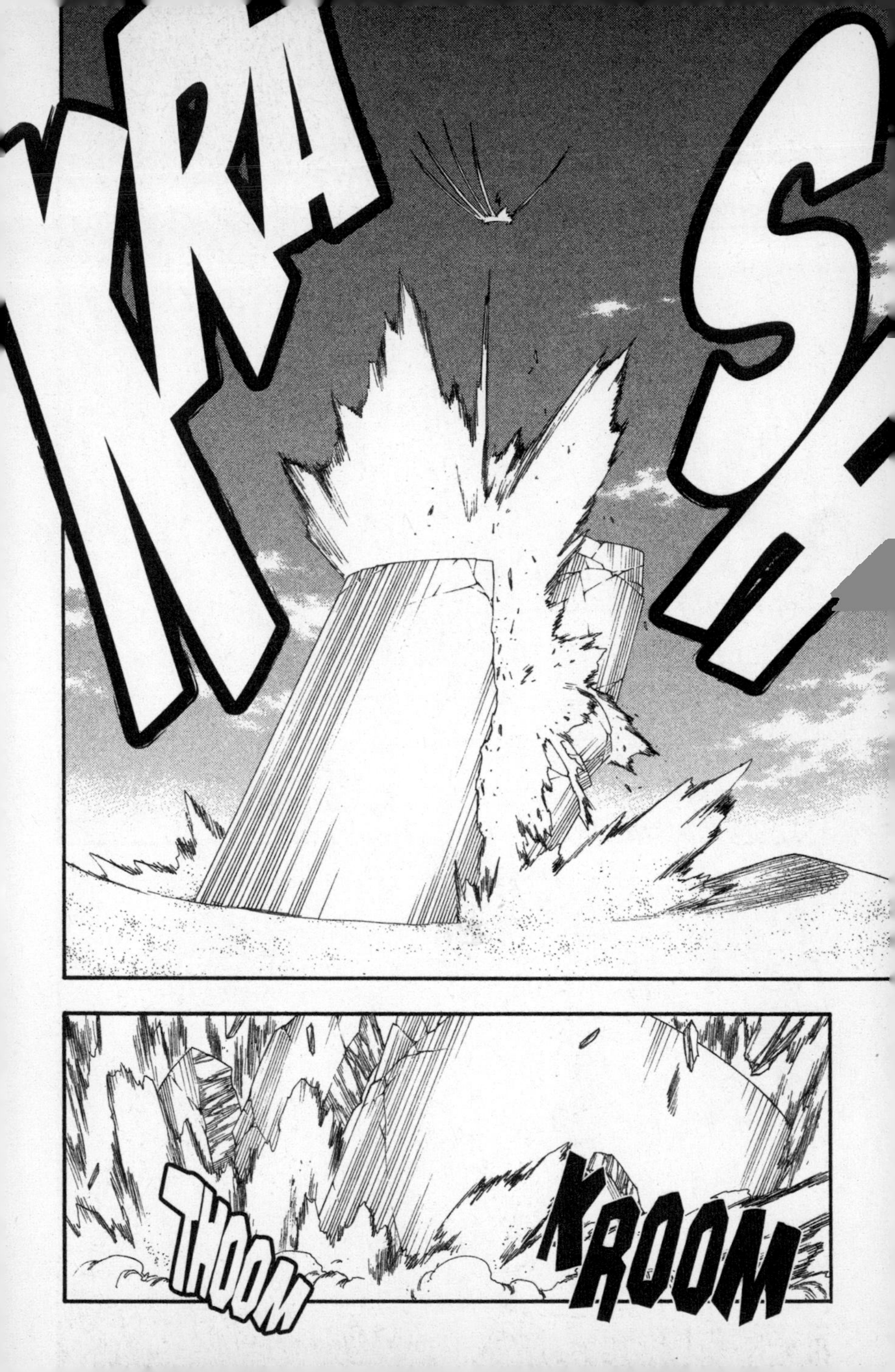
KRA
THOOM
KROOM

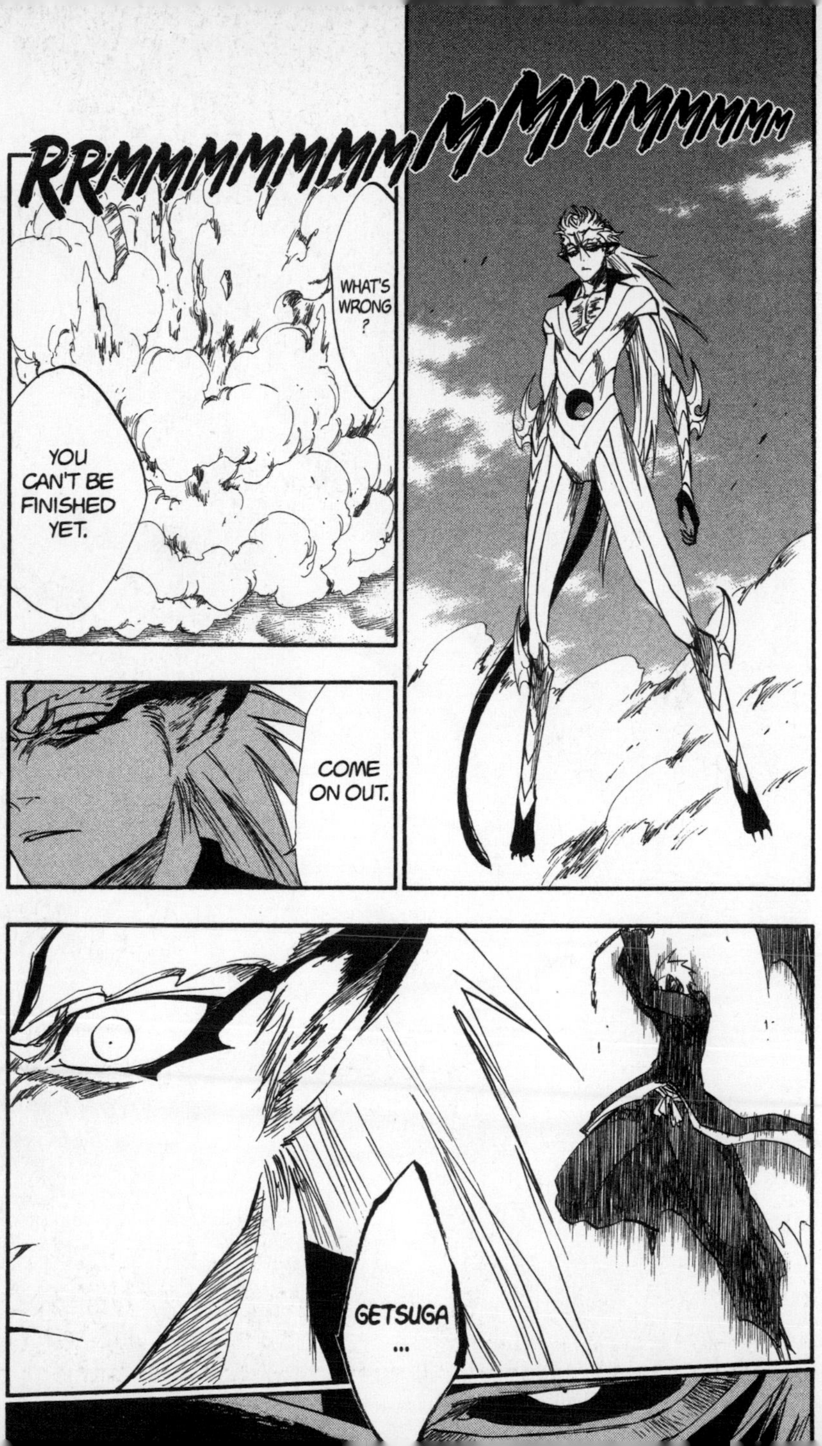
RRMMMMMMMMMMMMMMMMMMMMMMM
WHAT'S WRONG?
YOU CAN'T BE FINISHED YET.
COME ON OUT.
GETSUGA...

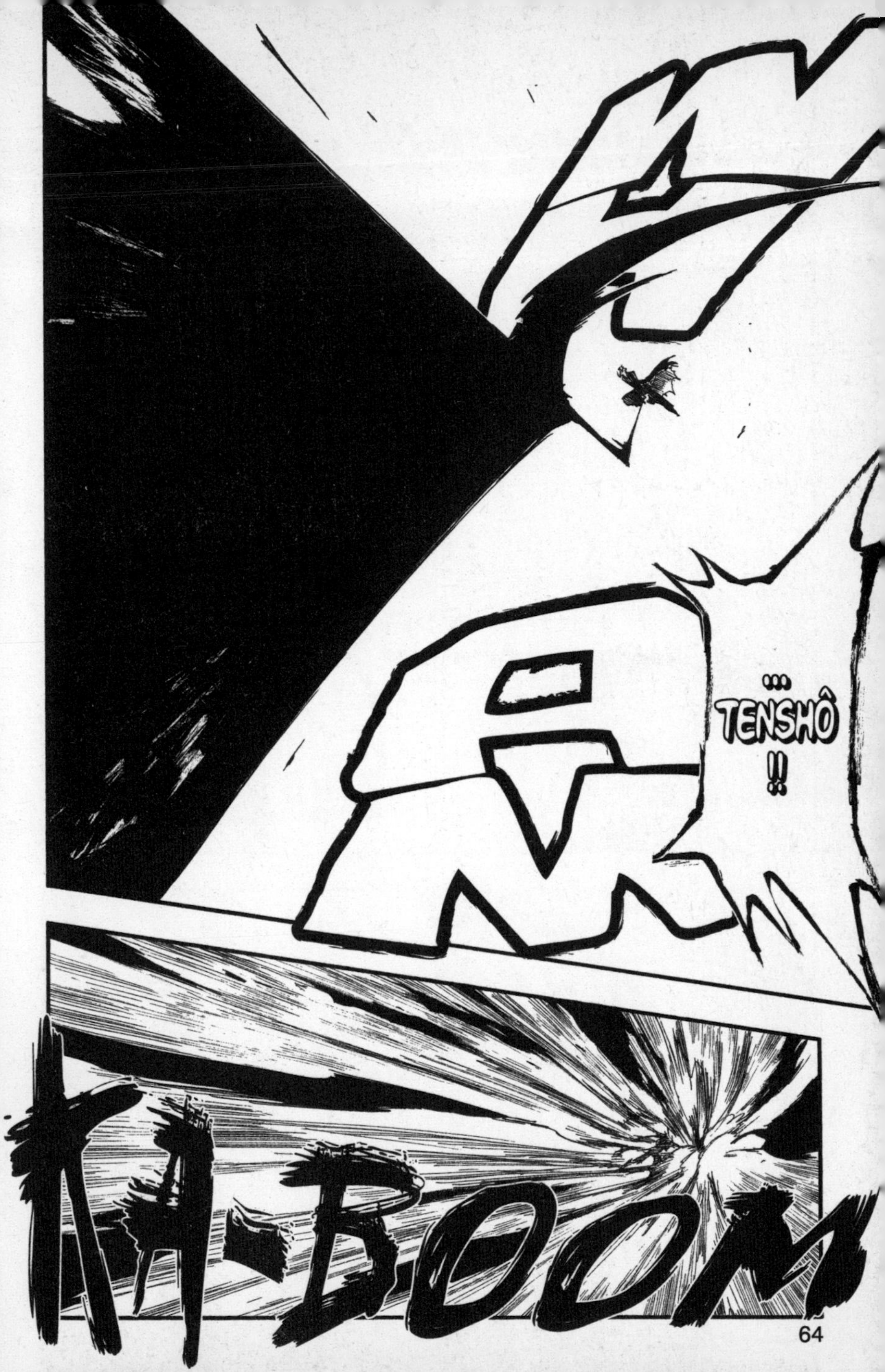
...TENSHÔ !!
KA-BOOM

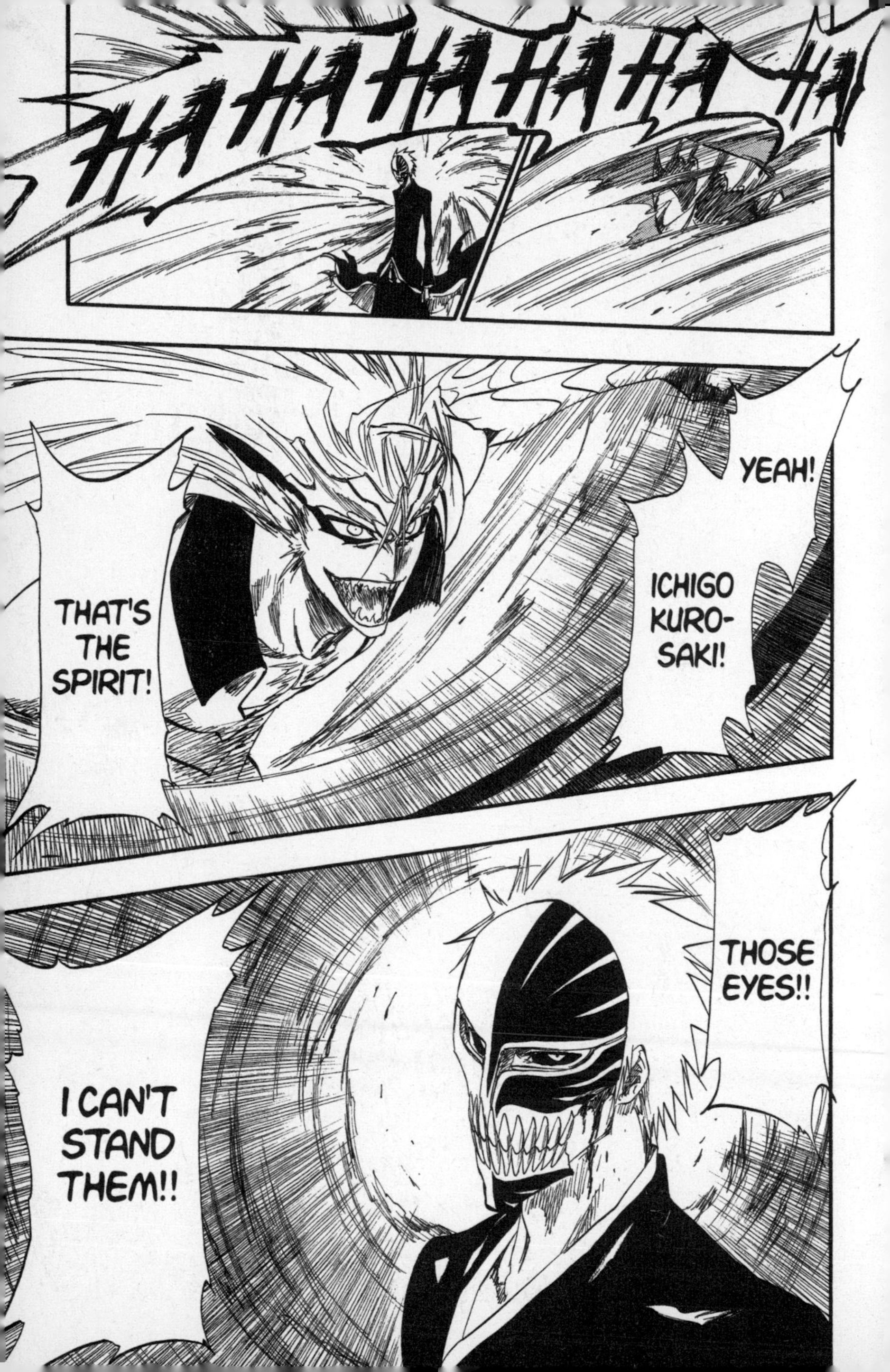
HAHAHAHAHAHAHA
YEAH!
ICHIGO KURO-SAKI!
THAT'S THE SPIRIT!
THOSE EYES!!
I CAN'T STAND THEM!!

282. THE PRIMAL FEAR

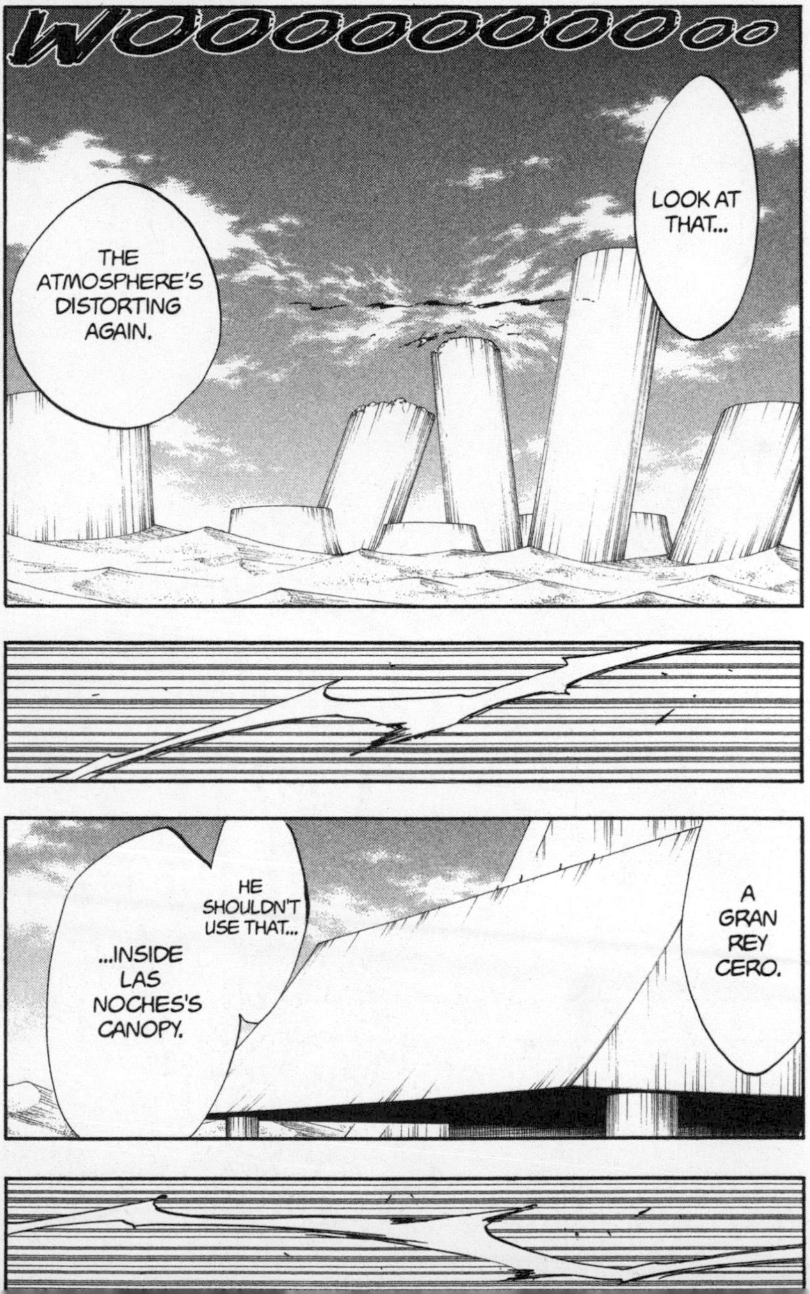
WOOOOOOOOOoo
LOOK AT THAT...
THE ATMOSPHERE'S DISTORTING AGAIN.
A GRAN REY CERO.
HE SHOULDN'T USE THAT...
...INSIDE LAS NOCHES'S CANOPY.

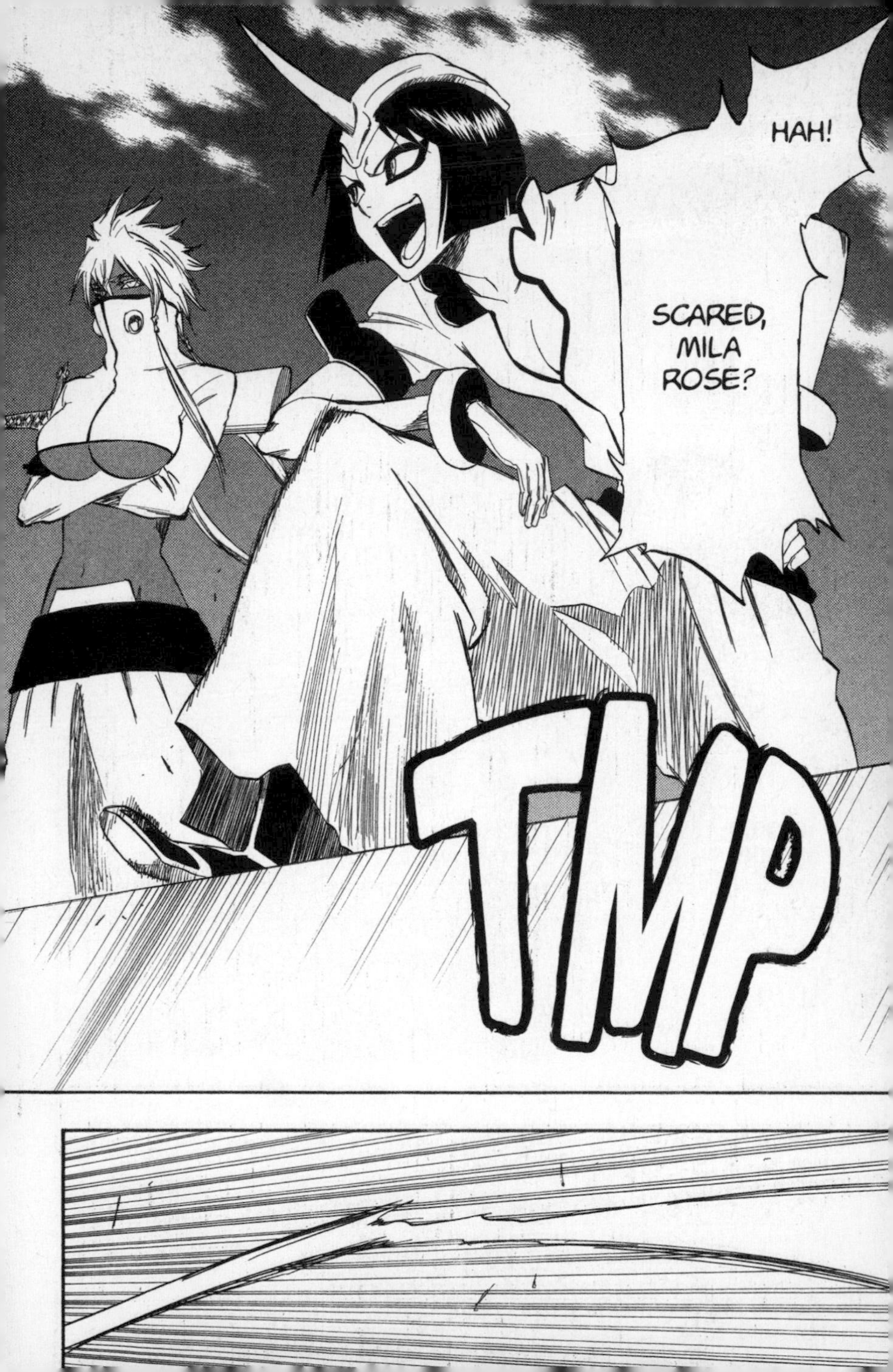
HAH!
SCARED, MILA ROSE?
TMP

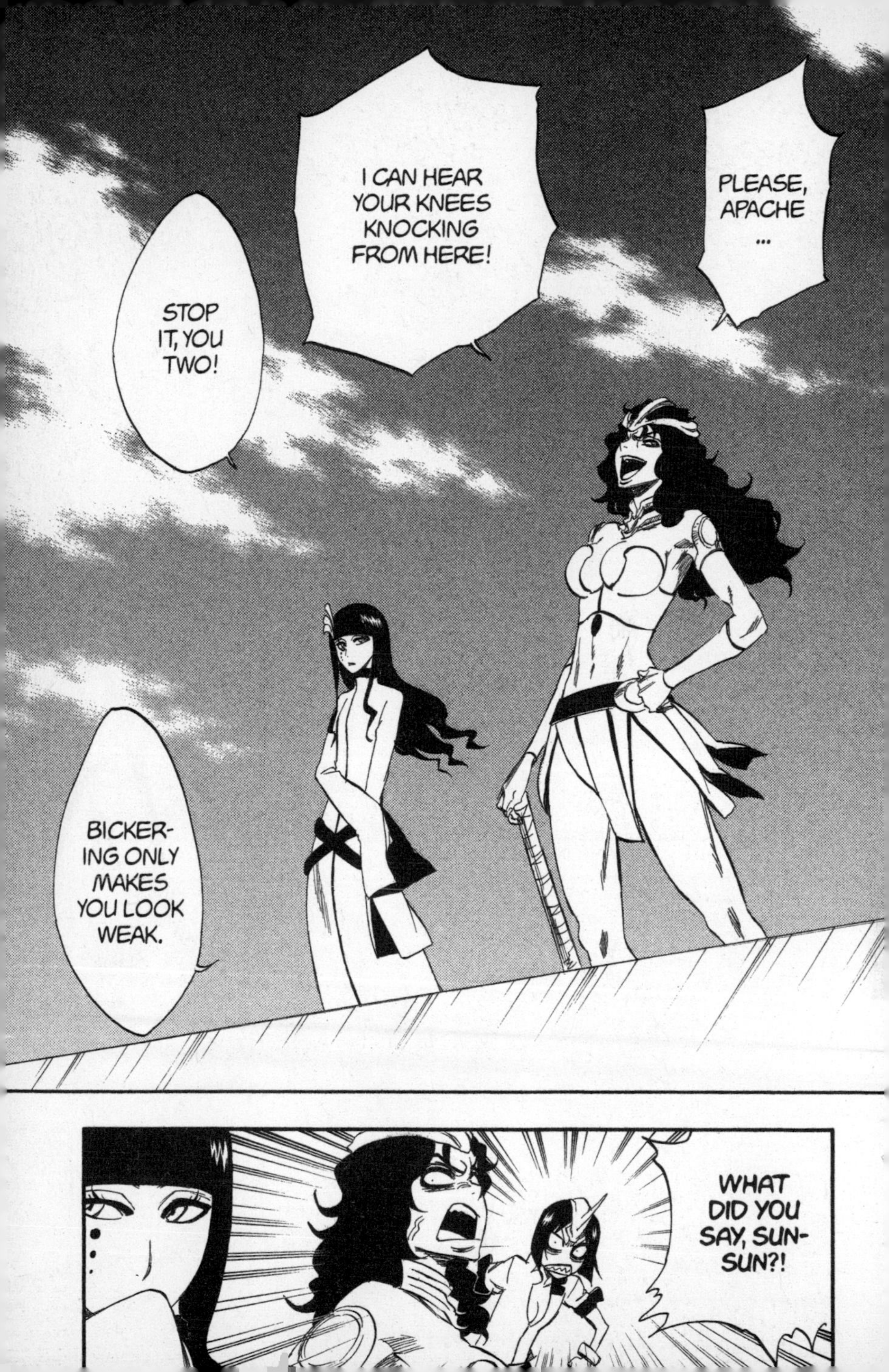
PLEASE, APACHE ...
I CAN HEAR YOUR KNEES KNOCKING FROM HERE!
STOP IT, YOU TWO!
BICKERING ONLY MAKES YOU LOOK WEAK.
WHAT DID YOU SAY, SUN-SUN?!

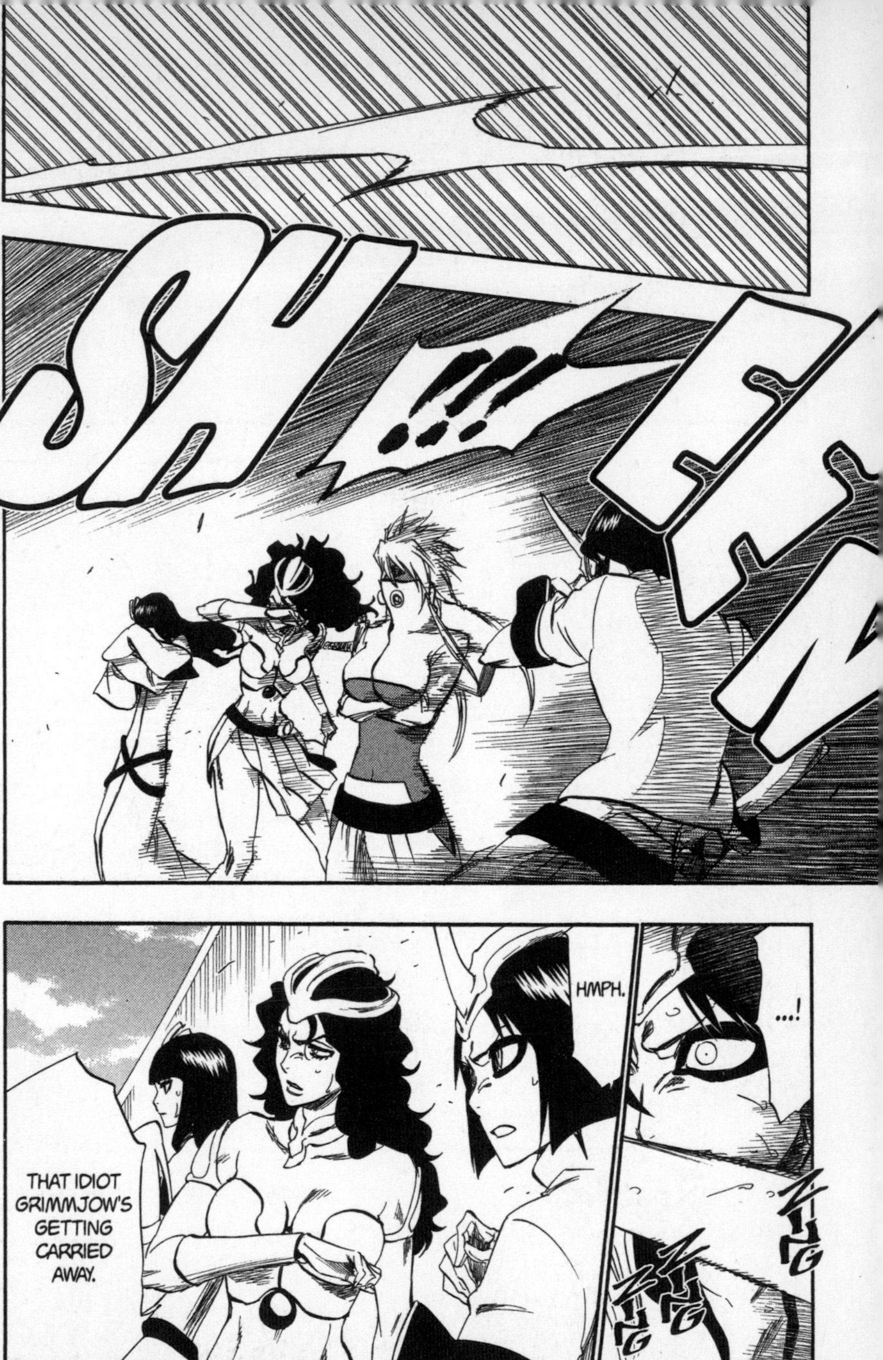
SHEEN
HMPH.
...!
THAT IDIOT GRIMMJOW'S GETTING CARRIED AWAY.

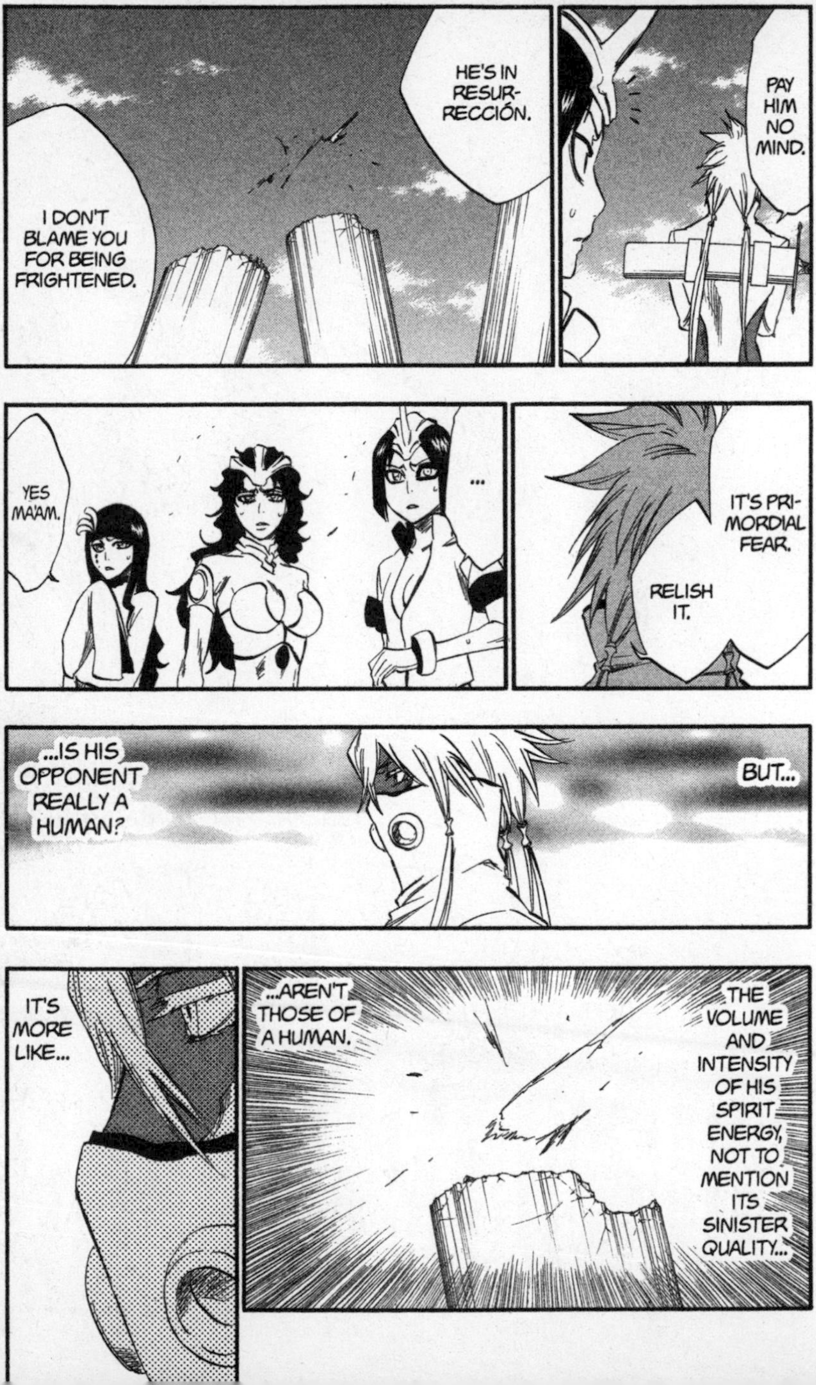
PAY HIM NO MIND.
HE'S IN RESUR-RECCIÓN.
I DON'T BLAME YOU FOR BEING FRIGHTENED.
IT'S PRI-MORDIAL FEAR.
RELISH IT.
...
YES MA'AM.
BUT...
...IS HIS OPPONENT REALLY A HUMAN?
THE VOLUME AND INTENSITY OF HIS SPIRIT ENERGY, NOT TO MENTION ITS SINISTER QUALITY...
...AREN'T THOSE OF A HUMAN.
IT'S MORE LIKE...

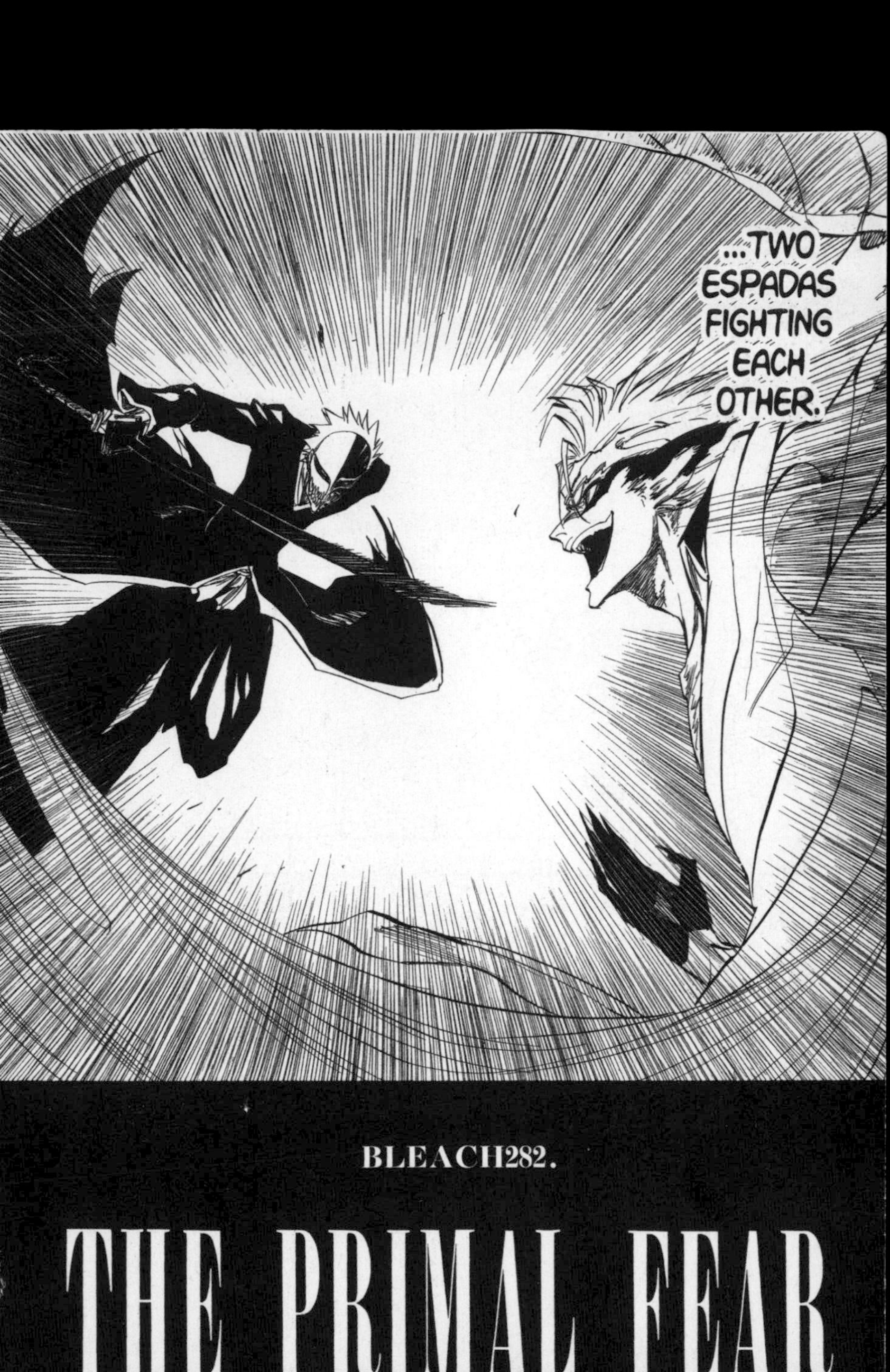
...TWO ESPADAS FIGHTING EACH OTHER.

BLEACH282.

THE PRIMAL FEAR

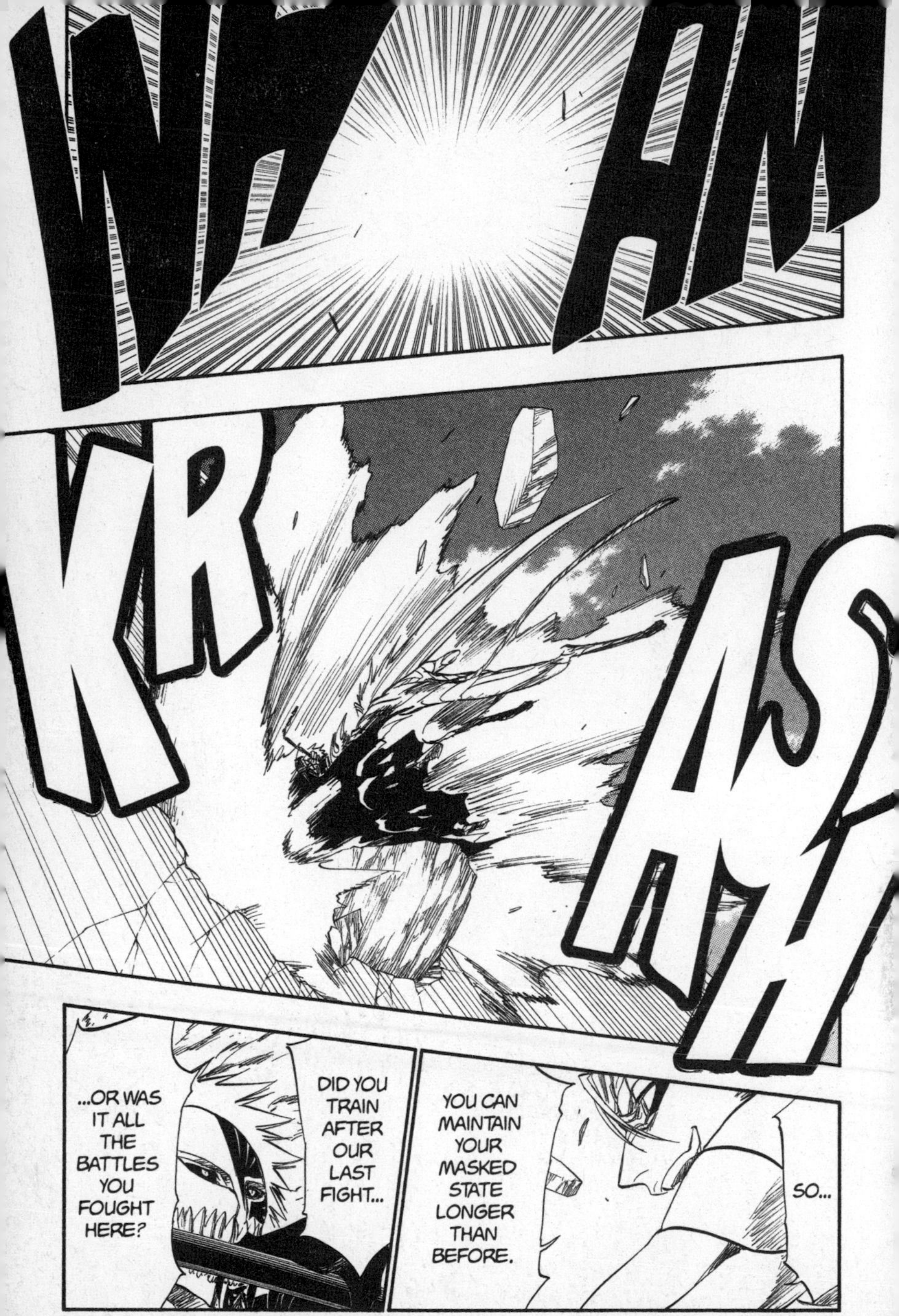
WHAM
KRASH
SO...
YOU CAN MAINTAIN YOUR MASKED STATE LONGER THAN BEFORE.
DID YOU TRAIN AFTER OUR LAST FIGHT...
...OR WAS IT ALL THE BATTLES YOU FOUGHT HERE?

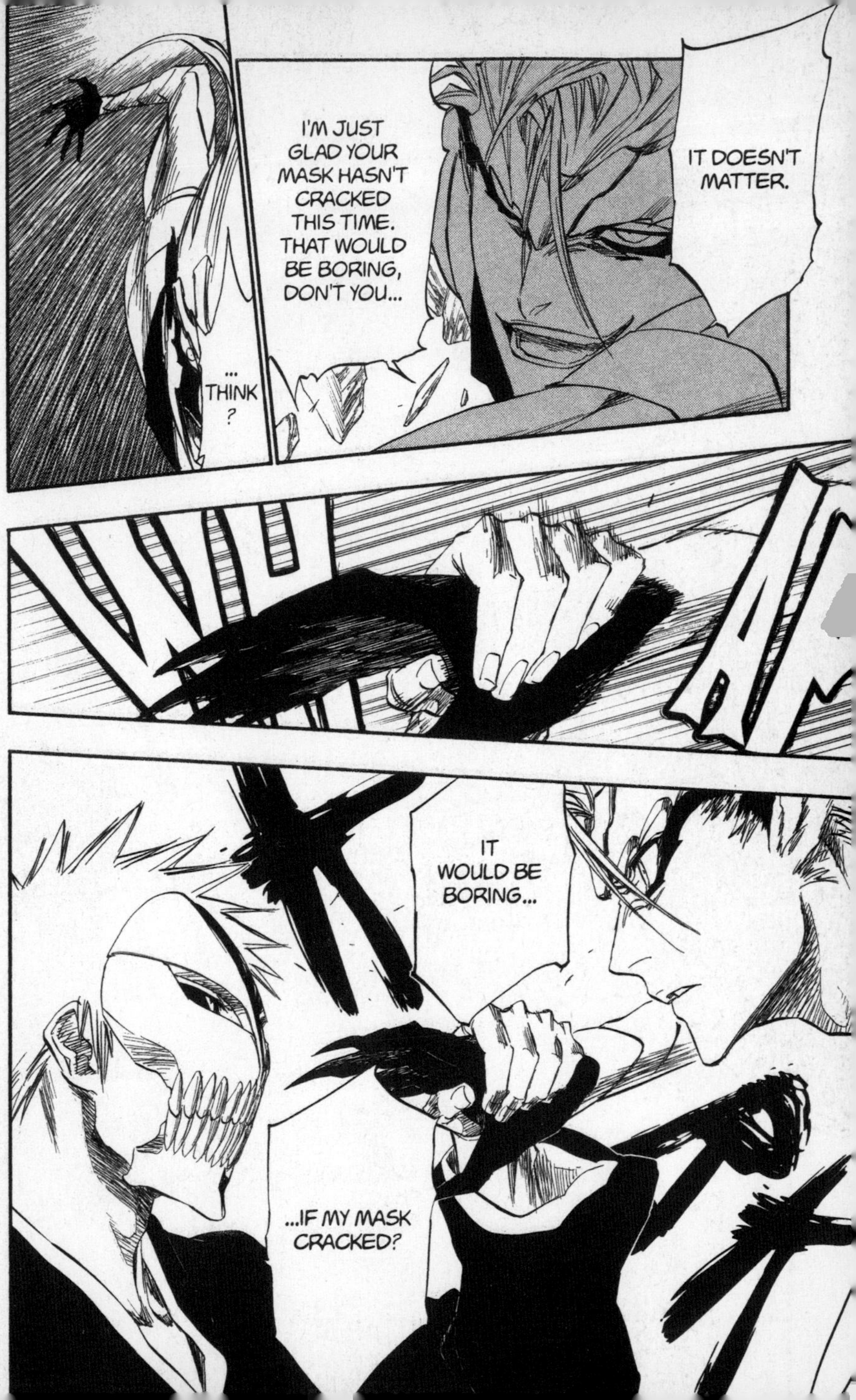
IT DOESN'T MATTER.
I'M JUST GLAD YOUR MASK HASN'T CRACKED THIS TIME. THAT WOULD BE BORING, DON'T YOU...
...THINK?
IT WOULD BE BORING...
...IF MY MASK CRACKED?

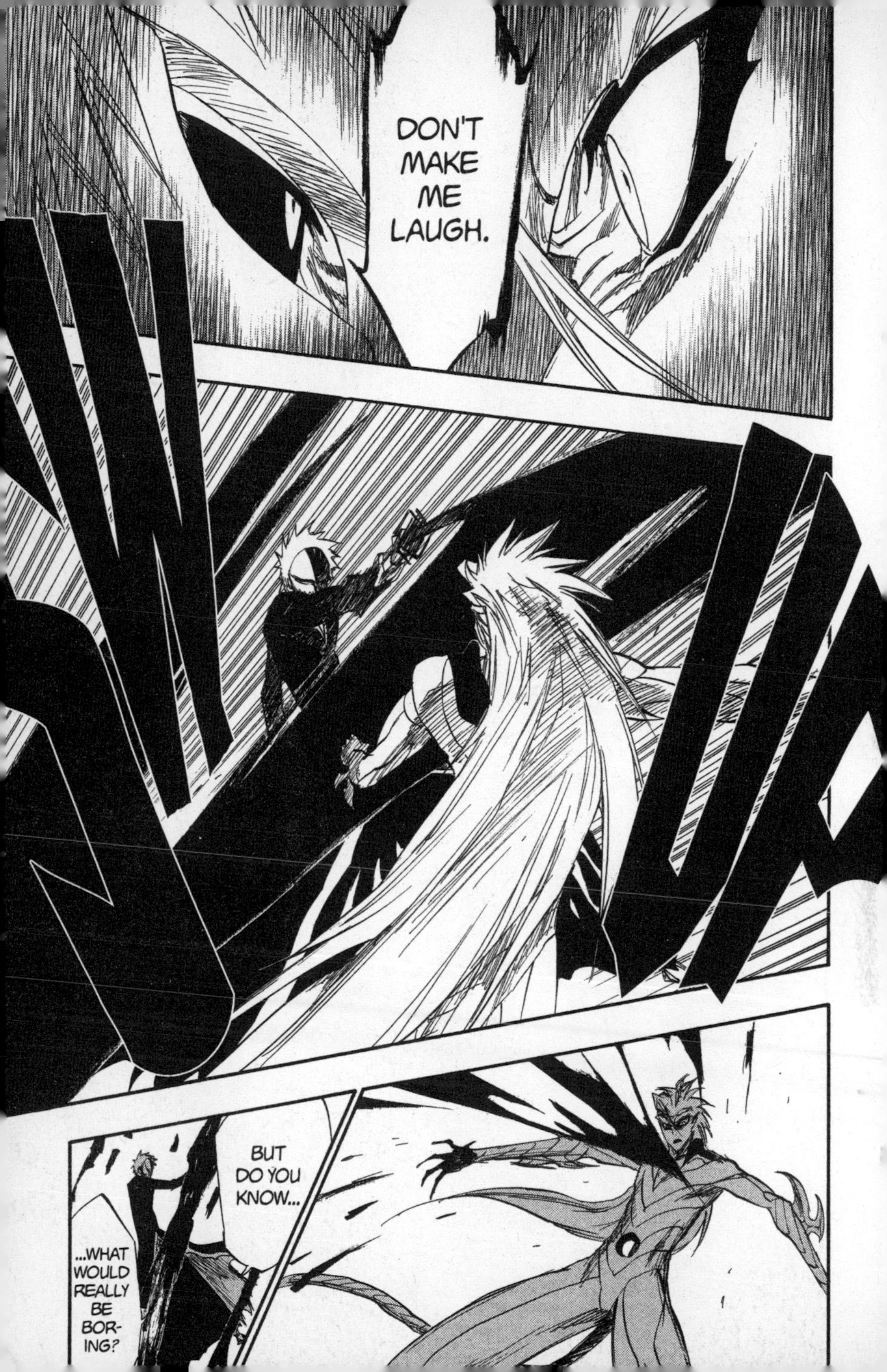
DON'T MAKE ME LAUGH.
BUT DO YOU KNOW...
...WHAT WOULD REALLY BE BOR-ING?

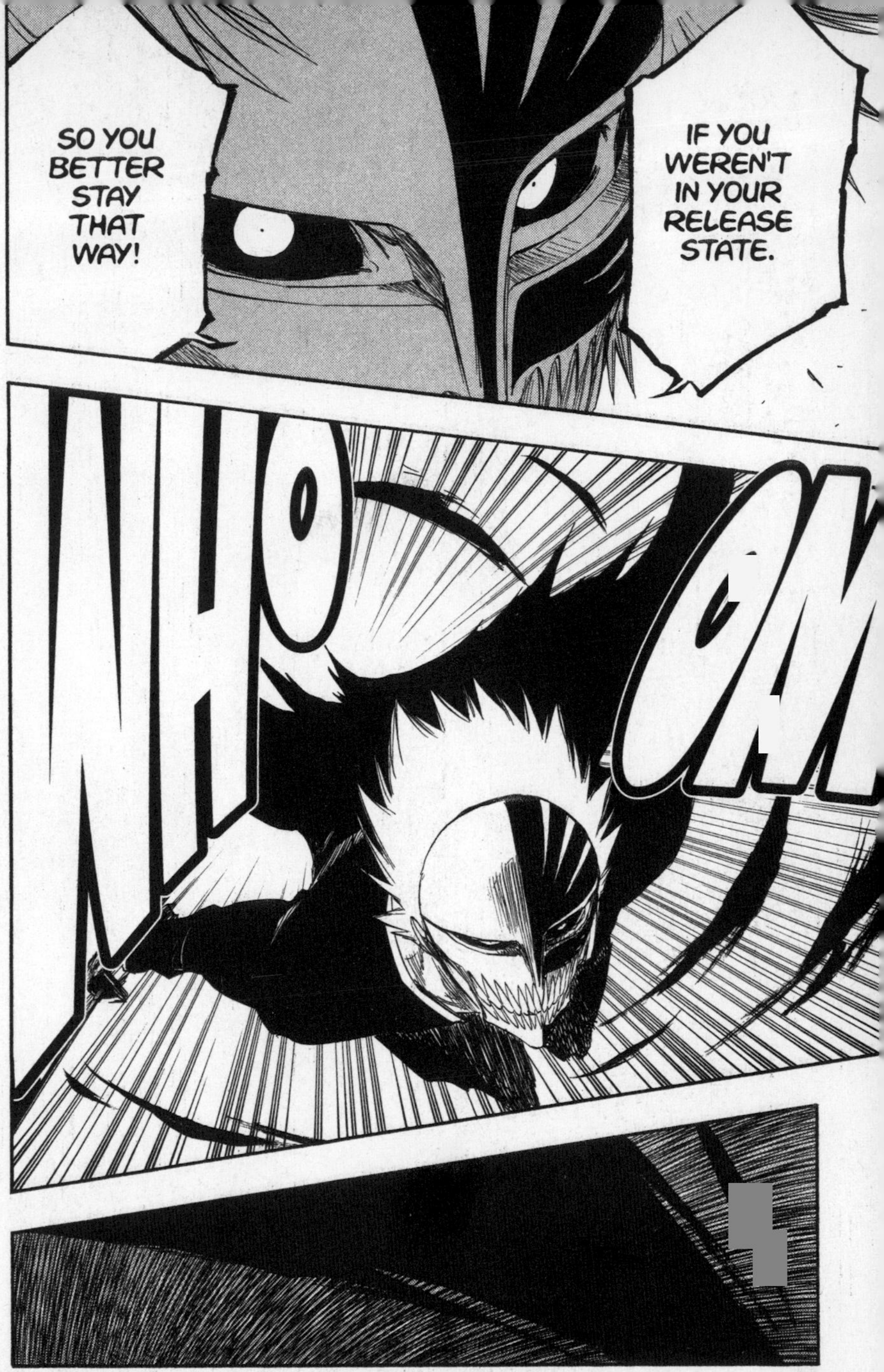
IF YOU WEREN'T IN YOUR RELEASE STATE.
SO YOU BETTER STAY THAT WAY!
WHOOM

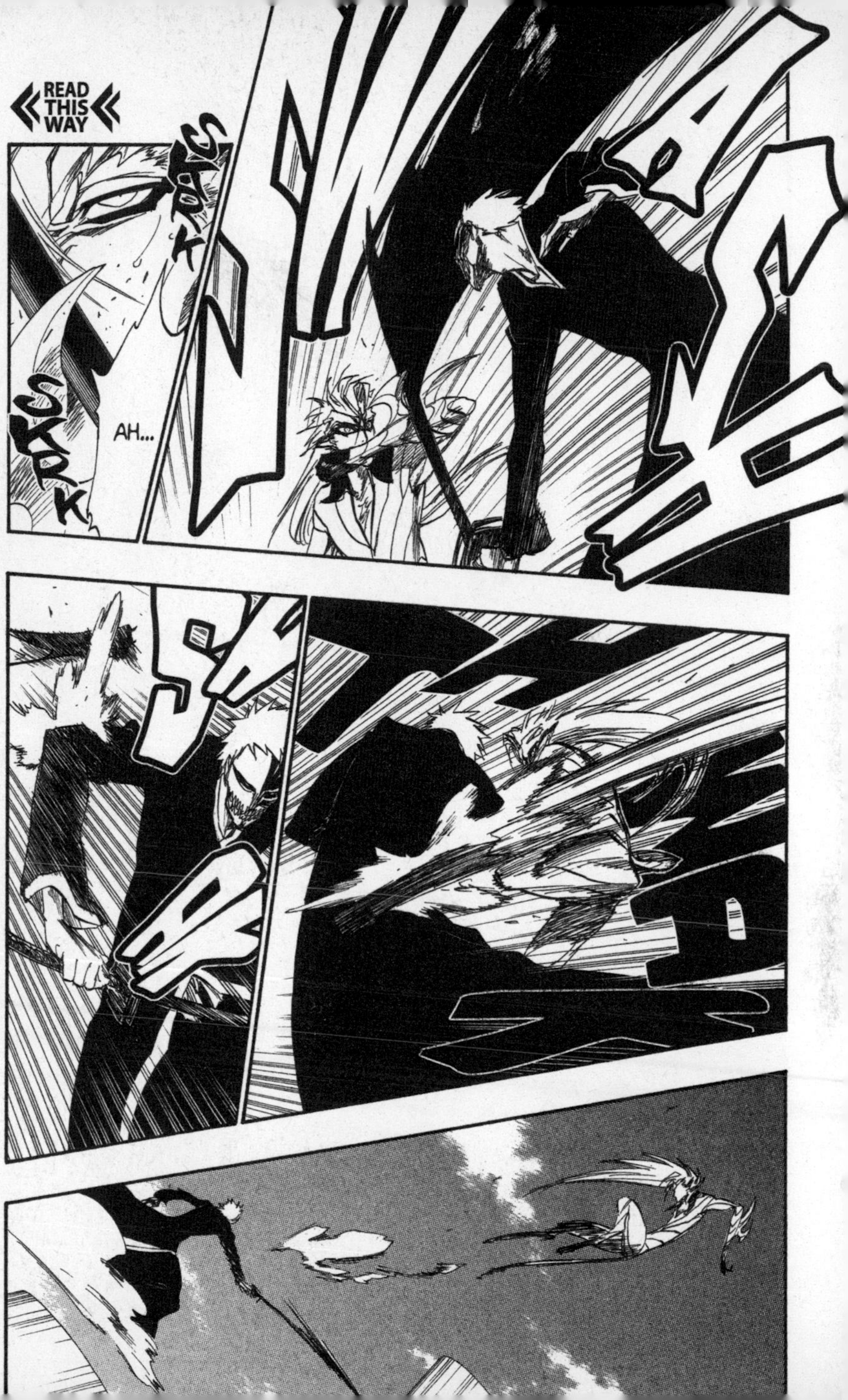
READ THIS WAY
STRK STRK
STRK
AH...

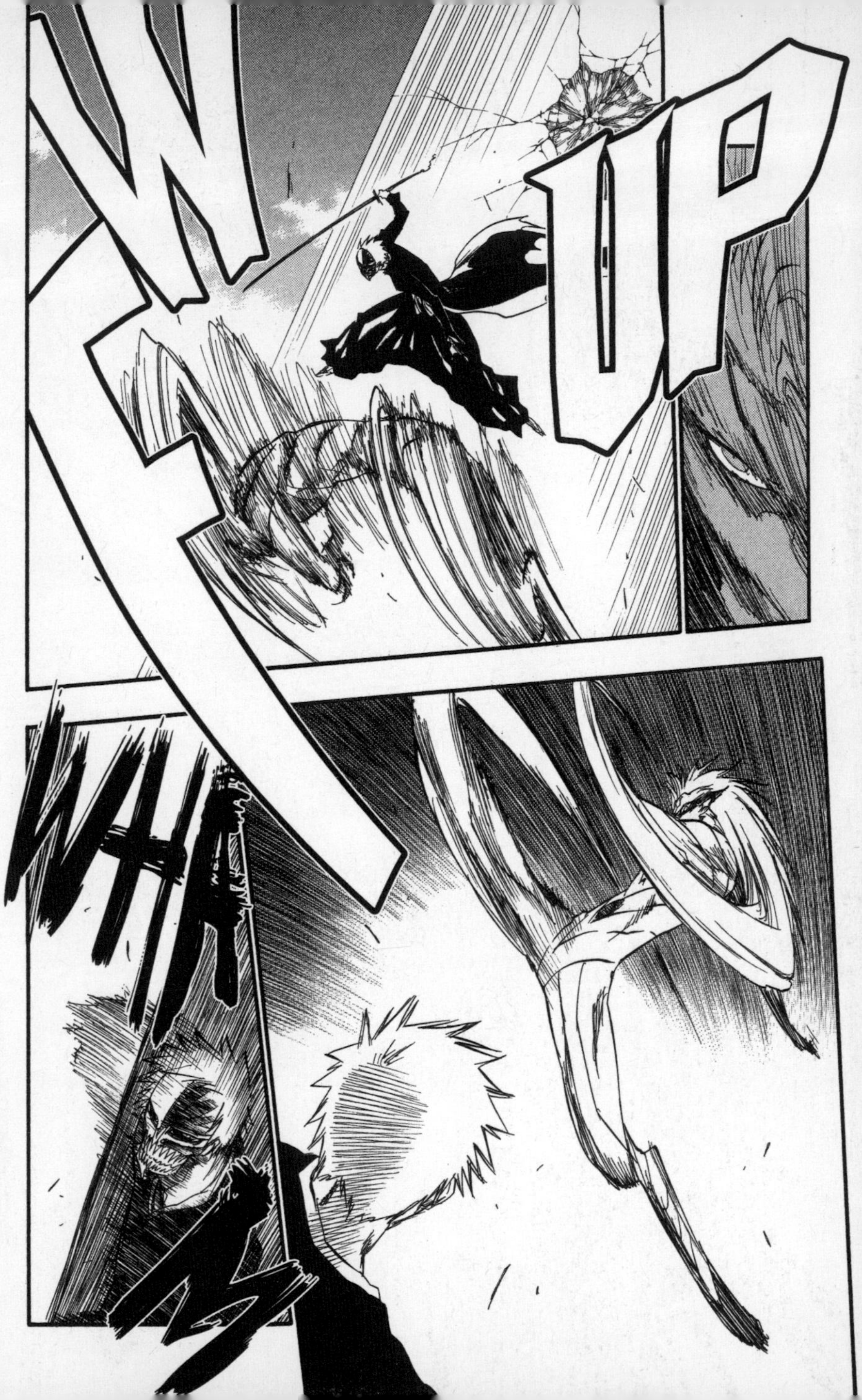
WHUP
WHAS

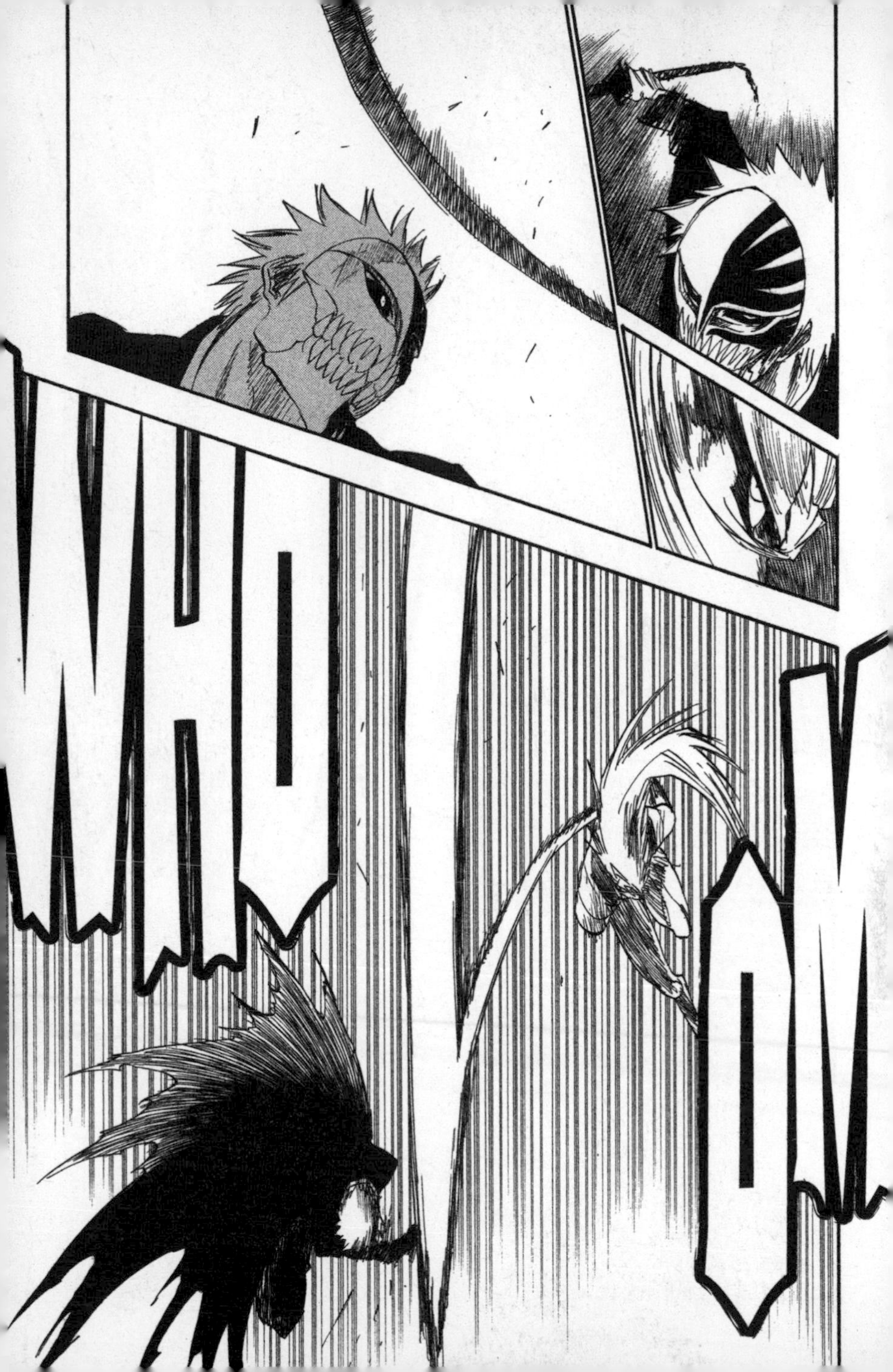
WHOOM

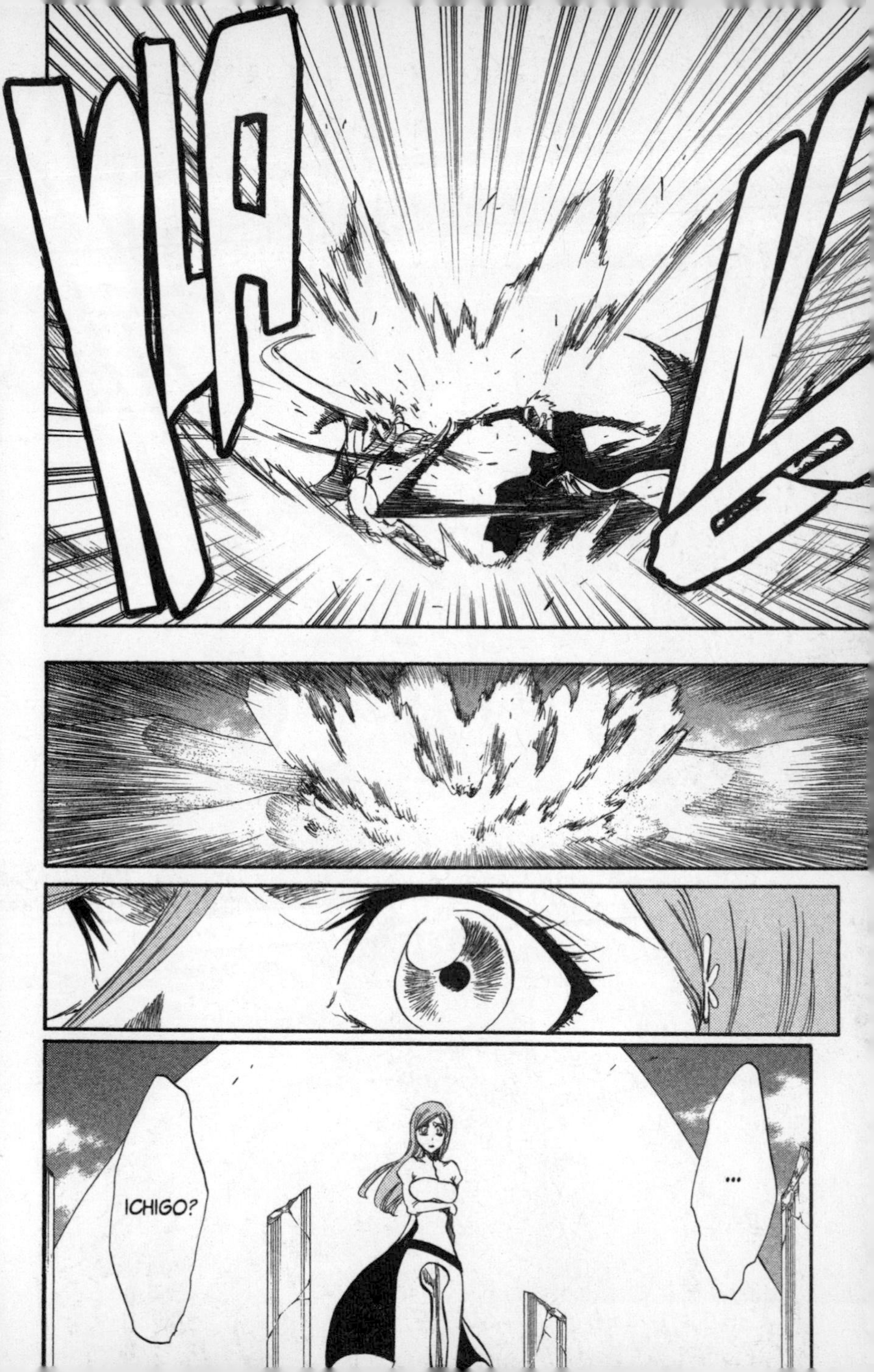

KA-WAM
...
ICHIGO?

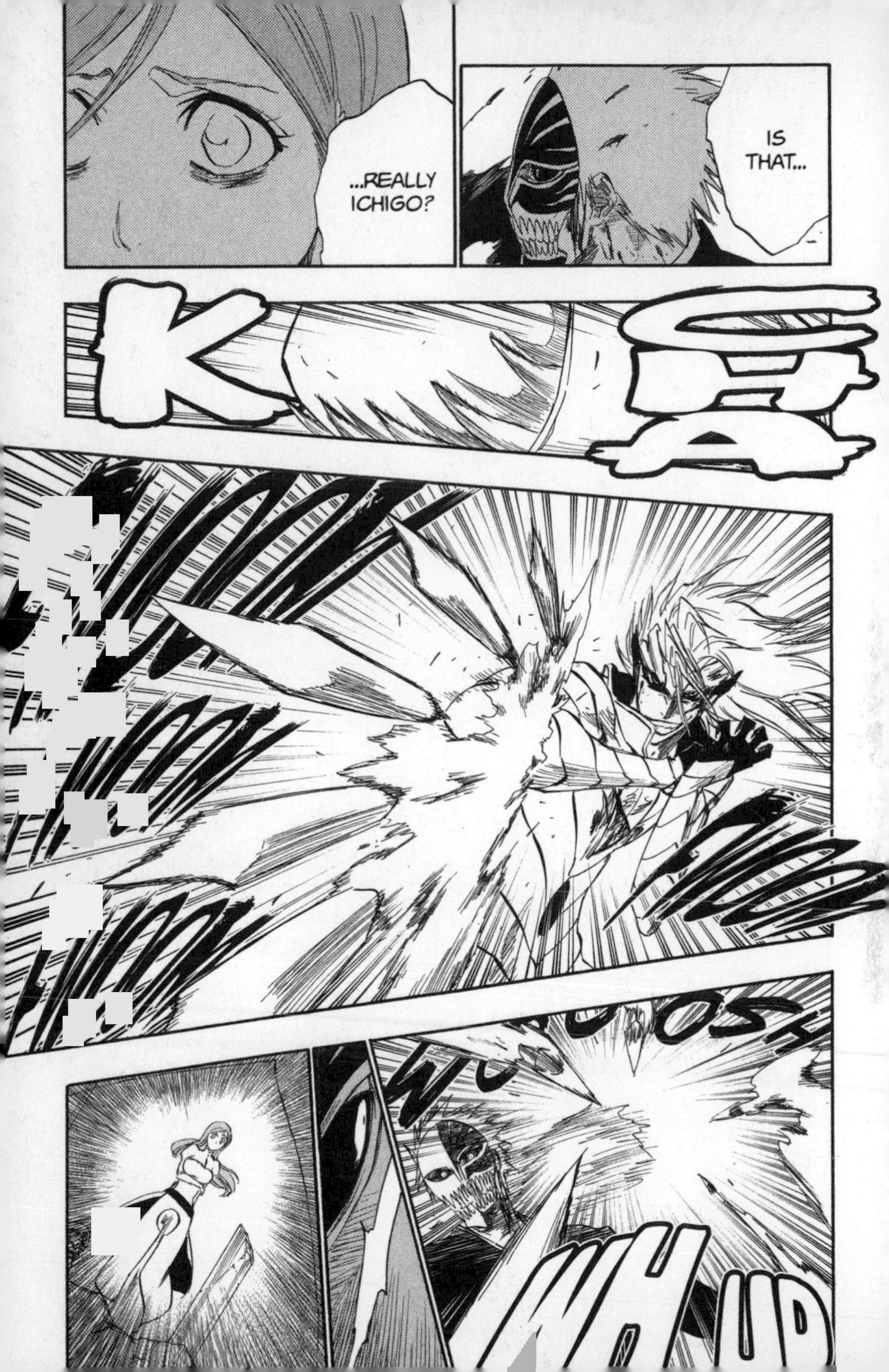
IS THAT...
...REALLY ICHIGO?

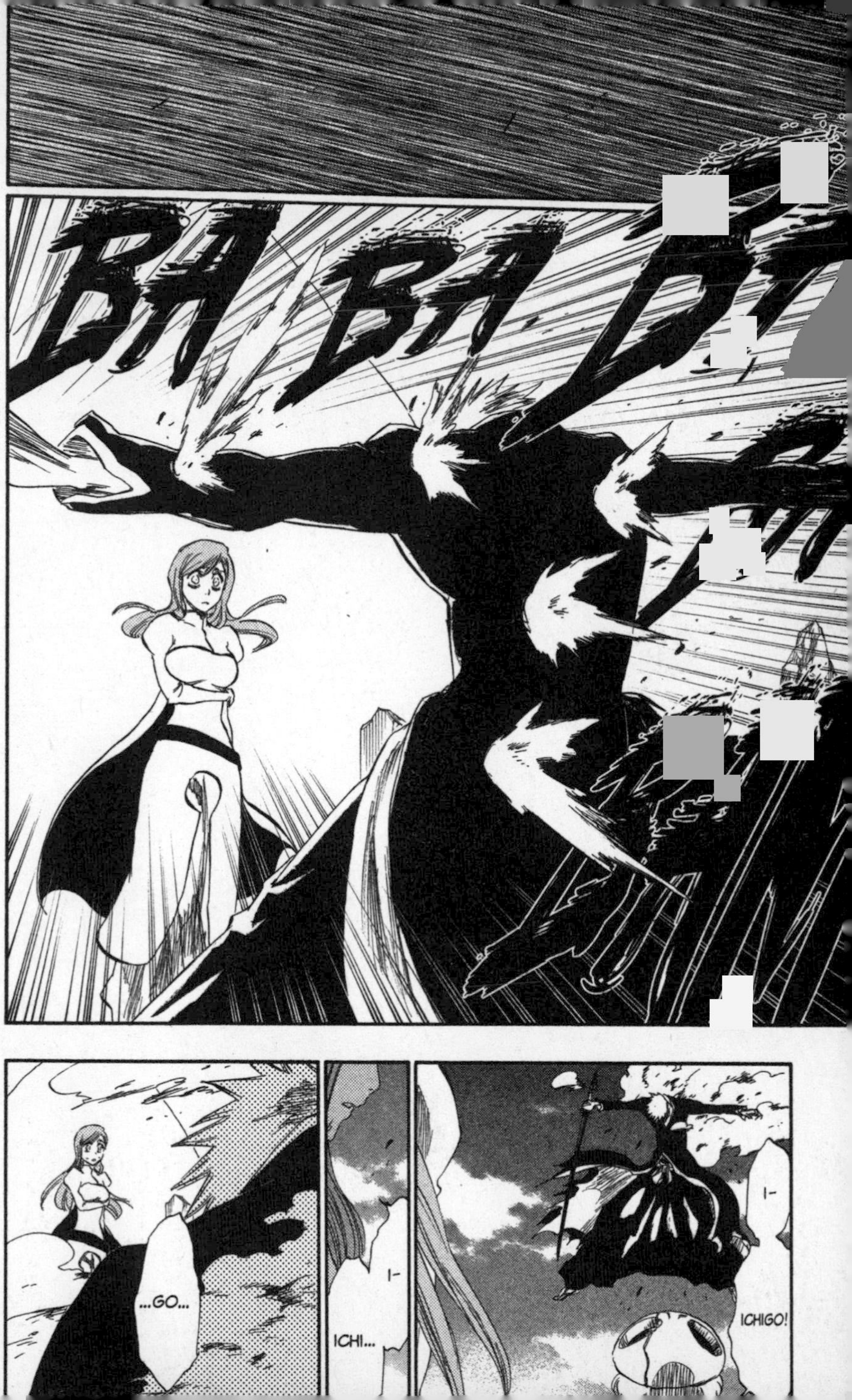
I-
ICHIGO!
I-
ICHI...
...GO...

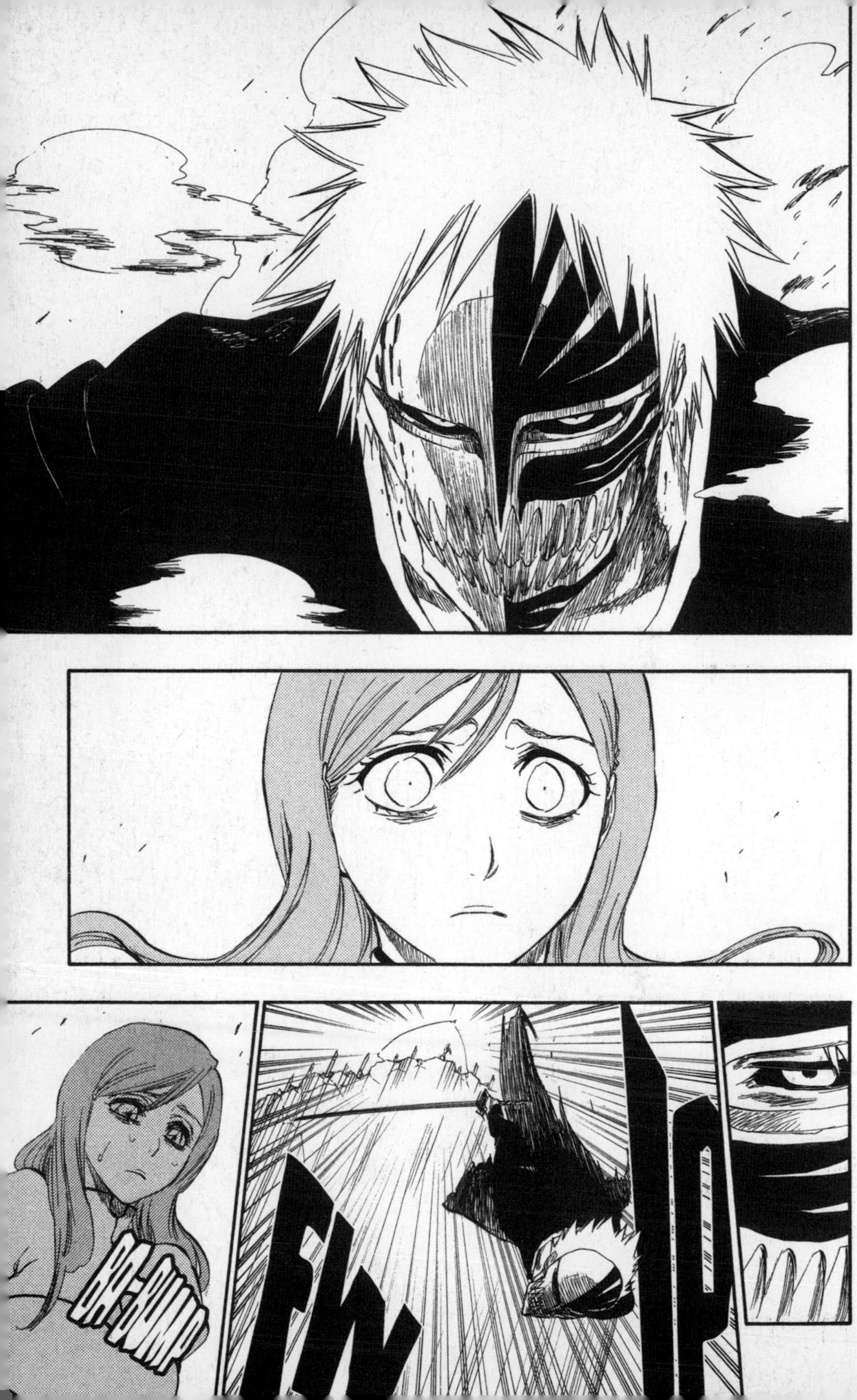
FWIP
BA-BUMP

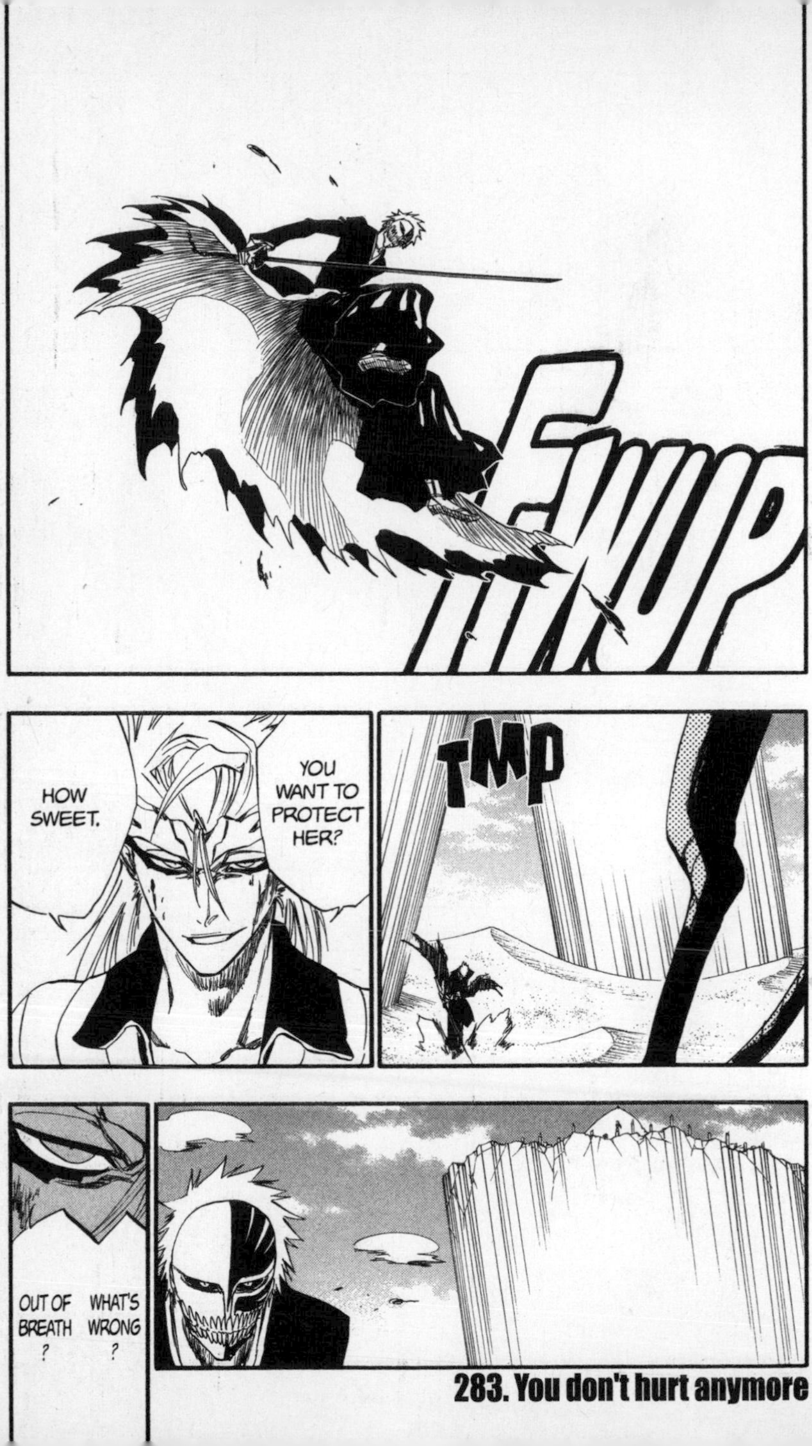
TMP
YOU WANT TO PROTECT HER?
HOW SWEET.
WHAT'S WRONG?
OUT OF BREATH?

283. You don't hurt anymore

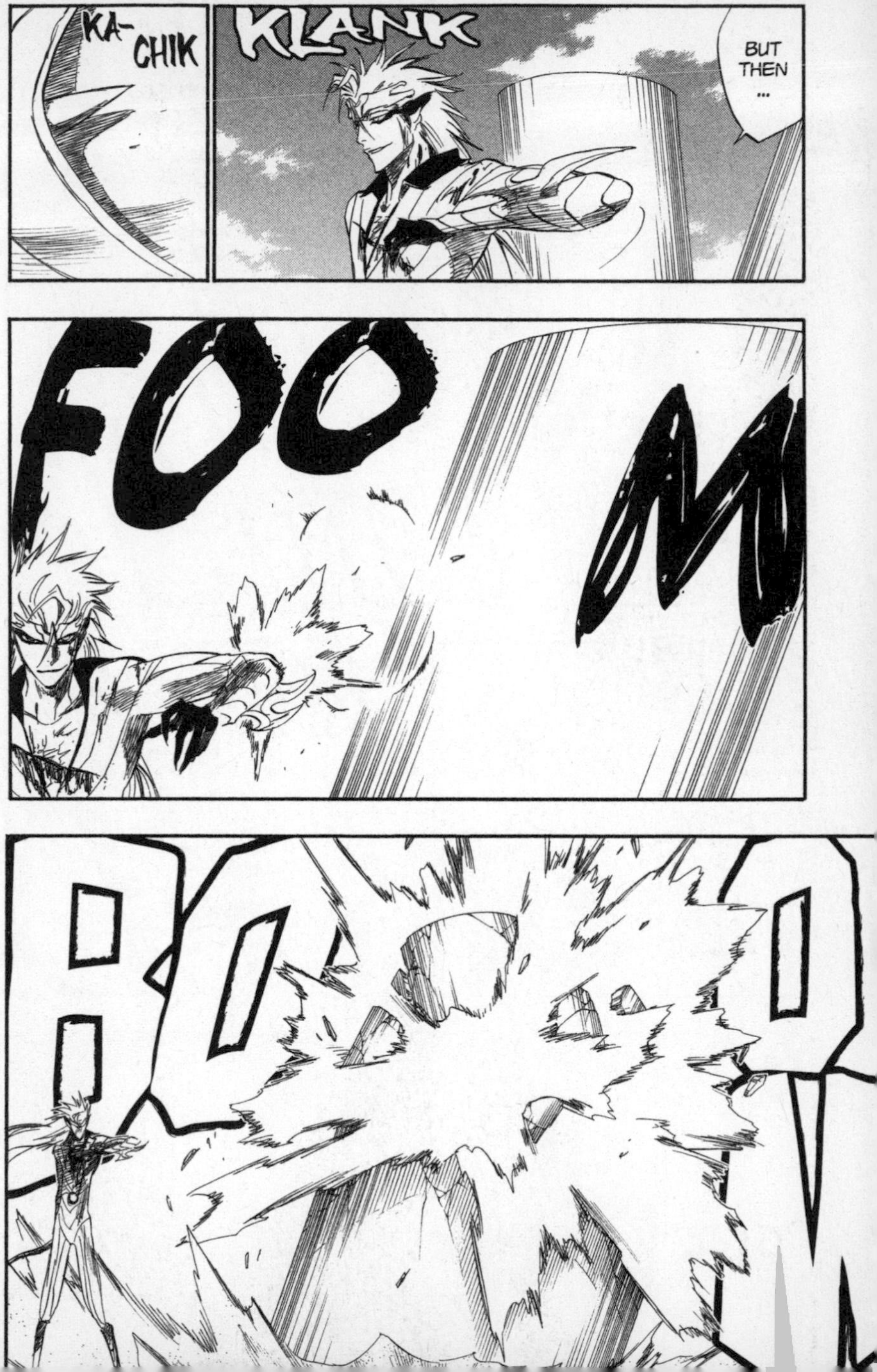
BUT THEN ...
KLANK
KA-CHIK
FOOM
BOOM

READ THIS WAY

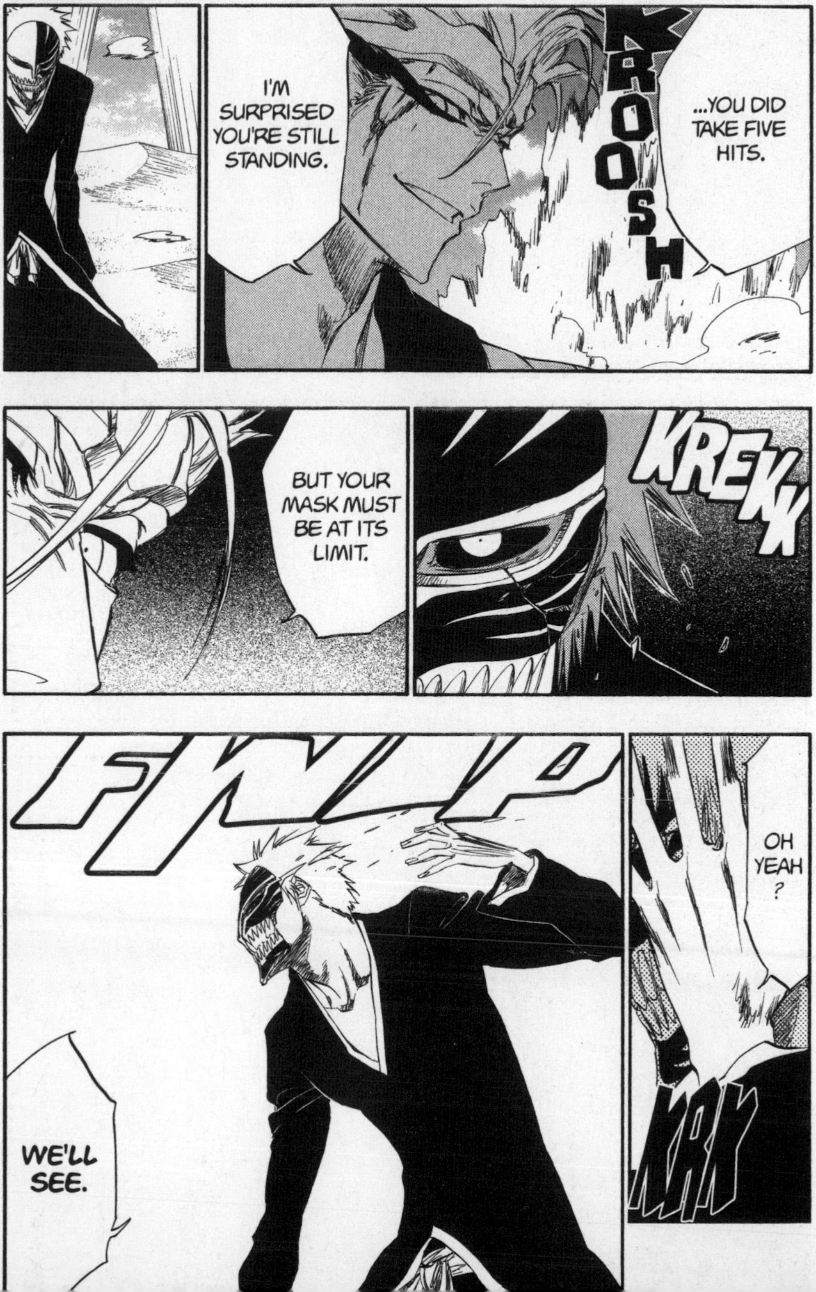

I'M SURPRISED YOU'RE STILL STANDING.
KROOSH
...YOU DID TAKE FIVE HITS.
KREKK
BUT YOUR MASK MUST BE AT ITS LIMIT.
OH YEAH?
KRK
FWIP
WE'LL SEE.

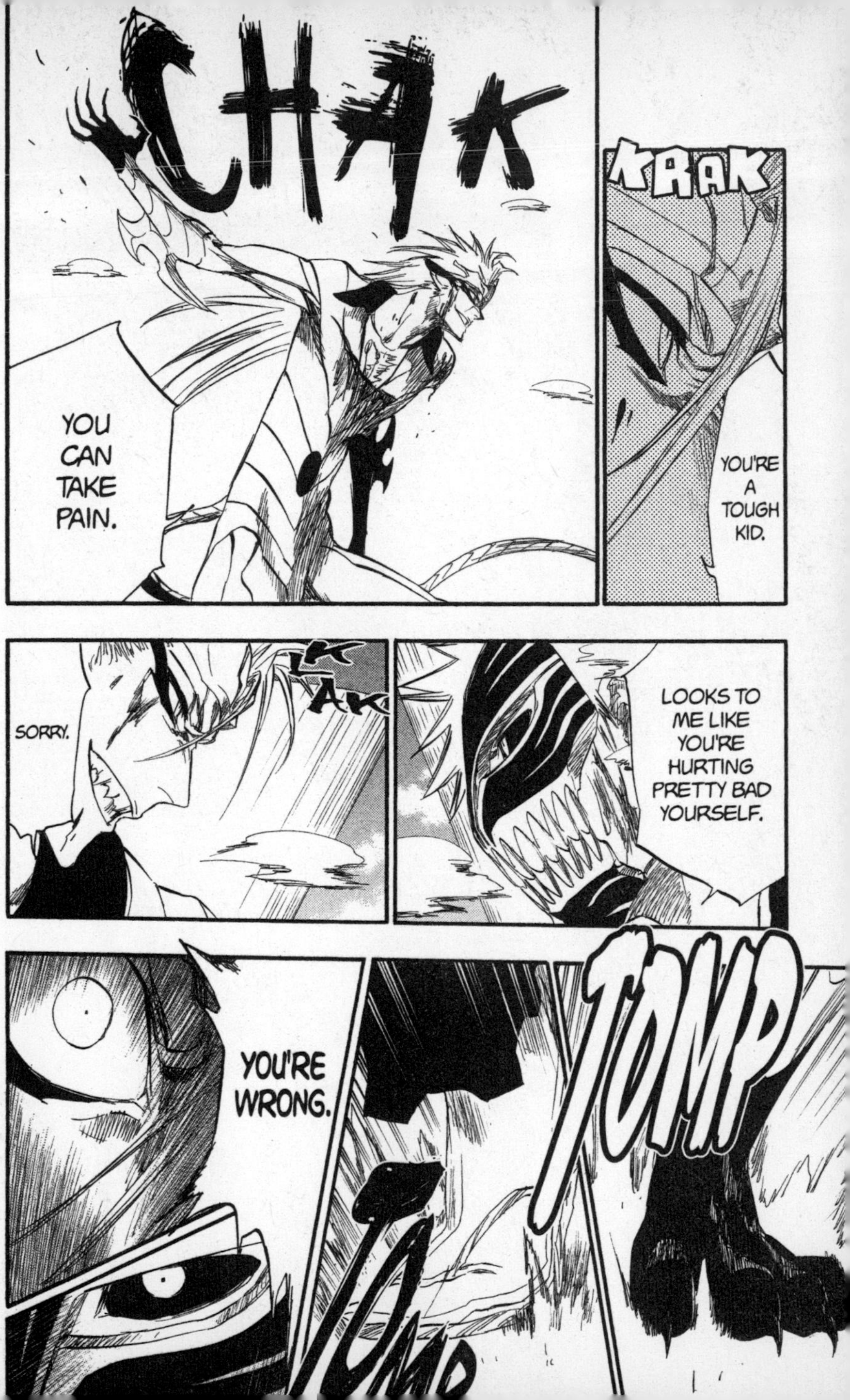
CHAK
YOU CAN TAKE PAIN.
KRAK
YOU'RE A TOUGH KID.
LOOKS TO ME LIKE YOU'RE HURTING PRETTY BAD YOURSELF.
KRAK
SORRY.
TOMP
YOU'RE WRONG.
TOMP

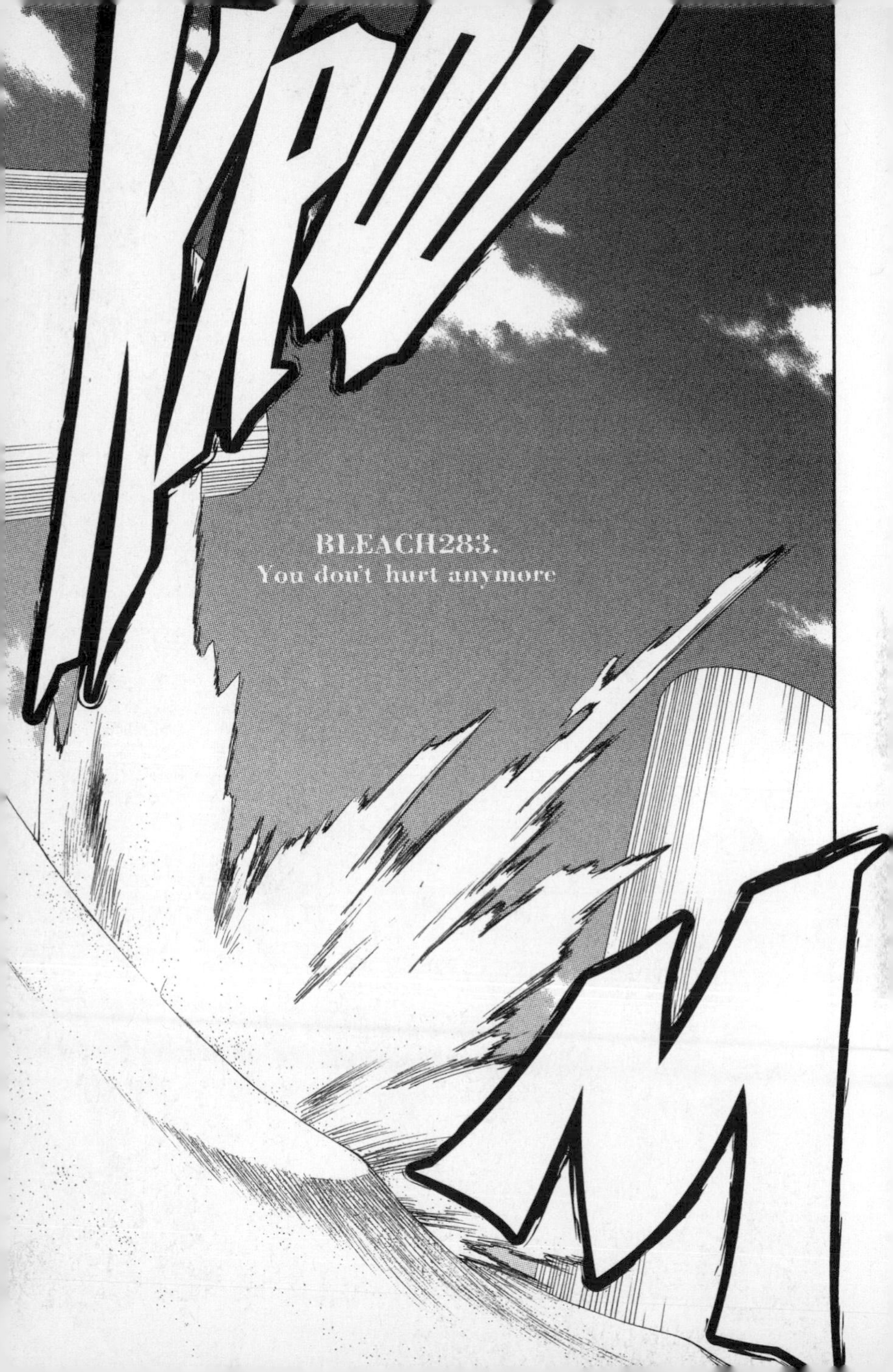
BLEACH283.
You don't hurt anymore

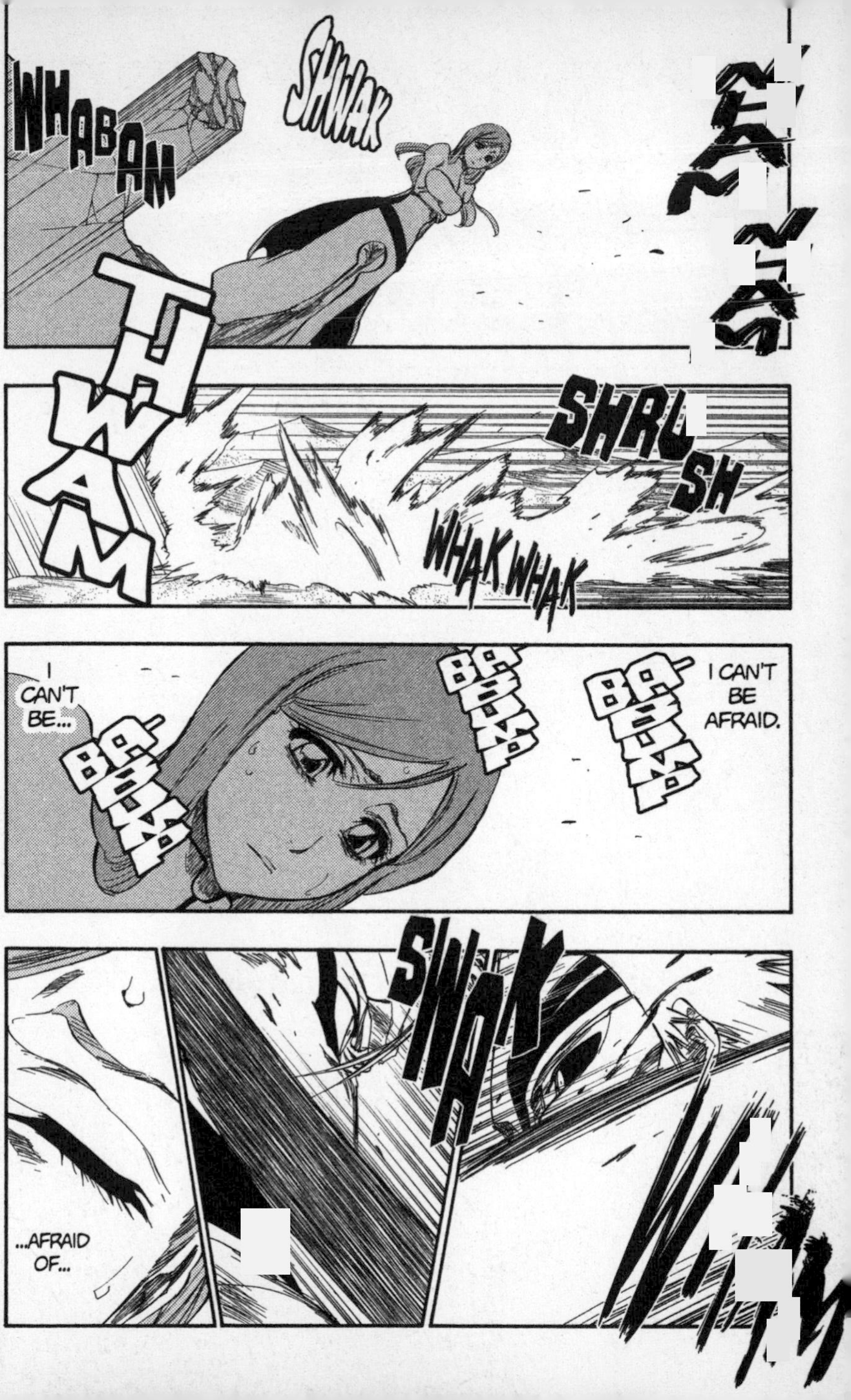
SHWAK
WHABAM
THWAM
WHAK WHAK
I CAN'T BE AFRAID.
I CAN'T BE...
SHWAK
...AFRAID OF...

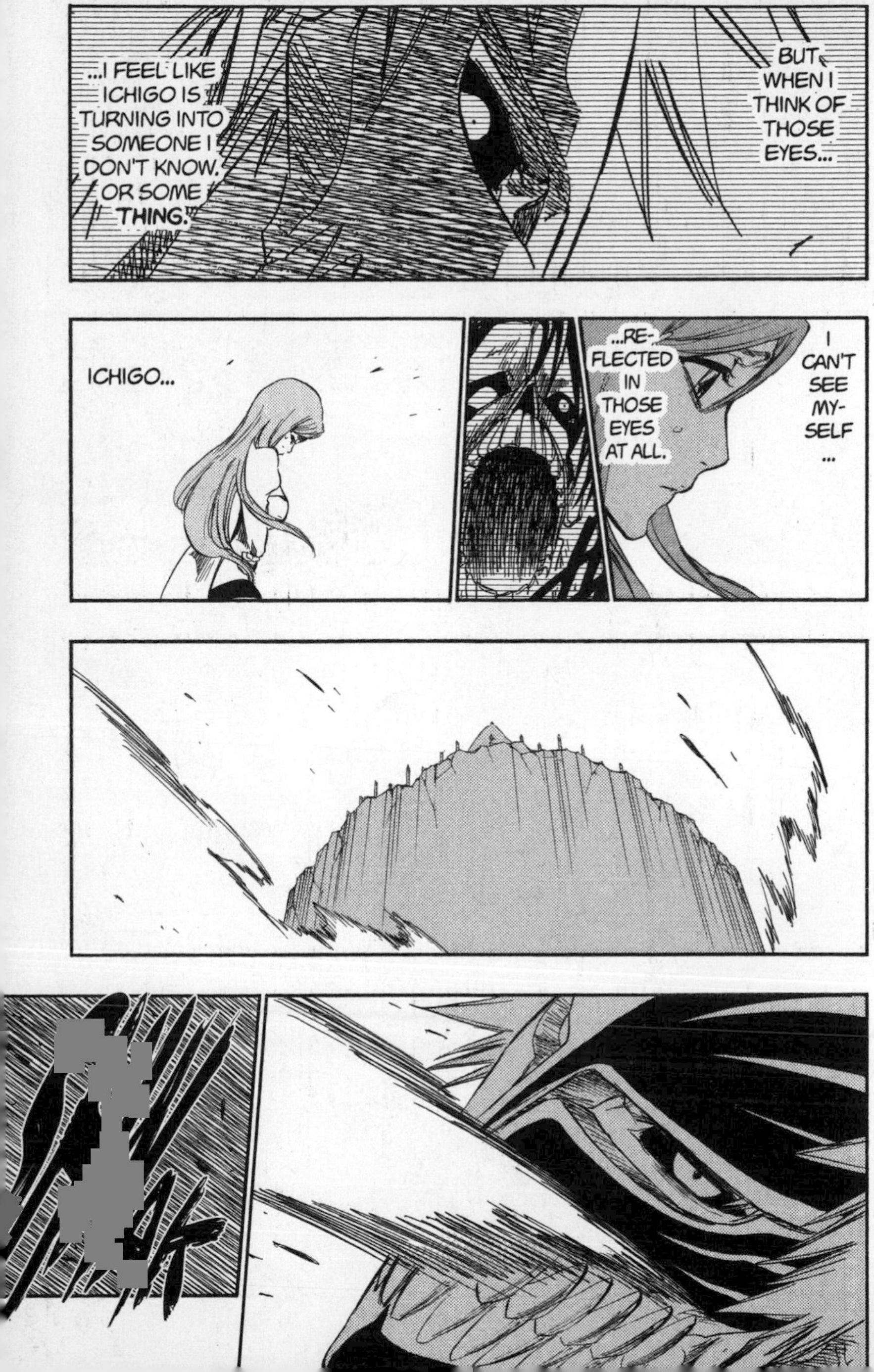
BUT WHEN I THINK OF THOSE EYES...
...I FEEL LIKE ICHIGO IS TURNING INTO SOMEONE I DON'T KNOW. OR SOME THING.
I CAN'T SEE MY-SELF ...
...RE-FLECTED IN THOSE EYES AT ALL.
ICHIGO...

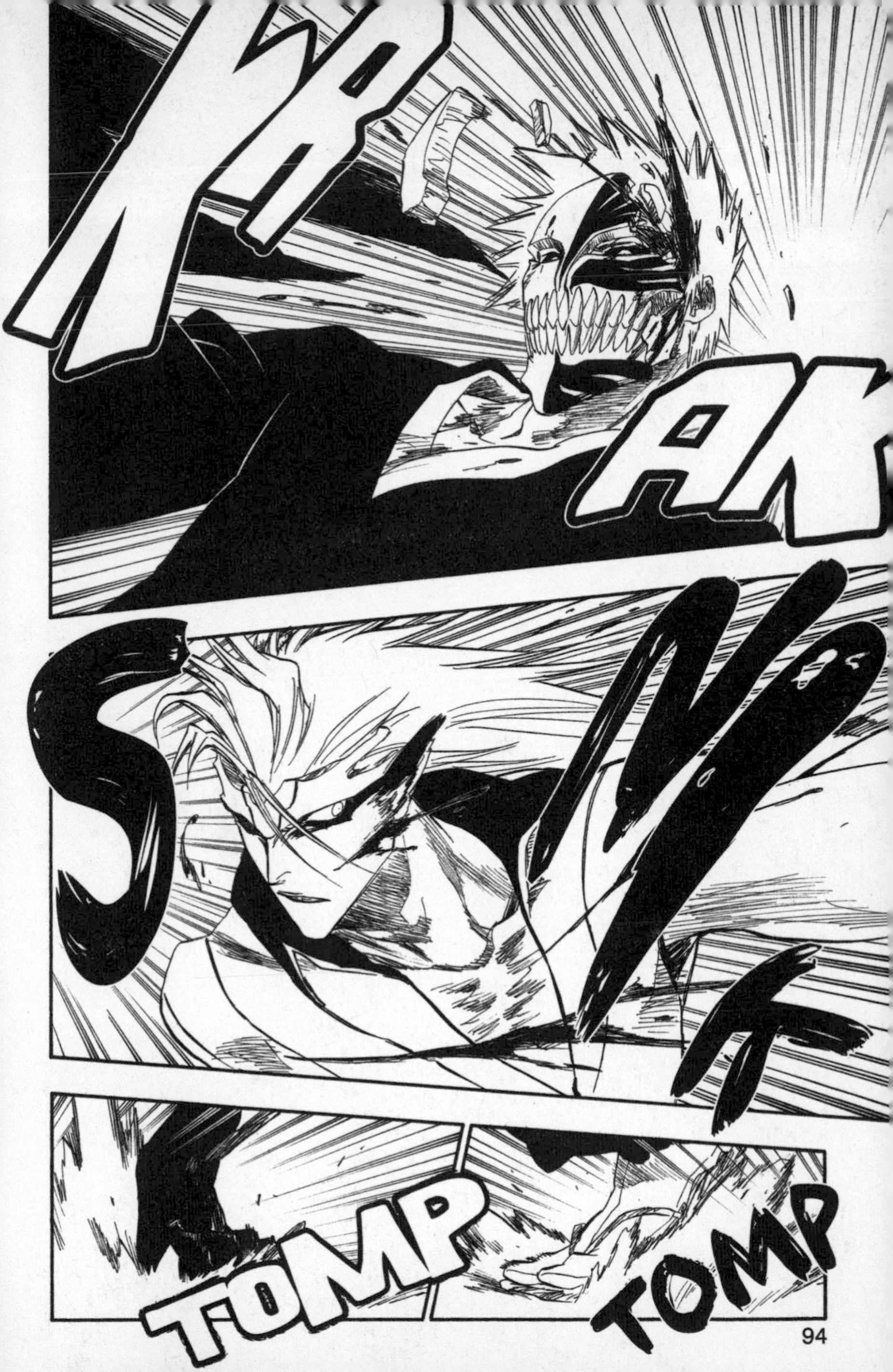
TOMP
TOMP

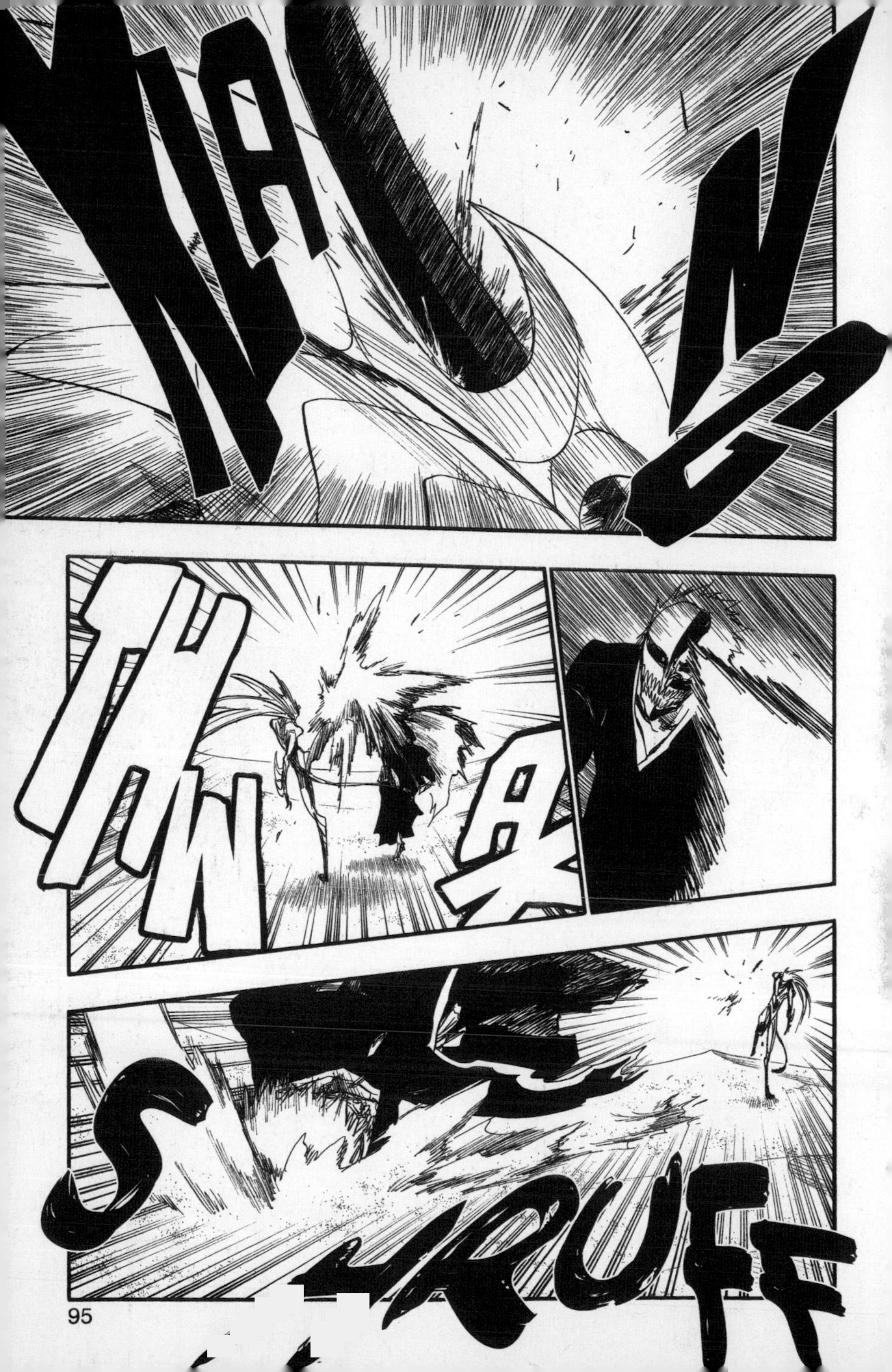
WANG
THWA
SHRUFF

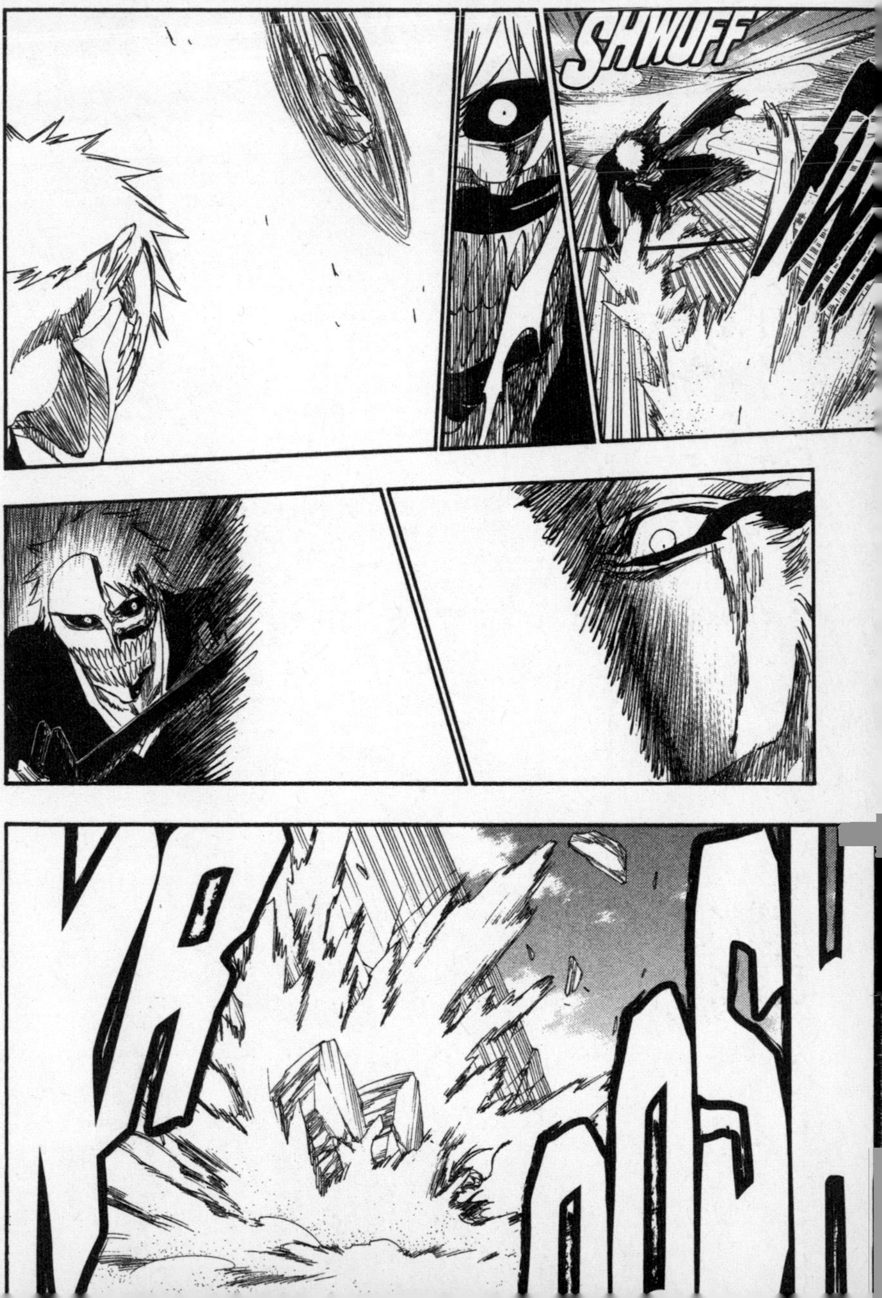
SHWUFF

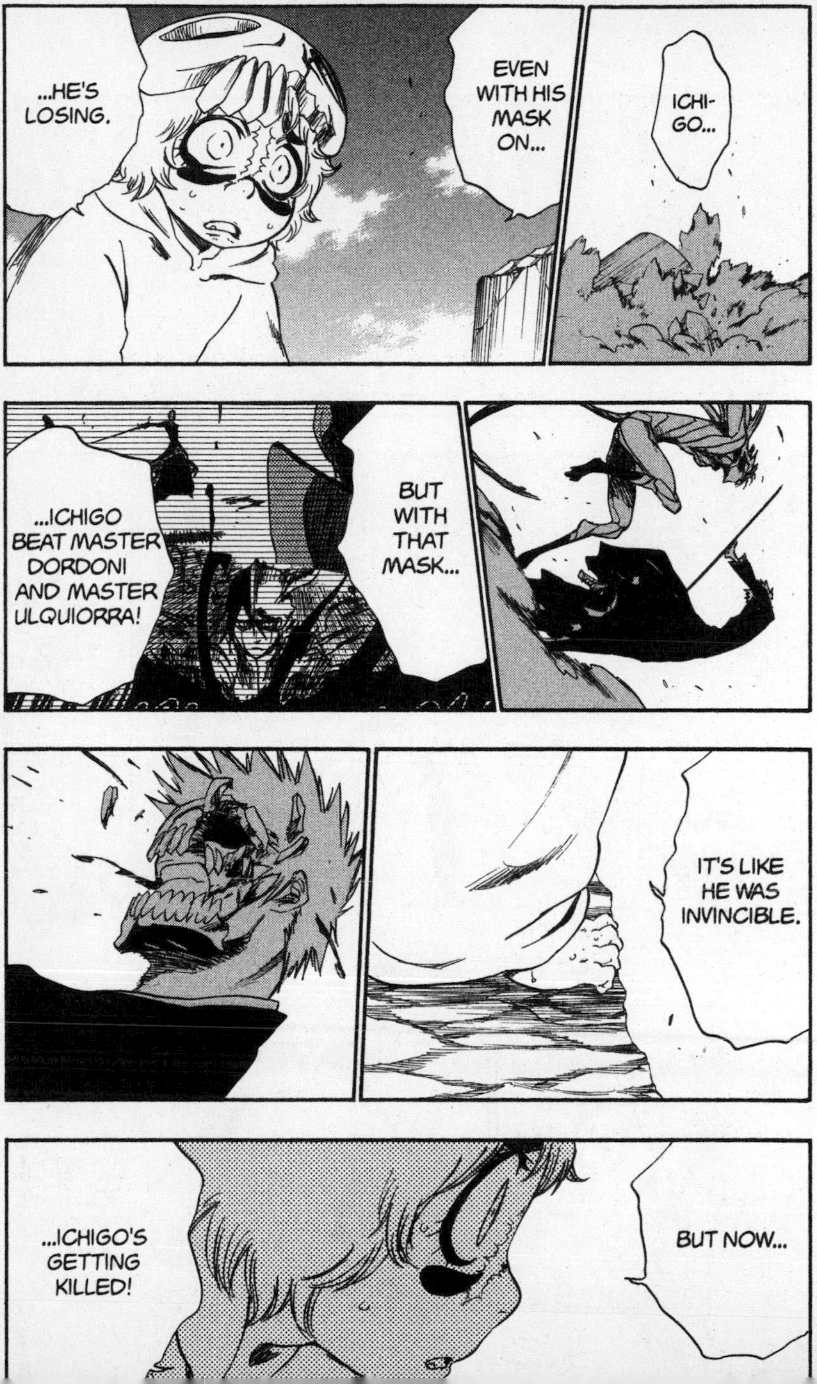
ICHI-
GO...
EVEN
WITH HIS
MASK
ON...
...HE'S
LOSING.
BUT
WITH
THAT
MASK...
...ICHIGO
BEAT MASTER
DORDONI
AND MASTER
ULQUIORRA!
IT'S LIKE
HE WAS
INVINCIBLE.
BUT NOW...
...ICHIGO'S
GETTING
KILLED!

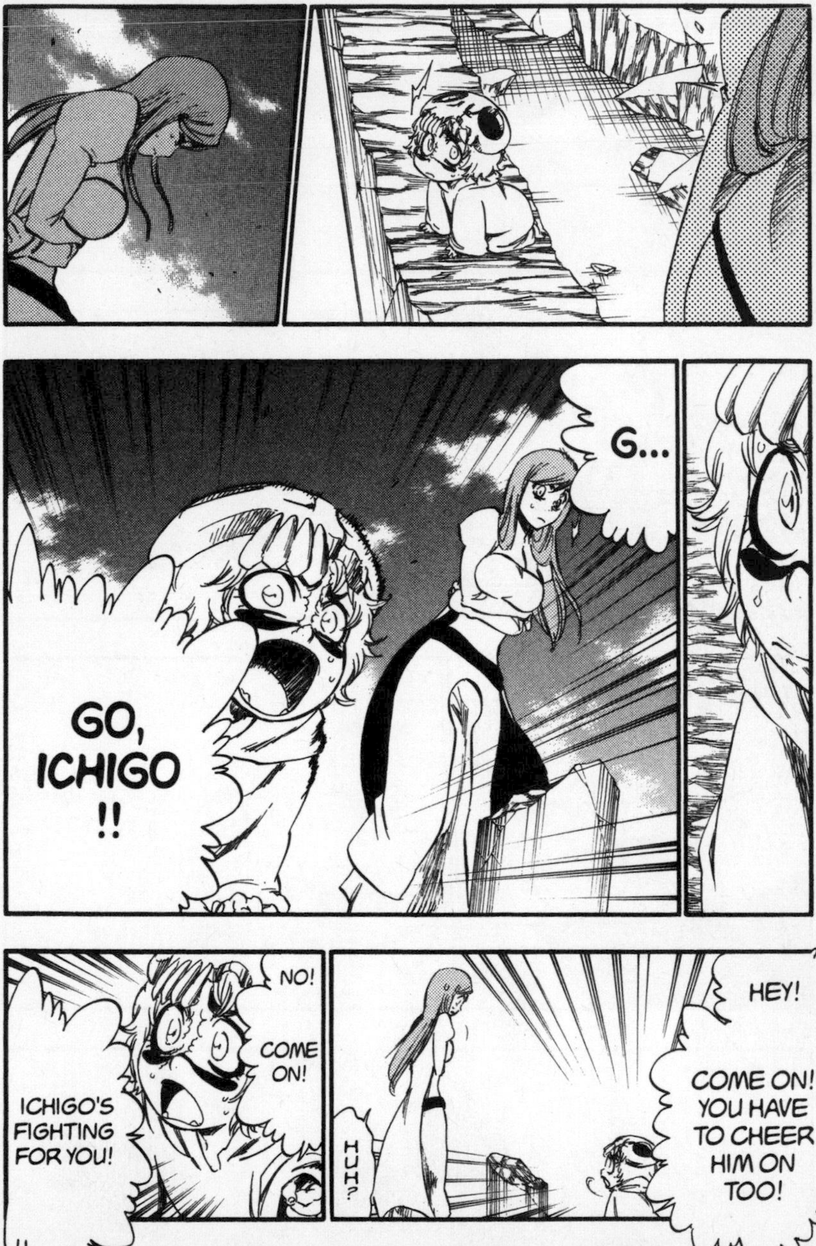

G...
GO, ICHIGO !!
HEY!
COME ON! YOU HAVE TO CHEER HIM ON TOO!
HUH?
NO!
COME ON!
ICHIGO'S FIGHTING FOR YOU!

READ THIS WAY

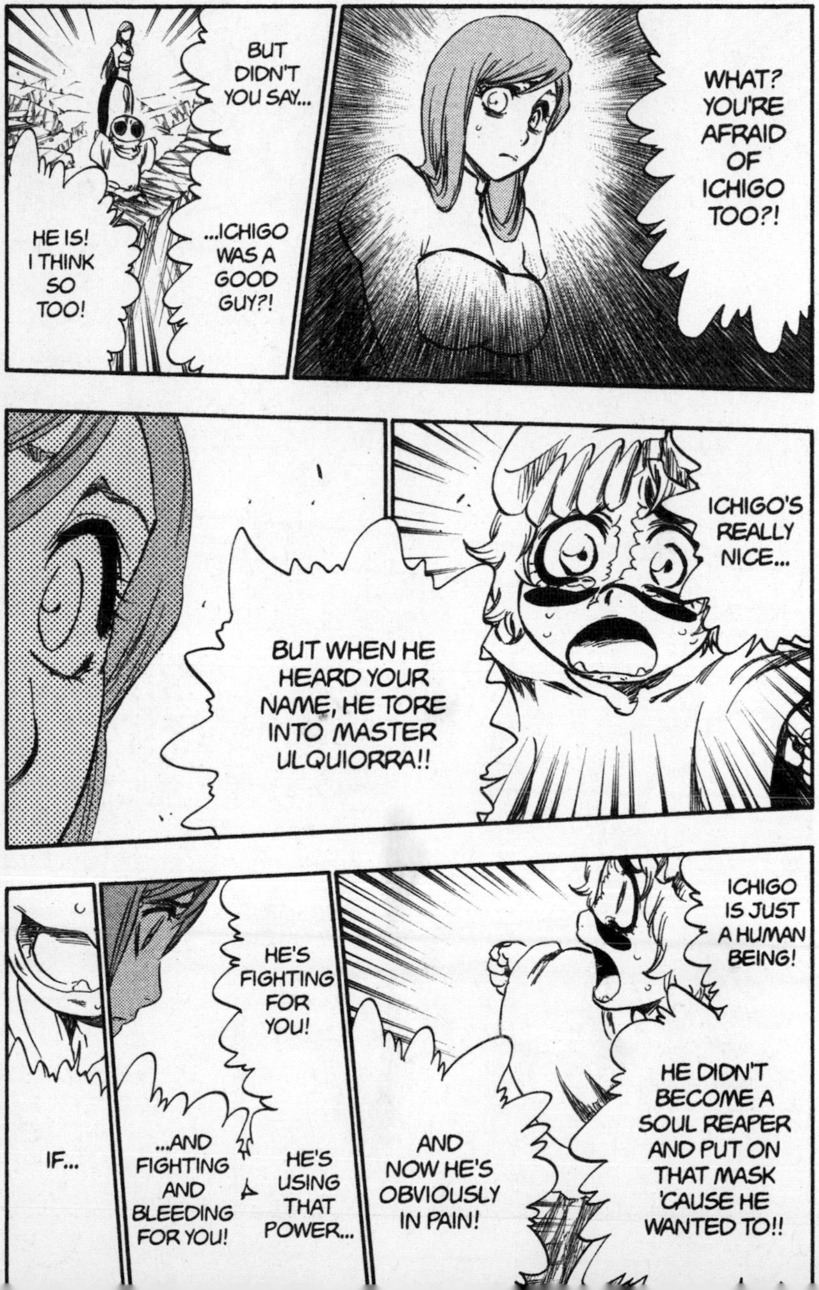
WHAT? YOU'RE AFRAID OF ICHIGO TOO?!
BUT DIDN'T YOU SAY...
...ICHIGO WAS A GOOD GUY?!
HE IS! I THINK SO TOO!
ICHIGO'S REALLY NICE...
BUT WHEN HE HEARD YOUR NAME, HE TORE INTO MASTER ULQUIORRA!!
ICHIGO IS JUST A HUMAN BEING!
HE DIDN'T BECOME A SOUL REAPER AND PUT ON THAT MASK 'CAUSE HE WANTED TO!!
AND NOW HE'S OBVIOUSLY IN PAIN!
HE'S FIGHTING FOR YOU!
HE'S USING THAT POWER...
...AND FIGHTING AND BLEEDING FOR YOU!
IF...

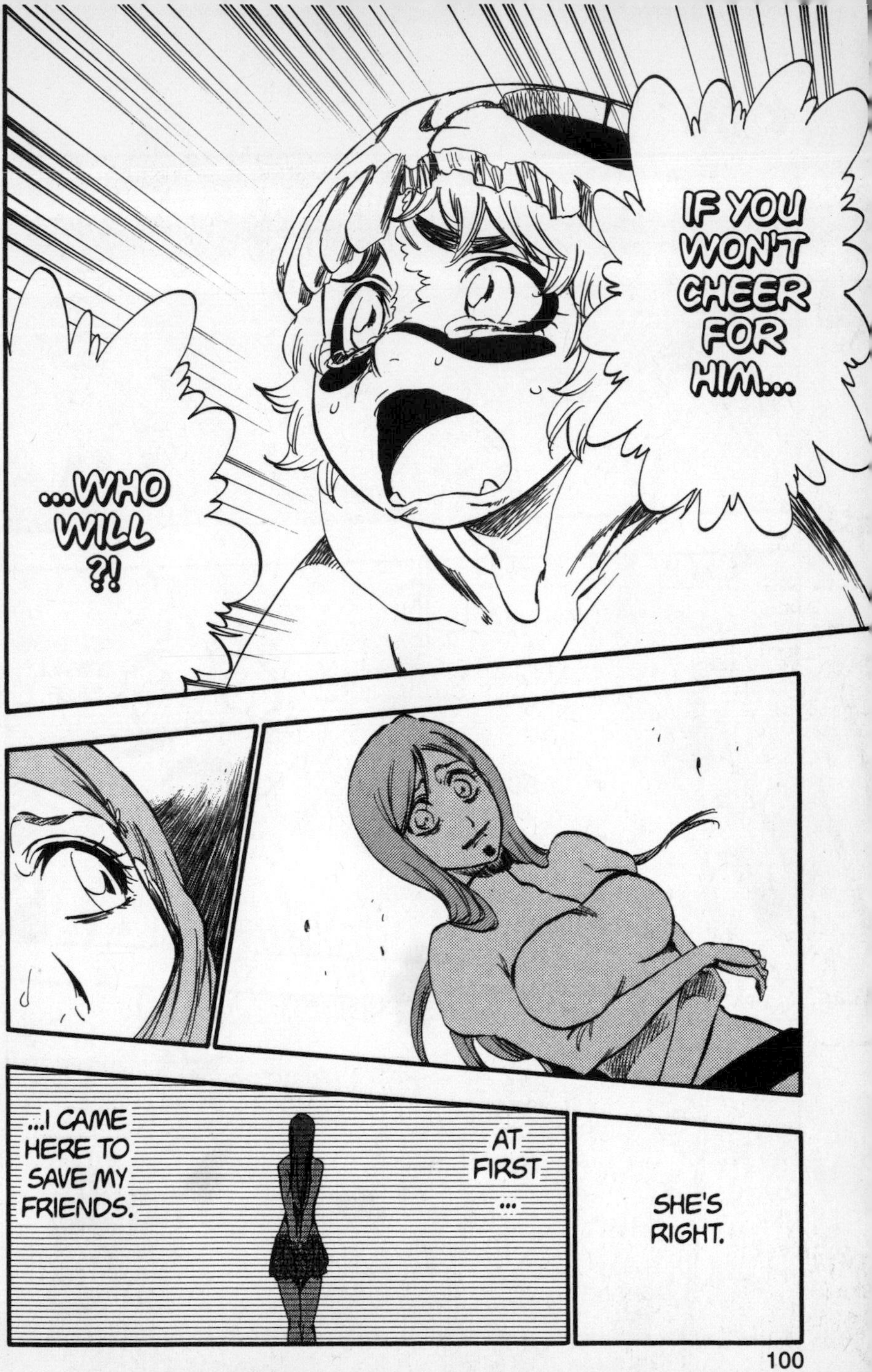
IF YOU WON'T CHEER FOR HIM...
...WHO WILL ?!
SHE'S RIGHT.
AT FIRST ...
...I CAME HERE TO SAVE MY FRIENDS.

READ THIS WAY

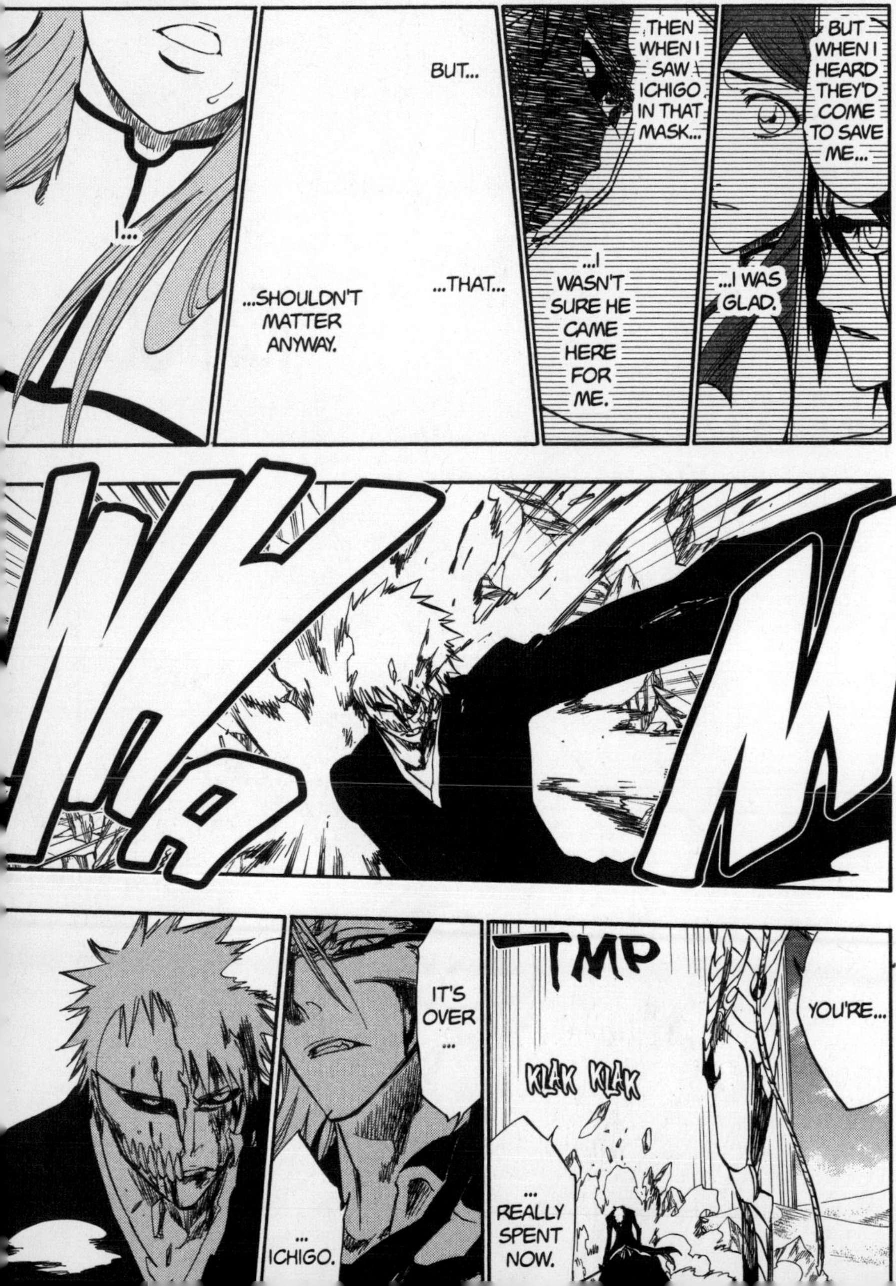
BUT WHEN I HEARD THEY'D COME TO SAVE ME...
...I WAS GLAD.
THEN WHEN I SAW ICHIGO IN THAT MASK...
...I WASN'T SURE HE CAME HERE FOR ME.
BUT...
...THAT...
...SHOULDN'T MATTER ANYWAY.
I...
WHAM
YOU'RE...
TMP
KLAK KLAK
...REALLY SPENT NOW.
IT'S OVER...
...ICHIGO.

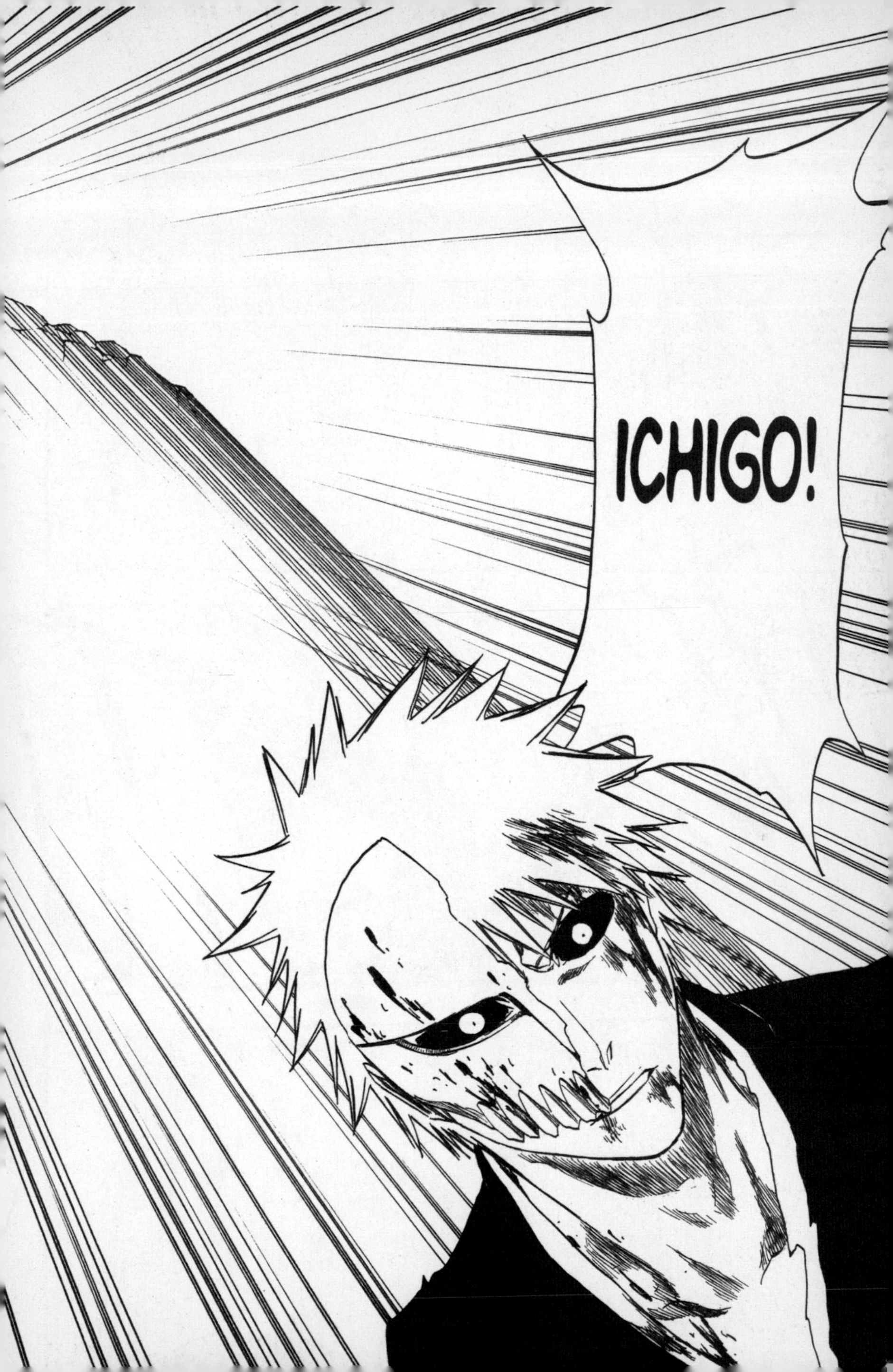
ICHIGO!

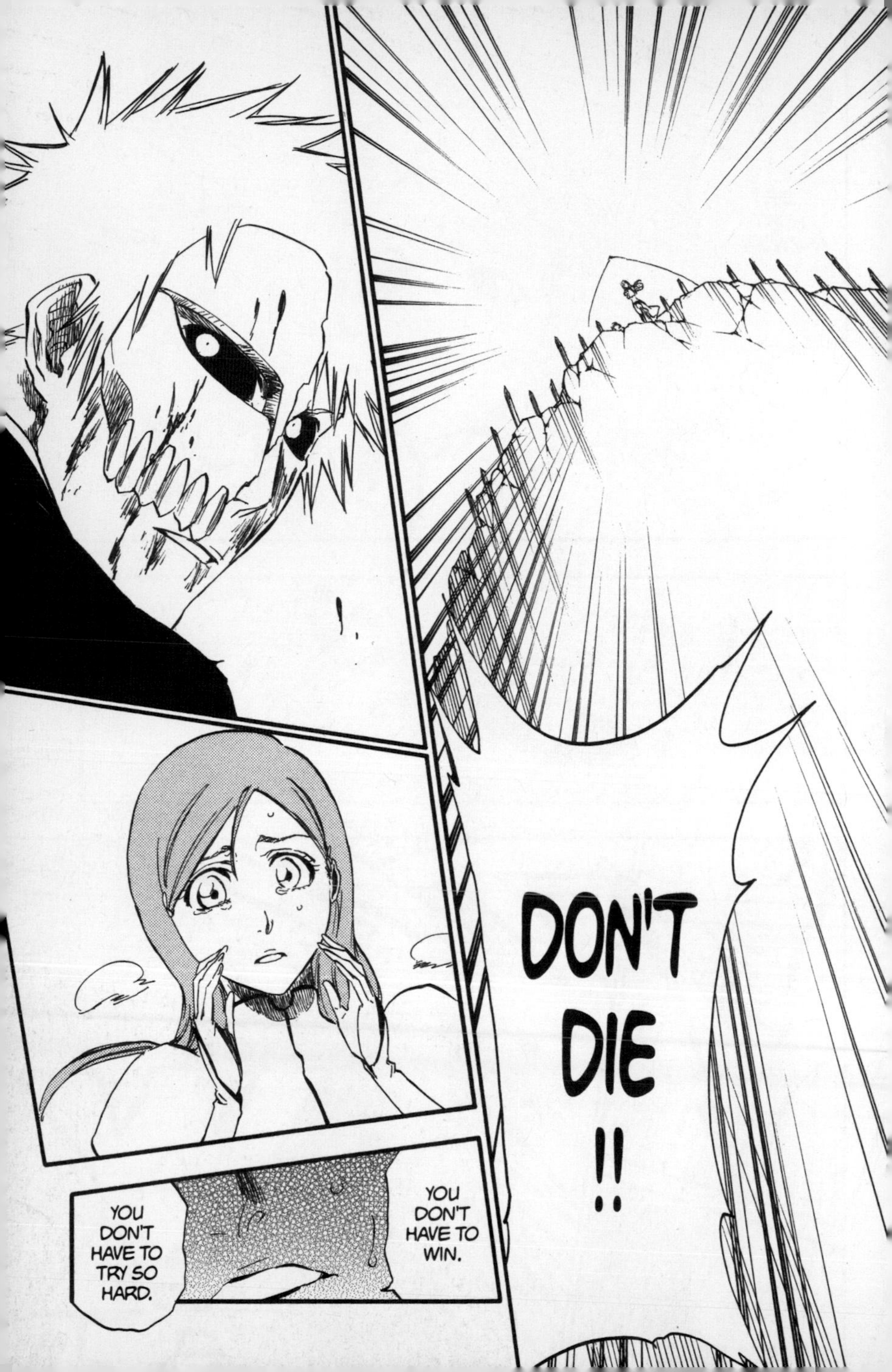
DON'T DIE !!
YOU DON'T HAVE TO WIN.
YOU DON'T HAVE TO TRY SO HARD.

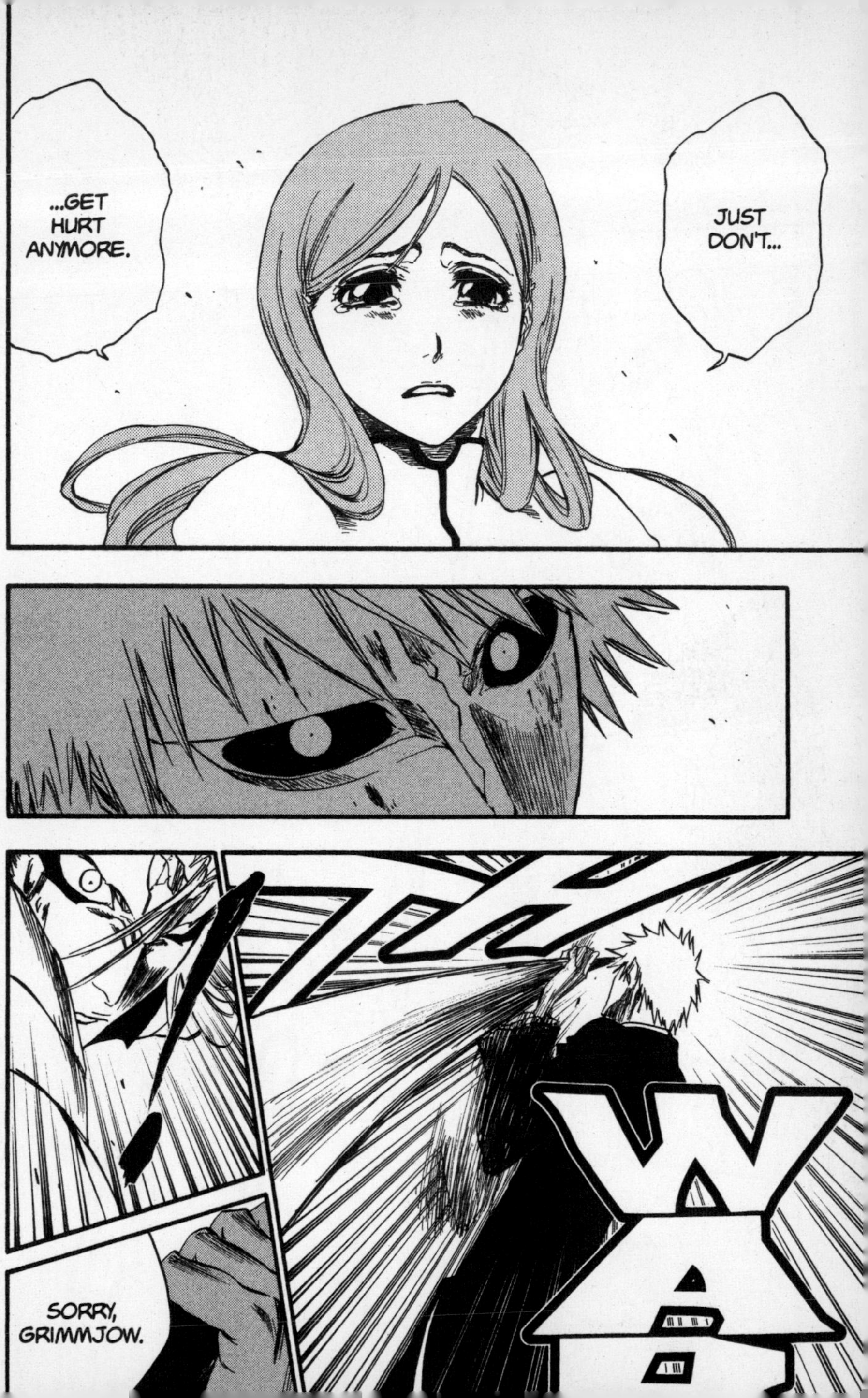
JUST DON'T...
...GET HURT ANYMORE.
SORRY, GRIMMJOW.

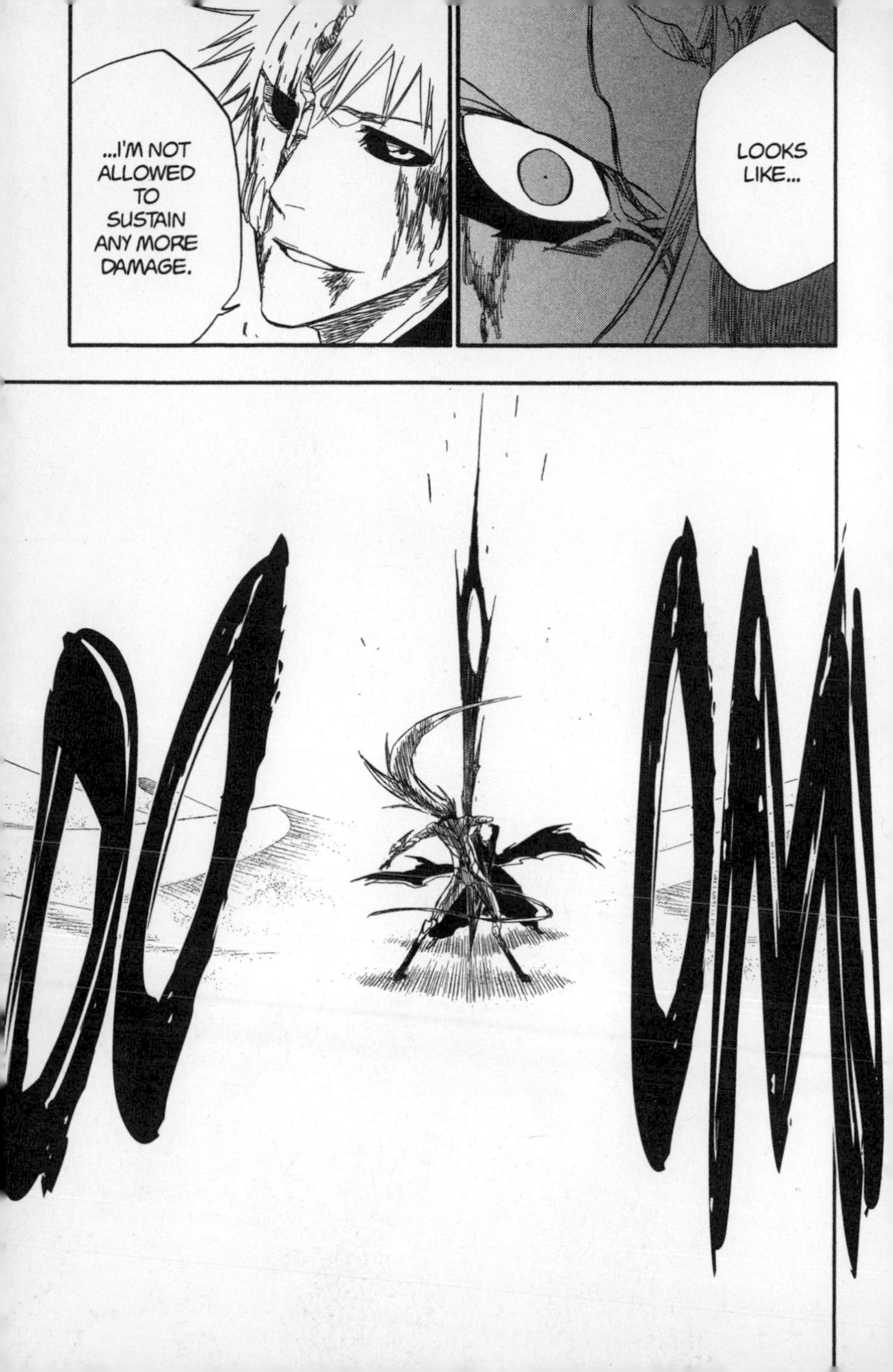
LOOKS LIKE...
...I'M NOT ALLOWED TO SUSTAIN ANY MORE DAMAGE.

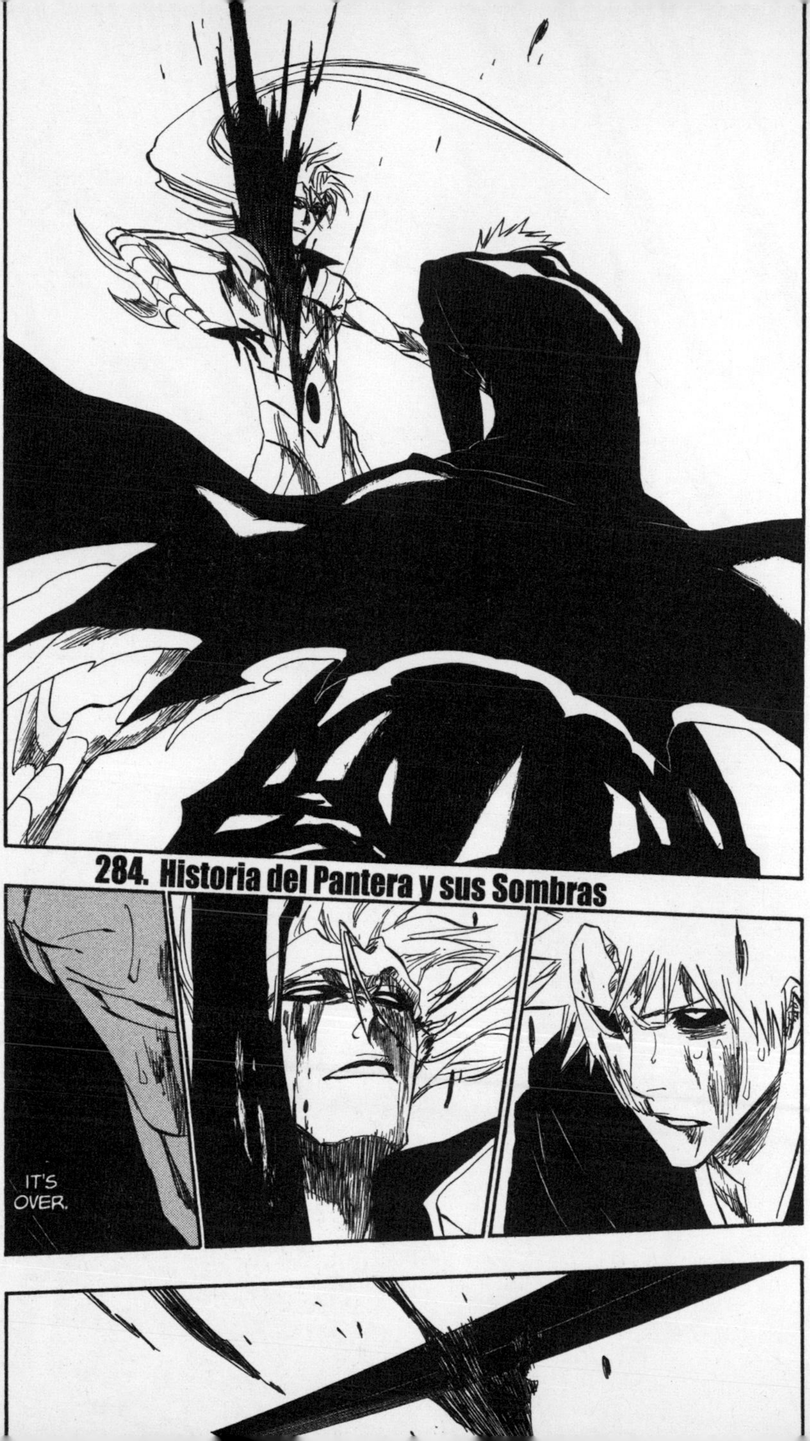
284. Historia del Pantera y sus Sombras
IT'S OVER.

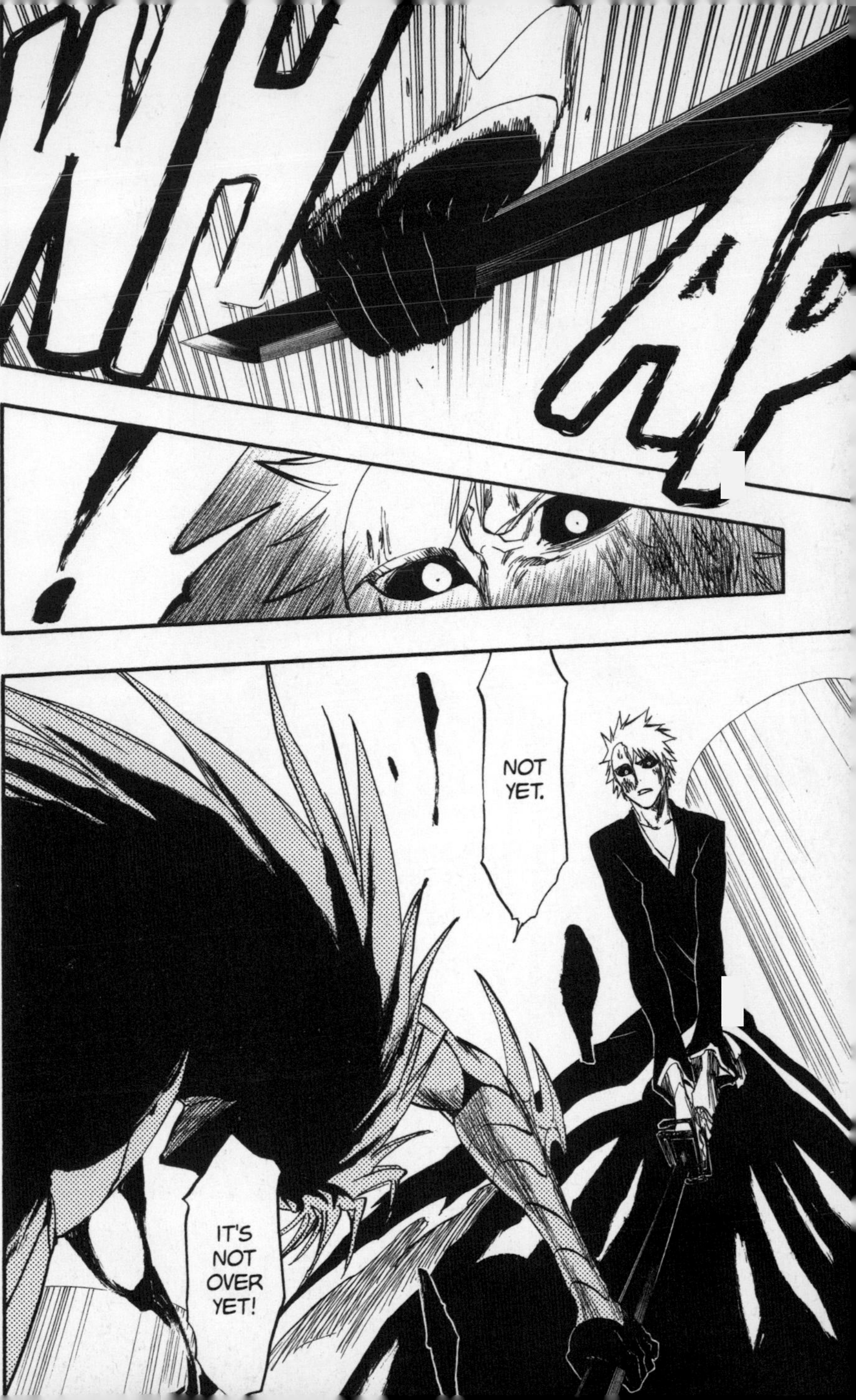
NOT YET.
IT'S NOT OVER YET!

READ THIS WAY

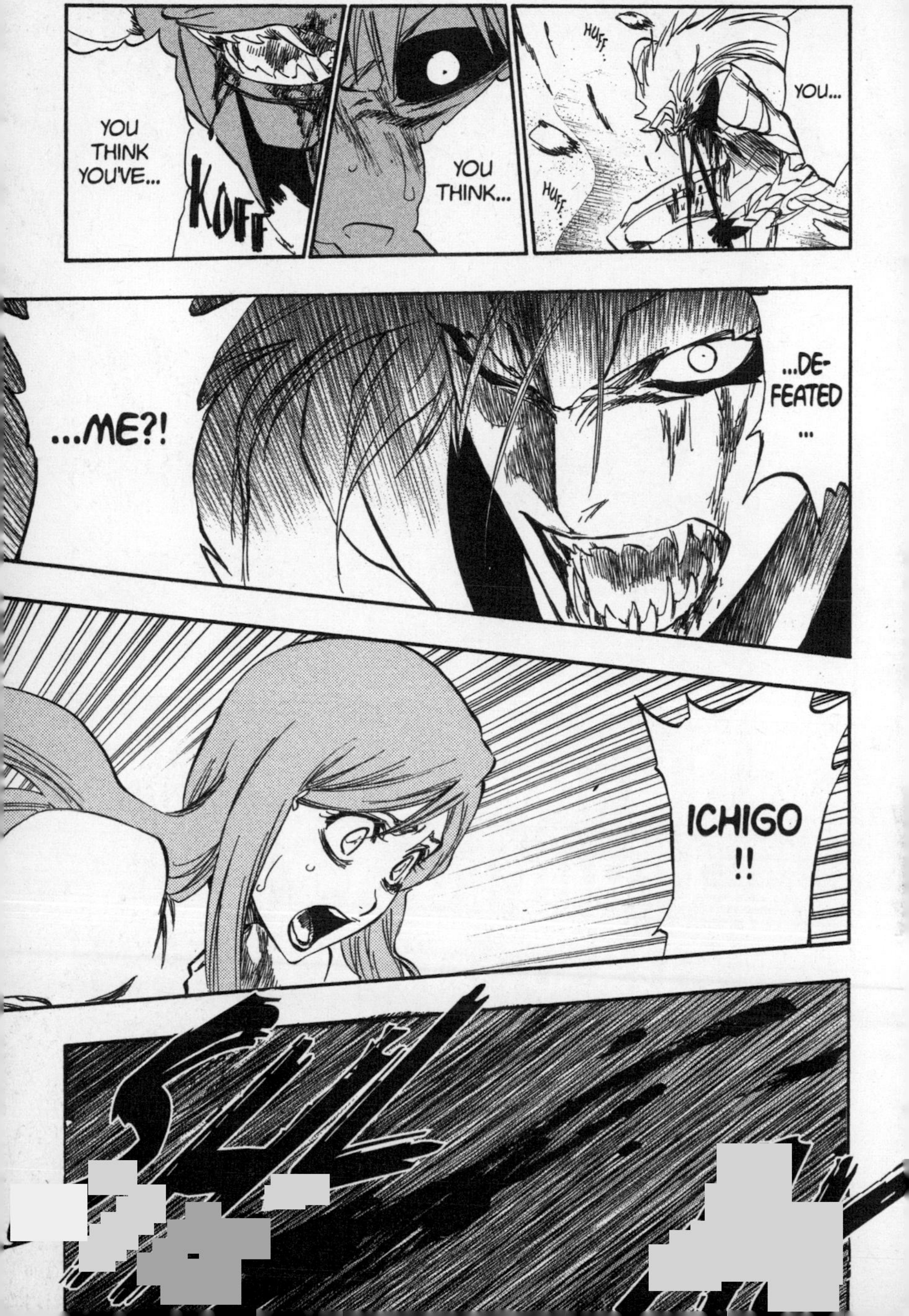
HUFF
HUFF
YOU...
YOU THINK...
YOU THINK YOU'VE...
KOFF
...DE-FEATED...
...ME?!
ICHIGO!!

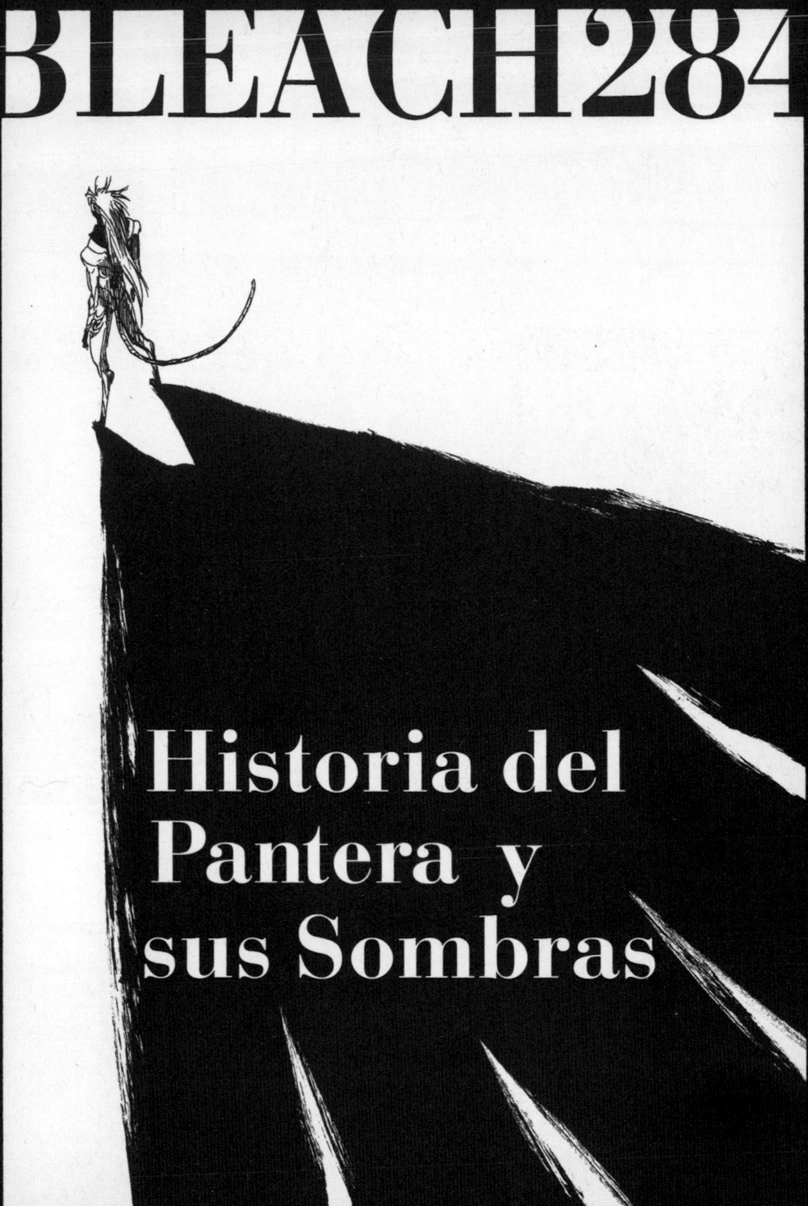
BLEACH284
Historia del Pantera y sus Sombras

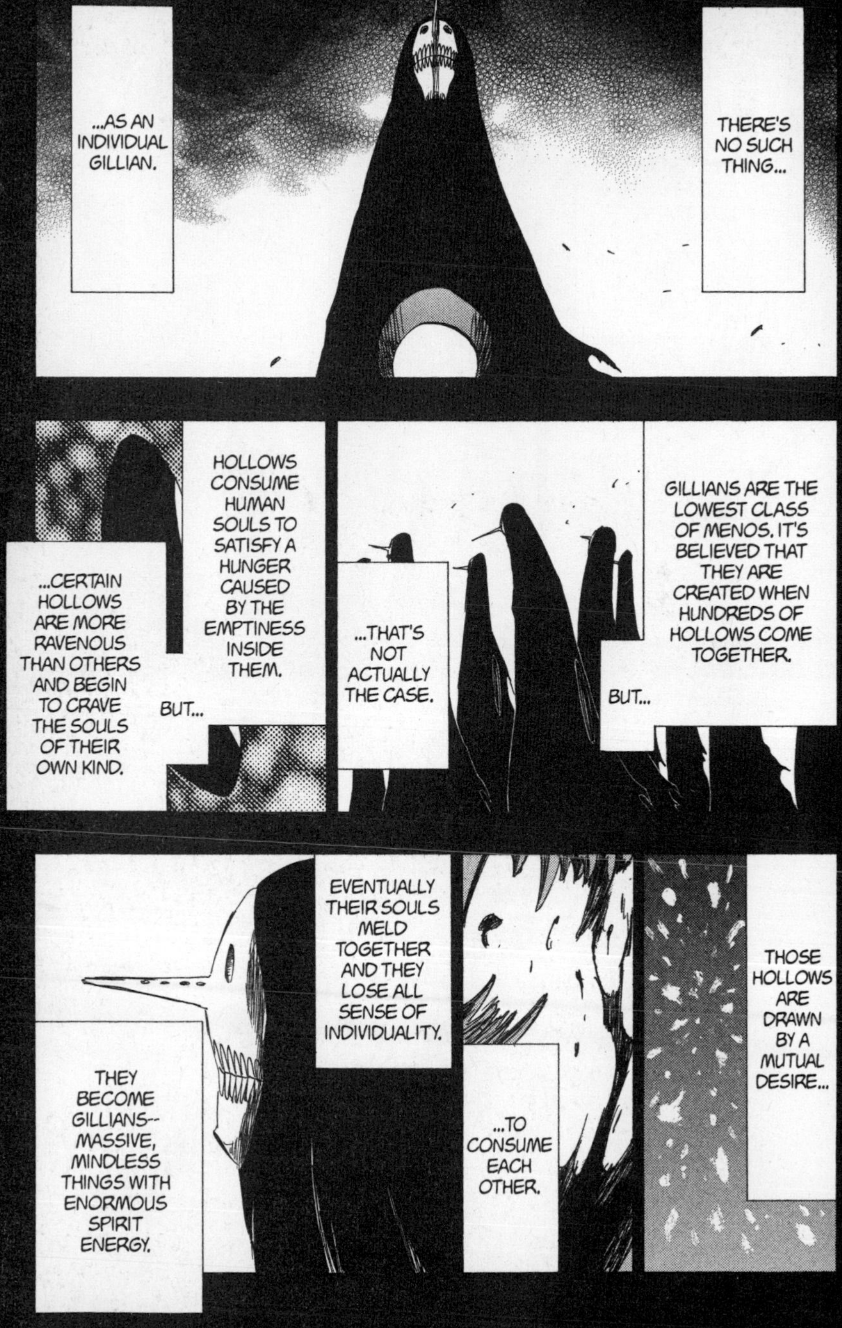
THERE'S NO SUCH THING...
...AS AN INDIVIDUAL GILLIAN.
GILLIANS ARE THE LOWEST CLASS OF MENOS. IT'S BELIEVED THAT THEY ARE CREATED WHEN HUNDREDS OF HOLLOWS COME TOGETHER.
BUT...
...THAT'S NOT ACTUALLY THE CASE.
HOLLOWS CONSUME HUMAN SOULS TO SATISFY A HUNGER CAUSED BY THE EMPTINESS INSIDE THEM.
BUT...
...CERTAIN HOLLOWS ARE MORE RAVENOUS THAN OTHERS AND BEGIN TO CRAVE THE SOULS OF THEIR OWN KIND.
THOSE HOLLOWS ARE DRAWN BY A MUTUAL DESIRE...
...TO CONSUME EACH OTHER.
EVENTUALLY THEIR SOULS MELD TOGETHER AND THEY LOSE ALL SENSE OF INDIVIDUALITY.
THEY BECOME GILLIANS--MASSIVE, MINDLESS THINGS WITH ENORMOUS SPIRIT ENERGY.

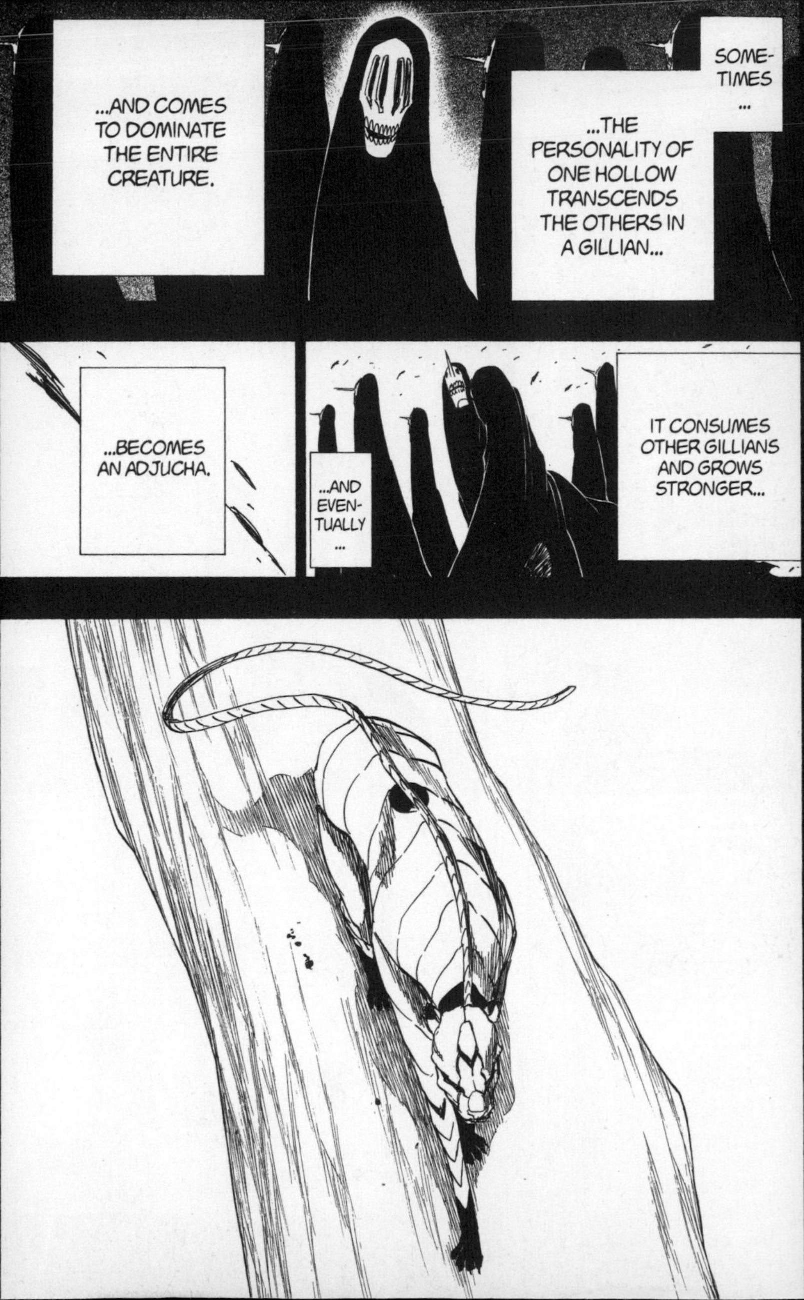
SOMETIMES...
...THE PERSONALITY OF ONE HOLLOW TRANSCENDS THE OTHERS IN A GILLIAN...
...AND COMES TO DOMINATE THE ENTIRE CREATURE.
IT CONSUMES OTHER GILLIANS AND GROWS STRONGER...
...AND EVENTUALLY...
...BECOMES AN ADJUCHA.

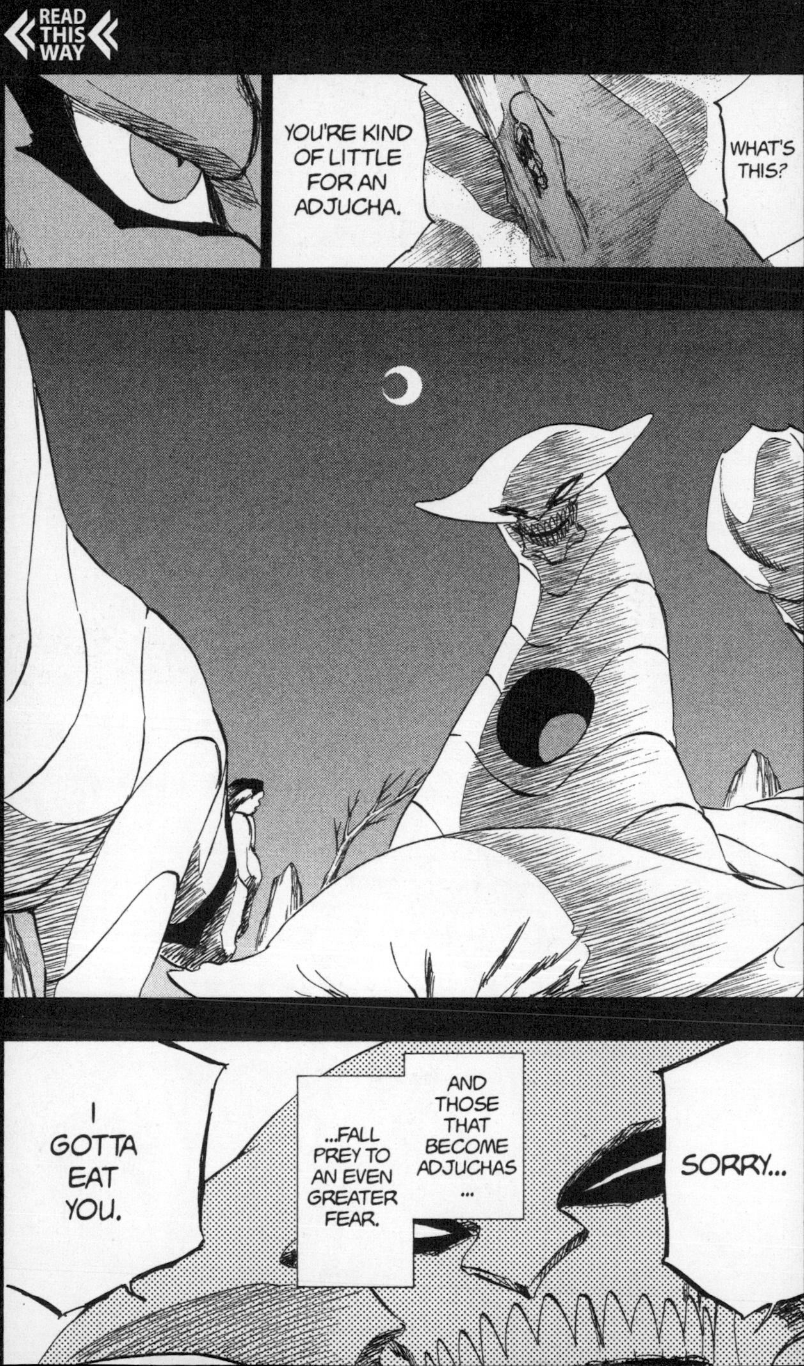
READ THIS WAY
WHAT'S THIS?
YOU'RE KIND OF LITTLE FOR AN ADJUCHA.
SORRY...
AND THOSE THAT BECOME ADJUCHAS...
...FALL PREY TO AN EVEN GREATER FEAR.
I GOTTA EAT YOU.

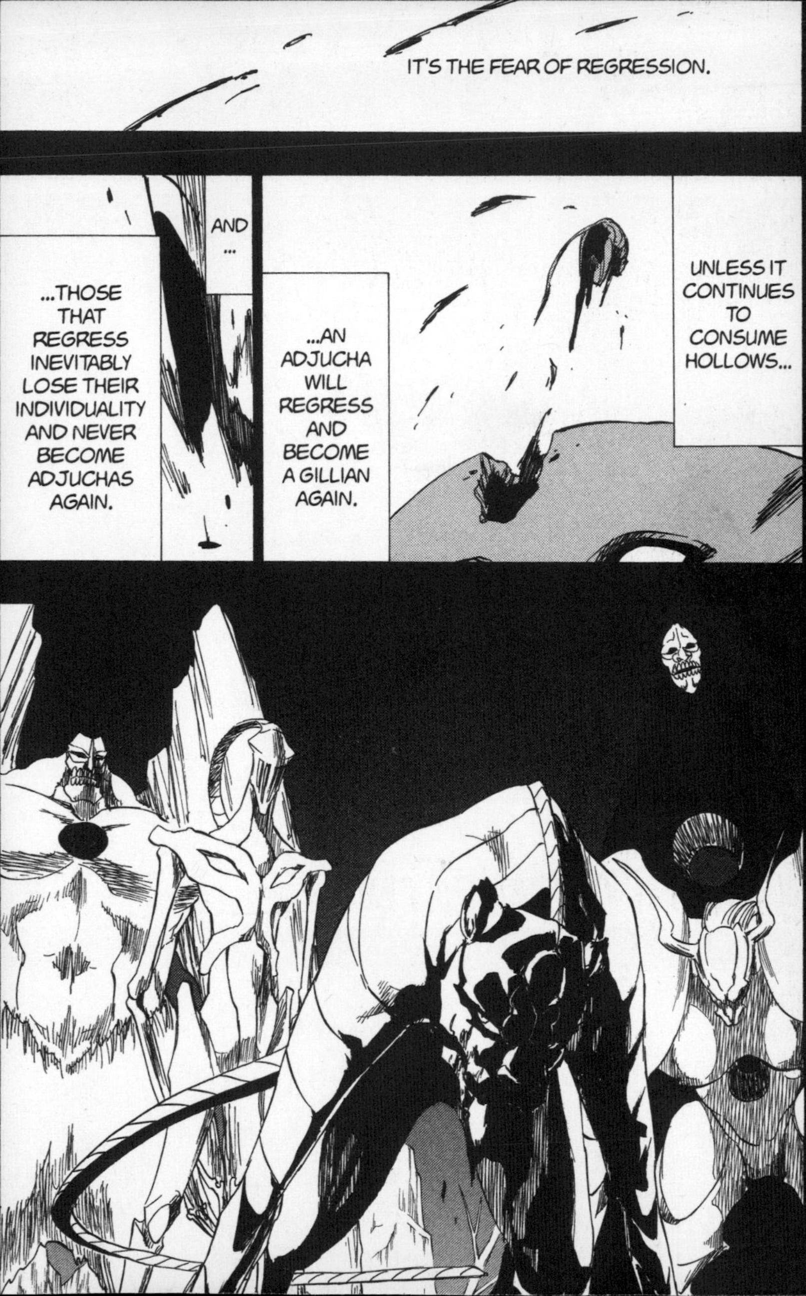
IT'S THE FEAR OF REGRESSION.
UNLESS IT CONTINUES TO CONSUME HOLLOWS...
...AN ADJUCHA WILL REGRESS AND BECOME A GILLIAN AGAIN.
AND ...
...THOSE THAT REGRESS INEVITABLY LOSE THEIR INDIVIDUALITY AND NEVER BECOME ADJUCHAS AGAIN.

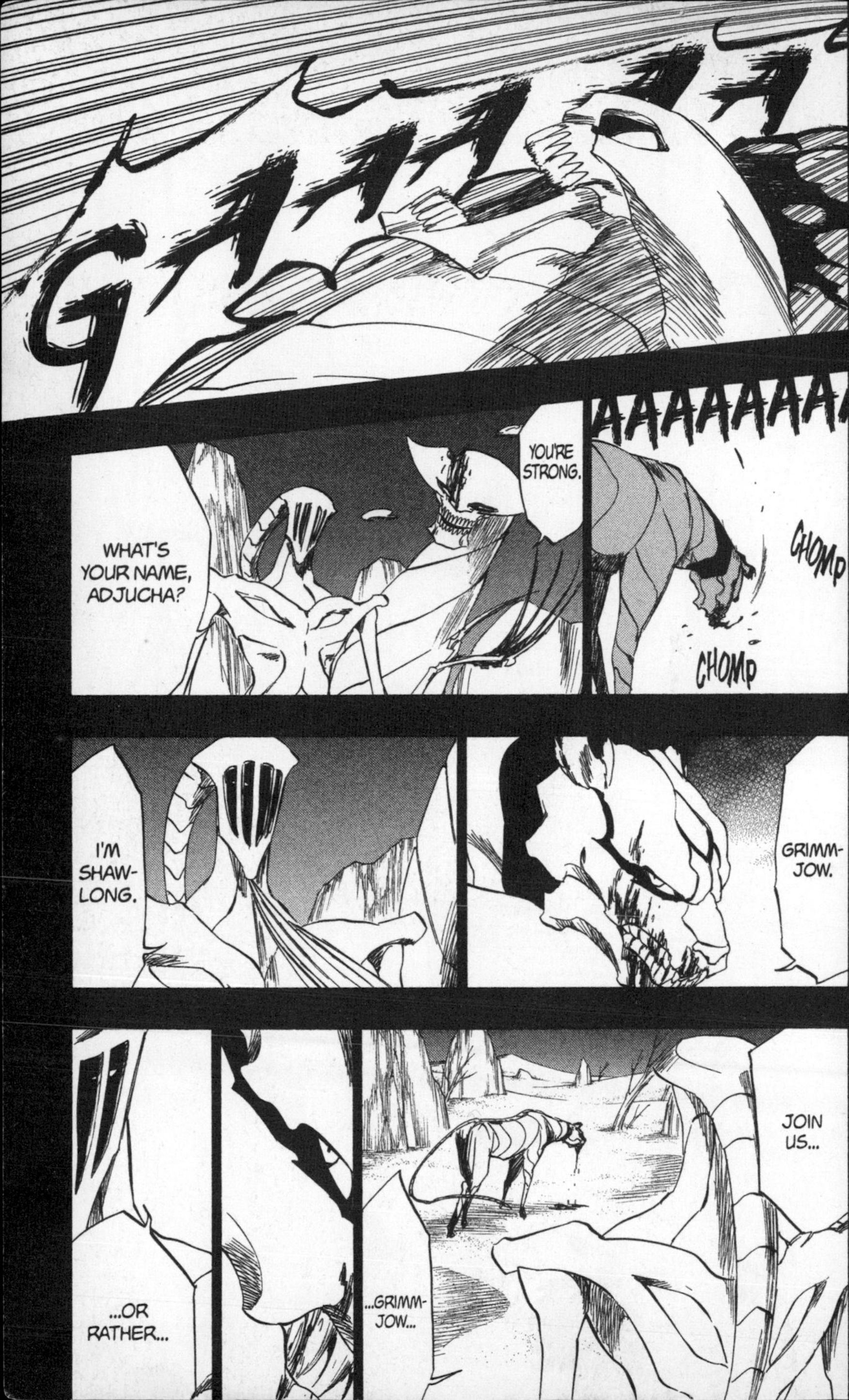
GAAAAA
AAAAAAAA
CHOMP
CHOMP
YOU'RE STRONG.
WHAT'S YOUR NAME, ADJUCHA?
GRIMM-JOW.
I'M SHAW-LONG.
JOIN US...
...GRIMM-JOW...
...OR RATHER...

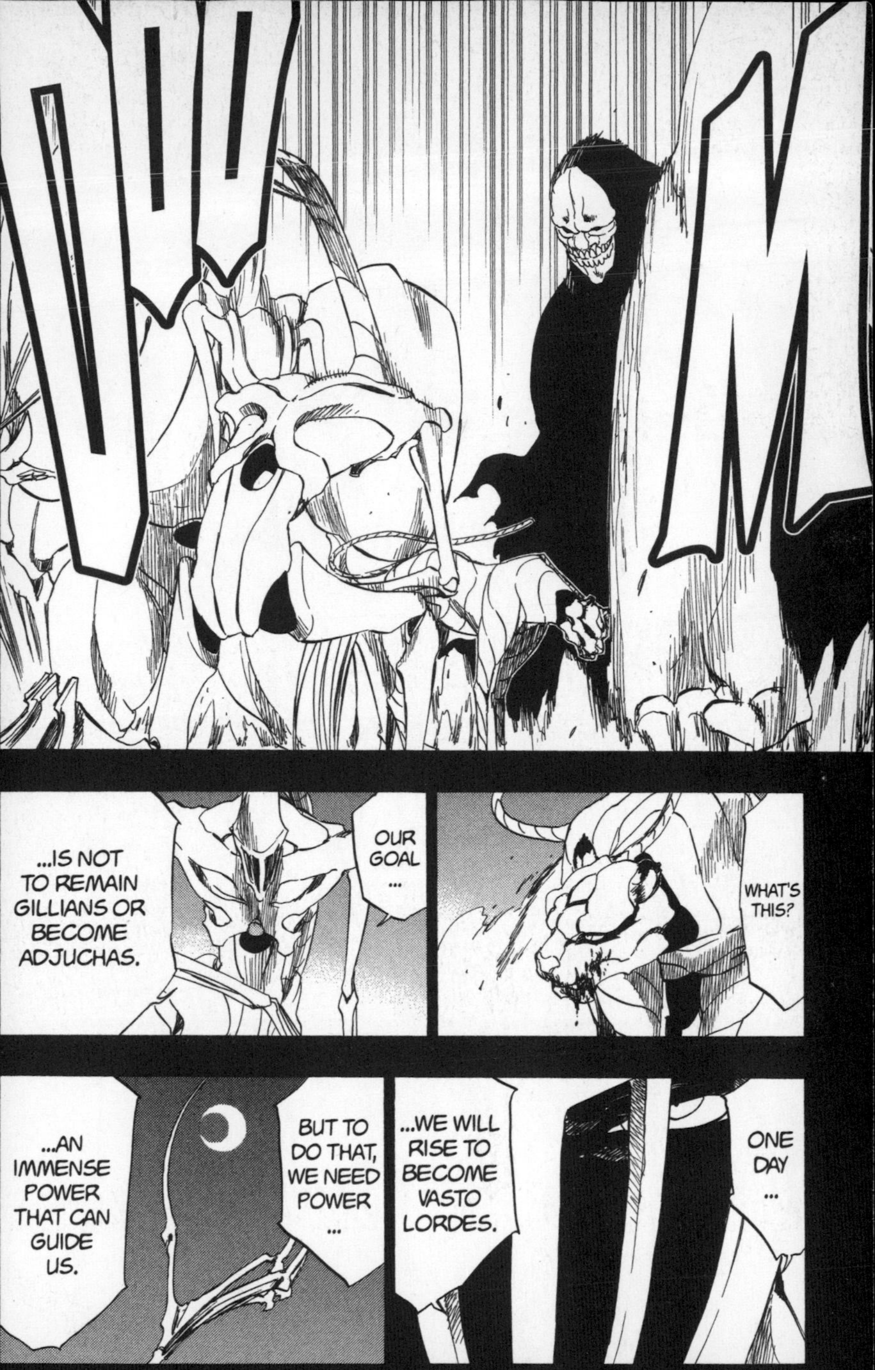
WHAT'S THIS?
OUR GOAL ...
...IS NOT TO REMAIN GILLIANS OR BECOME ADJUCHAS.
ONE DAY ...
...WE WILL RISE TO BECOME VASTO LORDES.
BUT TO DO THAT, WE NEED POWER ...
...AN IMMENSE POWER THAT CAN GUIDE US.

READ THIS WAY

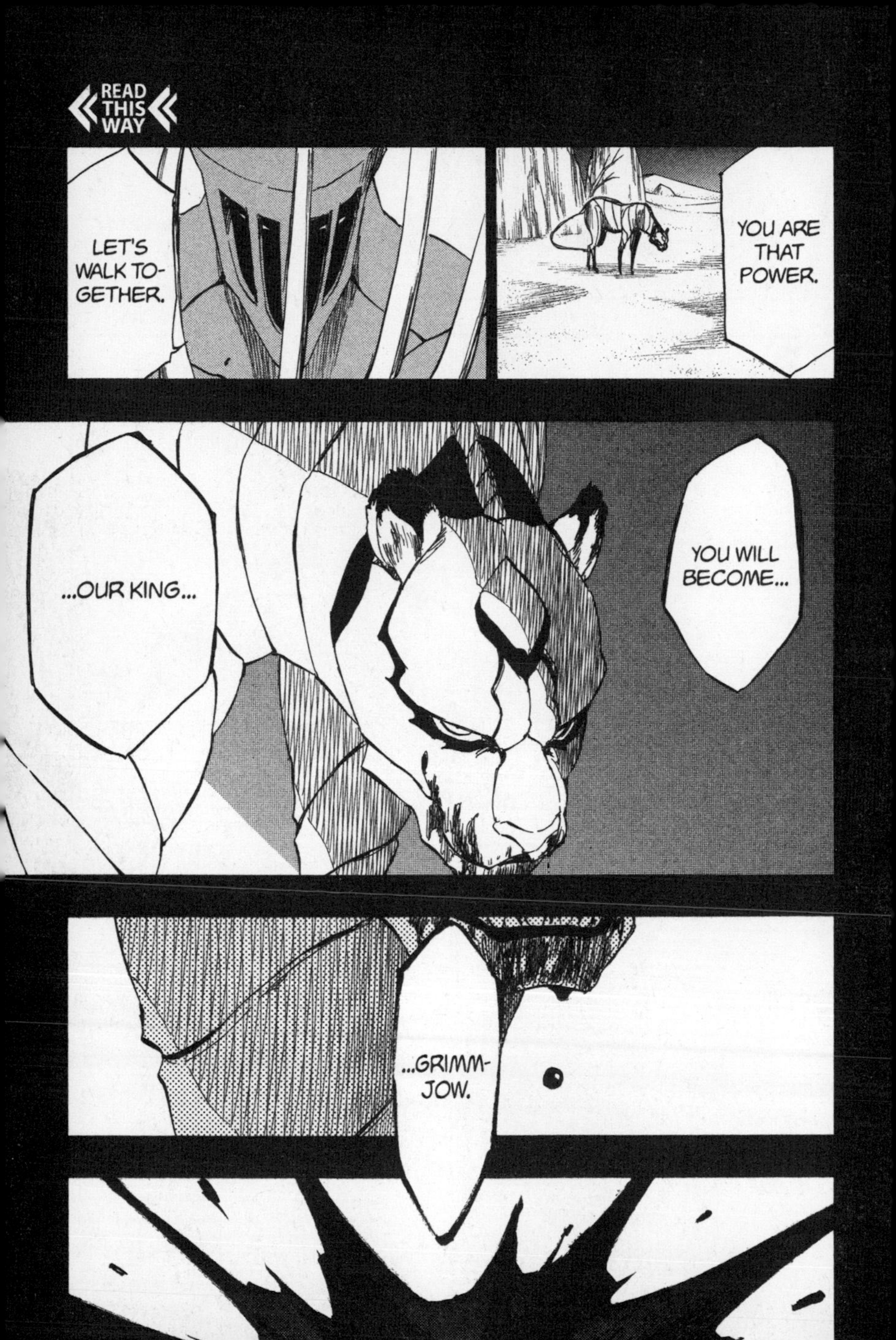

YOU ARE THAT POWER.
LET'S WALK TO-GETHER.
YOU WILL BECOME...
...OUR KING...
...GRIMM-JOW.

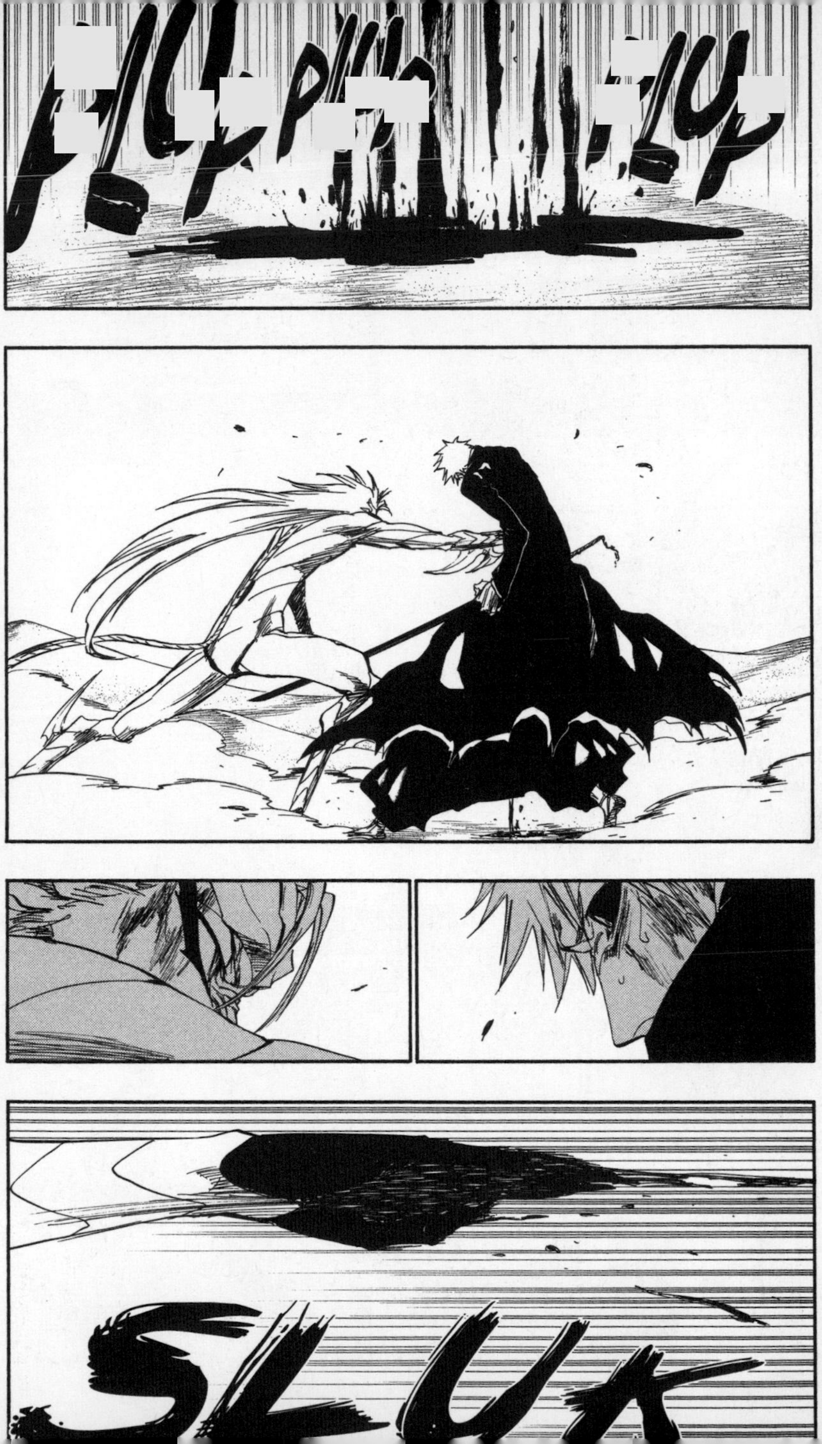
SLUK

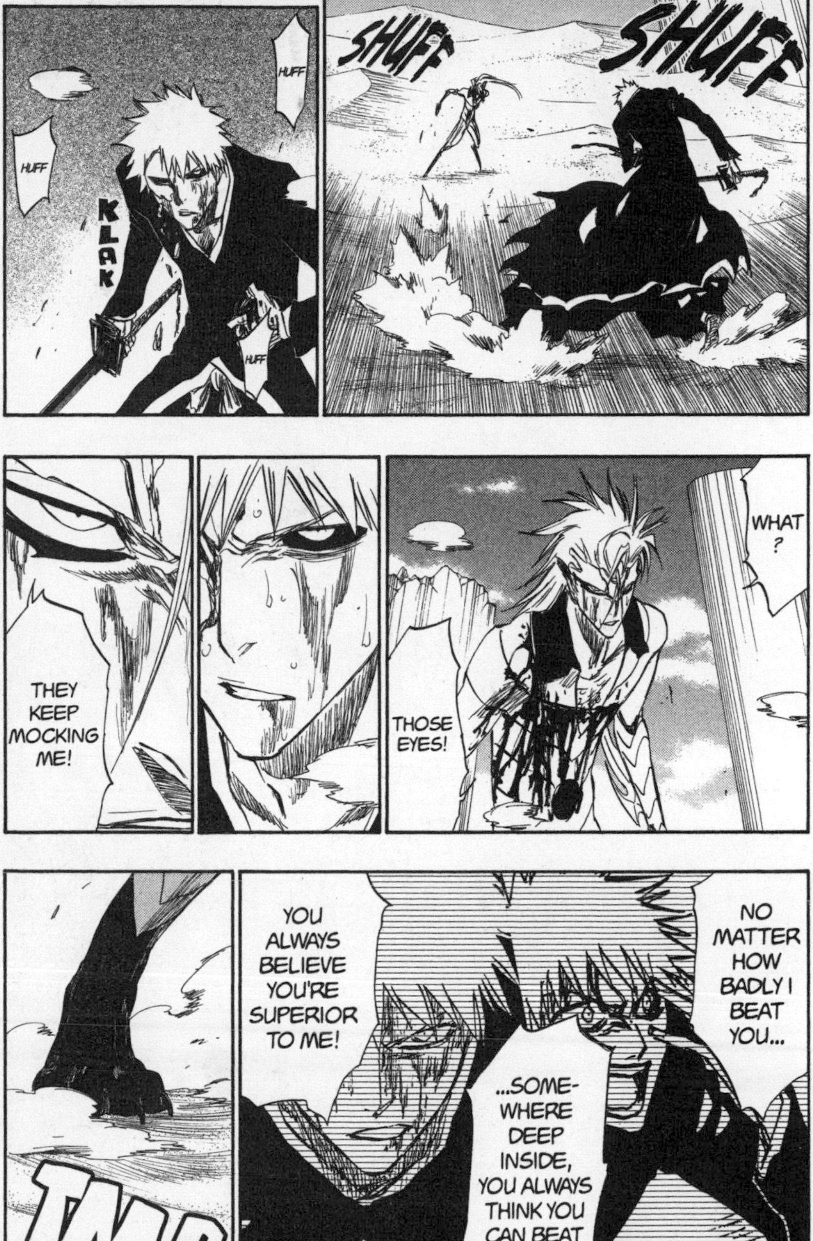
SHUFF
SHUFF
HUFF
HUFF
KLAK
HUFF
WHAT?
THOSE EYES!
THEY KEEP MOCKING ME!
NO MATTER HOW BADLY I BEAT YOU...
...SOME-WHERE DEEP INSIDE, YOU ALWAYS THINK YOU CAN BEAT ME.
YOU ALWAYS BELIEVE YOU'RE SUPERIOR TO ME!
TMP

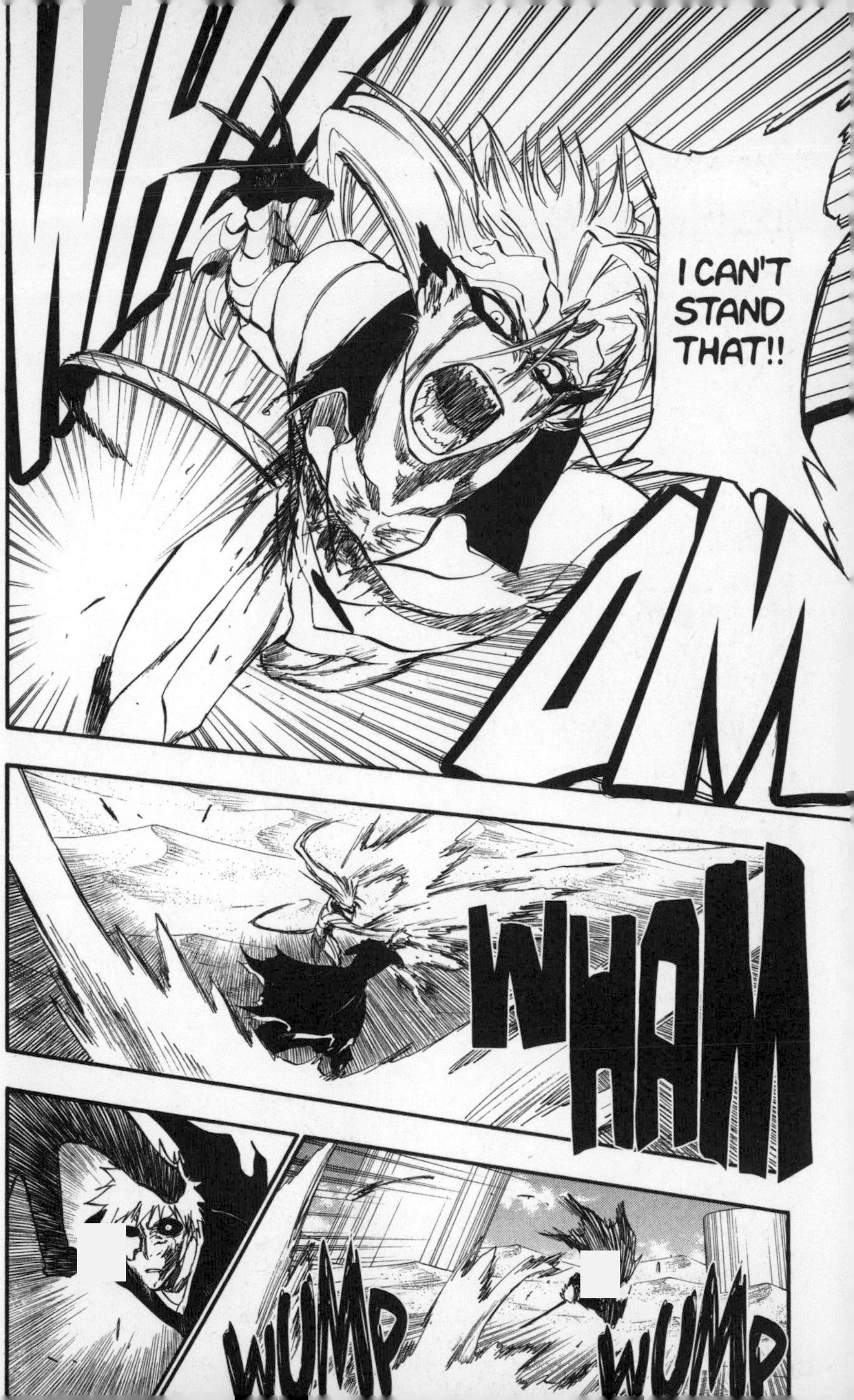
I CAN'T STAND THAT!!
WHAM
WHAM
WUMP
WUMP

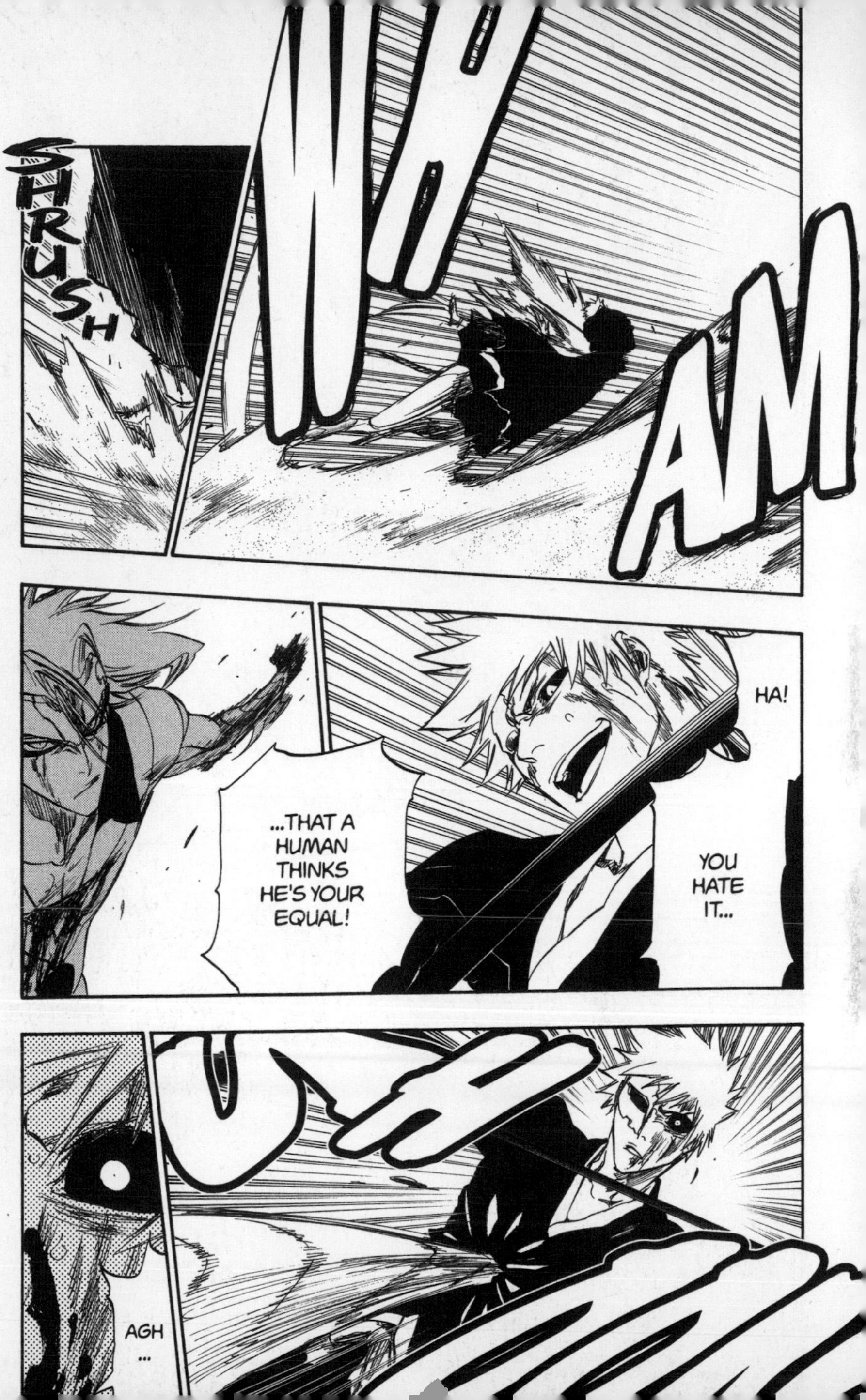
WHAM
SHRUSH
HA!
YOU HATE IT...
...THAT A HUMAN THINKS HE'S YOUR EQUAL!
AGH ...

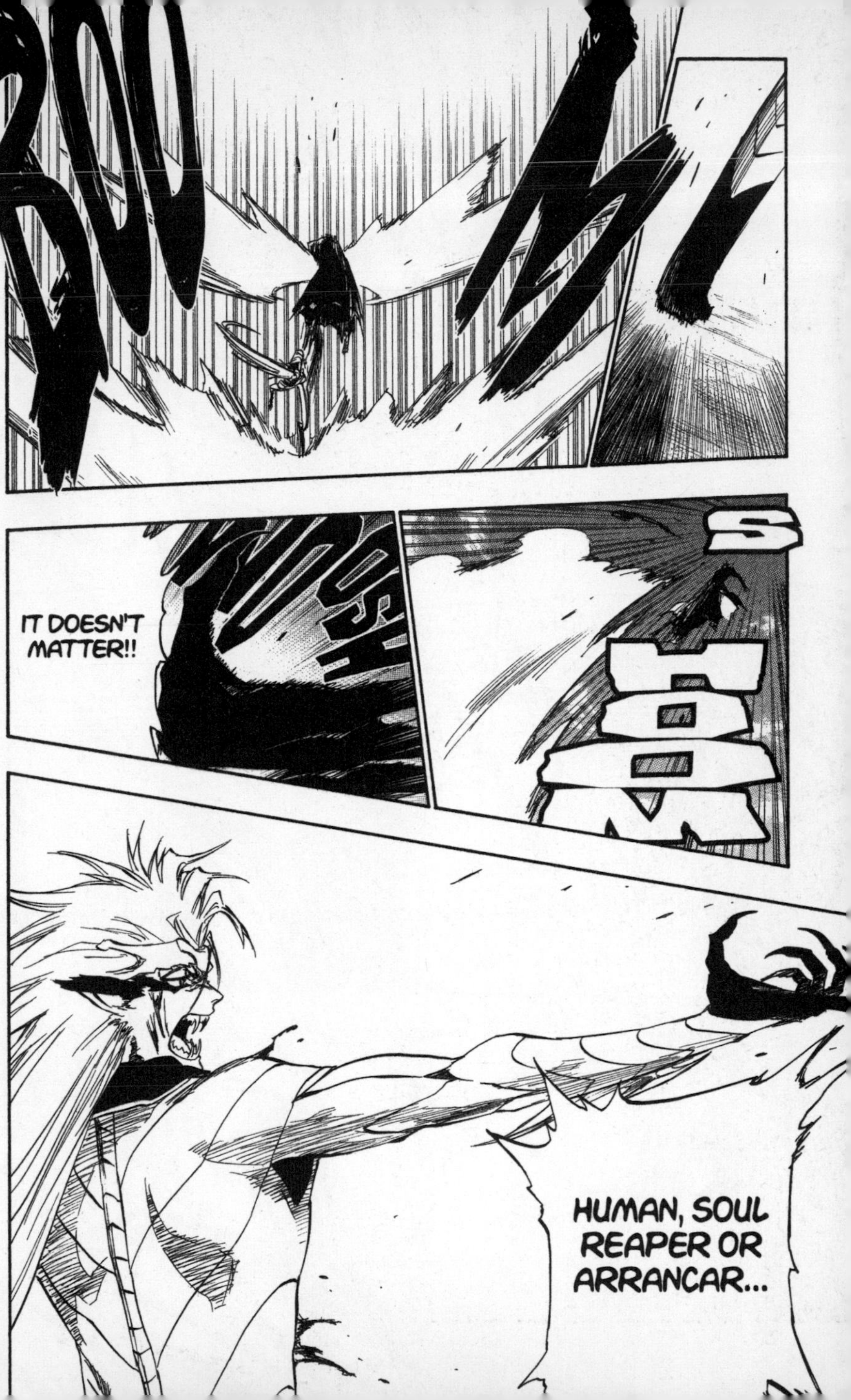
WHOOSH!
IT DOESN'T MATTER!!
HUMAN, SOUL REAPER OR ARRANCAR...

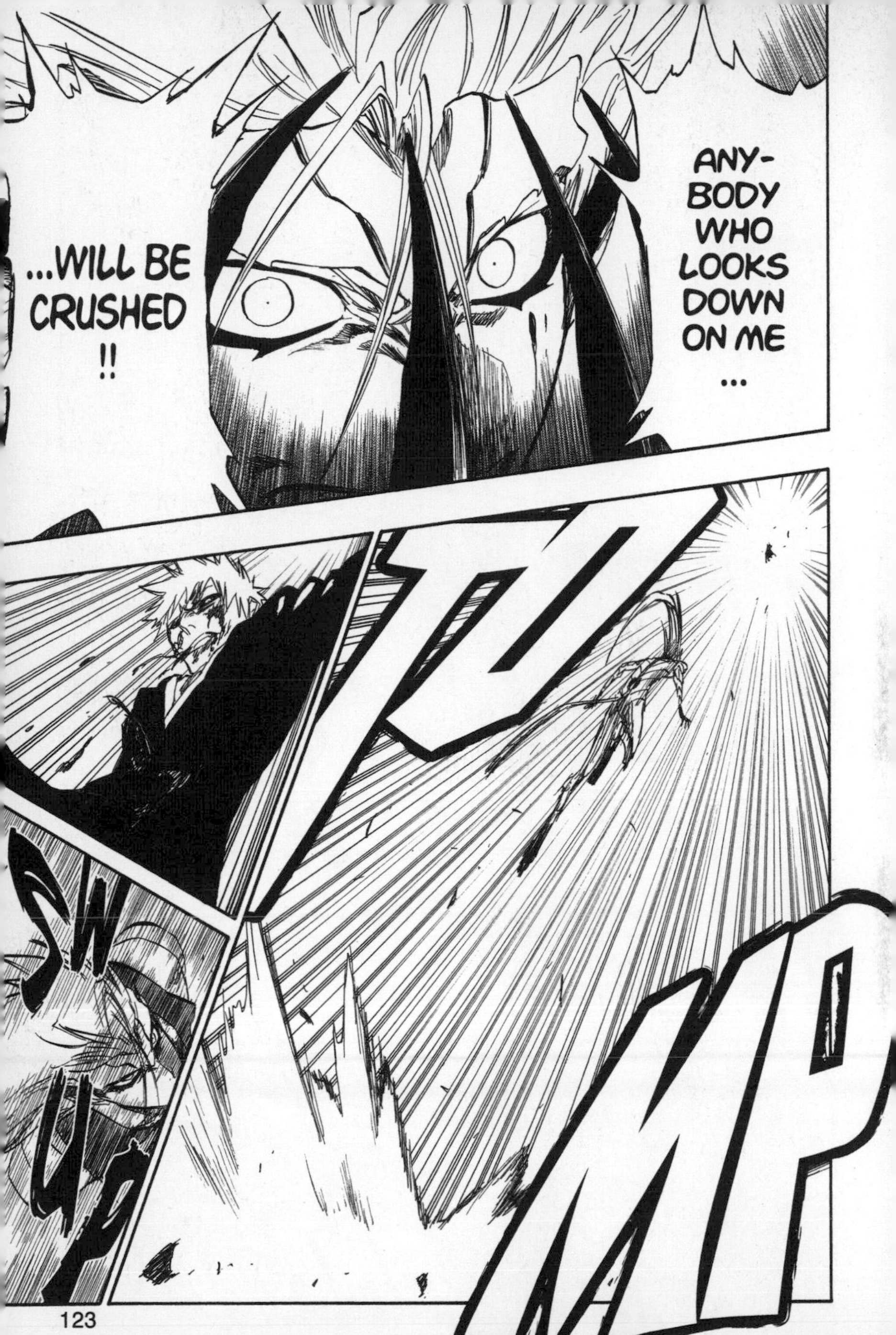
ANY-BODY WHO LOOKS DOWN ON ME ...
...WILL BE CRUSHED !!
ZU
SW
UP
ZAP

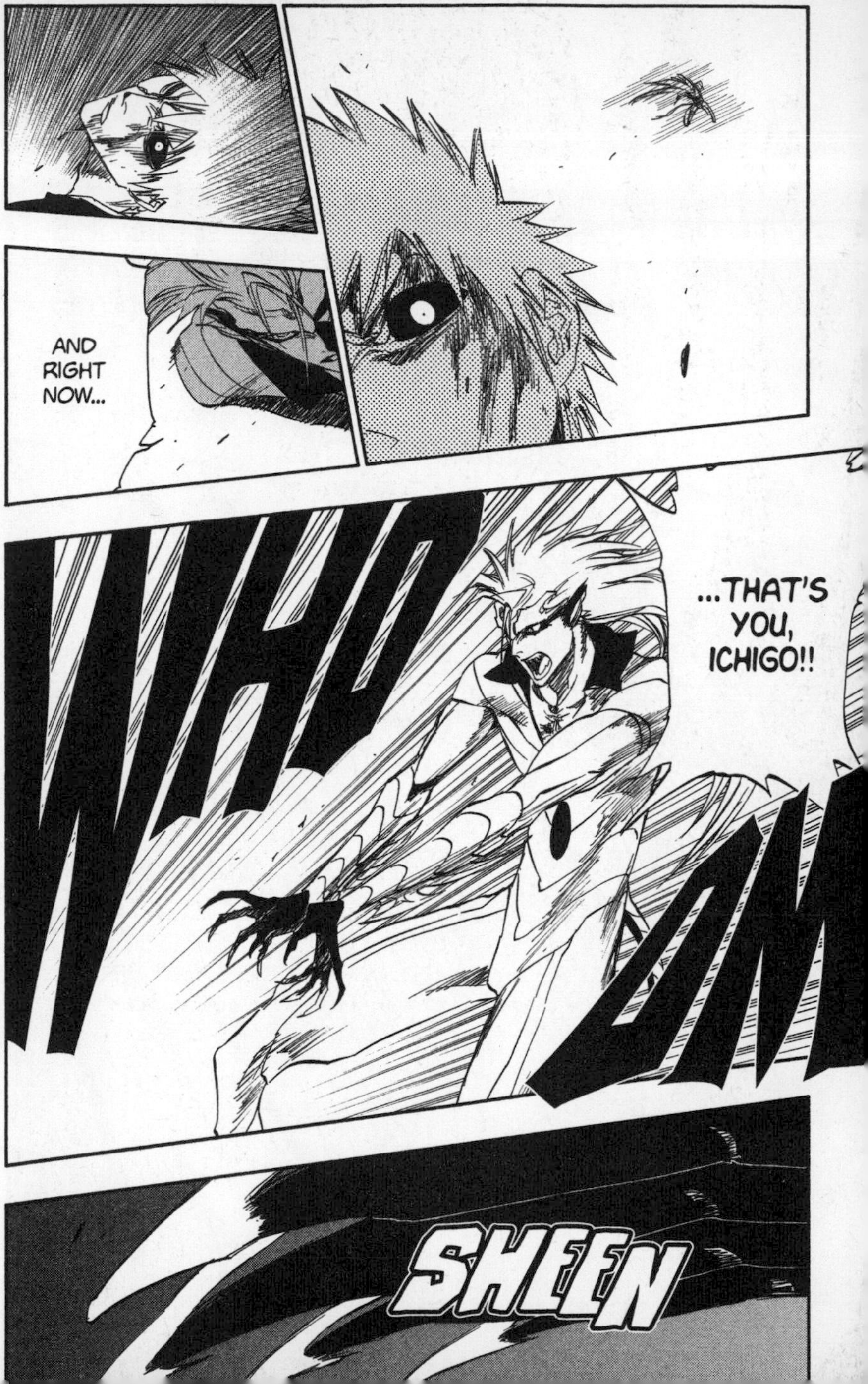
AND RIGHT NOW...
...THAT'S YOU, ICHIGO!!
WHOOM
SHEEN

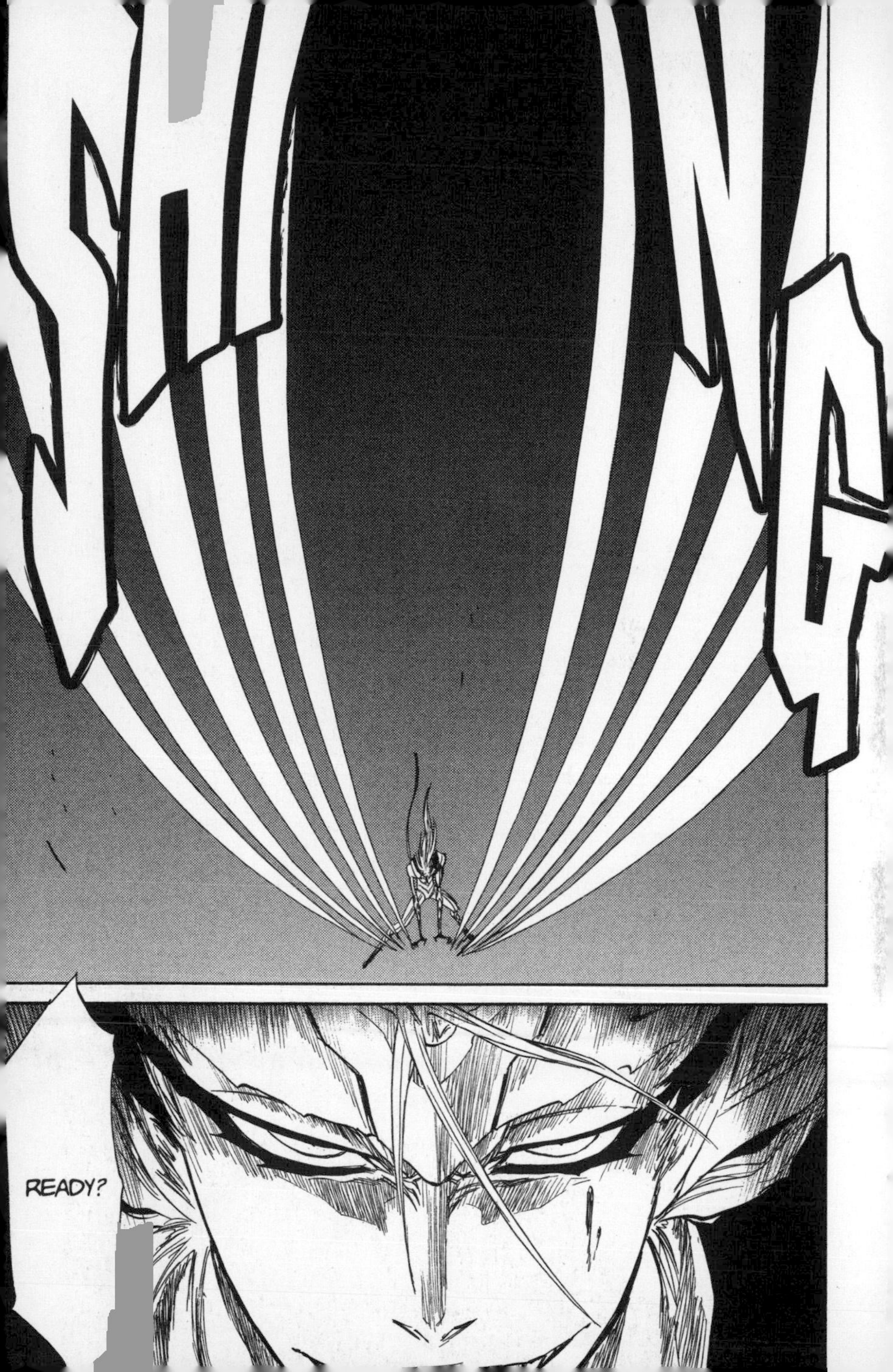
SHING
READY?

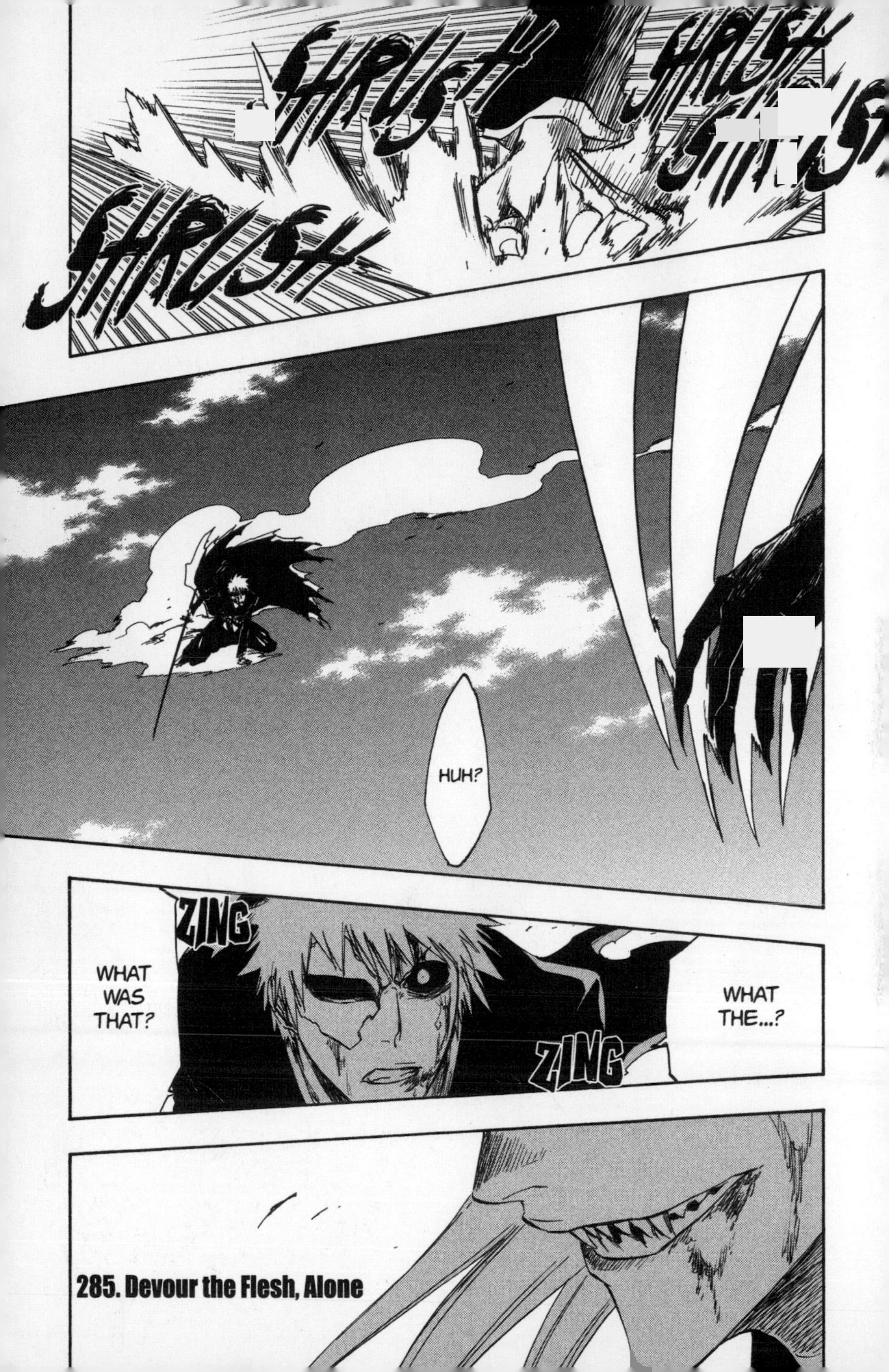
SHRUSH
SHRUSH
SHRUSH
HUH?
ZING
WHAT THE...?
WHAT WAS THAT?
ZING

285. Devour the Flesh, Alone

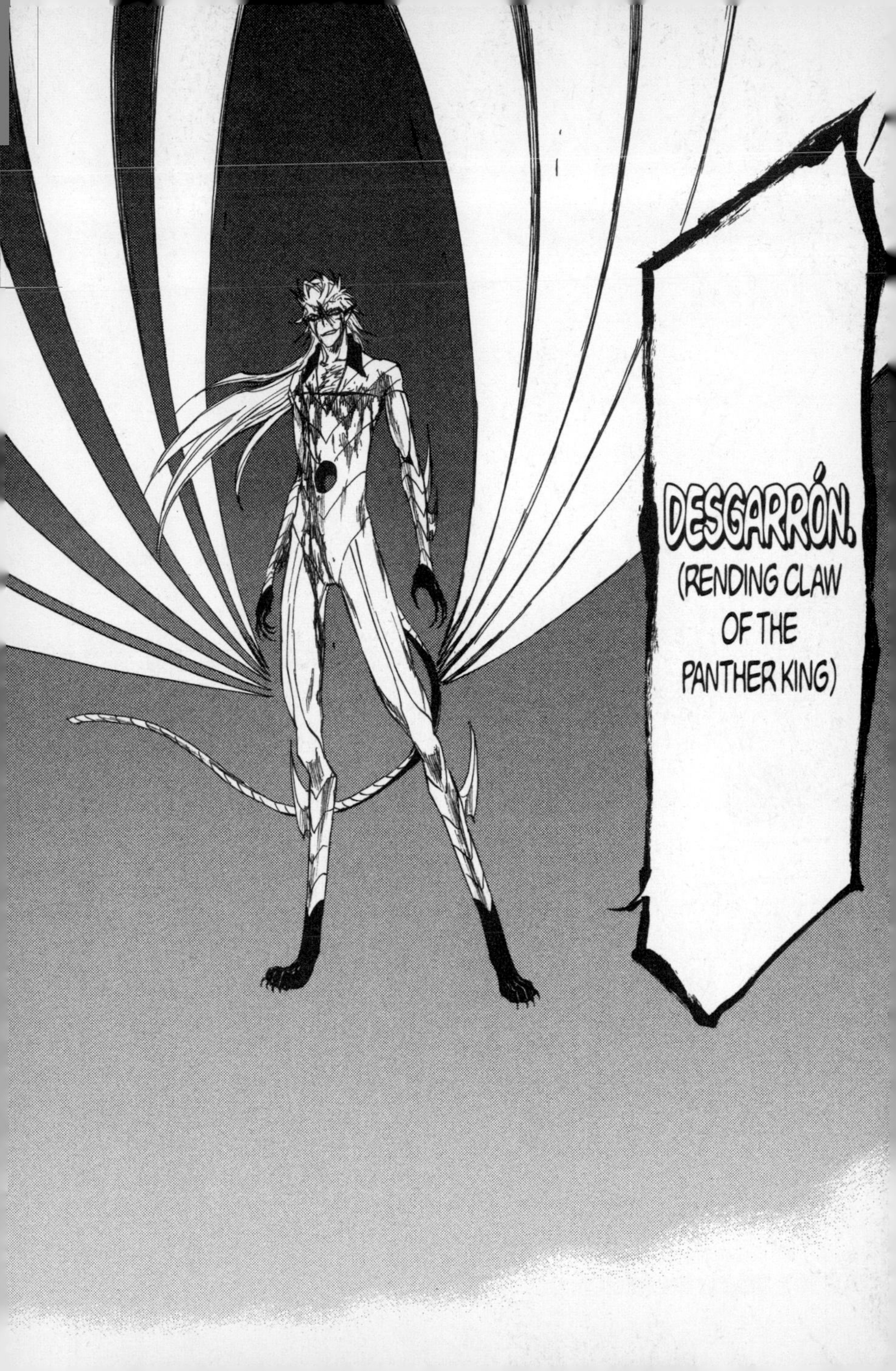
DESGARRÓN.
(RENDING CLAW OF THE PANTHER KING)

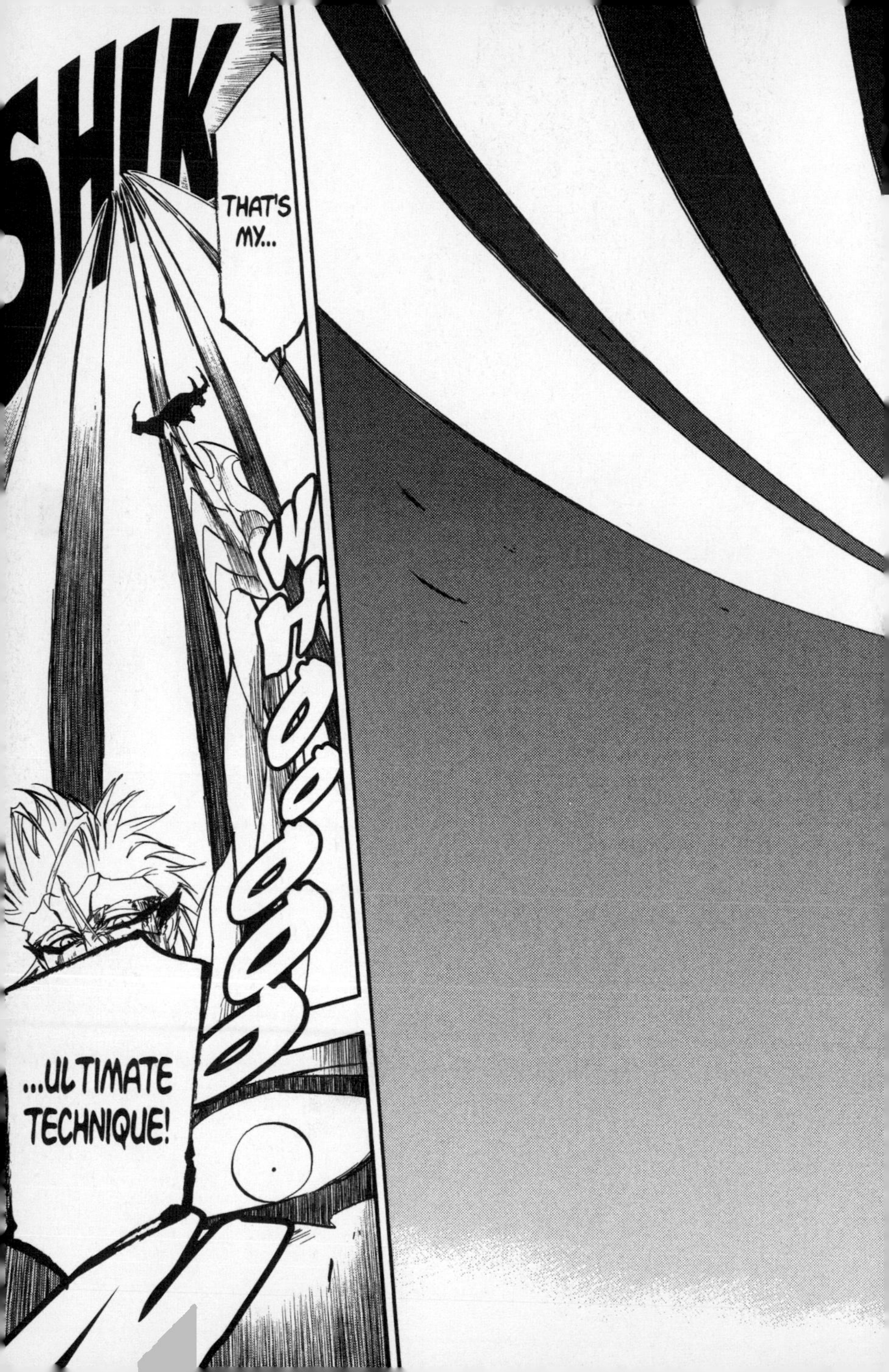
SHIK
THAT'S MY...
WHOOOOOO
...ULTIMATE TECHNIQUE!

BLEACH 285.

Devour the Flesh, Alone

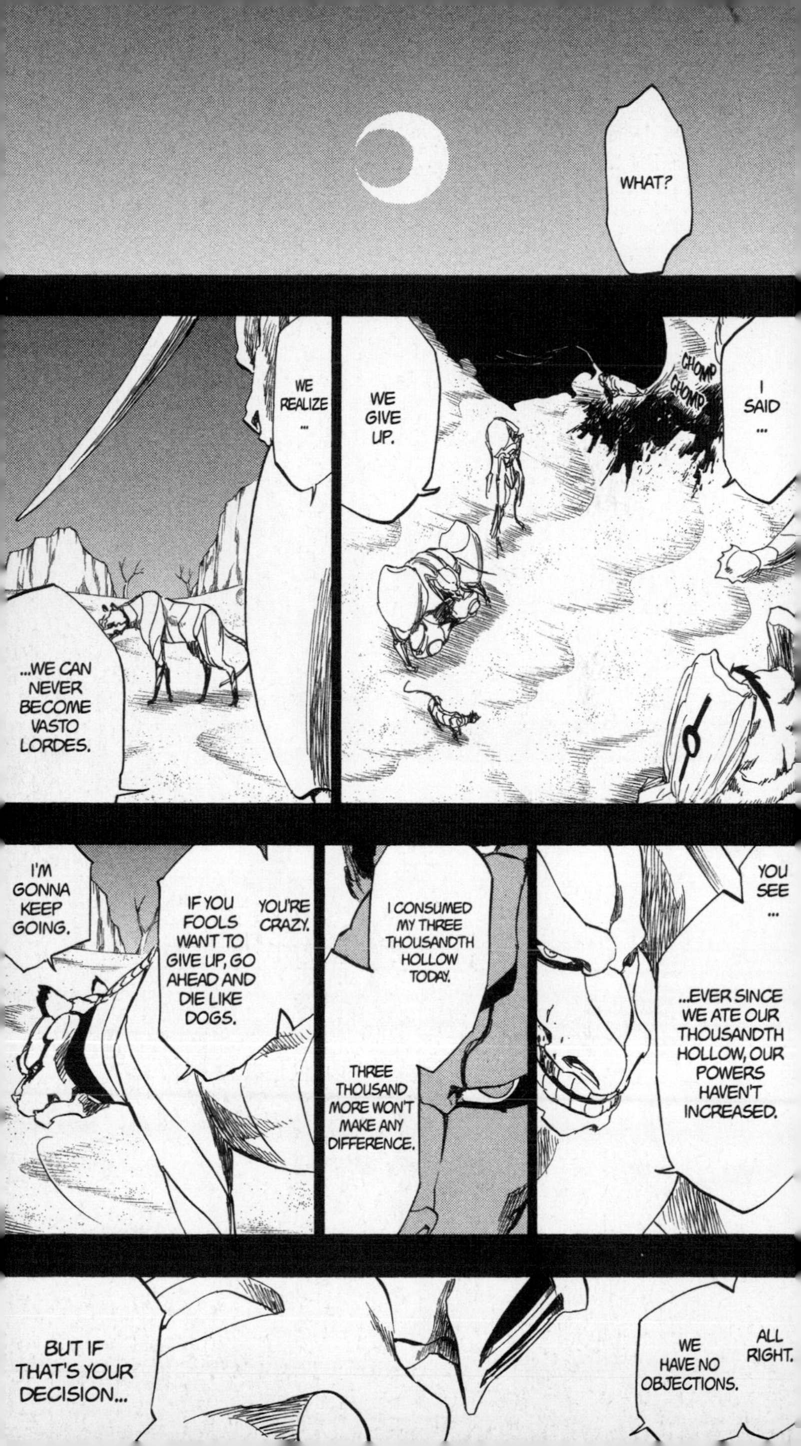
WHAT?
CHOMP CHOMP
I SAID ...
WE GIVE UP.
WE REALIZE ...
...WE CAN NEVER BECOME VASTO LORDES.
YOU SEE ...
...EVER SINCE WE ATE OUR THOUSANDTH HOLLOW, OUR POWERS HAVEN'T INCREASED.
I CONSUMED MY THREE THOUSANDTH HOLLOW TODAY.
THREE THOUSAND MORE WON'T MAKE ANY DIFFERENCE.
YOU'RE CRAZY.
IF YOU FOOLS WANT TO GIVE UP, GO AHEAD AND DIE LIKE DOGS.
I'M GONNA KEEP GOING.
ALL RIGHT.
WE HAVE NO OBJECTIONS.
BUT IF THAT'S YOUR DECISION...

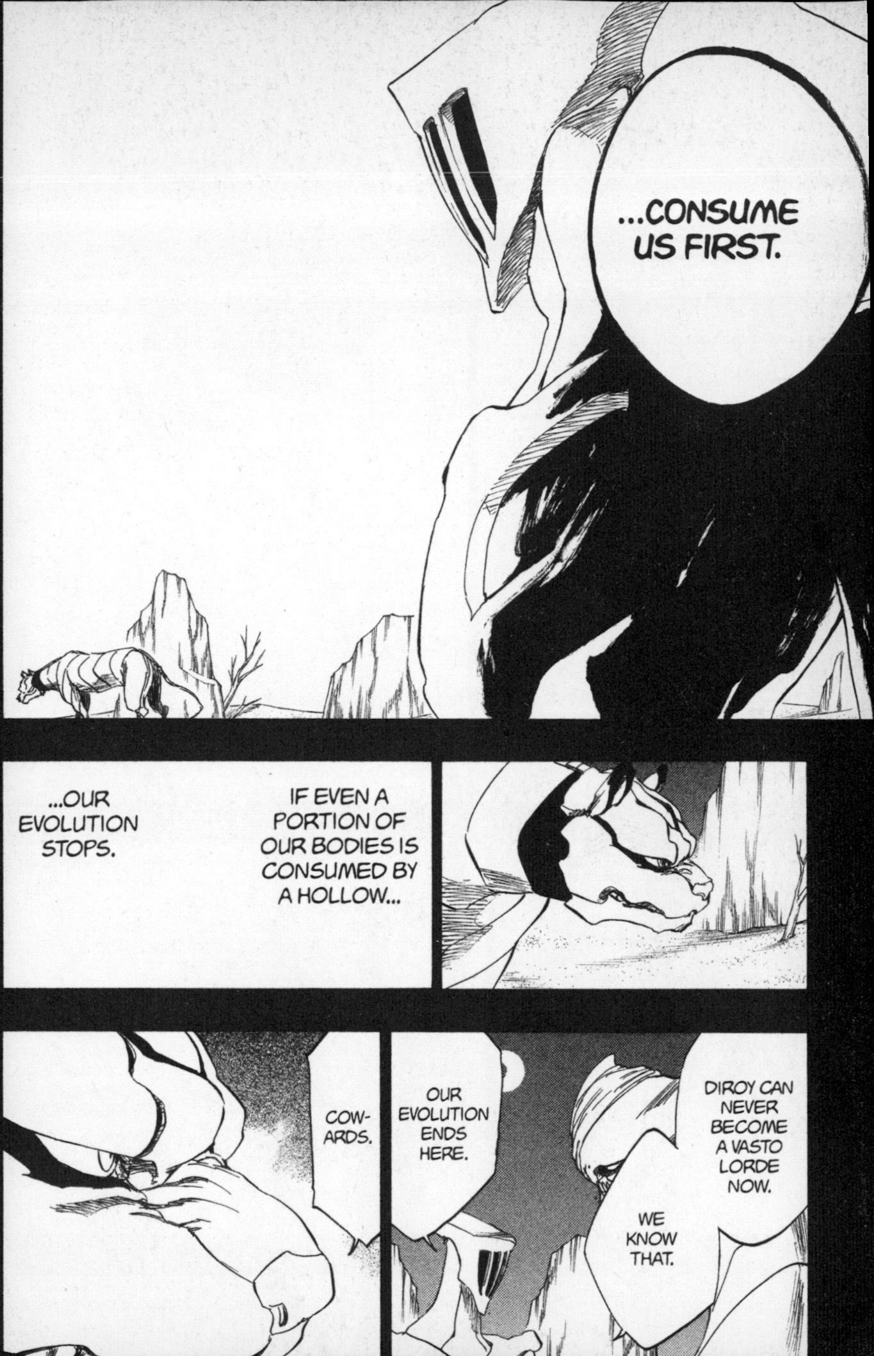
...CONSUME US FIRST.
IF EVEN A PORTION OF OUR BODIES IS CONSUMED BY A HOLLOW...
...OUR EVOLUTION STOPS.
DIROY CAN NEVER BECOME A VASTO LORDE NOW.
WE KNOW THAT.
OUR EVOLUTION ENDS HERE.
COW-ARDS.

READ THIS WAY

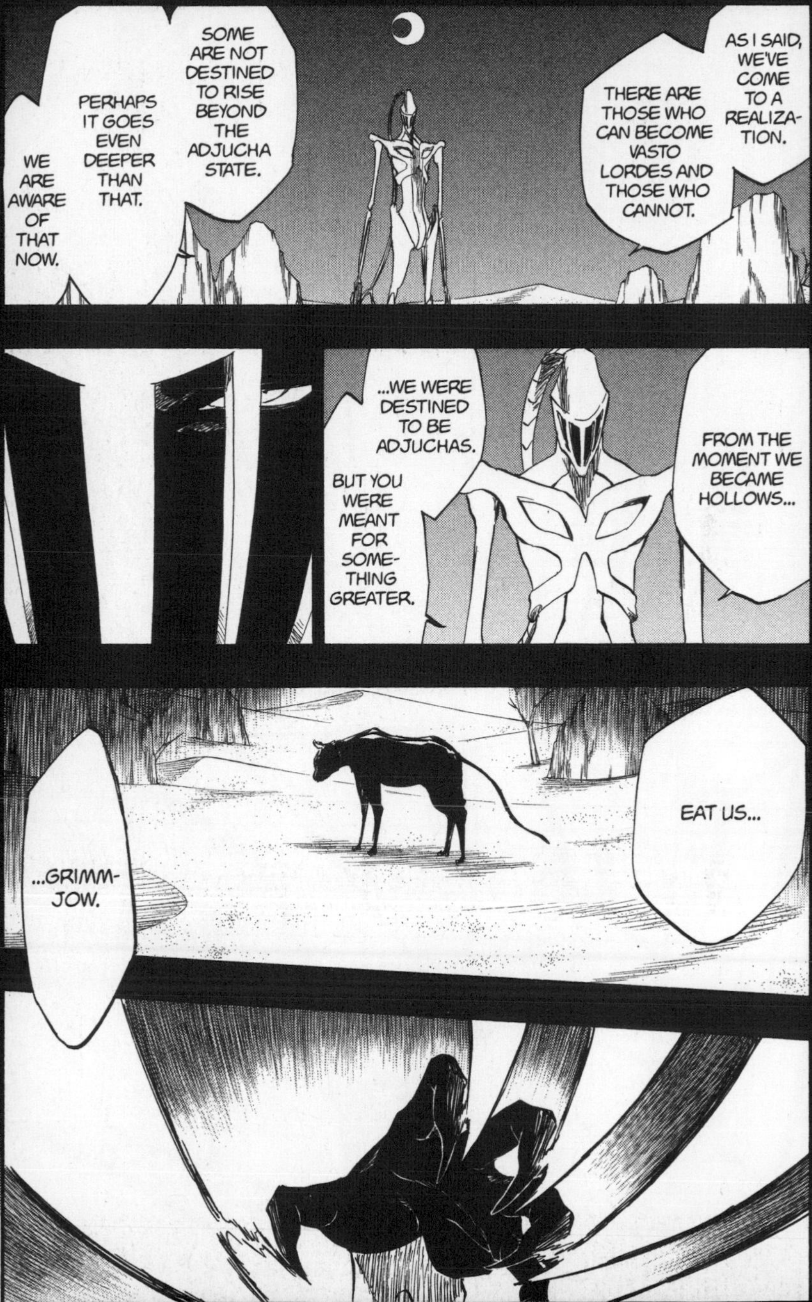
AS I SAID, WE'VE COME TO A REALIZATION.
THERE ARE THOSE WHO CAN BECOME VASTO LORDES AND THOSE WHO CANNOT.
SOME ARE NOT DESTINED TO RISE BEYOND THE ADJUCHA STATE.
PERHAPS IT GOES EVEN DEEPER THAN THAT.
WE ARE AWARE OF THAT NOW.
FROM THE MOMENT WE BECAME HOLLOWS...
...WE WERE DESTINED TO BE ADJUCHAS.
BUT YOU WERE MEANT FOR SOMETHING GREATER.
EAT US...
...GRIMM-JOW.

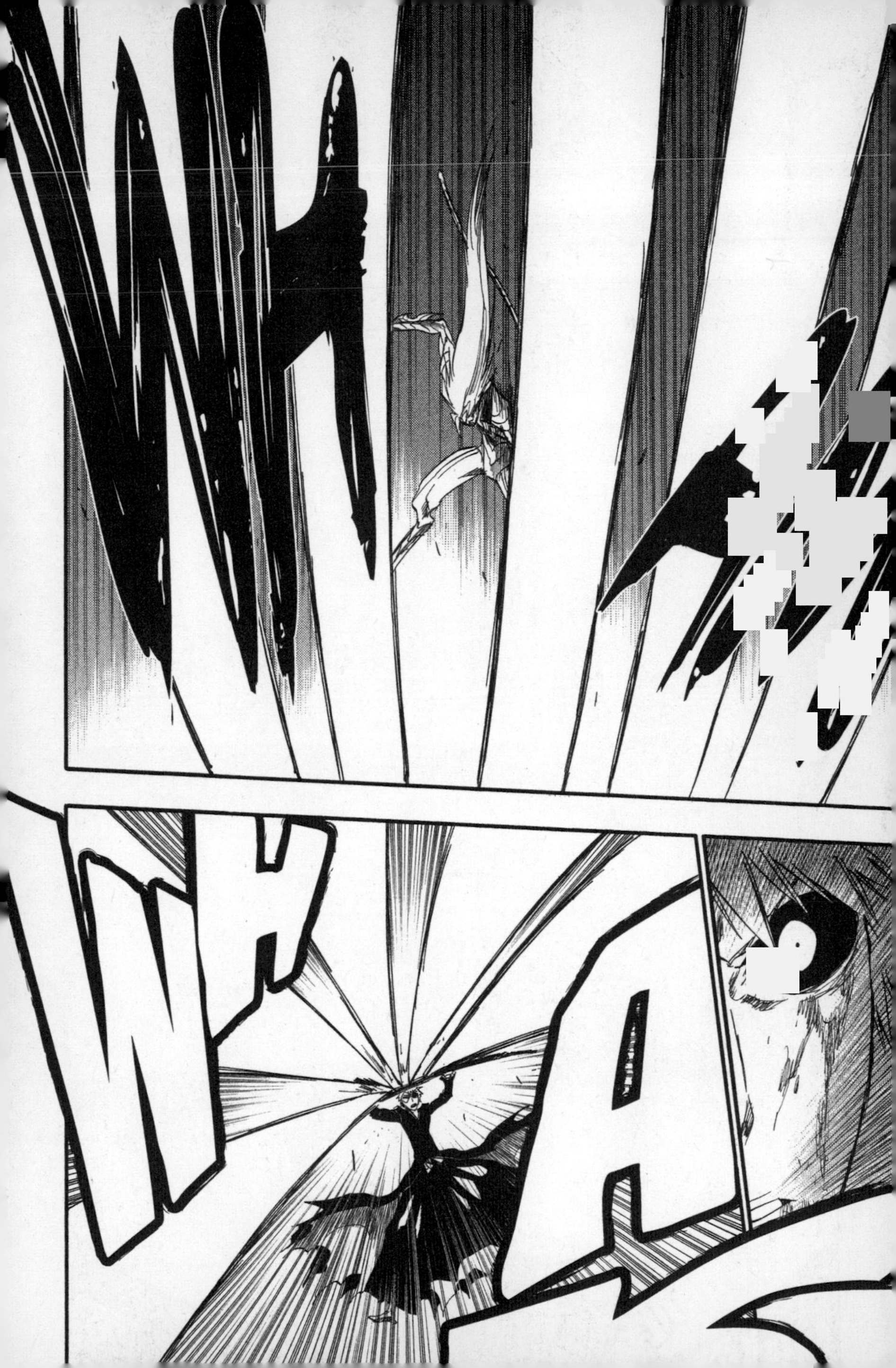
WHA

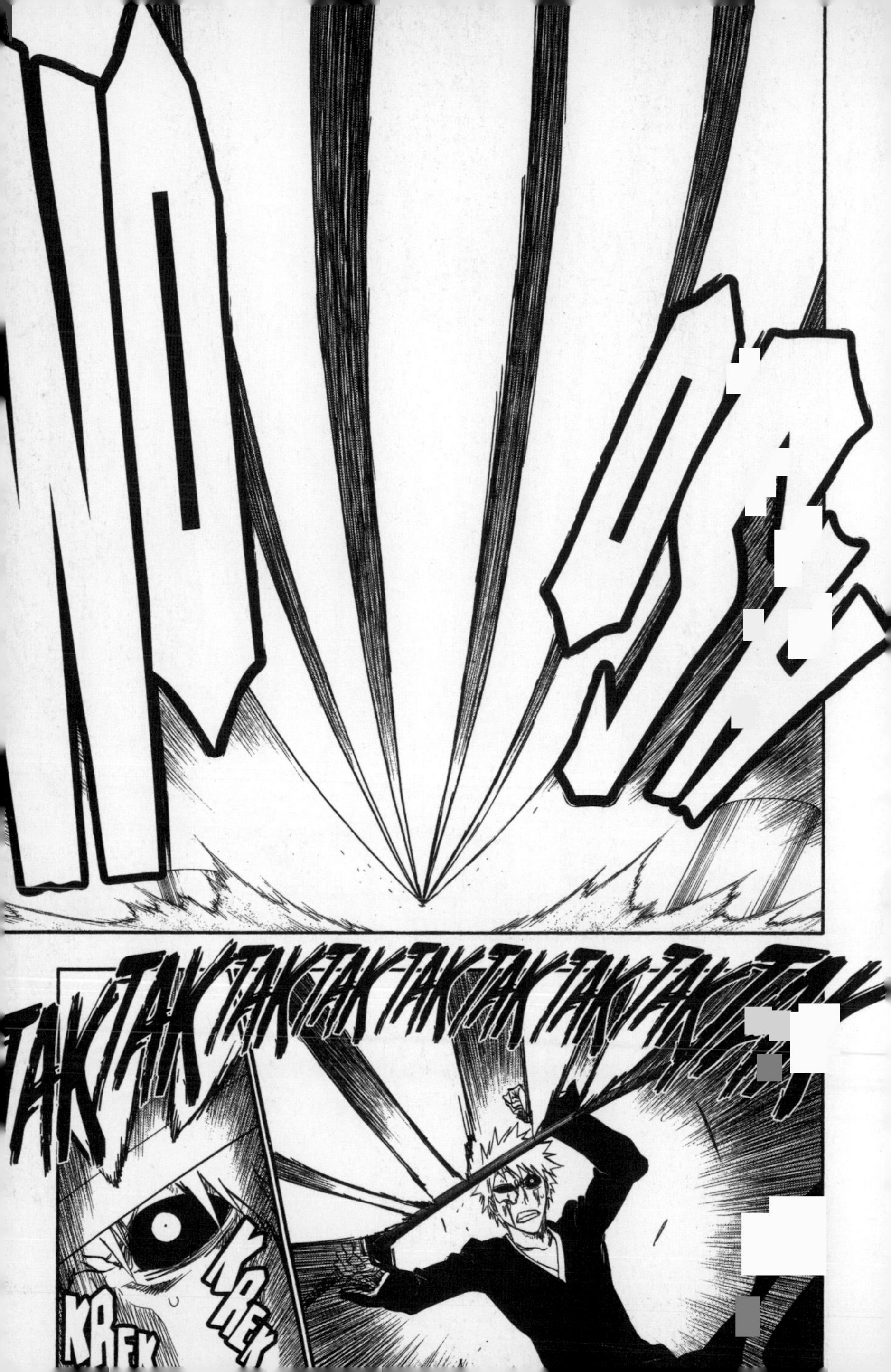
TAK TAK TAK TAK TAK TAK TAK TAK
KREK
KREK

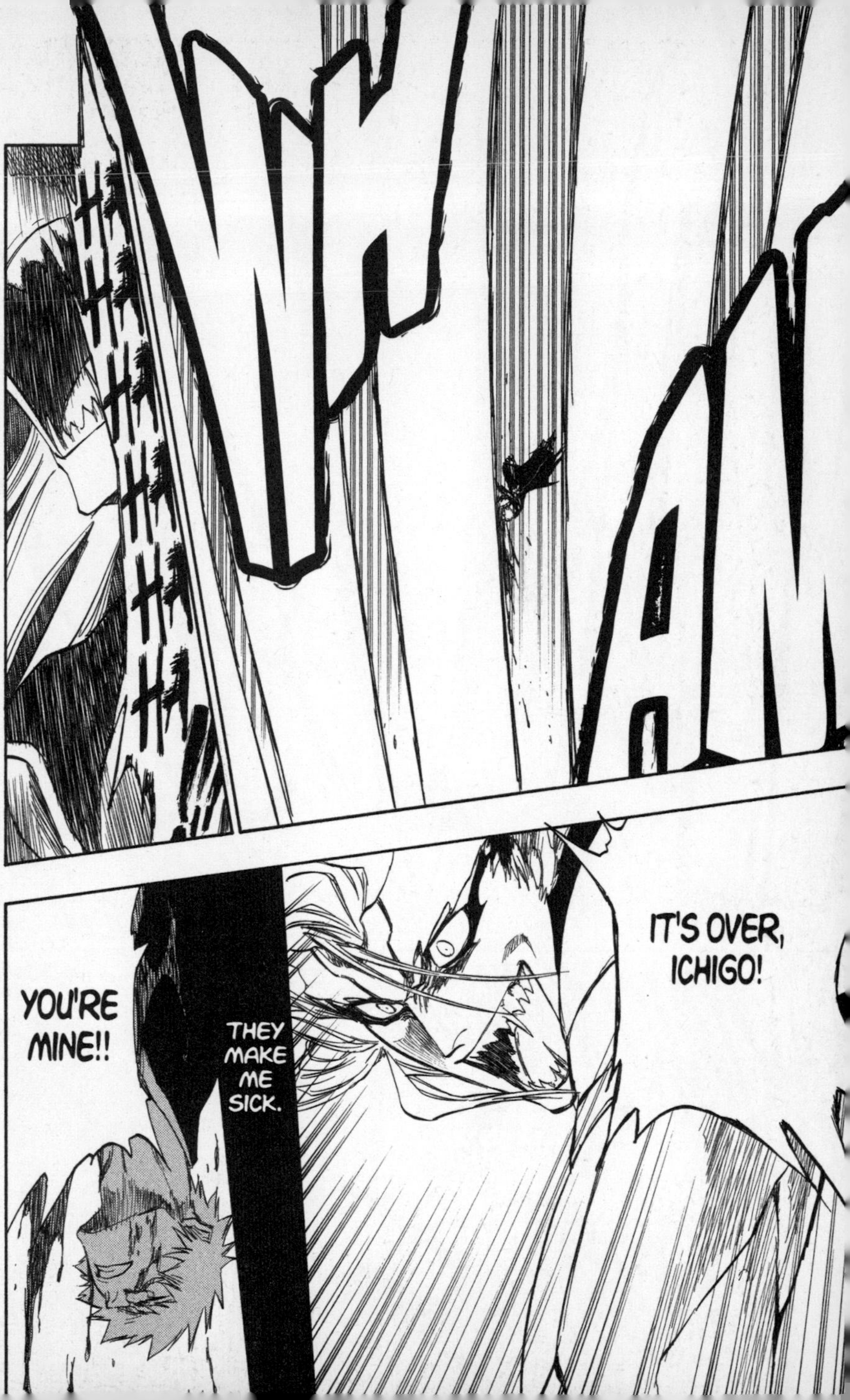
IT'S OVER, ICHIGO!
THEY MAKE ME SICK.
YOU'RE MINE!!

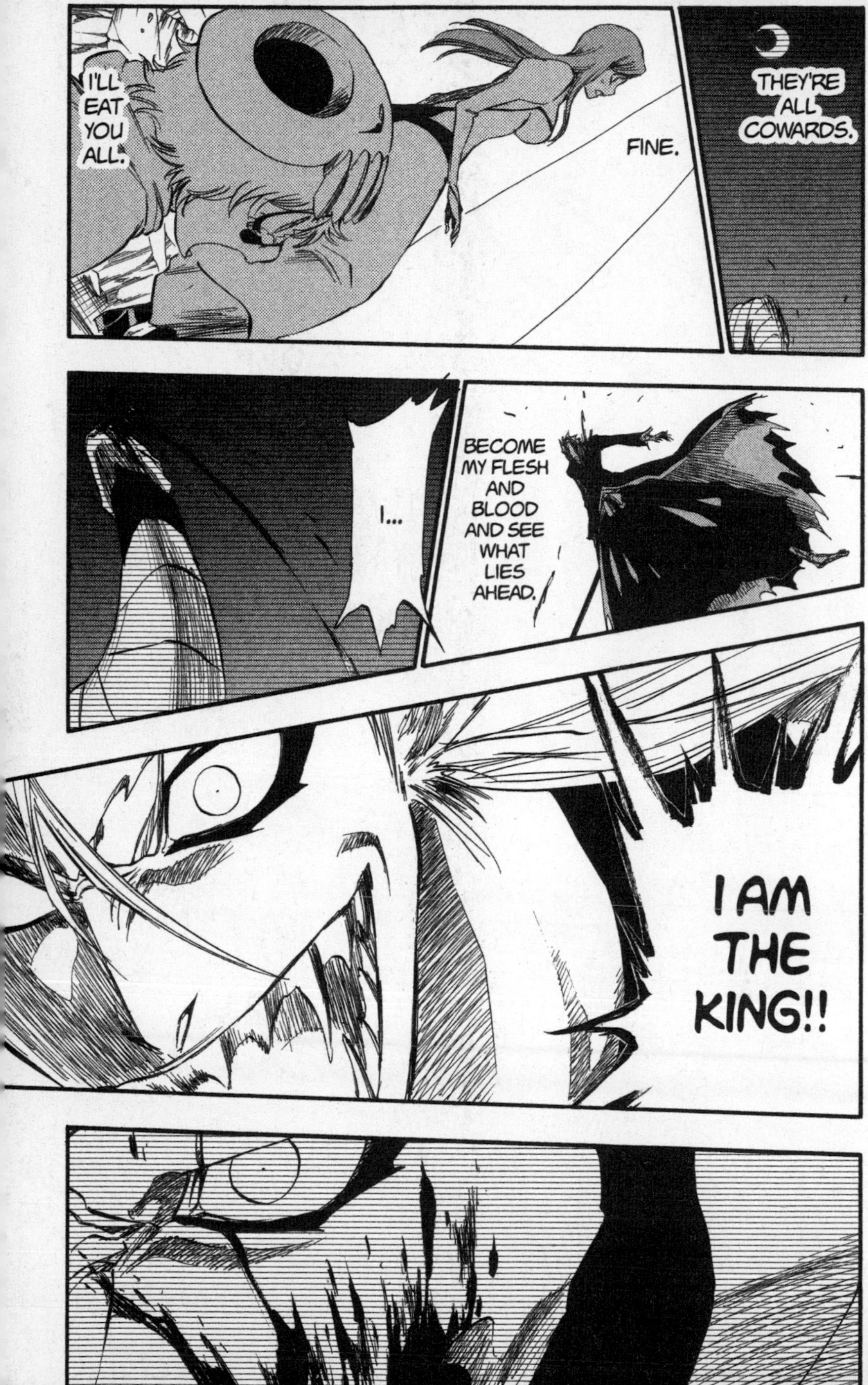
THEY'RE ALL COWARDS.
FINE.
I'LL EAT YOU ALL.
BECOME MY FLESH AND BLOOD AND SEE WHAT LIES AHEAD.
I...
I AM THE KING!!

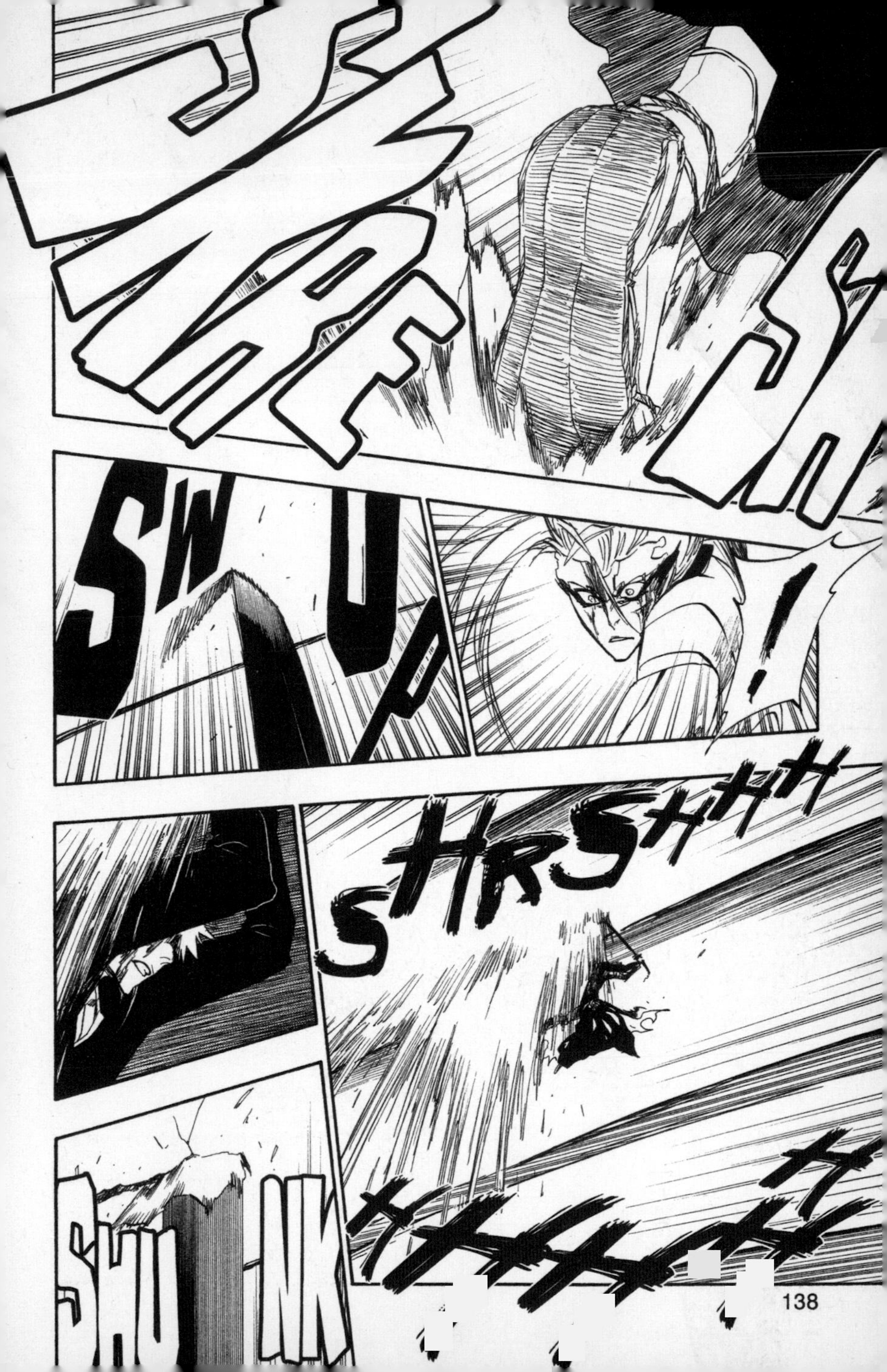
SWUP
!
SHRSHHH
SHUNK

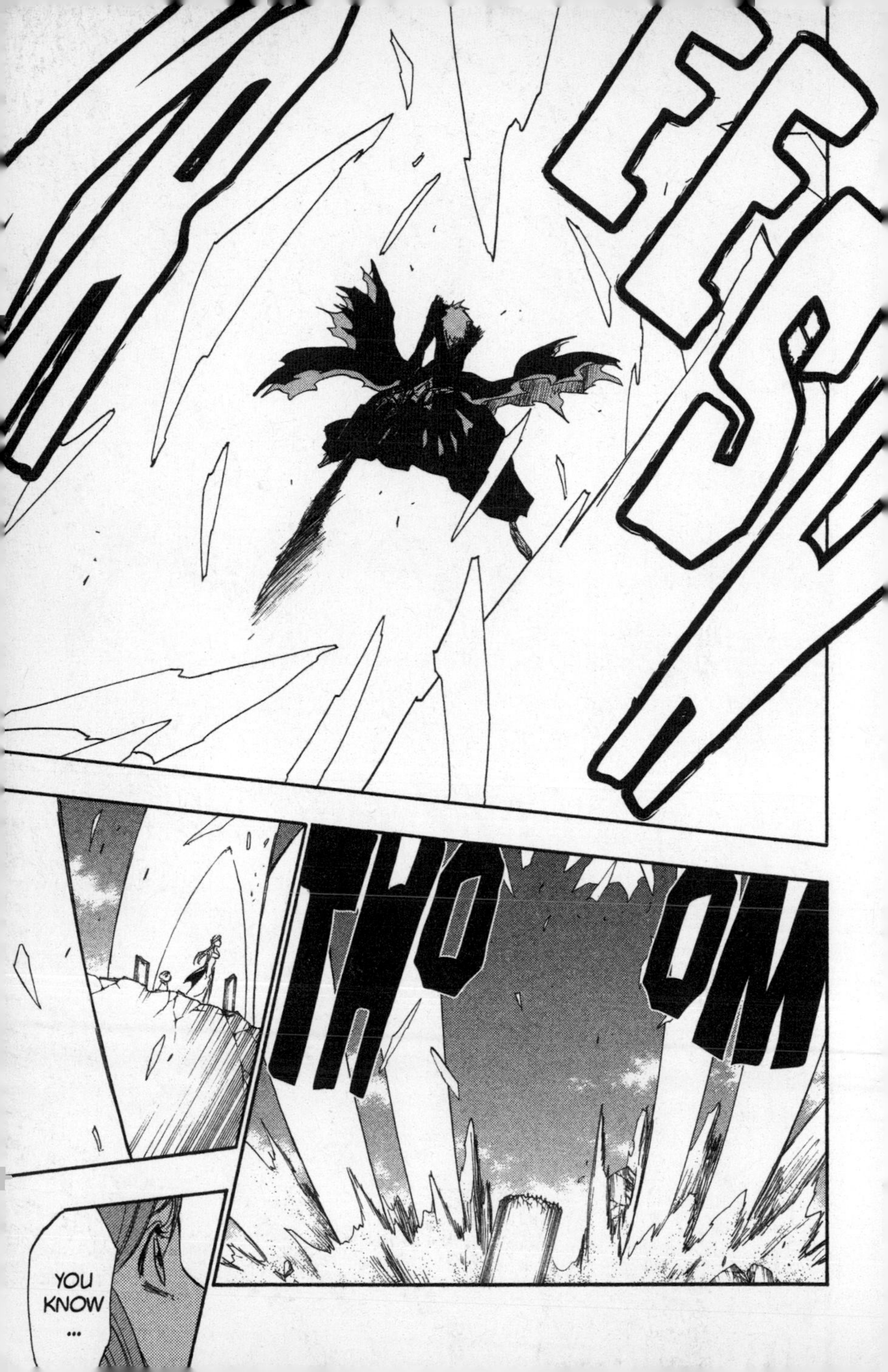
THOOM
YOU KNOW ...

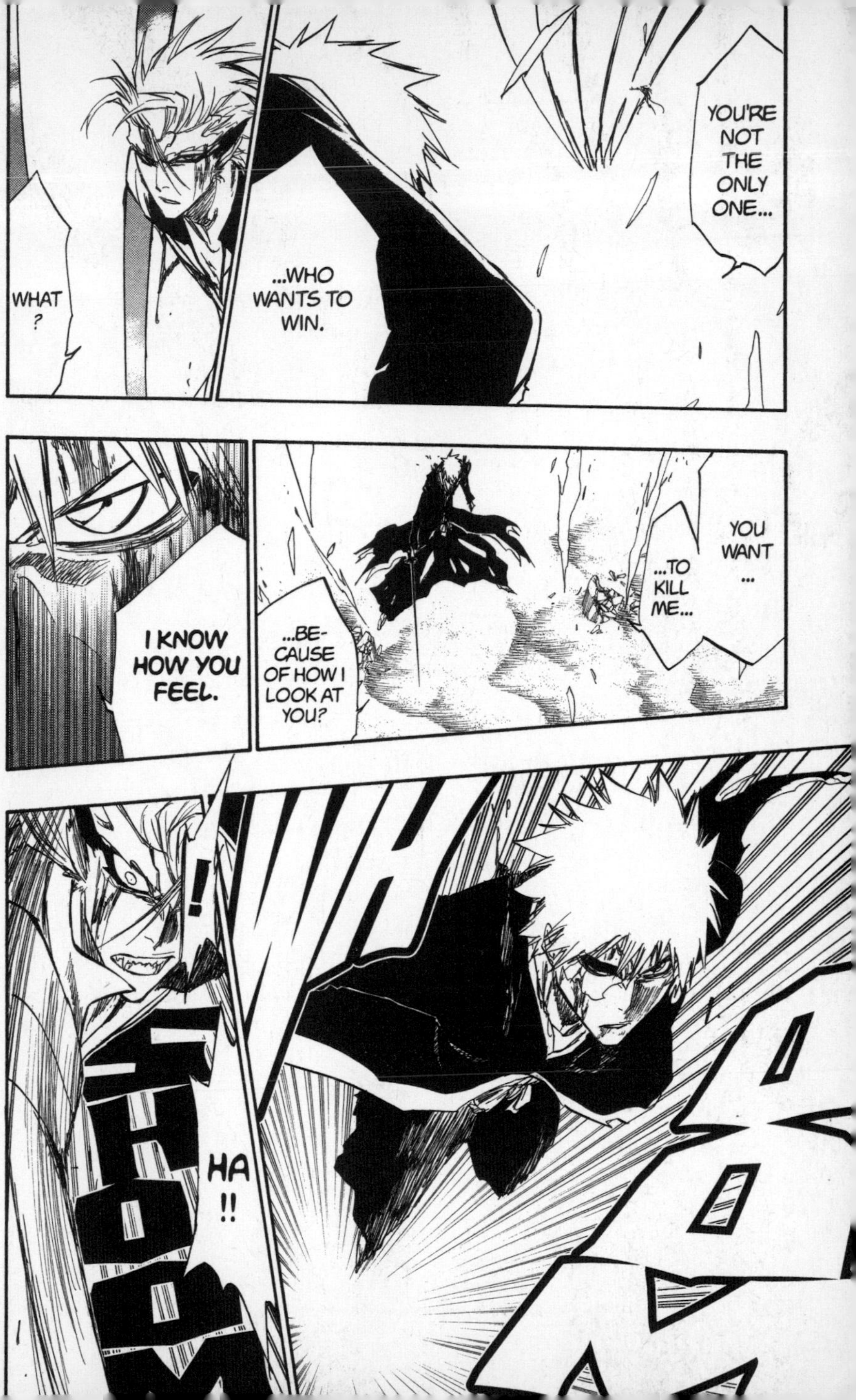
YOU'RE NOT THE ONLY ONE...
...WHO WANTS TO WIN.
WHAT?
YOU WANT...
...TO KILL ME...
...BE-CAUSE OF HOW I LOOK AT YOU?
I KNOW HOW YOU FEEL.
!
HA!!

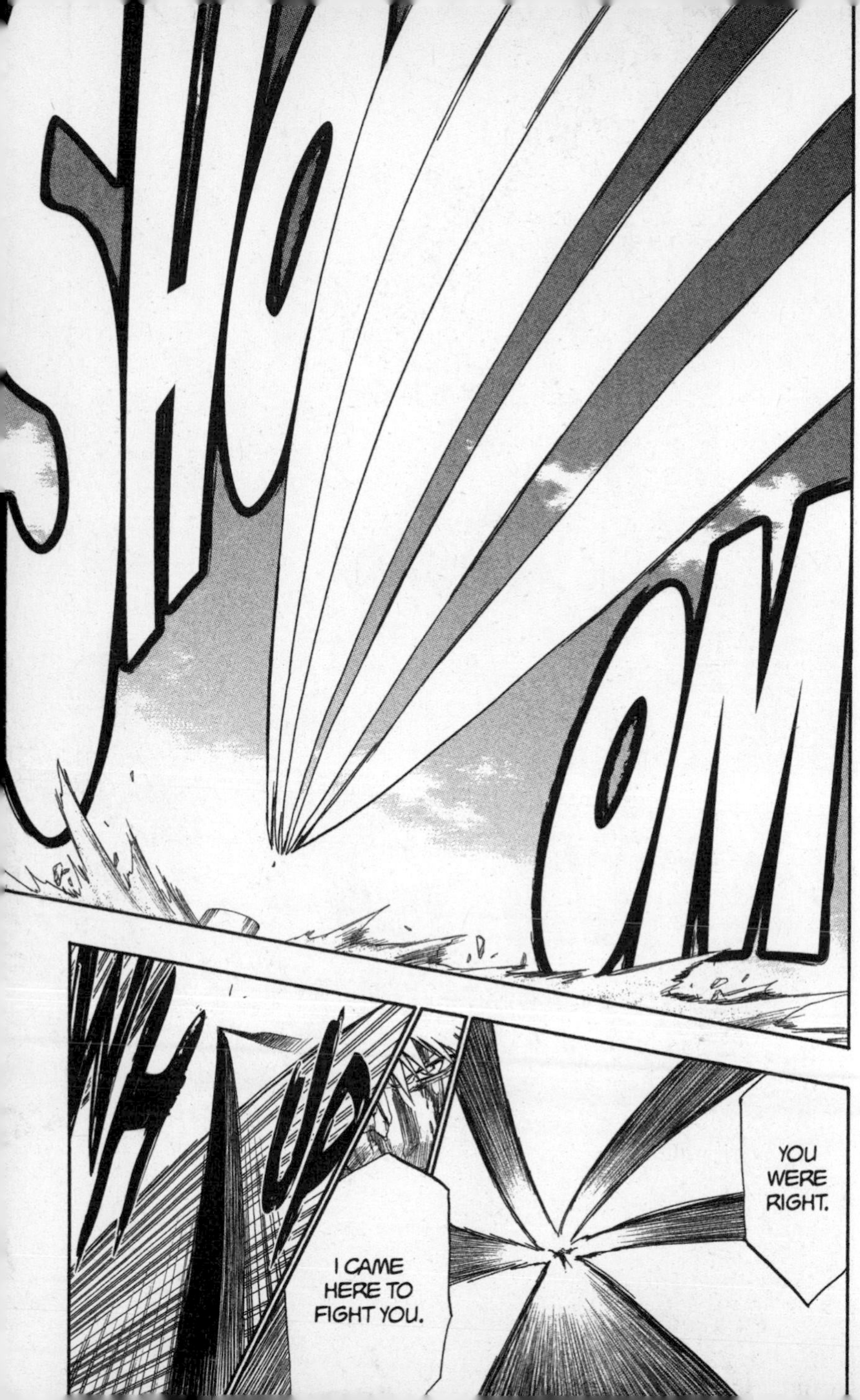
YOU WERE RIGHT.
I CAME HERE TO FIGHT YOU.

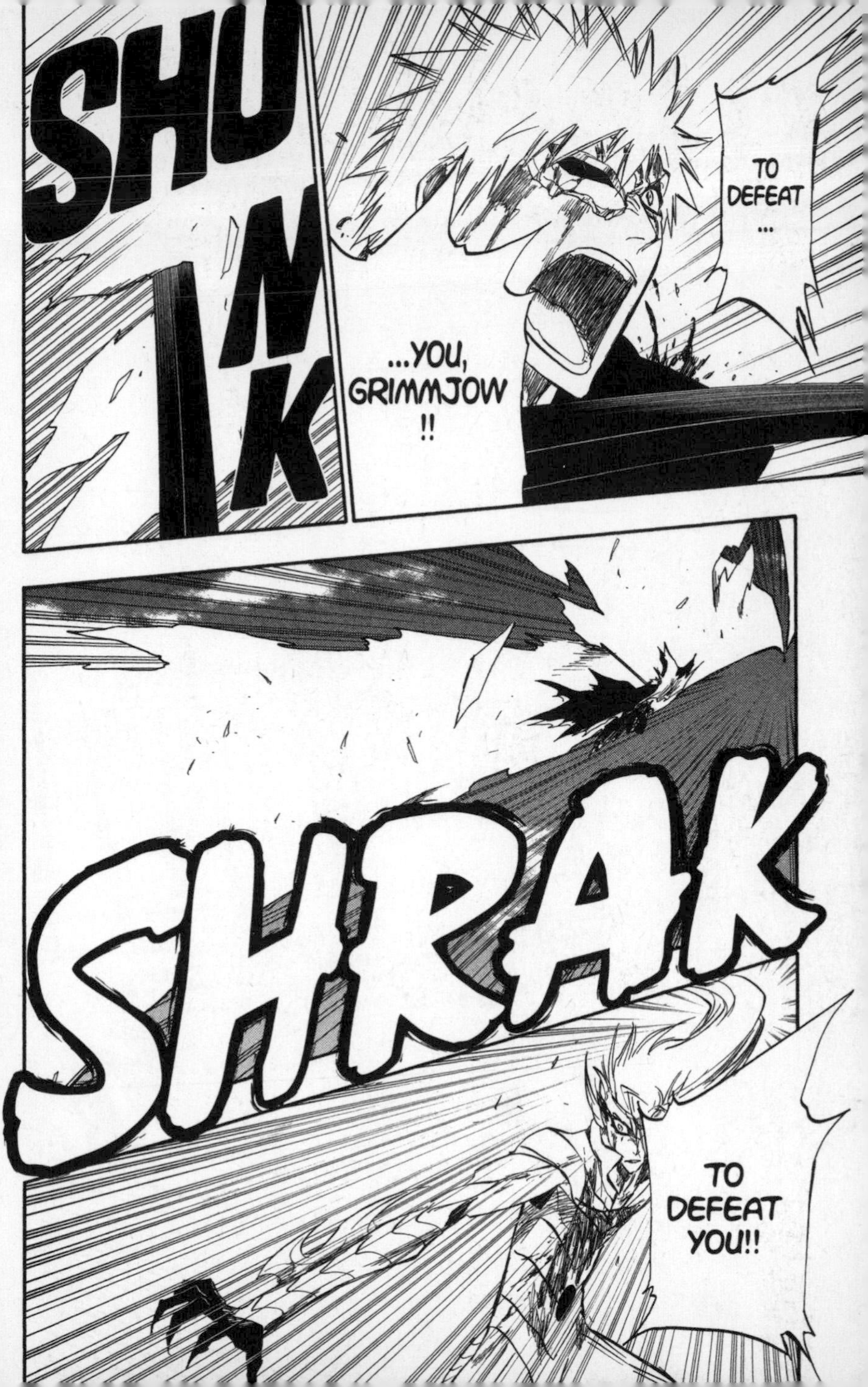
TO DEFEAT ...
...YOU, GRIMMJOW !!
SHUNK
SHRAK
TO DEFEAT YOU!!

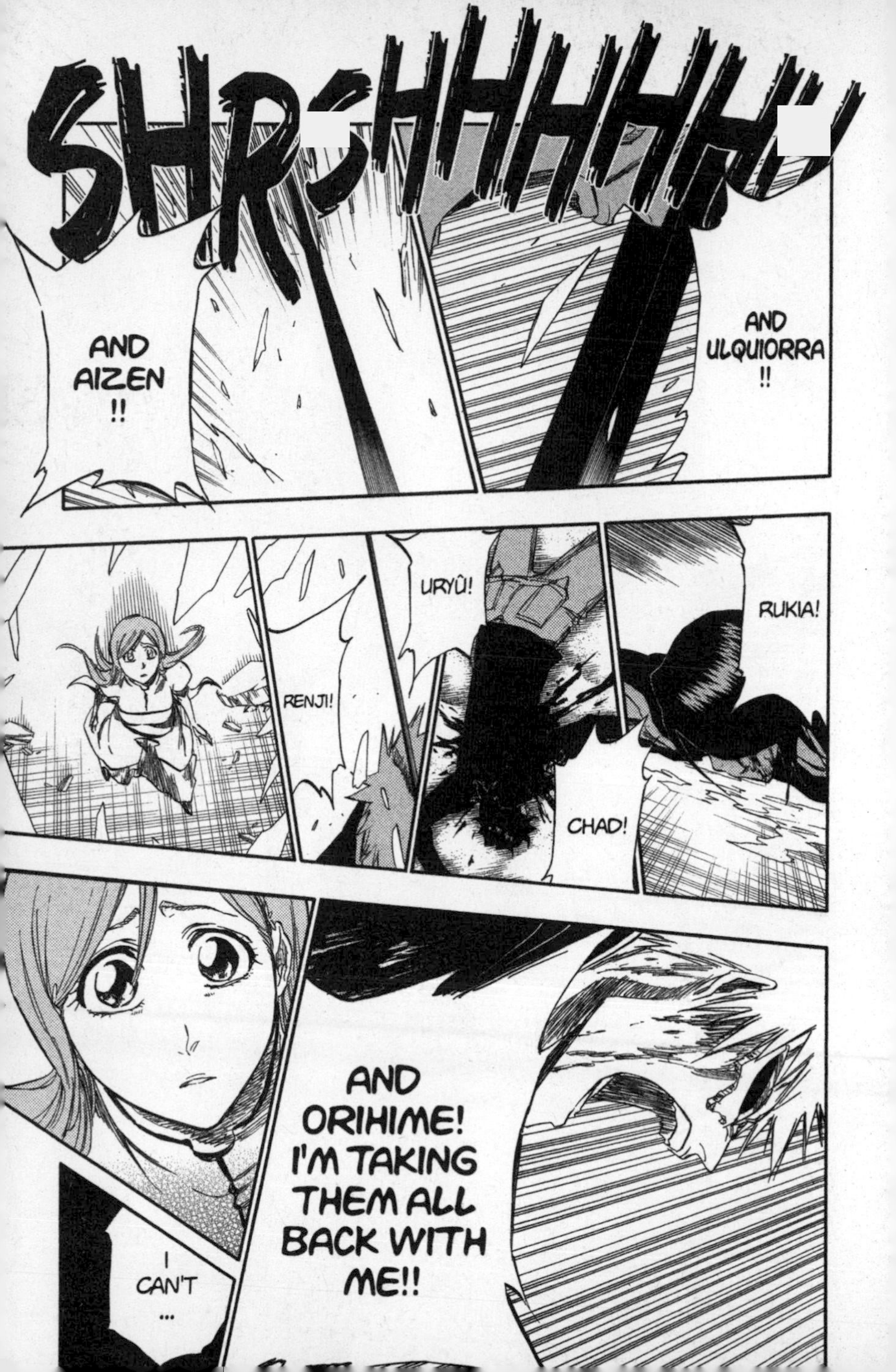
SHRSHHHHH
AND ULQUIORRA!!
AND AIZEN!!
RUKIA!
CHAD!
URYÛ!
RENJI!
AND ORIHIME! I'M TAKING THEM ALL BACK WITH ME!!
I CAN'T...

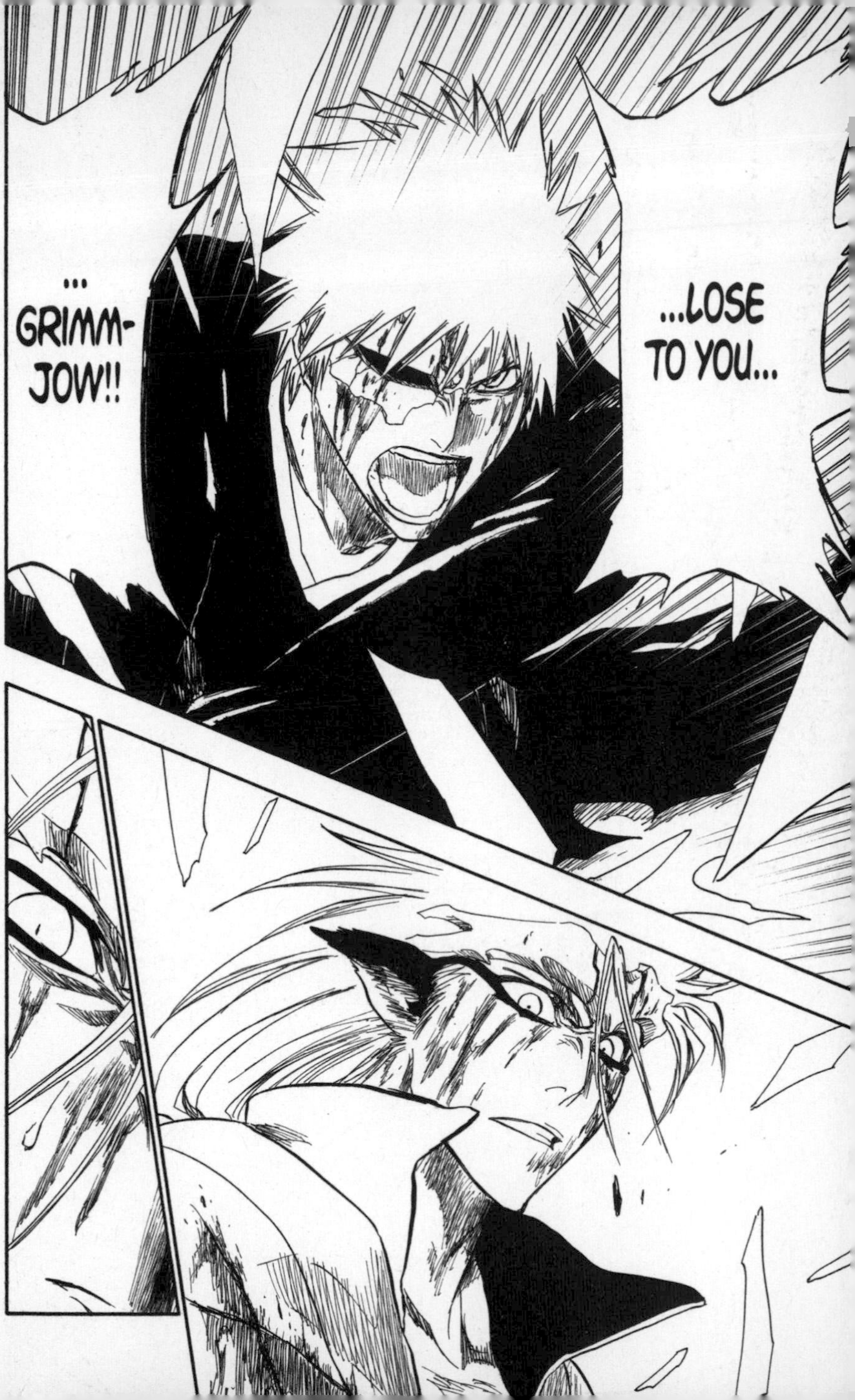
...LOSE TO YOU...
... GRIMM-JOW!!

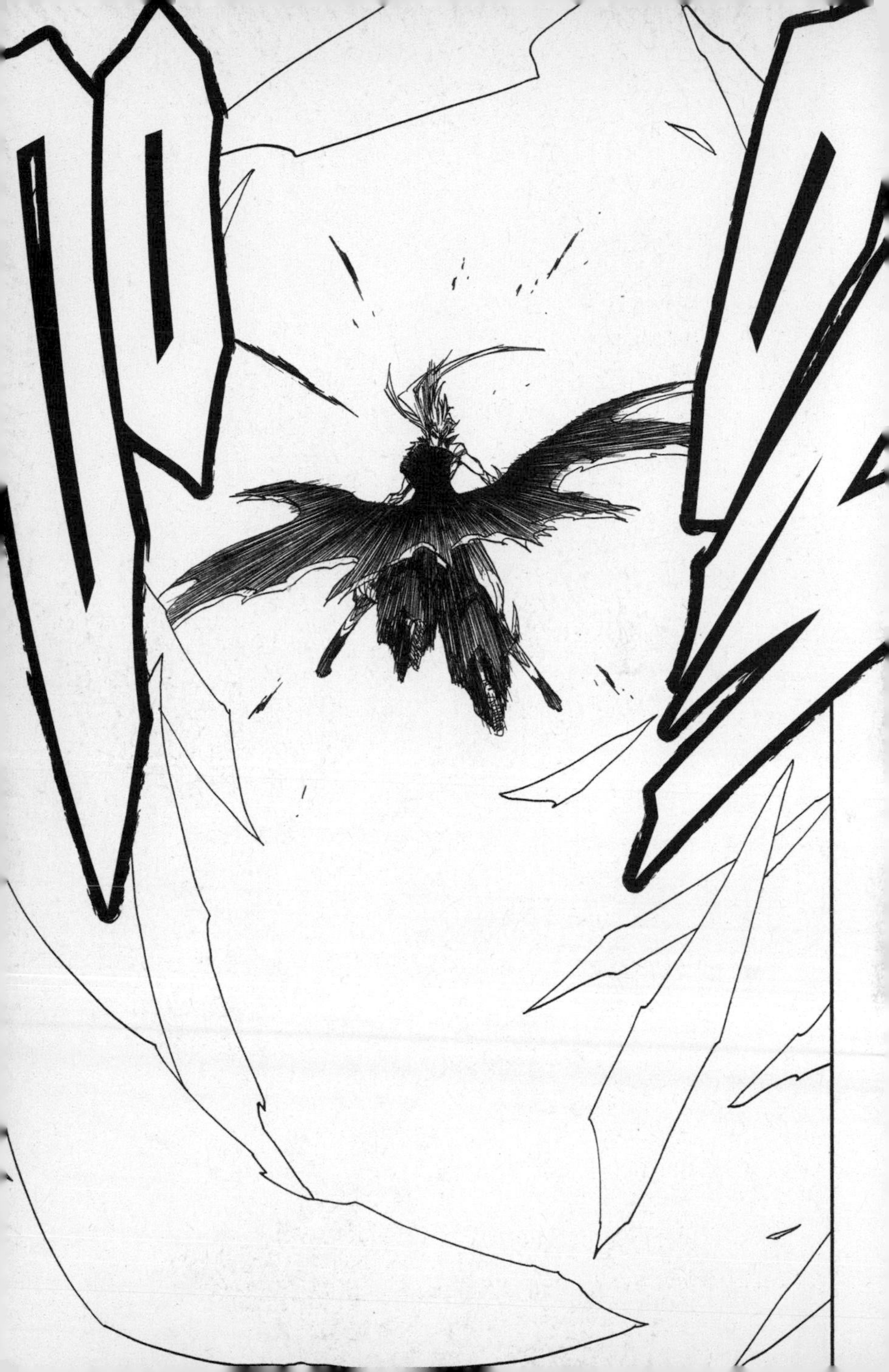

286. Guillotine You Standing

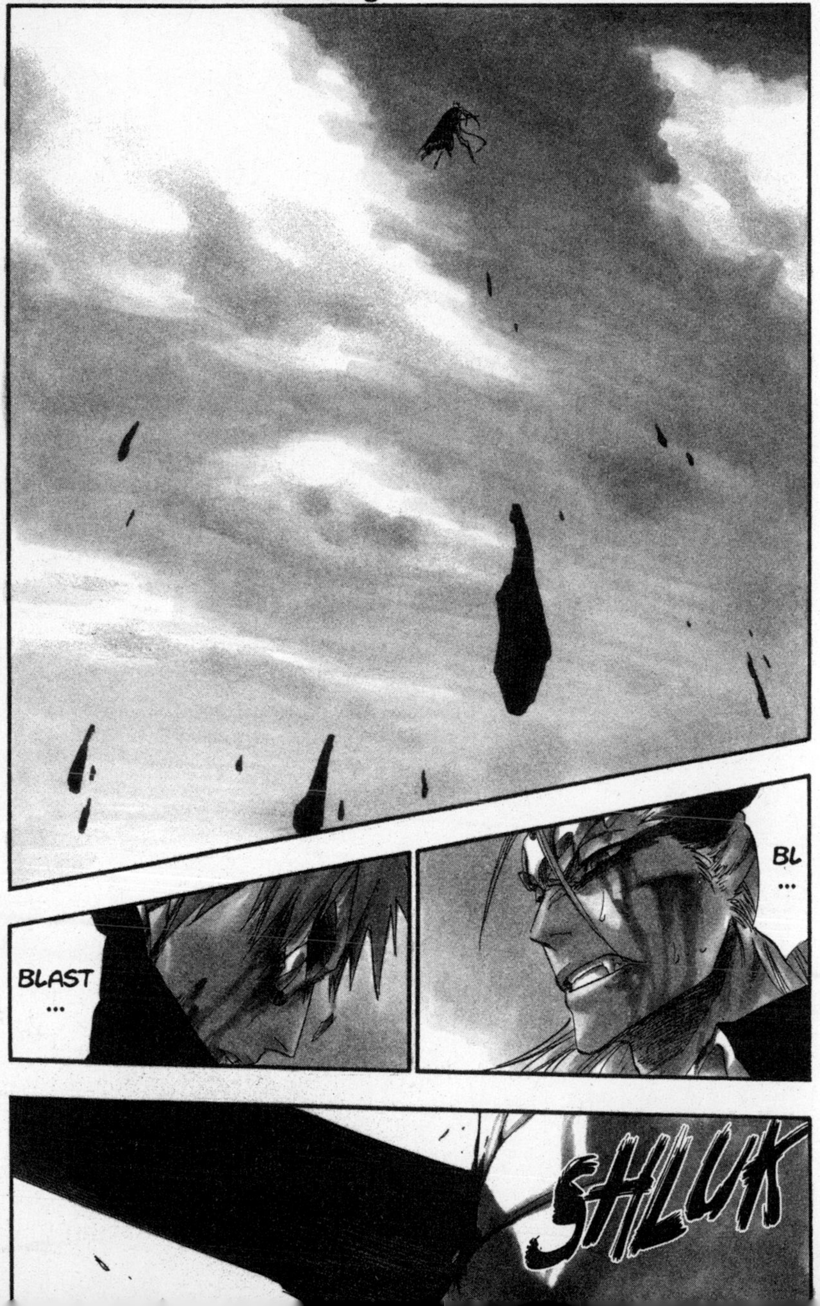
BL ...
BLAST ...
SHLUK

BLEACH
ブリーチ

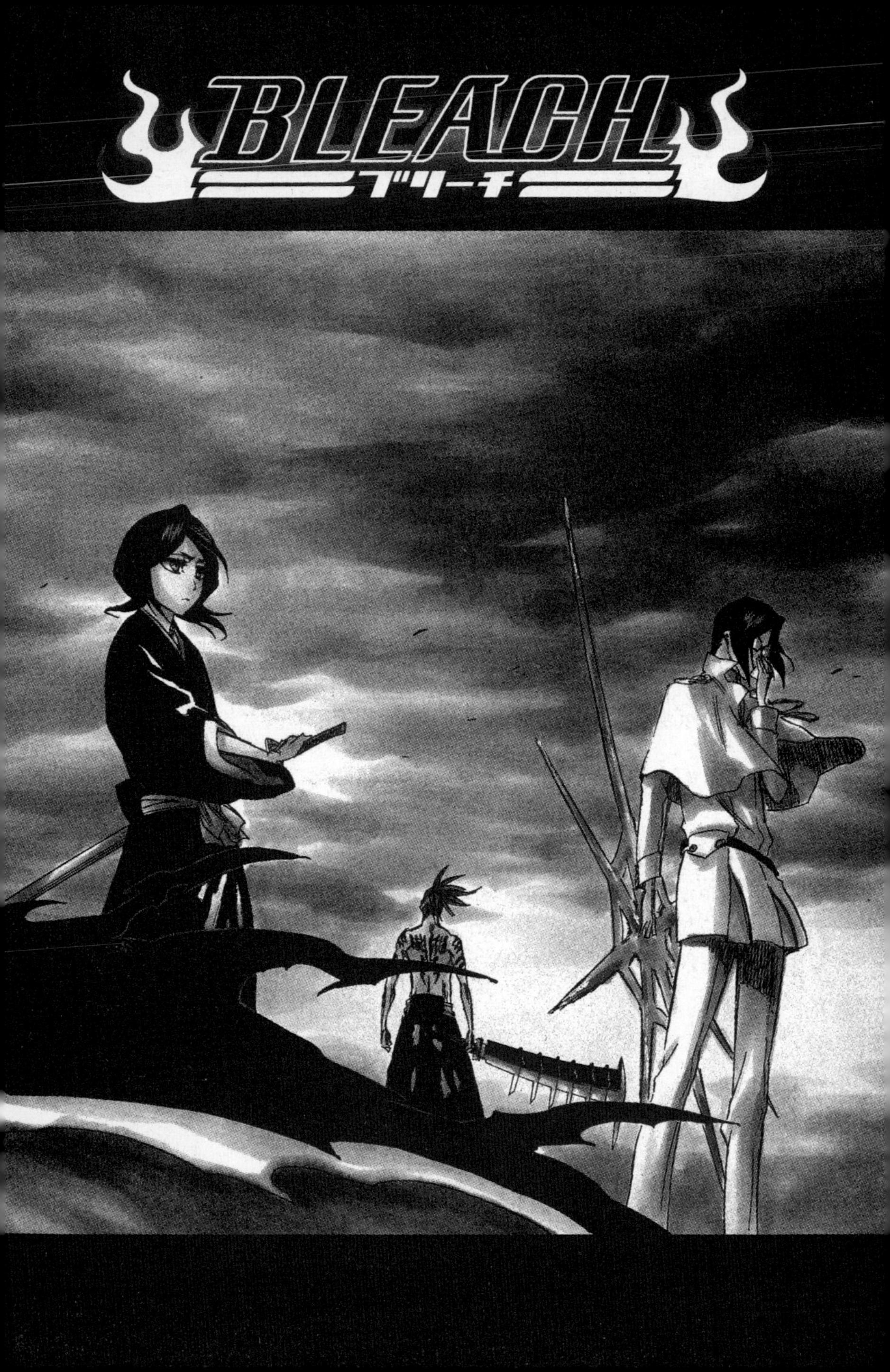

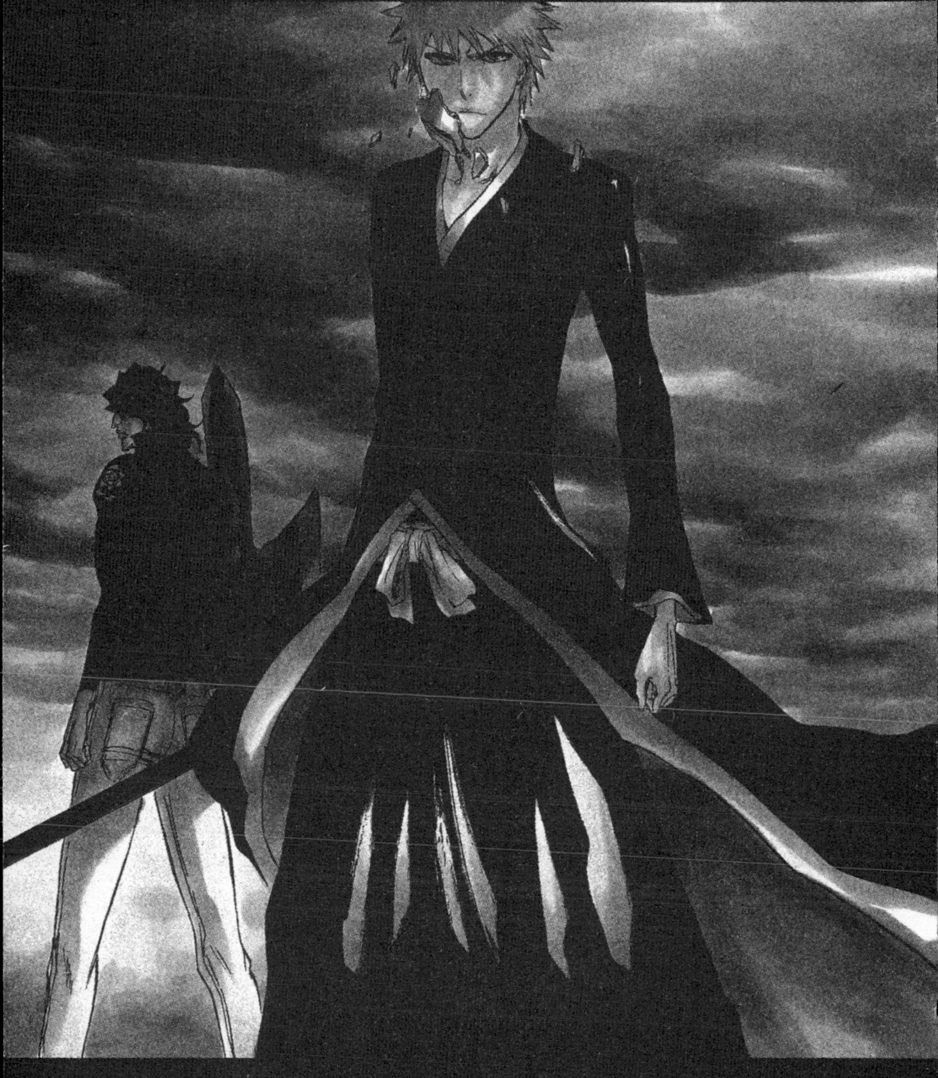

286.Guillotine You Standing

BLEACH
ブリーチ

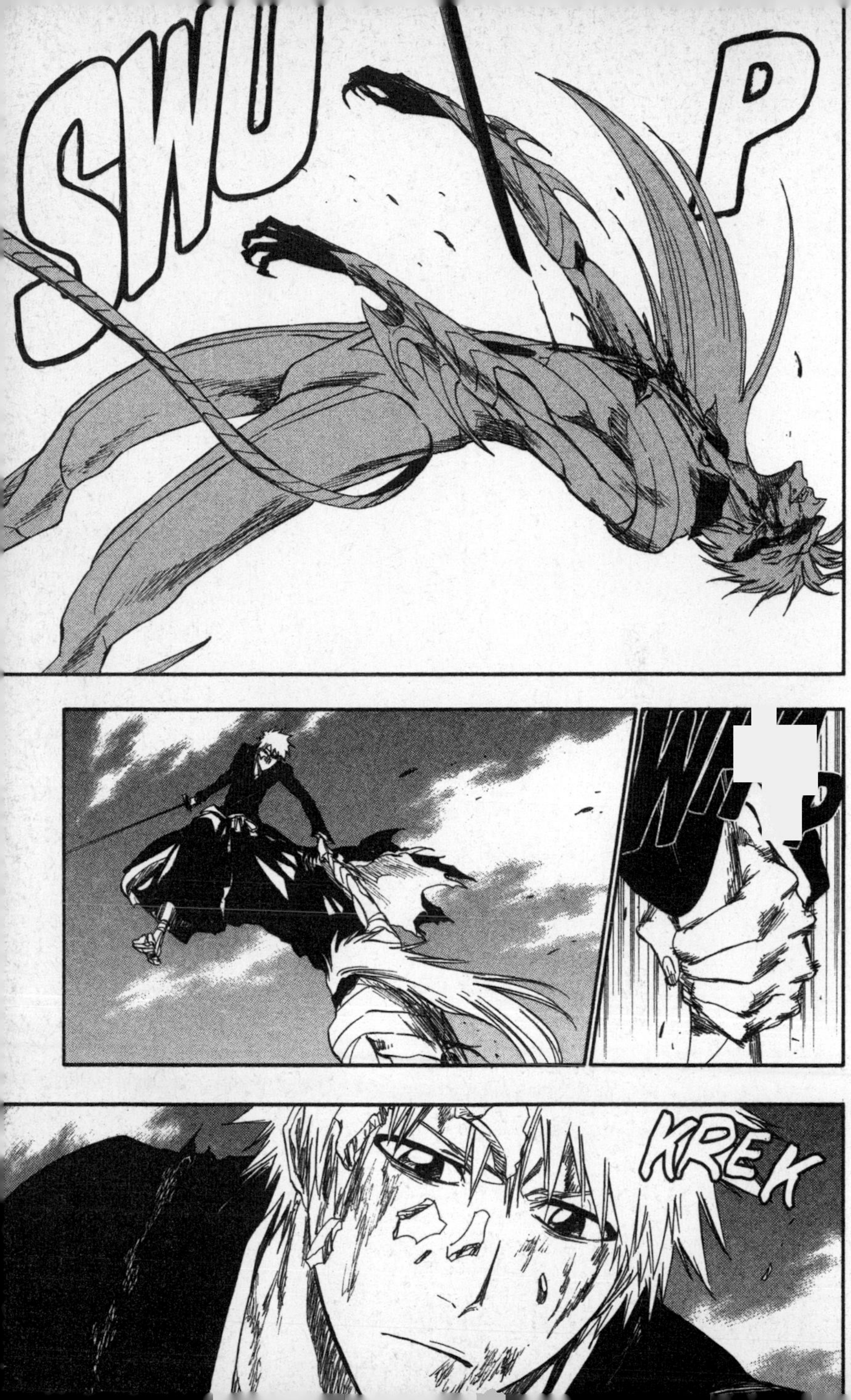
SWUP
KREK

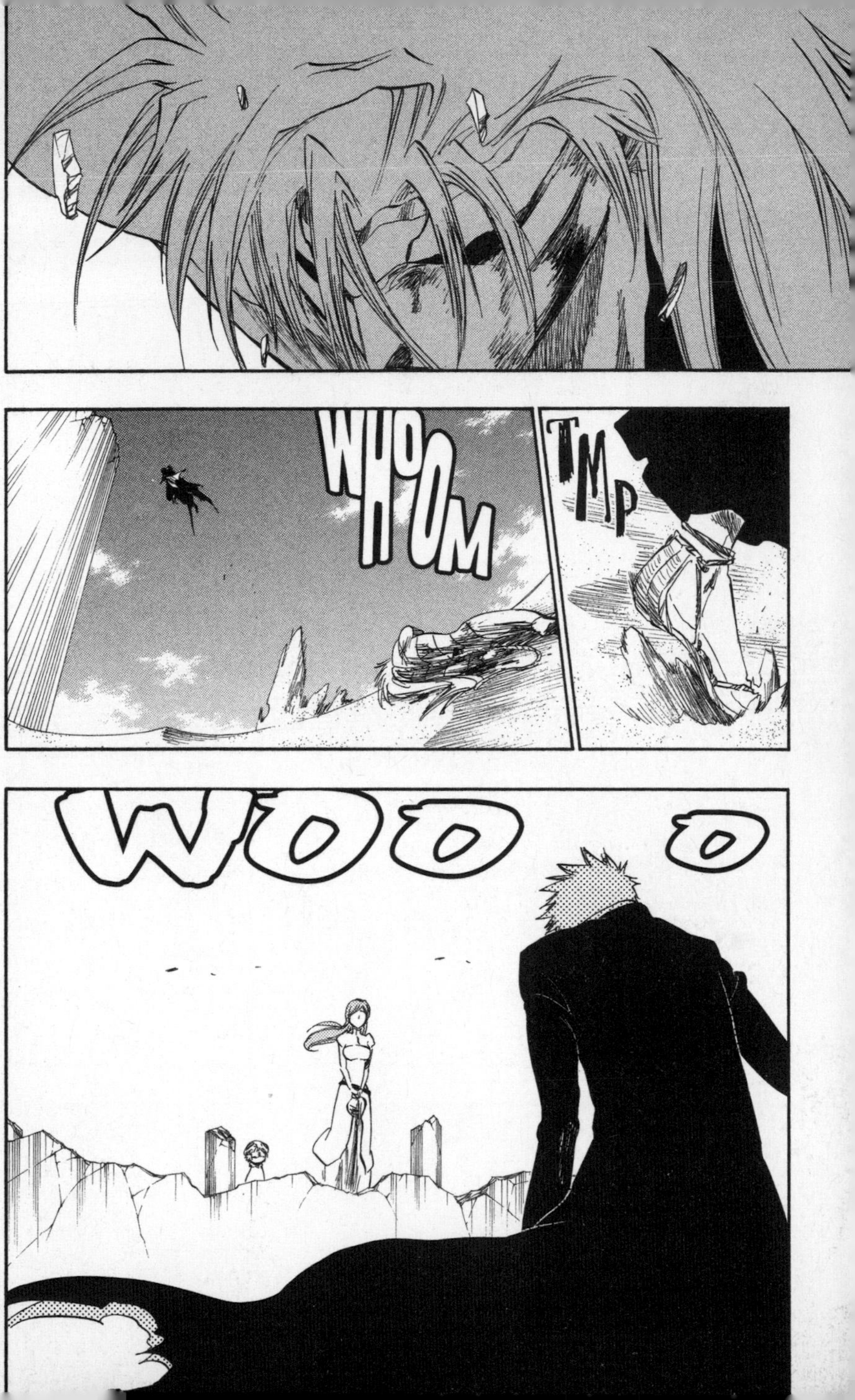
WHOOOM
TMP
WOOO

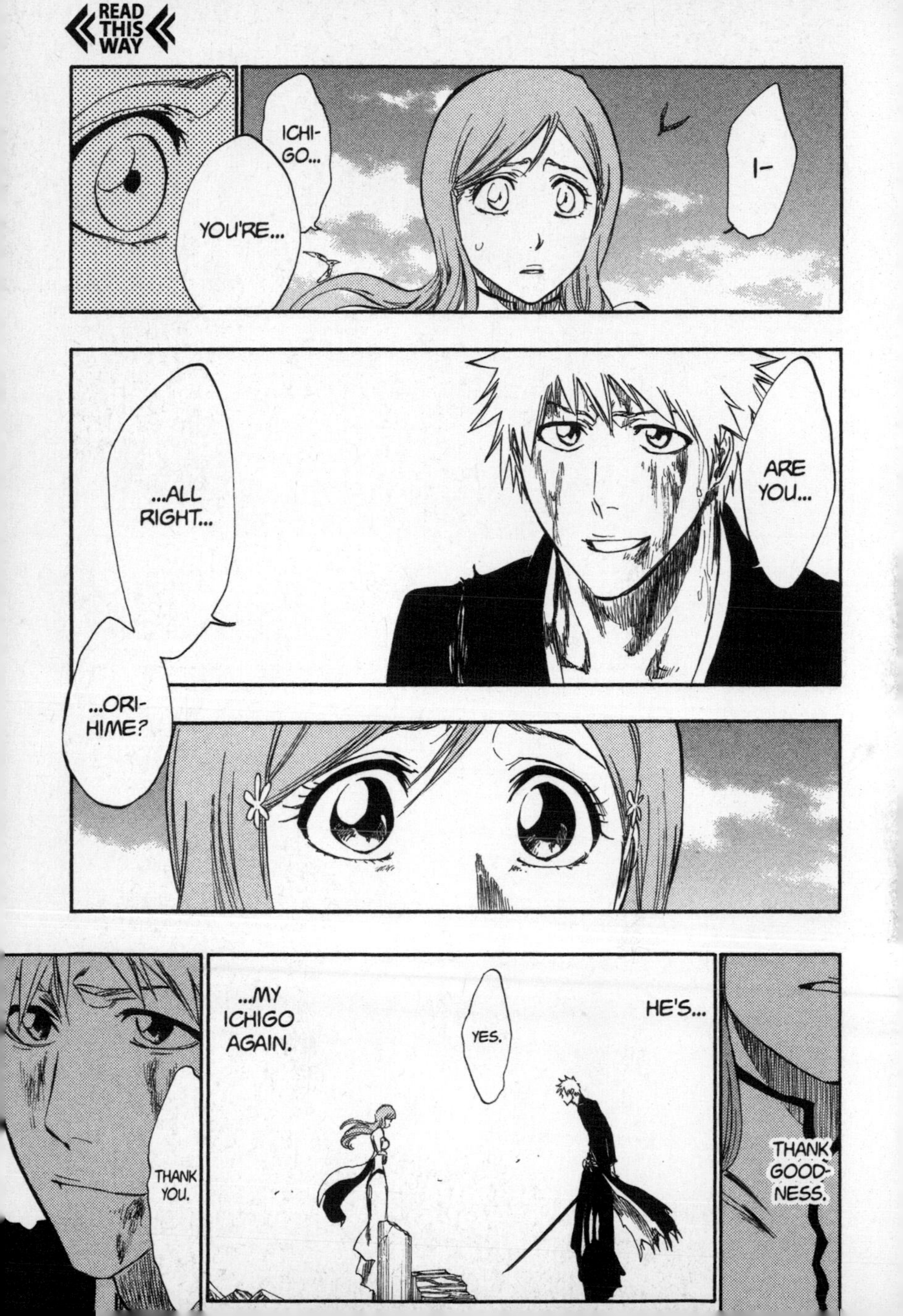
READ THIS WAY
I–
ICHIGO...
YOU'RE...
ARE YOU...
...ALL RIGHT...
...ORIHIME?
THANK GOODNESS.
HE'S...
YES.
...MY ICHIGO AGAIN.
THANK YOU.

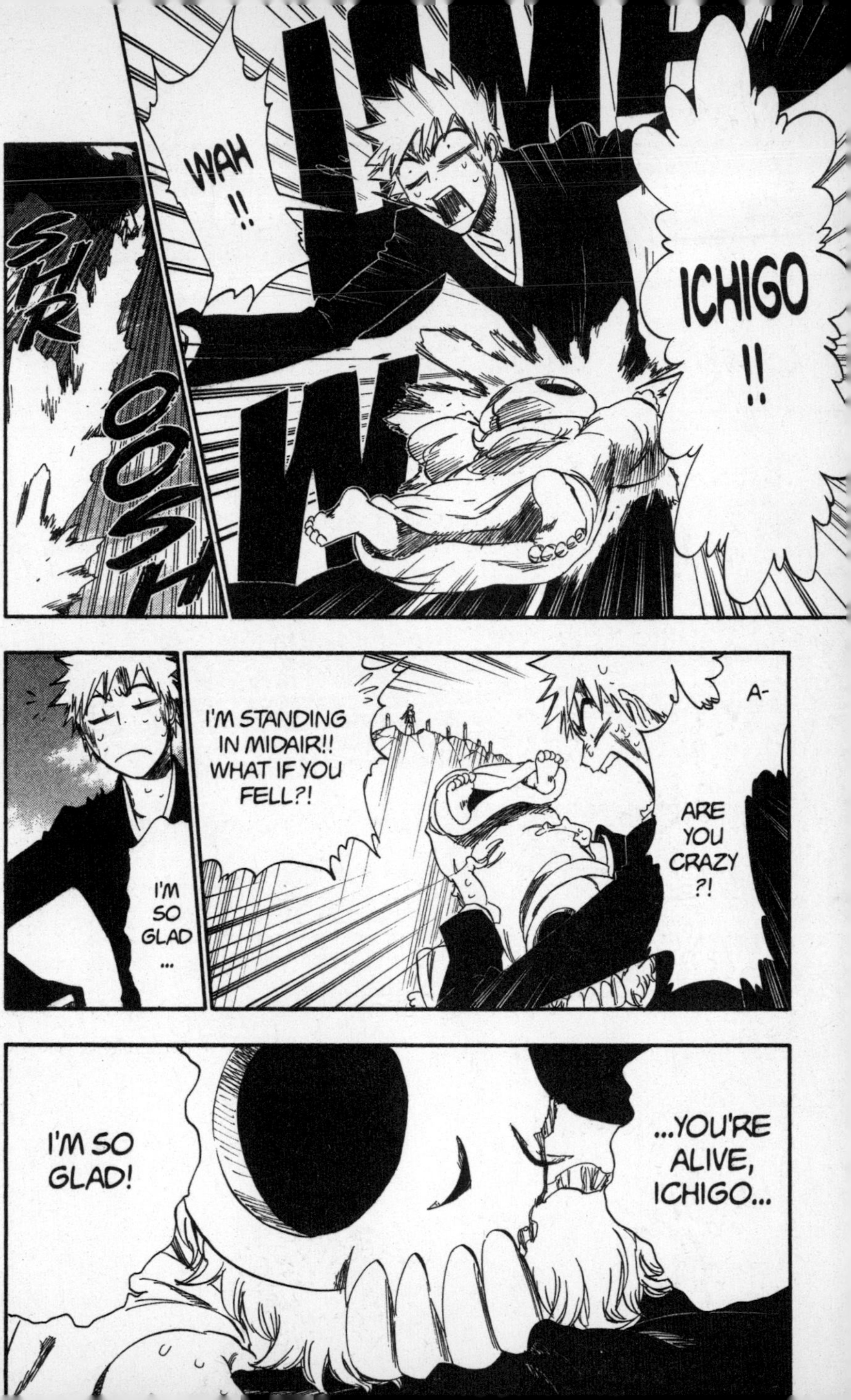
ICHIGO!!
WAH!!
SHR
OOSH
A-
ARE YOU CRAZY?!
I'M STANDING IN MIDAIR!! WHAT IF YOU FELL?!
I'M SO GLAD...
...YOU'RE ALIVE, ICHIGO...
I'M SO GLAD!

READ THIS WAY

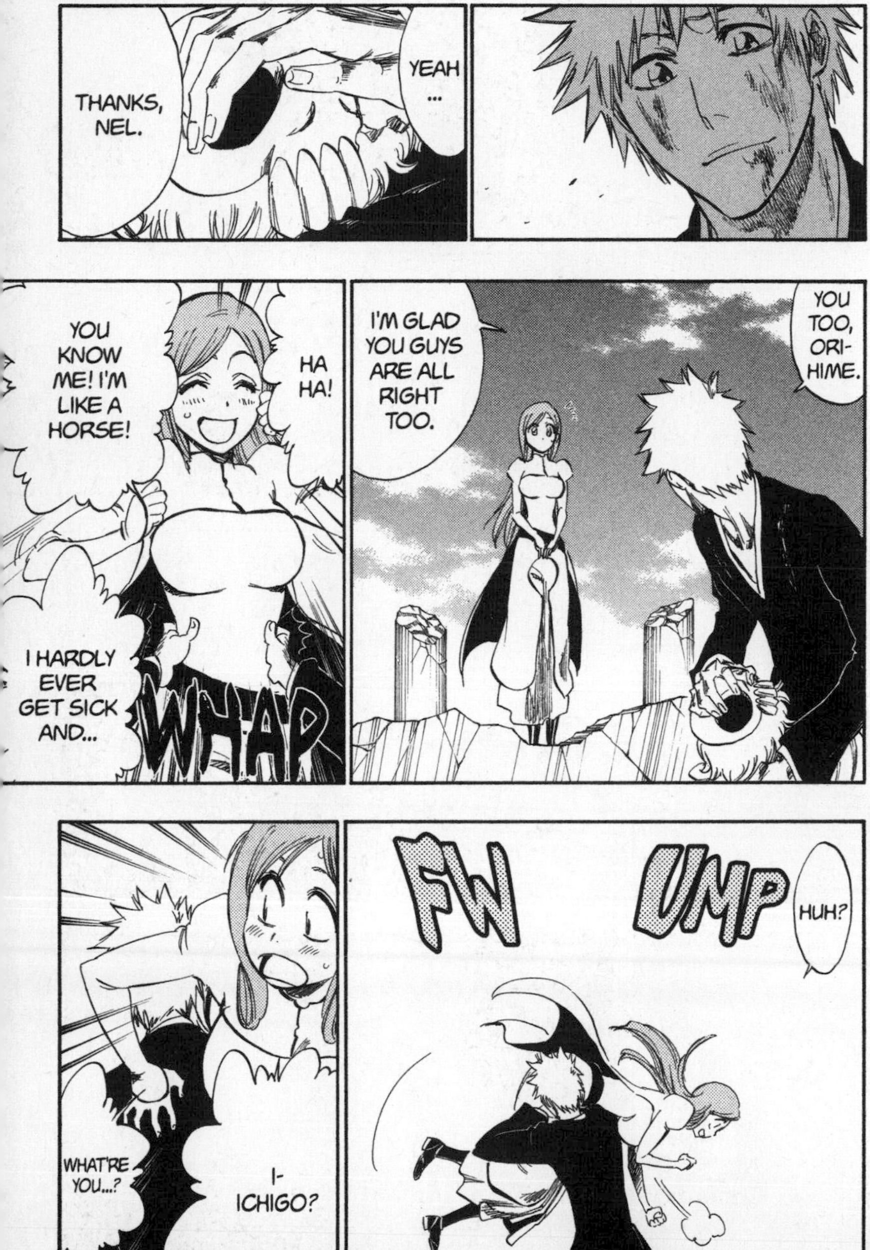
YEAH ...
THANKS, NEL.
YOU TOO, ORI-HIME.
I'M GLAD YOU GUYS ARE ALL RIGHT TOO.
HA HA!
YOU KNOW ME! I'M LIKE A HORSE!
I HARDLY EVER GET SICK AND...
WHAP
FWUMP
HUH?
I- ICHIGO?
WHAT'RE YOU...?

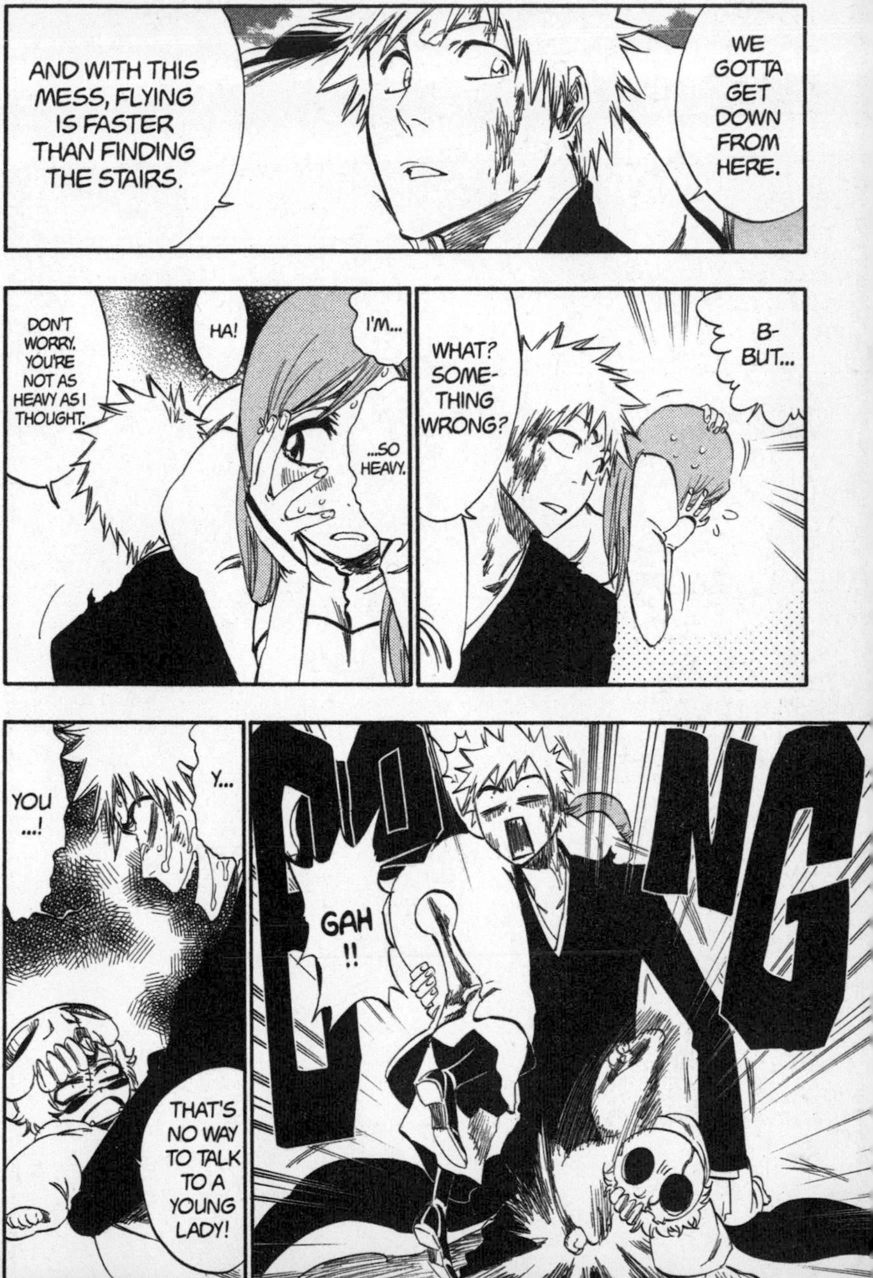
WE GOTTA GET DOWN FROM HERE.
AND WITH THIS MESS, FLYING IS FASTER THAN FINDING THE STAIRS.
B-BUT...
WHAT? SOME-THING WRONG?
I'M...
...SO HEAVY.
HA!
DON'T WORRY. YOU'RE NOT AS HEAVY AS I THOUGHT.
GAH !!
Y...
YOU ...!
THAT'S NO WAY TO TALK TO A YOUNG LADY!

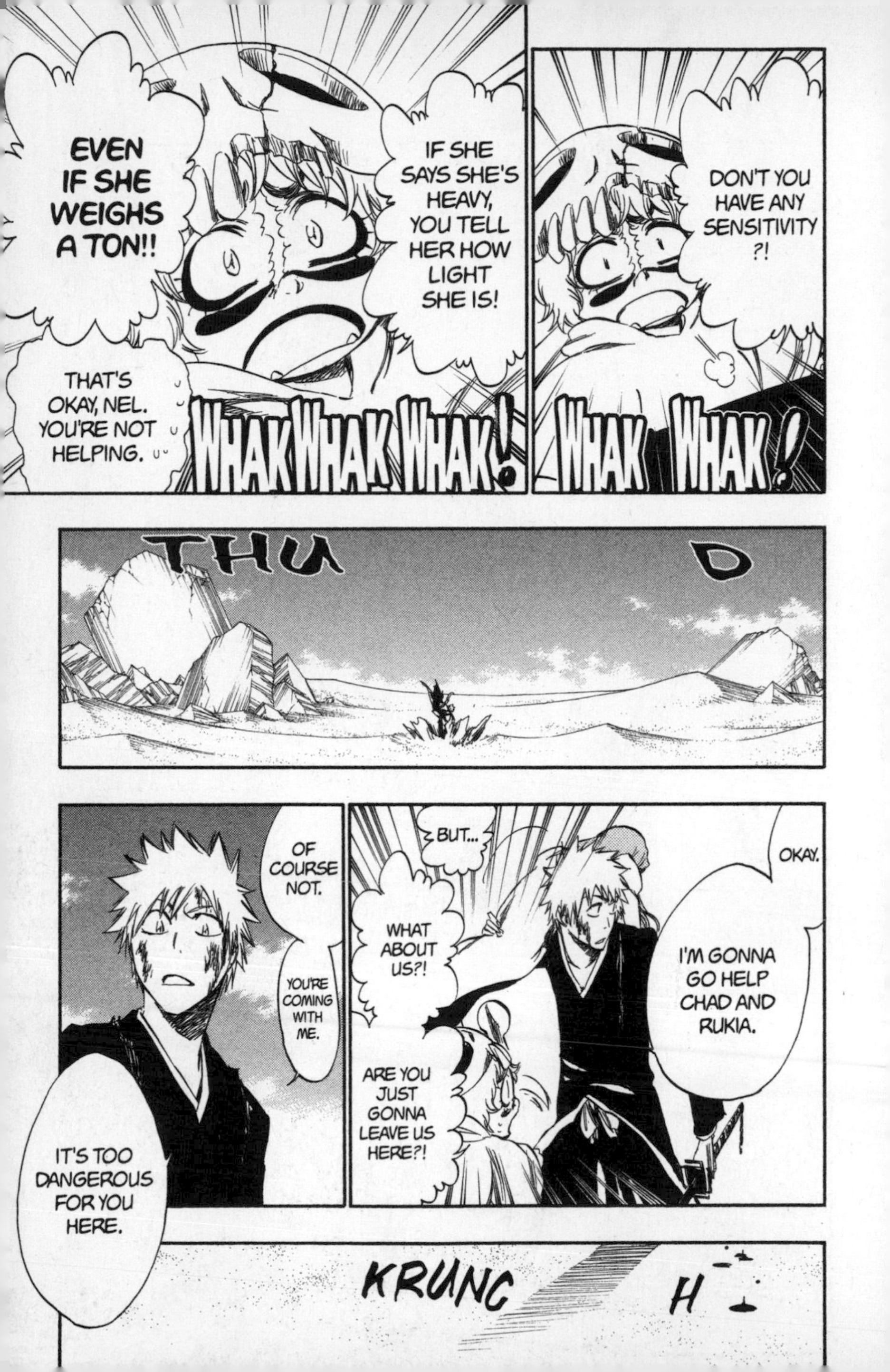
DON'T YOU HAVE ANY SENSITIVITY?!
WHAK WHAK!
IF SHE SAYS SHE'S HEAVY, YOU TELL HER HOW LIGHT SHE IS!
EVEN IF SHE WEIGHS A TON!!
THAT'S OKAY, NEL. YOU'RE NOT HELPING.
WHAKWHAK WHAK!
THUD
OKAY.
I'M GONNA GO HELP CHAD AND RUKIA.
BUT...
WHAT ABOUT US?!
ARE YOU JUST GONNA LEAVE US HERE?!
OF COURSE NOT.
YOU'RE COMING WITH ME.
IT'S TOO DANGEROUS FOR YOU HERE.
KRUNCH

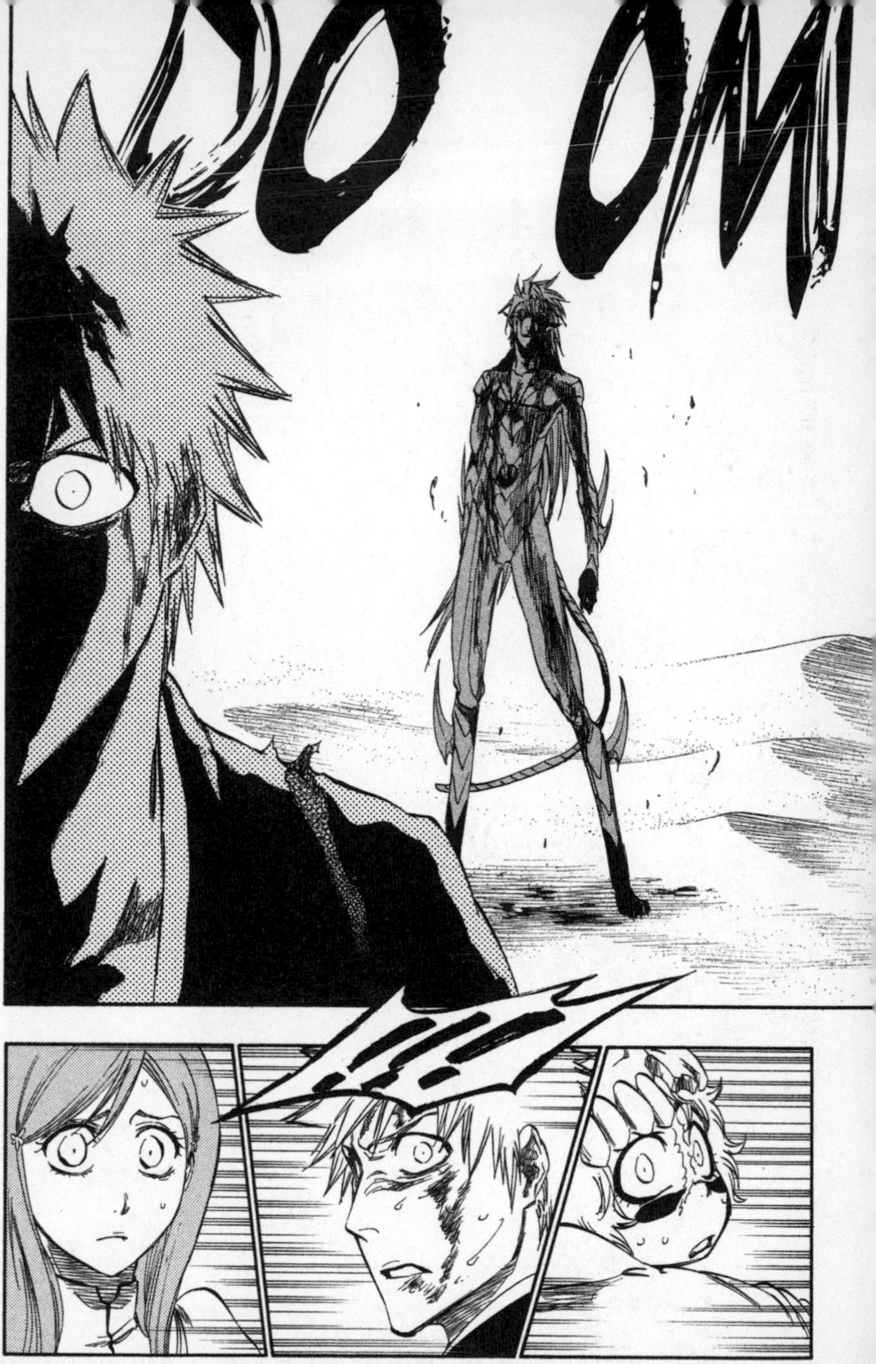
DOOM
!!

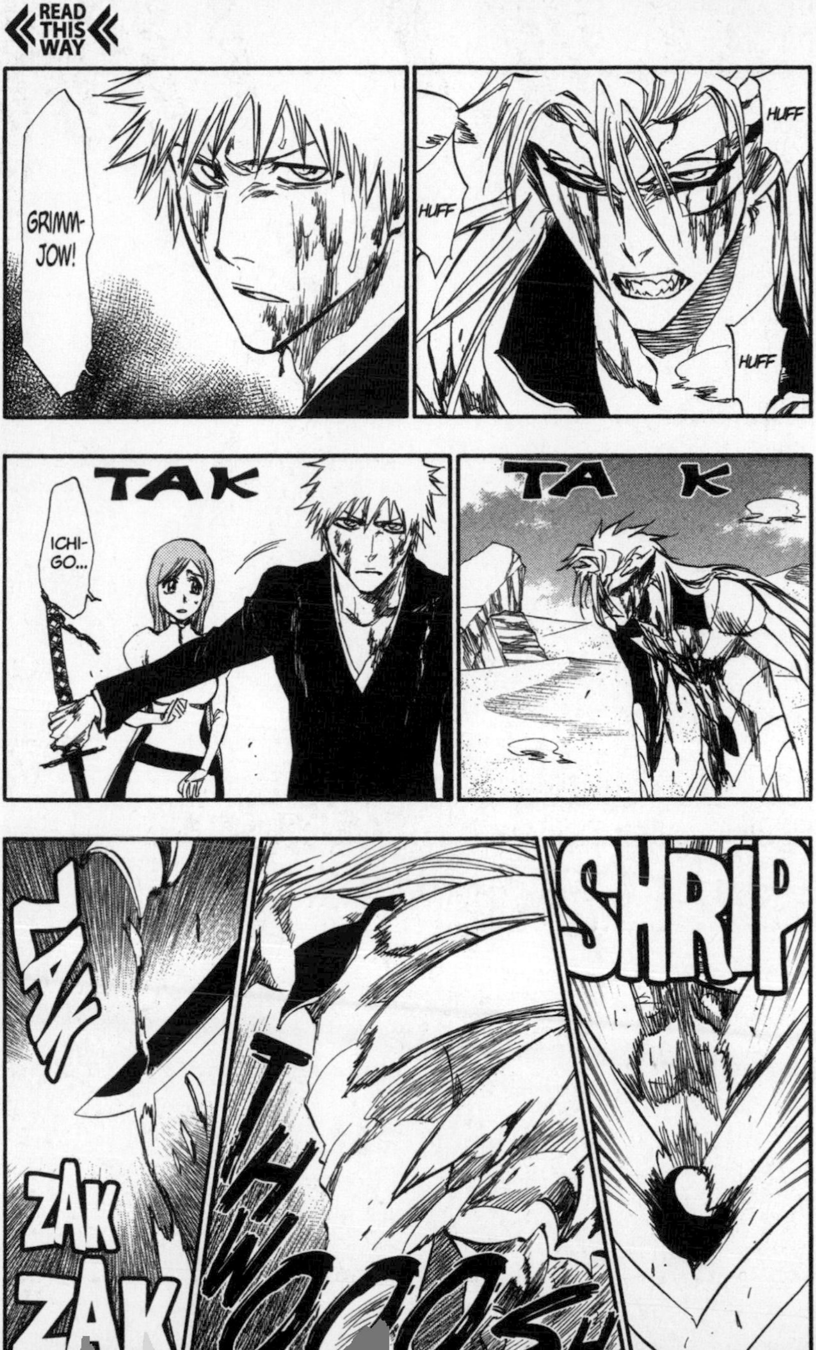
READ THIS WAY
HUFF
HUFF
HUFF
GRIMM-JOW!
TA K
TAK
ICHI-GO...
SHRIP
THWOOOSH
ZAK
ZAK ZAK

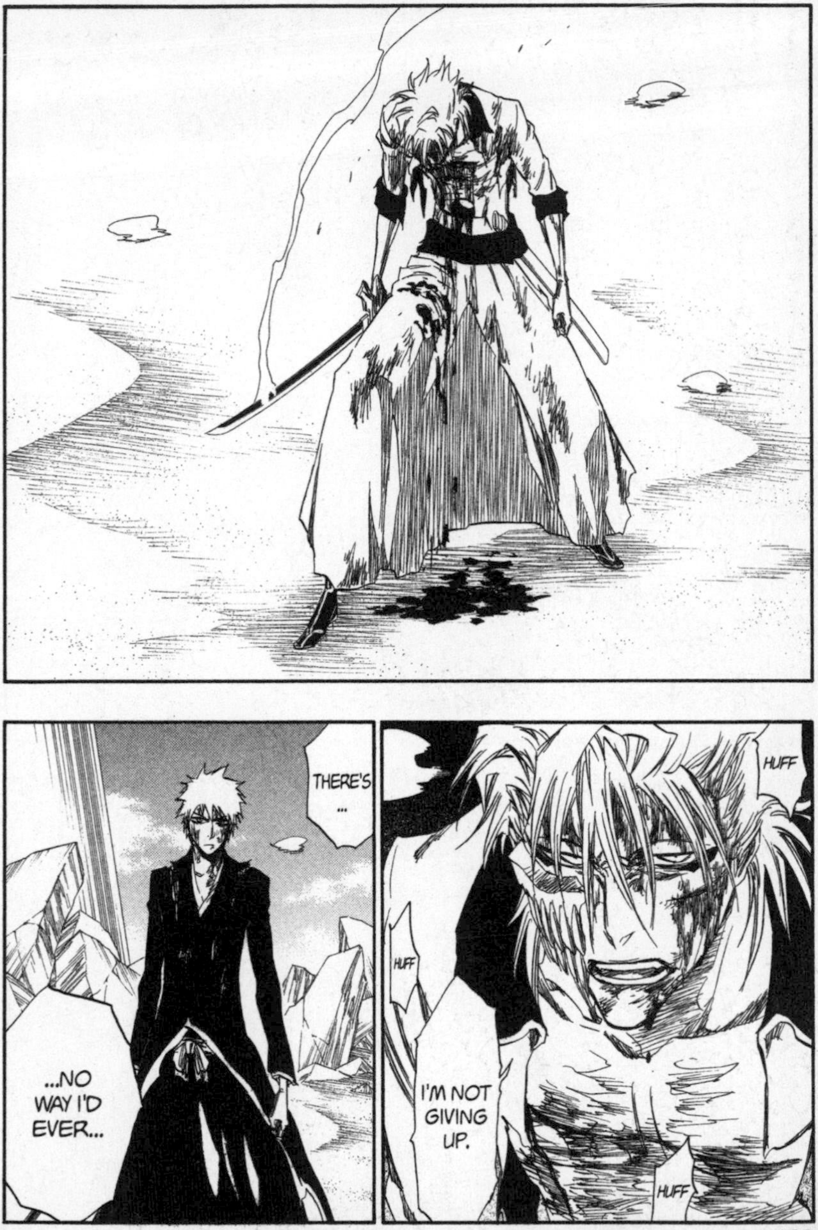
HUFF
HUFF
I'M NOT GIVING UP.
HUFF
THERE'S ...
...NO WAY I'D EVER...

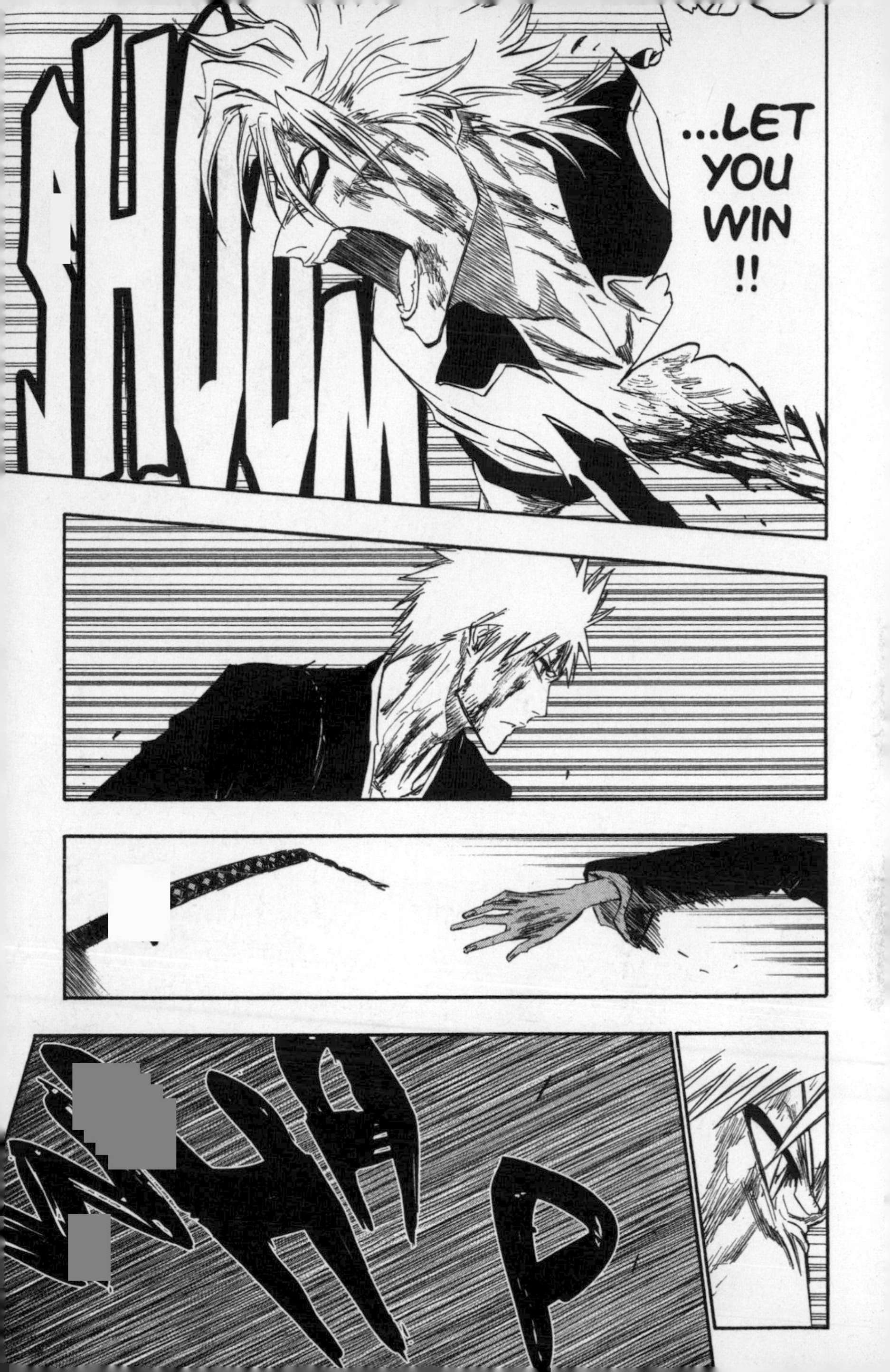
...LET YOU WIN !!

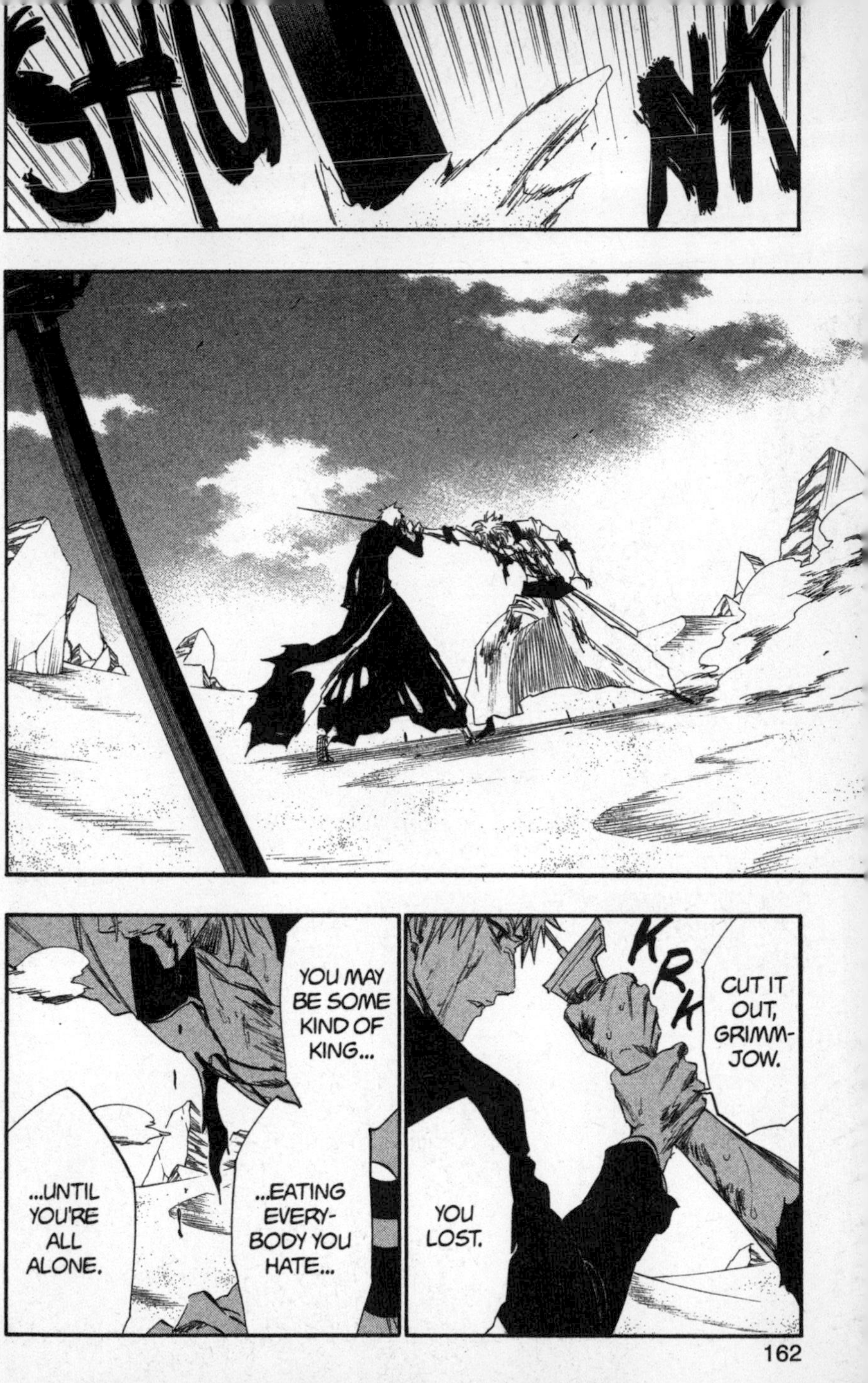
SHUNK
KRK
CUT IT OUT, GRIMM-JOW.
YOU LOST.
YOU MAY BE SOME KIND OF KING...
...EATING EVERY-BODY YOU HATE...
...UNTIL YOU'RE ALL ALONE.

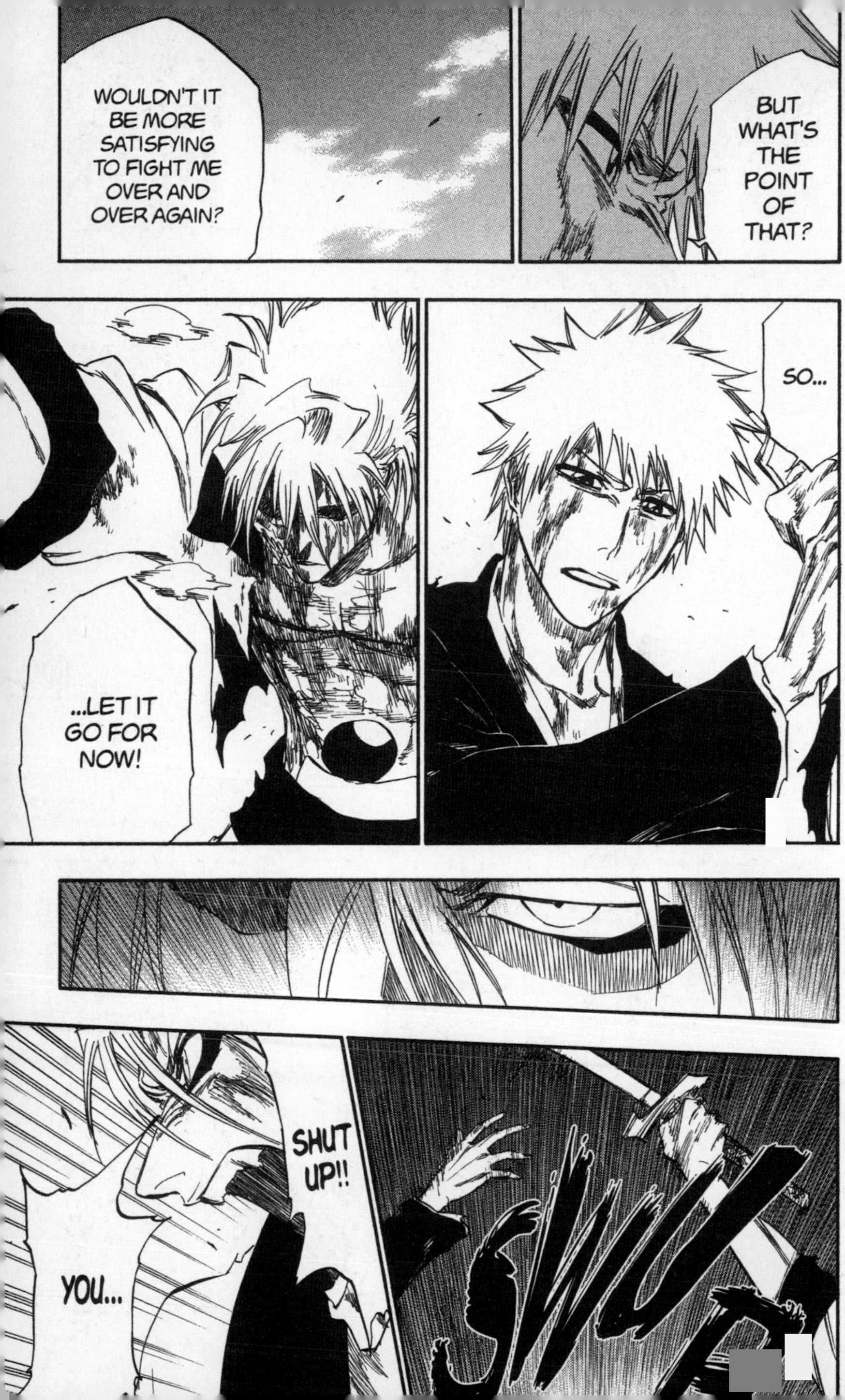
BUT WHAT'S THE POINT OF THAT?
WOULDN'T IT BE MORE SATISFYING TO FIGHT ME OVER AND OVER AGAIN?
SO...
...LET IT GO FOR NOW!
SHUT UP!!
YOU...

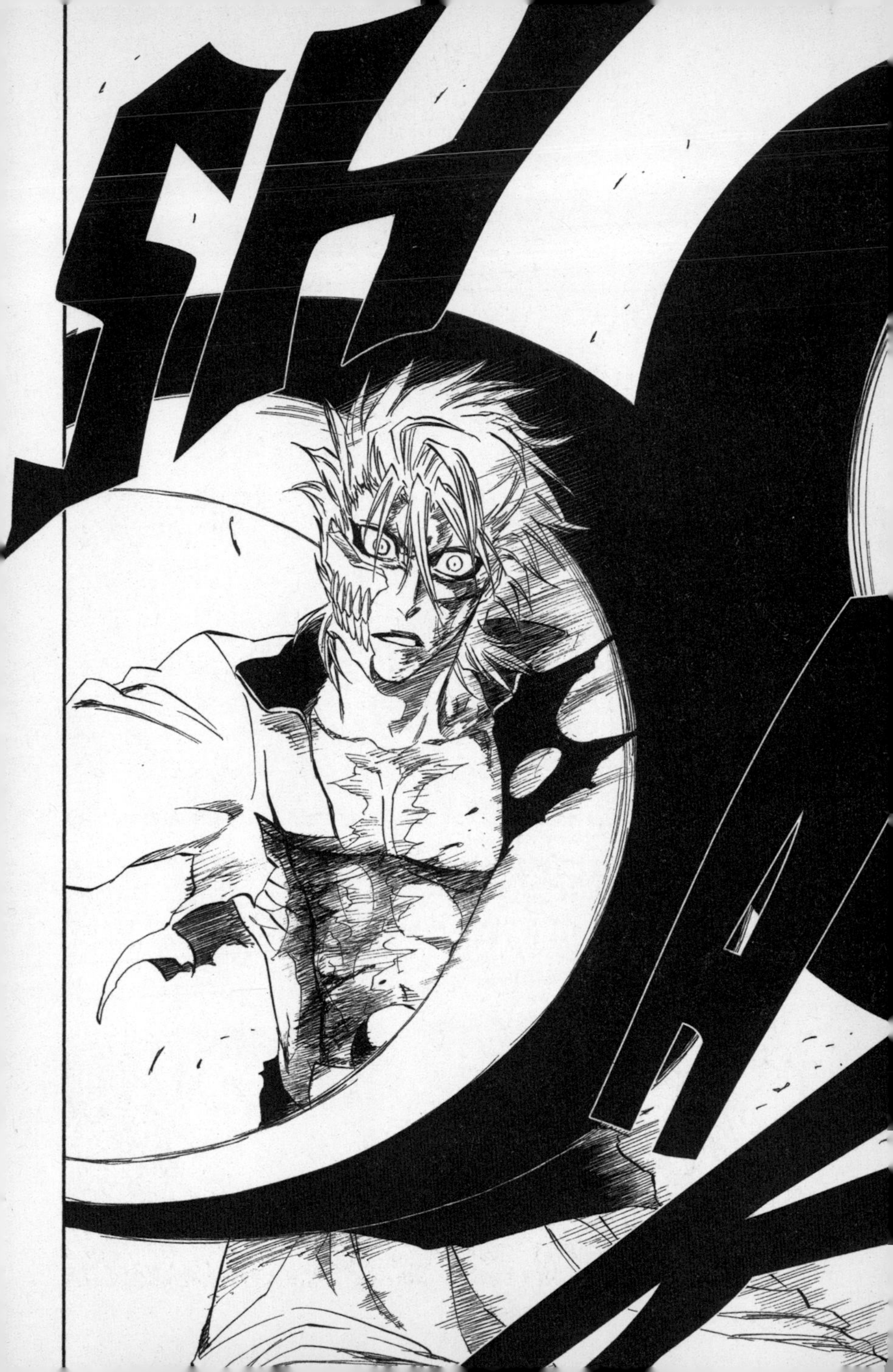

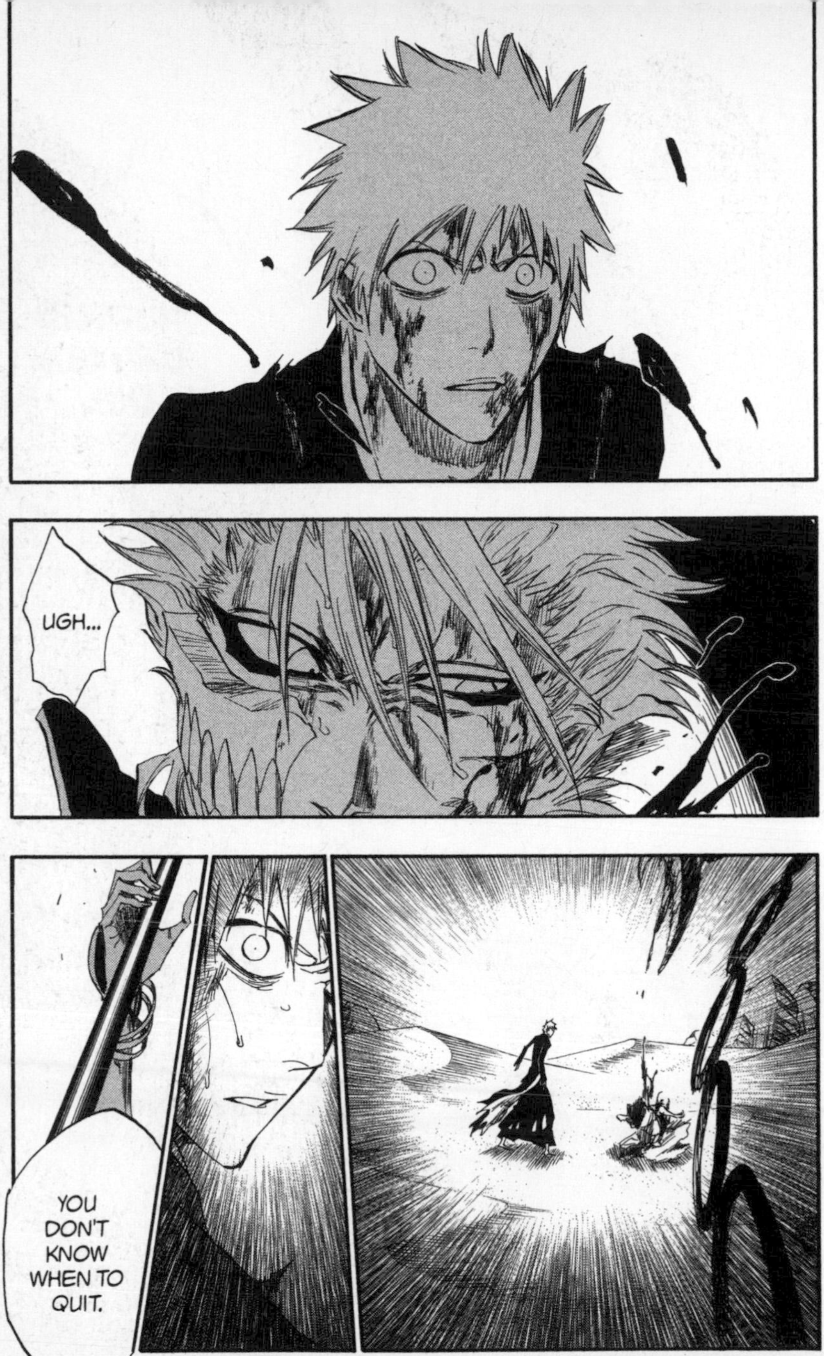
UGH...
YOU DON'T KNOW WHEN TO QUIT.

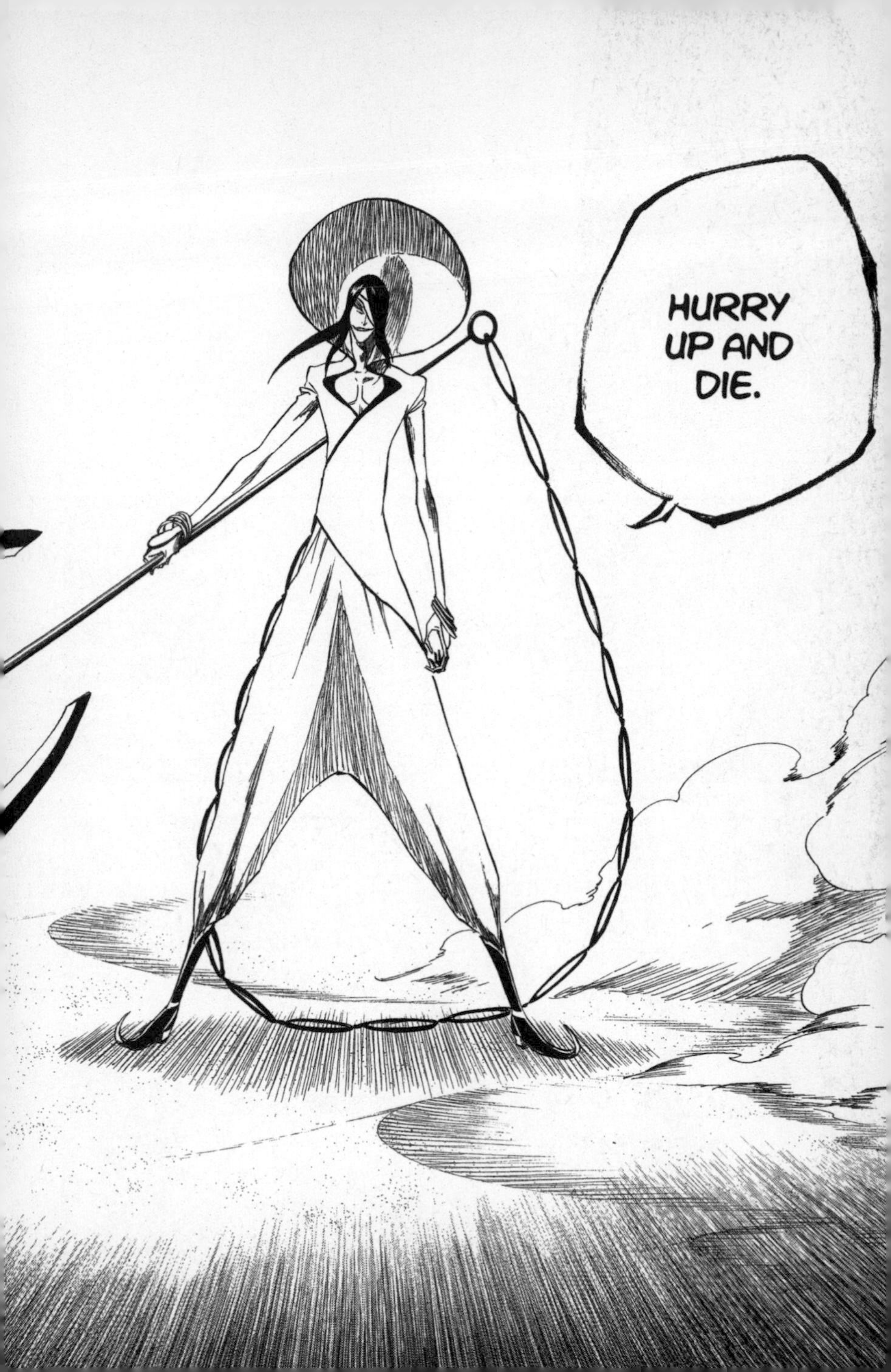
HURRY UP AND DIE.

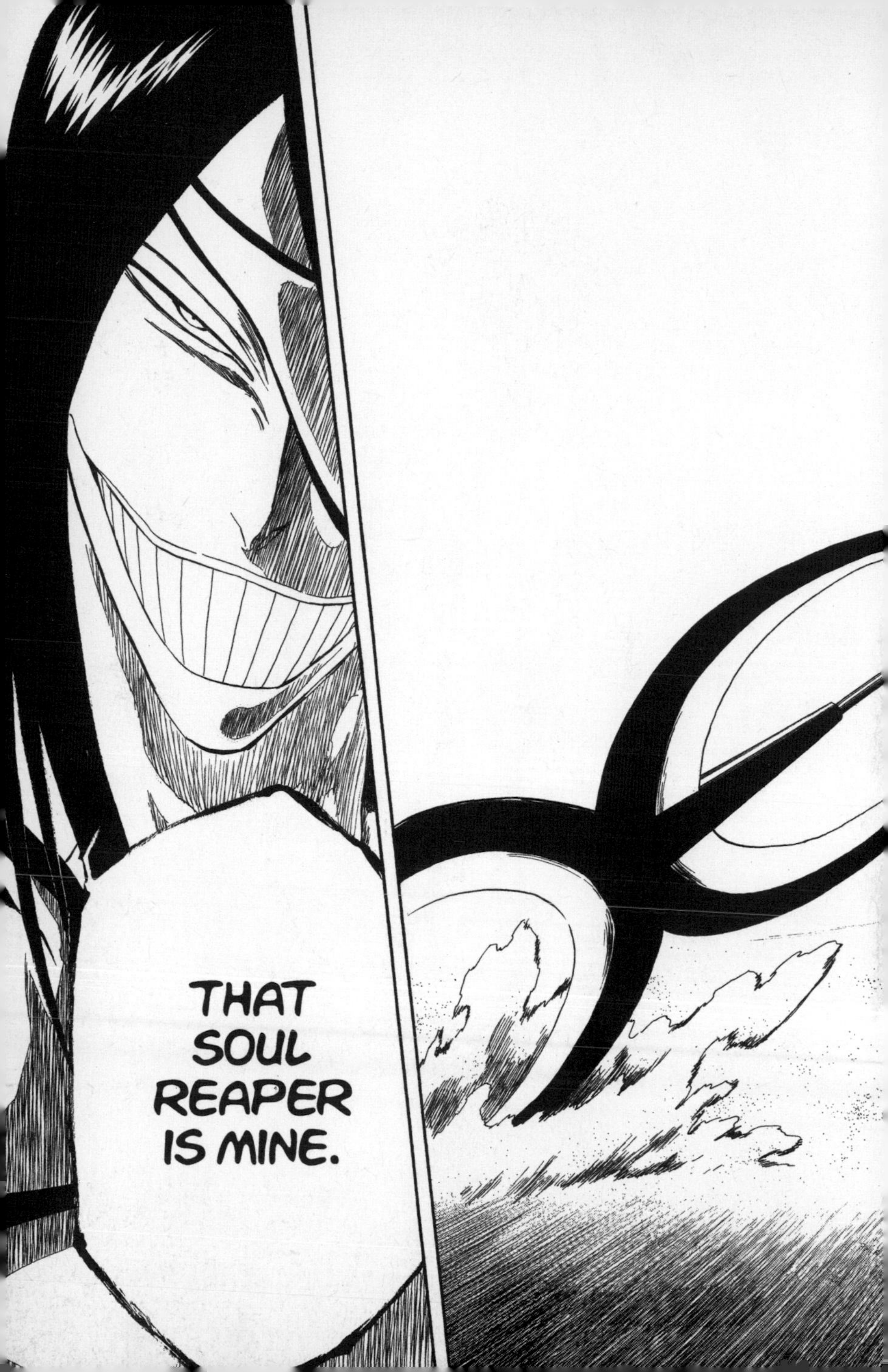
THAT SOUL REAPER IS MINE.

CONTI
NUED
IN
BLEACH
33

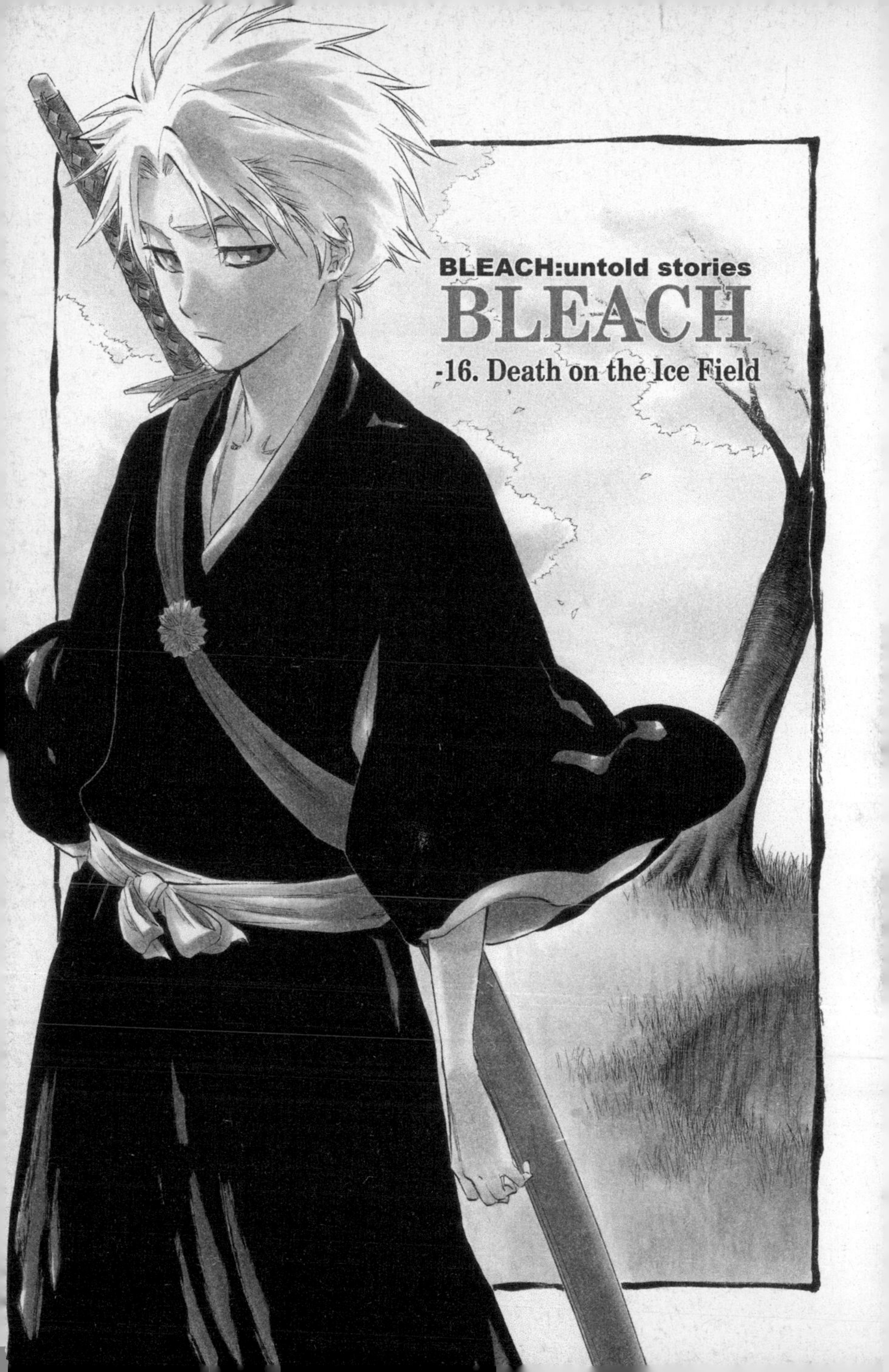
BLEACH:untold stories
BLEACH
-16. Death on the Ice Field

I DREAM
OF AN ICY
FIELD.

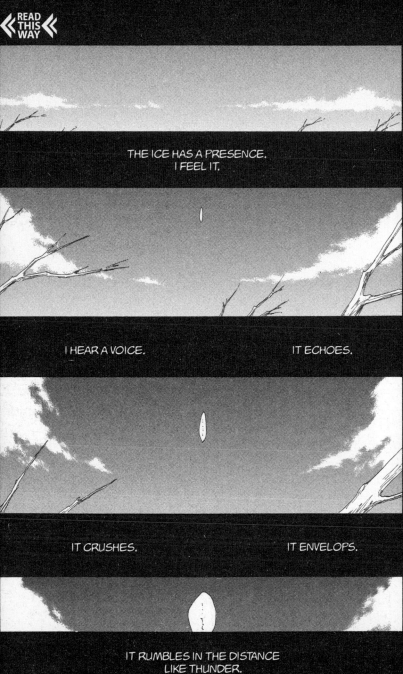

THE ICE HAS A PRESENCE.
I FEEL IT.

I HEAR A VOICE.   IT ECHOES.

IT CRUSHES.   IT ENVELOPS.

IT RUMBLES IN THE DISTANCE
LIKE THUNDER.

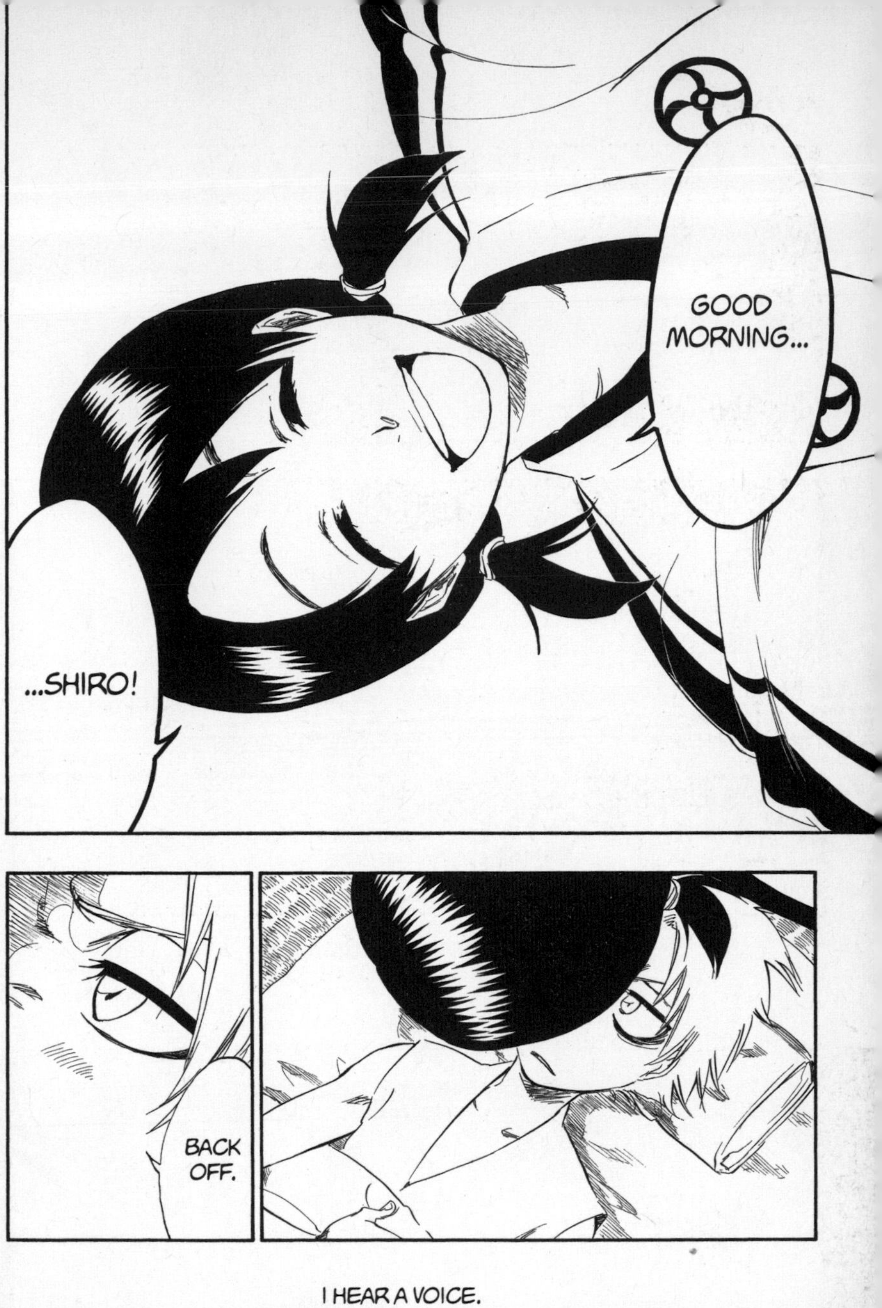
GOOD MORNING...
...SHIRO!
BACK OFF.

I HEAR A VOICE.

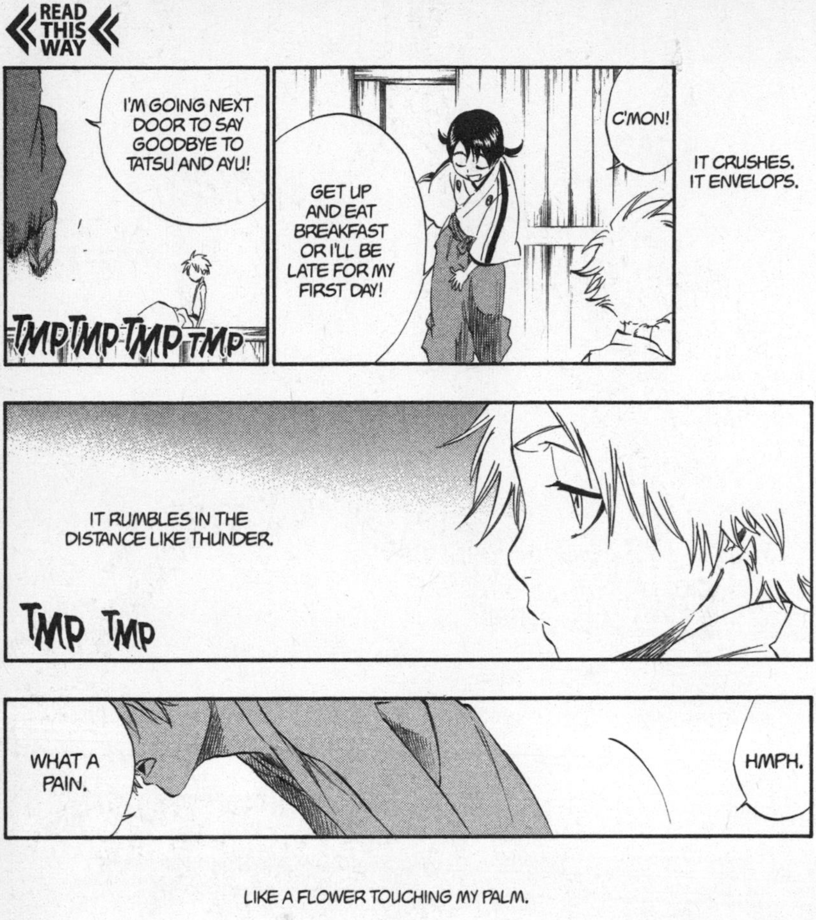
READ THIS WAY
IT CRUSHES. IT ENVELOPS.
C'MON!
GET UP AND EAT BREAKFAST OR I'LL BE LATE FOR MY FIRST DAY!
I'M GOING NEXT DOOR TO SAY GOODBYE TO TATSU AND AYU!
TMP TMP TMP TMP
IT RUMBLES IN THE DISTANCE LIKE THUNDER.
TMP TMP
HMPH.
WHAT A PAIN.
LIKE A FLOWER TOUCHING MY PALM.

bleach—16.

Death on the Ice Field

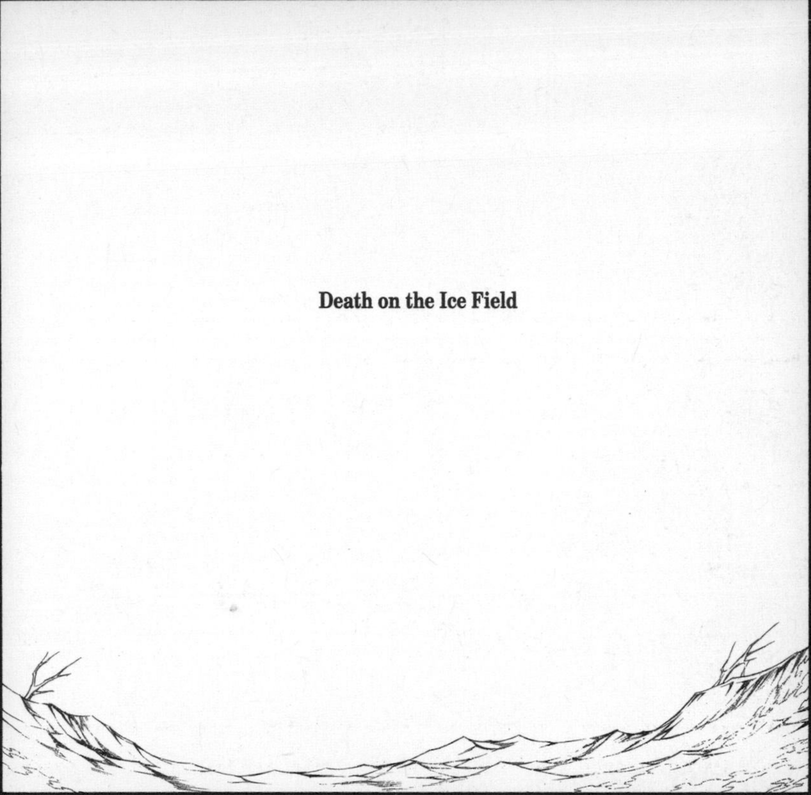

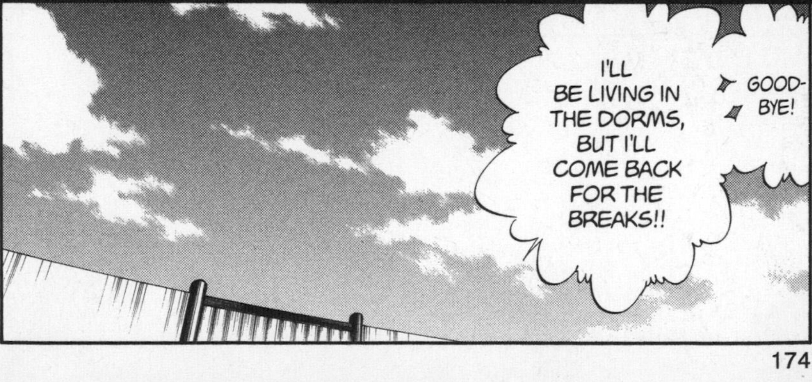
I'LL BE LIVING IN THE DORMS, BUT I'LL COME BACK FOR THE BREAKS!!
GOOD-BYE!

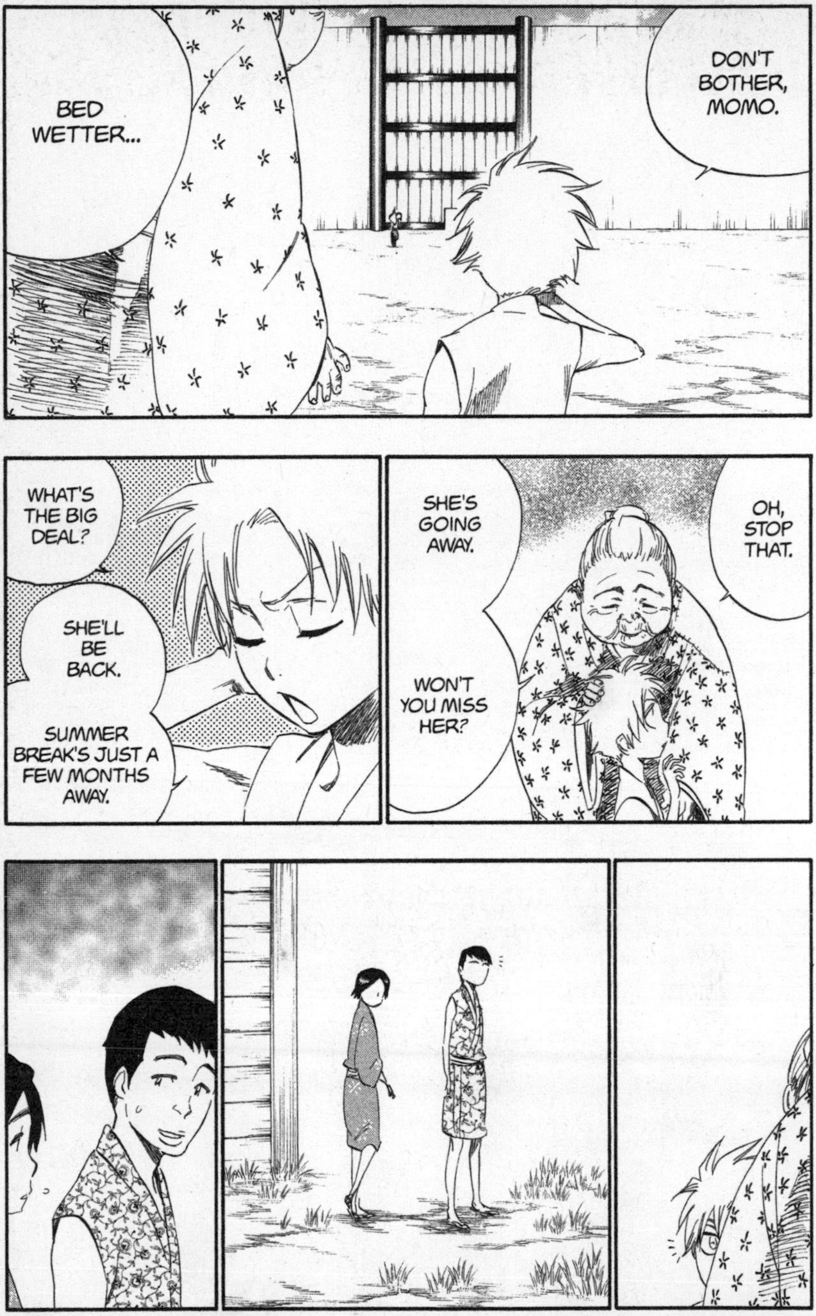
DON'T BOTHER, MOMO.
BED WETTER...
OH, STOP THAT.
SHE'S GOING AWAY.
WON'T YOU MISS HER?
WHAT'S THE BIG DEAL?
SHE'LL BE BACK.
SUMMER BREAK'S JUST A FEW MONTHS AWAY.

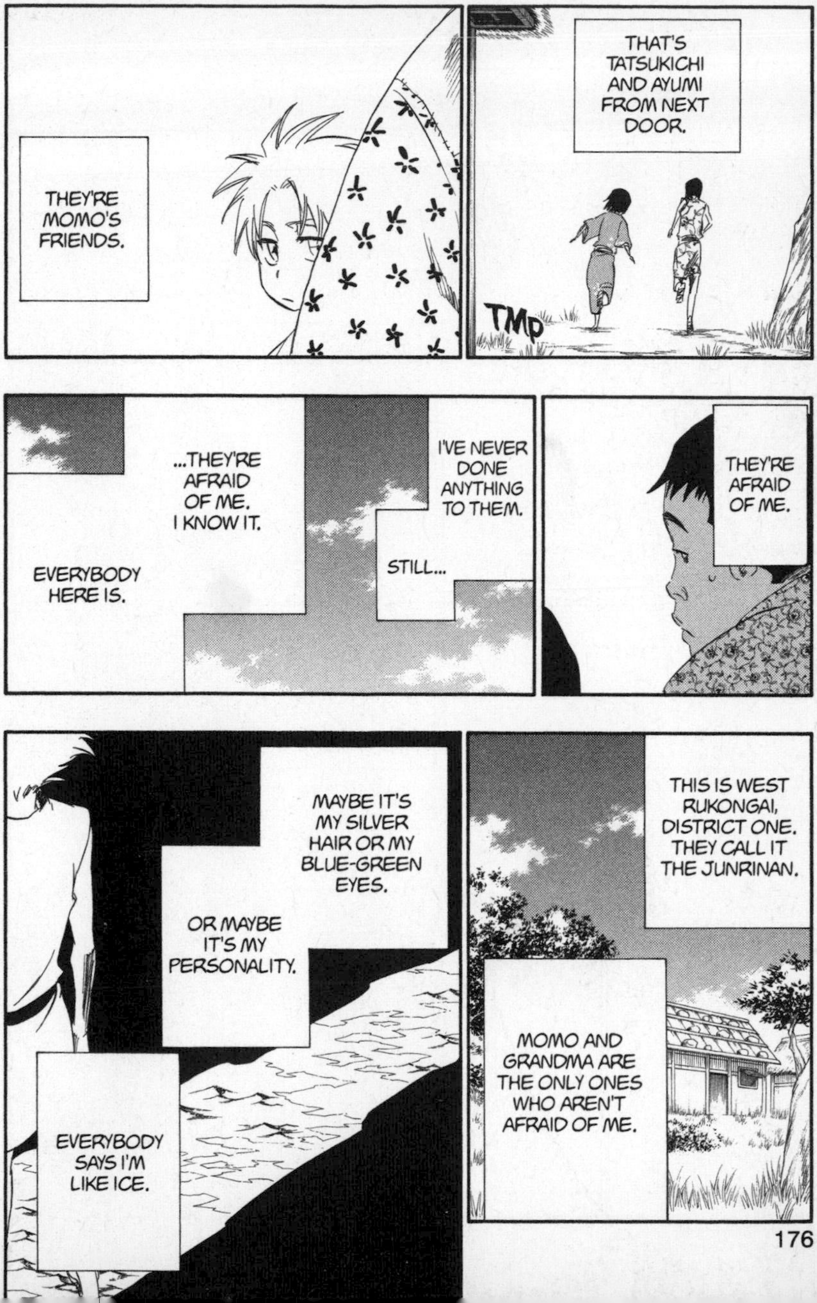
THAT'S TATSUKICHI AND AYUMI FROM NEXT DOOR.
TMP
THEY'RE MOMO'S FRIENDS.
THEY'RE AFRAID OF ME.
I'VE NEVER DONE ANYTHING TO THEM.
STILL...
...THEY'RE AFRAID OF ME. I KNOW IT.
EVERYBODY HERE IS.
THIS IS WEST RUKONGAI, DISTRICT ONE. THEY CALL IT THE JUNRINAN.
MOMO AND GRANDMA ARE THE ONLY ONES WHO AREN'T AFRAID OF ME.
MAYBE IT'S MY SILVER HAIR OR MY BLUE-GREEN EYES.
OR MAYBE IT'S MY PERSONALITY.
EVERYBODY SAYS I'M LIKE ICE.

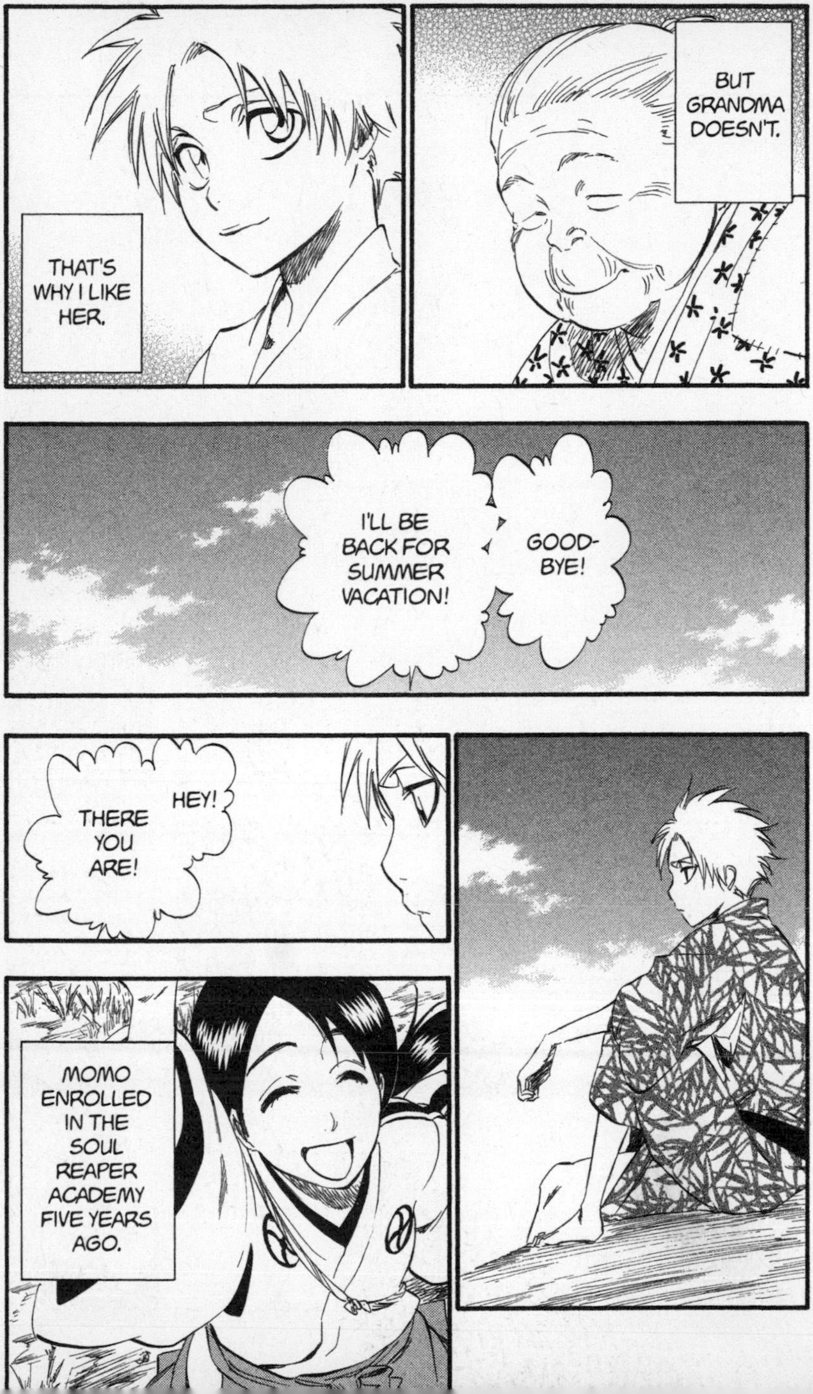
BUT GRANDMA DOESN'T.
THAT'S WHY I LIKE HER.
GOOD-BYE!
I'LL BE BACK FOR SUMMER VACATION!
HEY! THERE YOU ARE!
MOMO ENROLLED IN THE SOUL REAPER ACADEMY FIVE YEARS AGO.

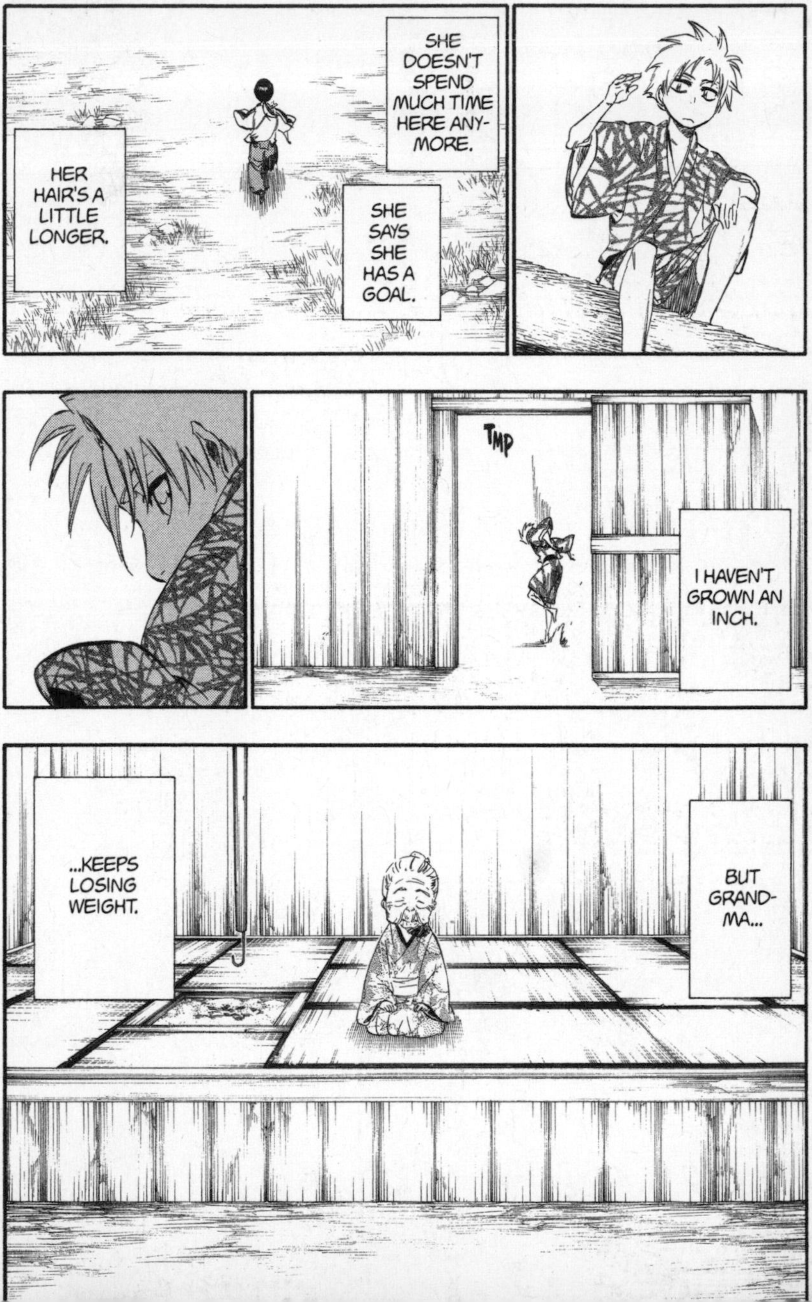
SHE DOESN'T SPEND MUCH TIME HERE ANY-MORE.
SHE SAYS SHE HAS A GOAL.
HER HAIR'S A LITTLE LONGER.
TMP
I HAVEN'T GROWN AN INCH.
BUT GRAND-MA...
...KEEPS LOSING WEIGHT.

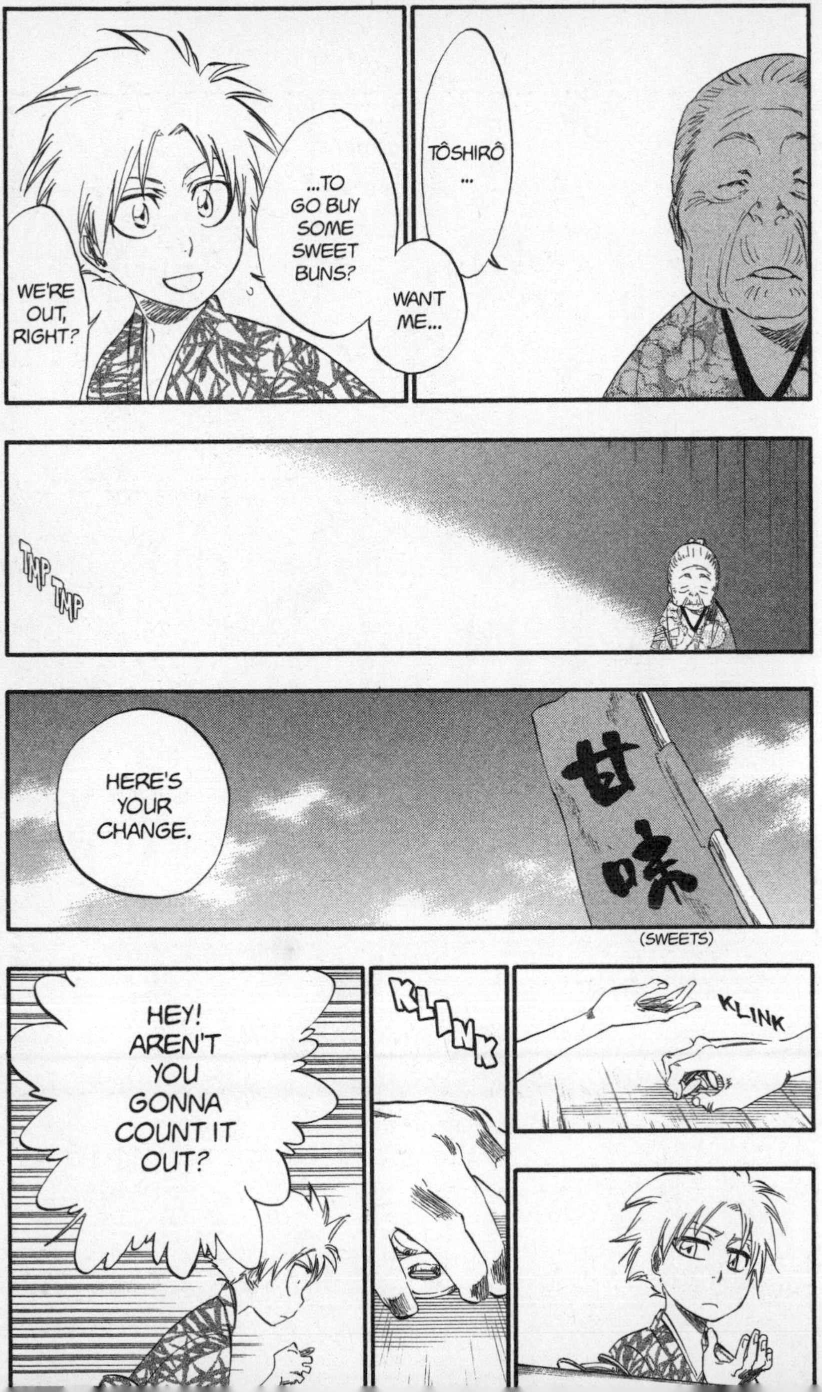
TÔSHIRÔ ...
WANT ME...
...TO GO BUY SOME SWEET BUNS?
WE'RE OUT, RIGHT?
TMP TMP
HERE'S YOUR CHANGE.
甘味
(SWEETS)
KLINK
KLINK
HEY! AREN'T YOU GONNA COUNT IT OUT?

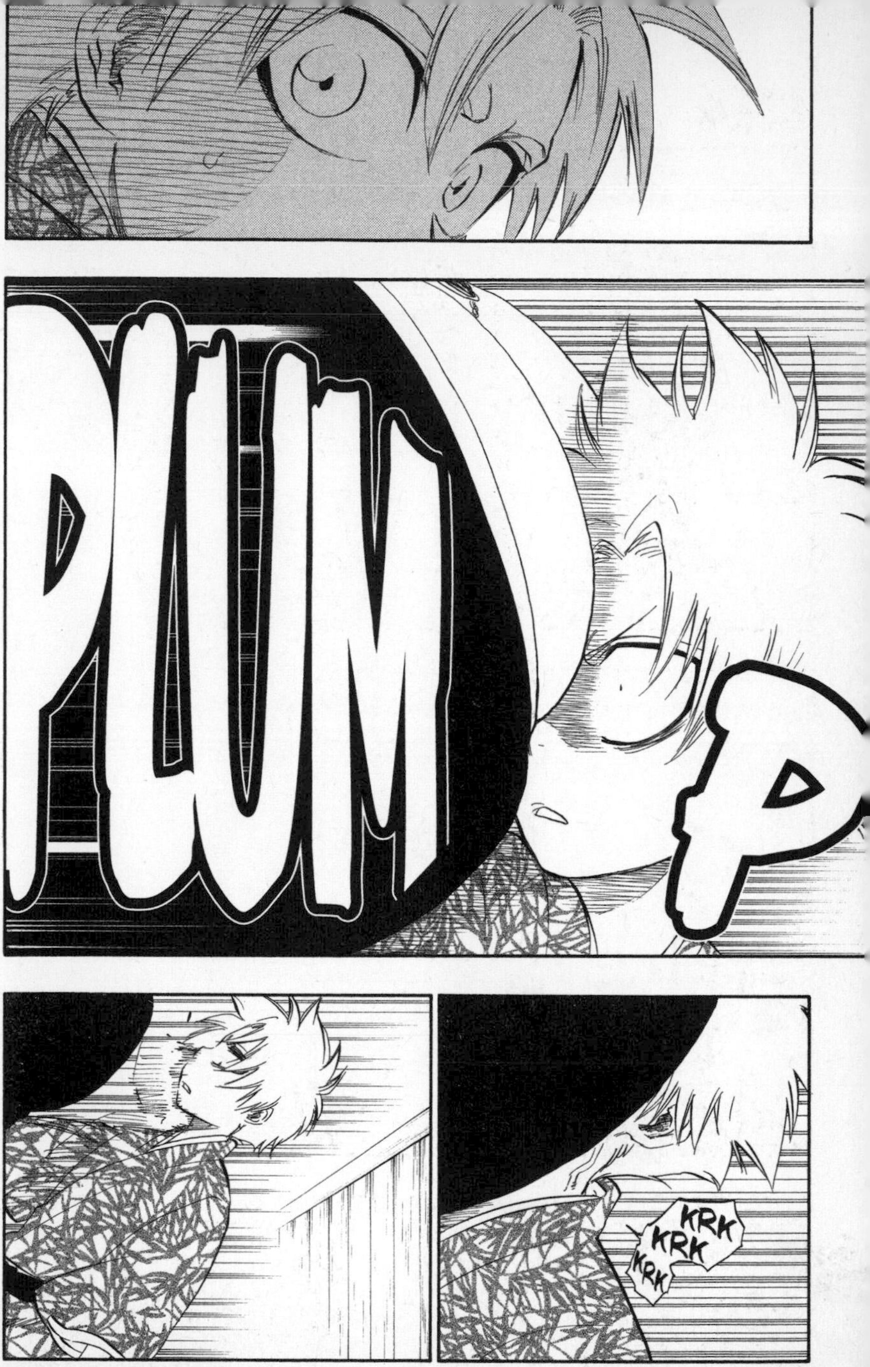
PLUMP
KRK
KRK
KRK

READ THIS WAY

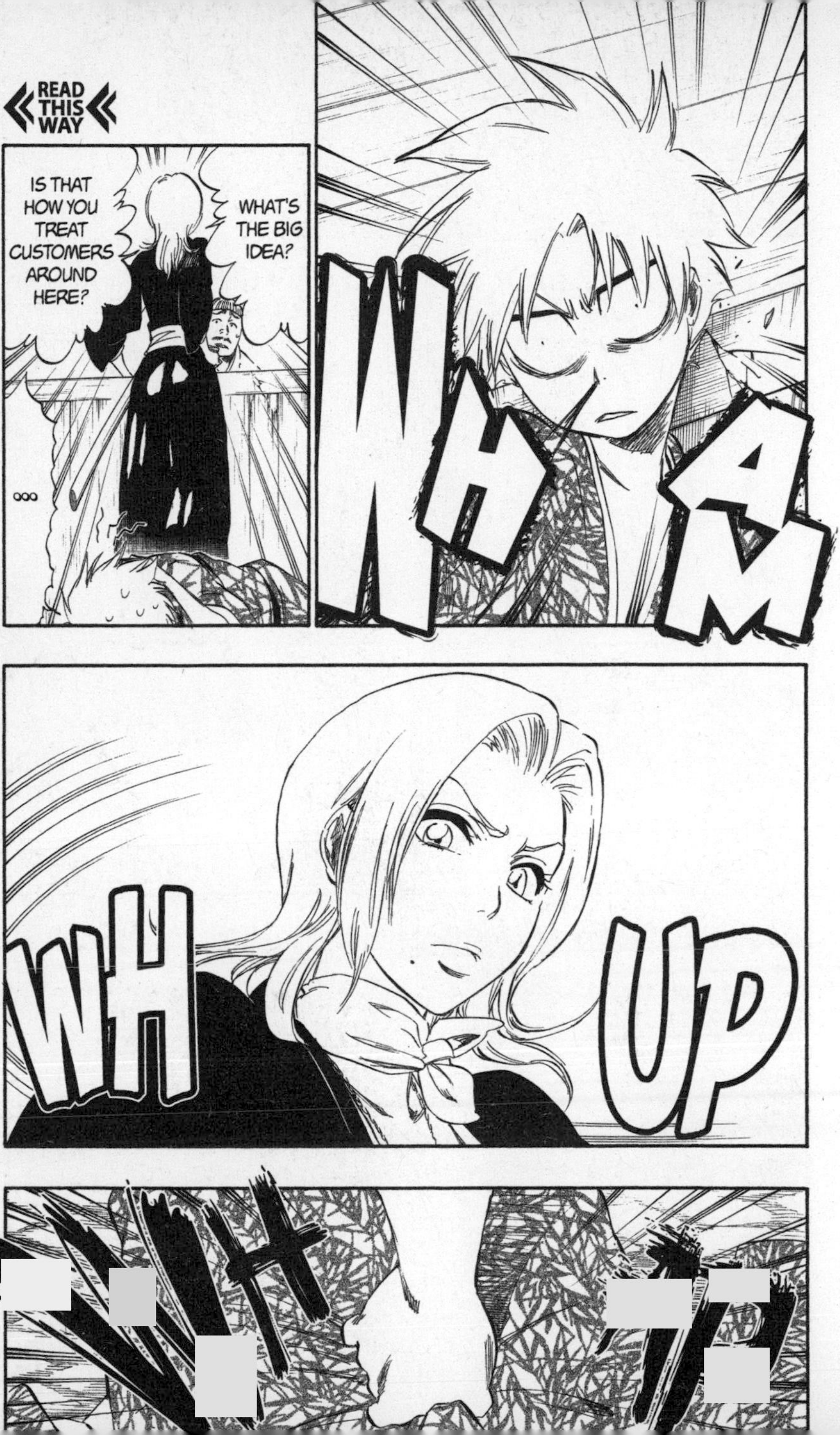
WHAM
WHAT'S THE BIG IDEA?
IS THAT HOW YOU TREAT CUSTOMERS AROUND HERE?
...
WHUP

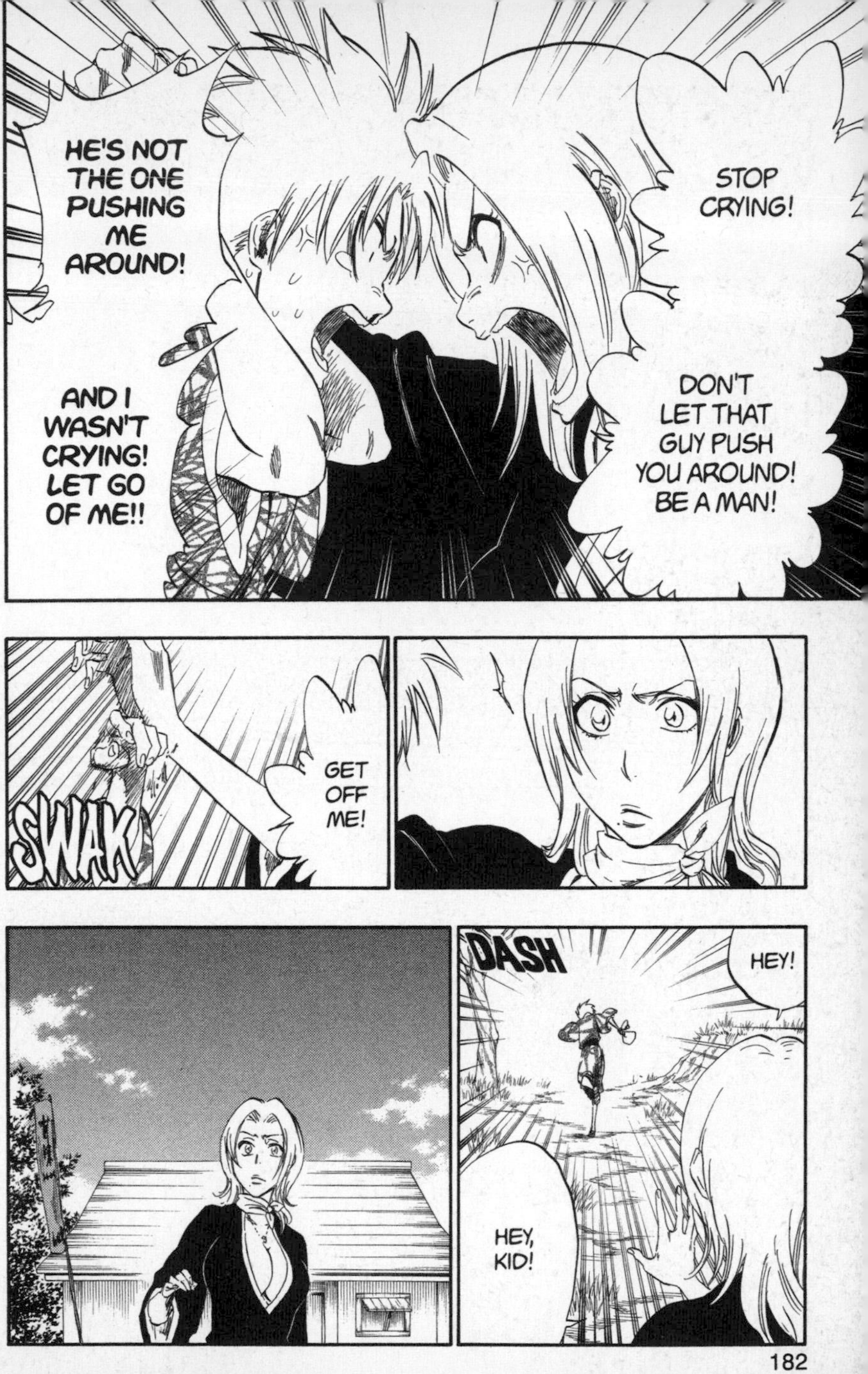
STOP CRYING!
DON'T LET THAT GUY PUSH YOU AROUND! BE A MAN!
HE'S NOT THE ONE PUSHING ME AROUND!
AND I WASN'T CRYING! LET GO OF ME!!
GET OFF ME!
SWAK
DASH
HEY!
HEY, KID!

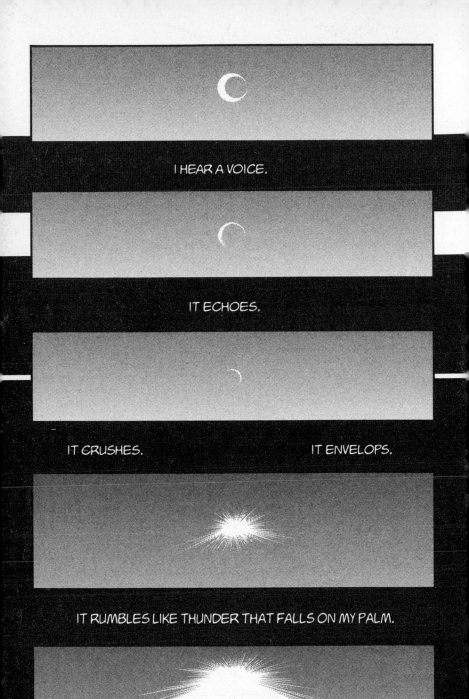

I HEAR A VOICE.

IT ECHOES.

IT CRUSHES.   IT ENVELOPS.

IT RUMBLES LIKE THUNDER THAT FALLS ON MY PALM.

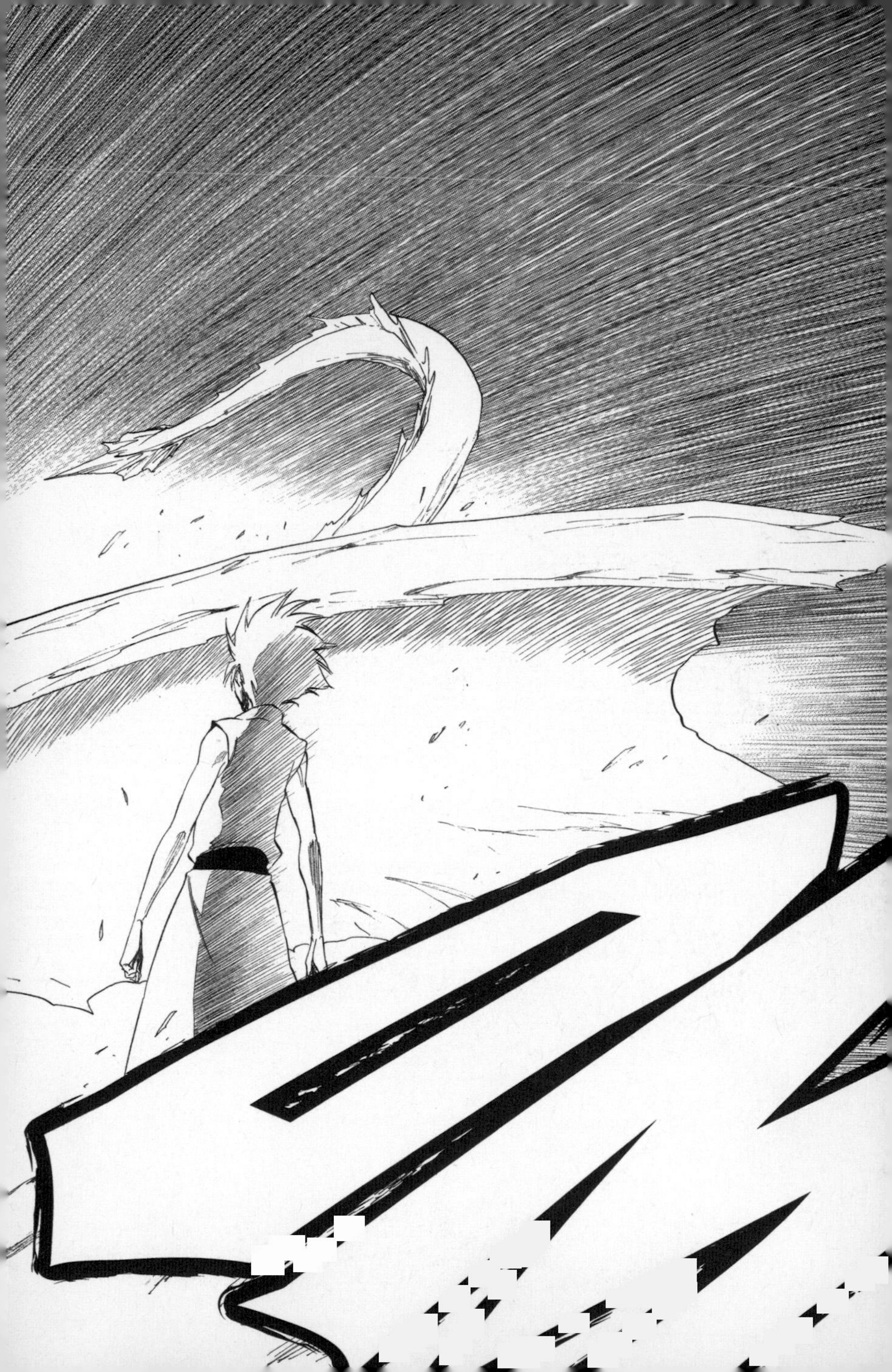

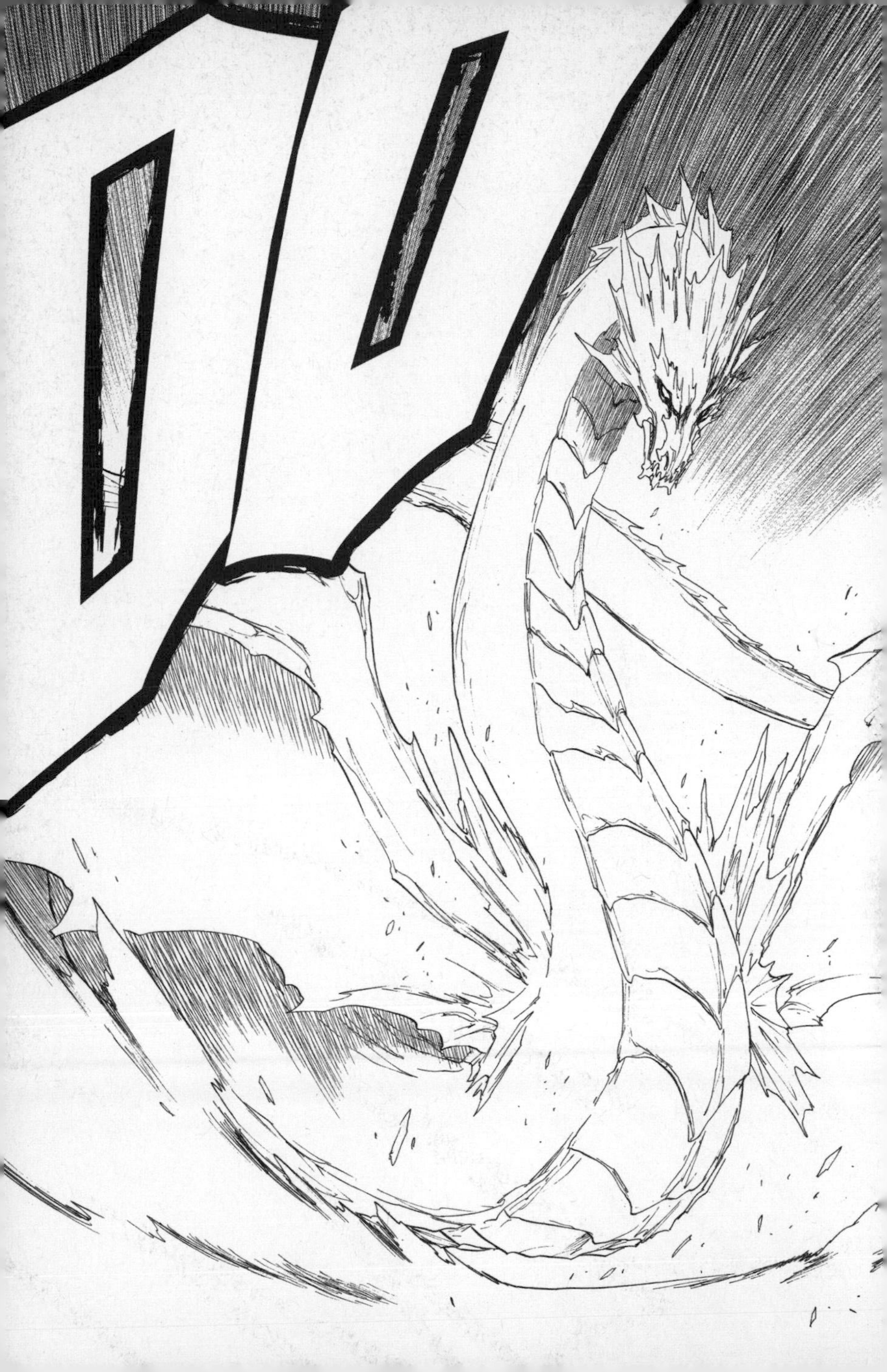

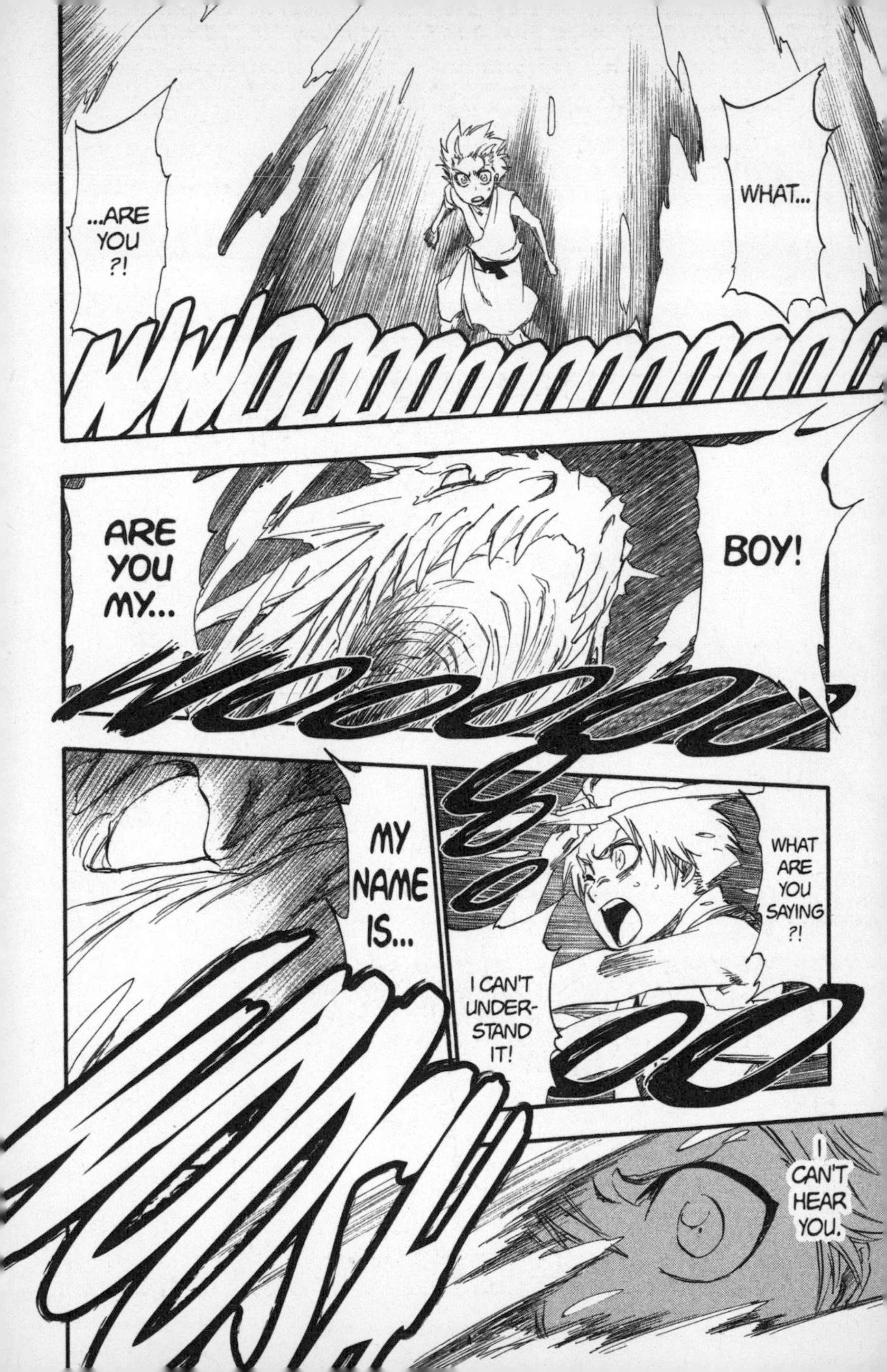
WHAT...
...ARE YOU ?!
BOY!
ARE YOU MY...
WHAT ARE YOU SAYING ?!
I CAN'T UNDER-STAND IT!
MY NAME IS...
I CAN'T HEAR YOU.

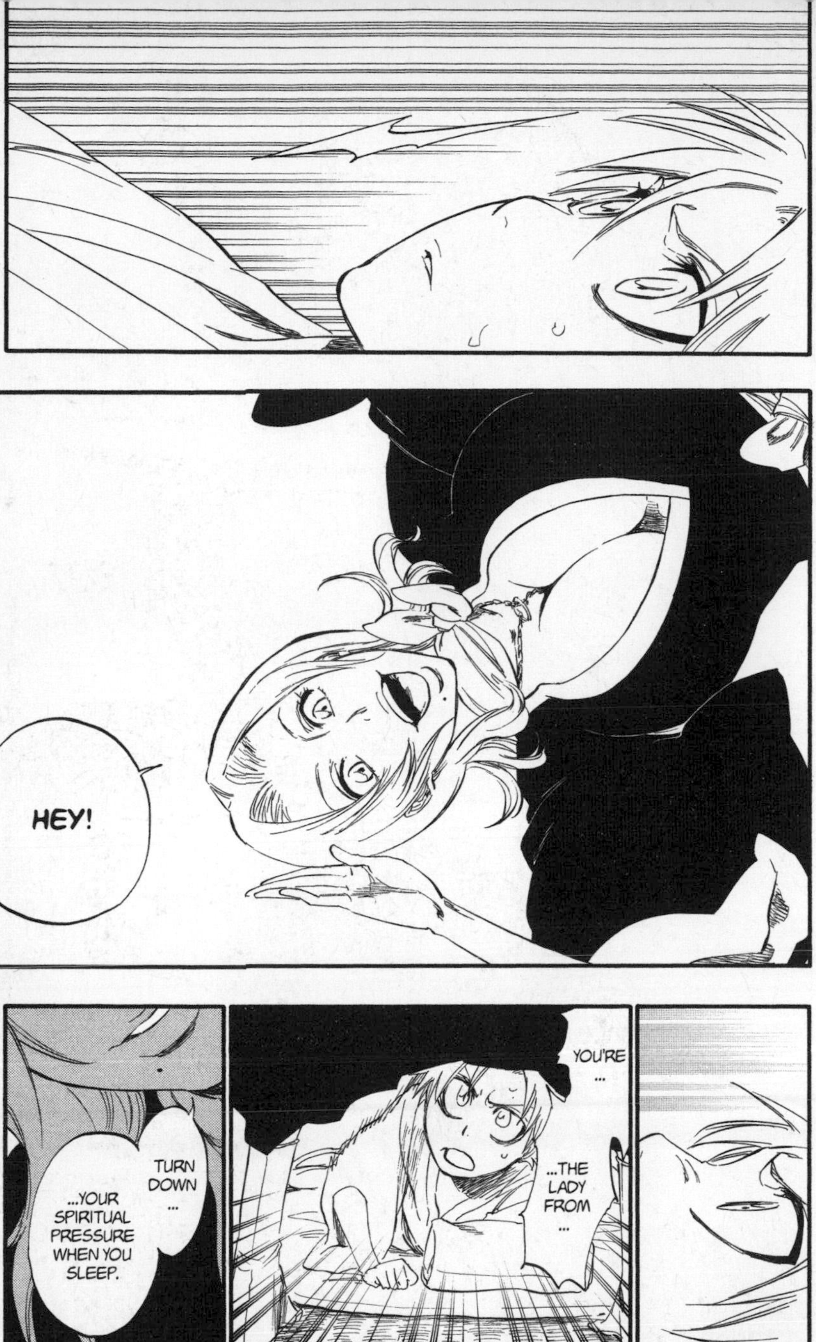
HEY!
YOU'RE ...
...THE LADY FROM ...
TURN DOWN ...
...YOUR SPIRITUAL PRESSURE WHEN YOU SLEEP.

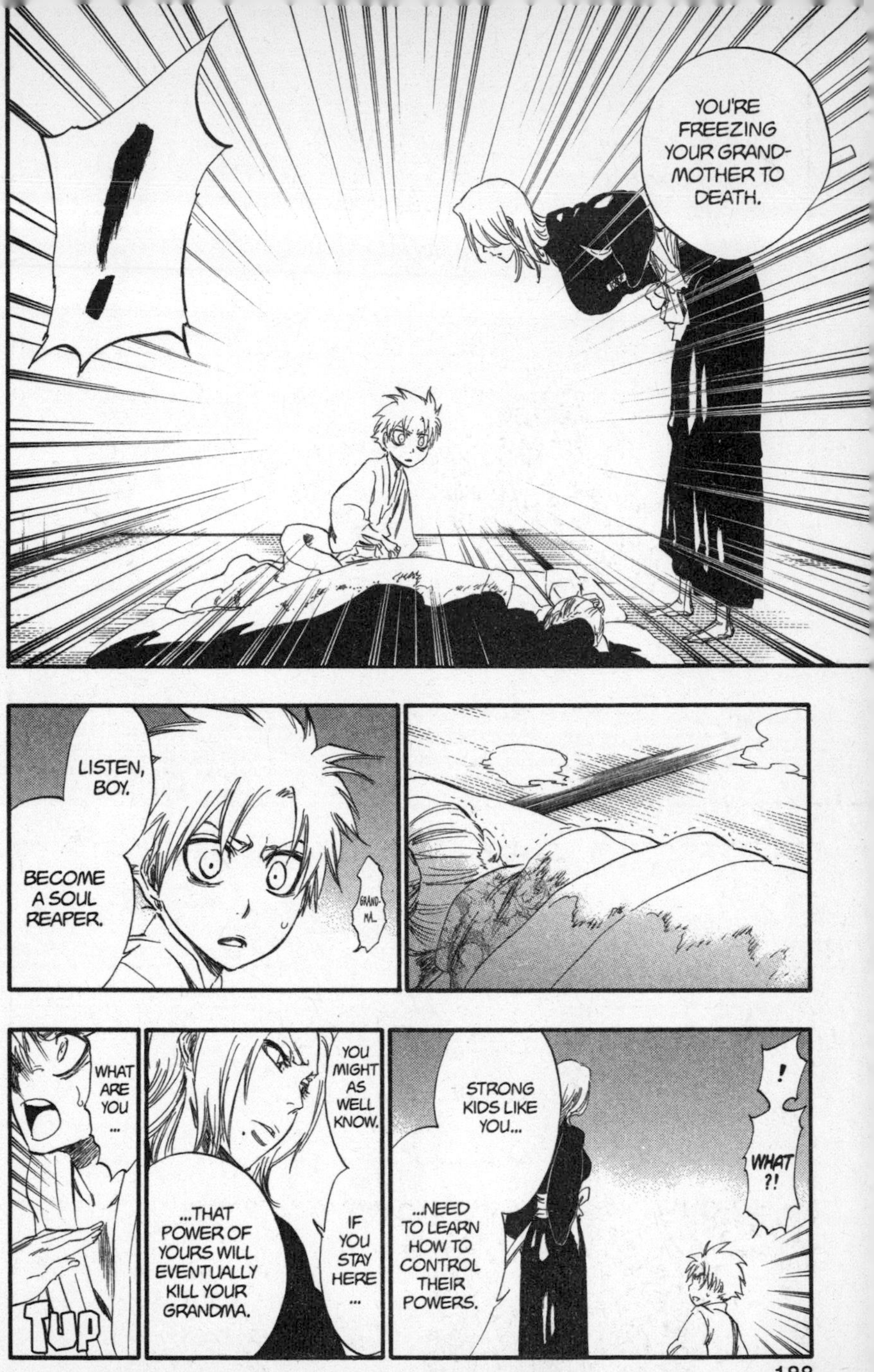
YOU'RE FREEZING YOUR GRAND-MOTHER TO DEATH.
!
GRAND-MA.
LISTEN, BOY.
BECOME A SOUL REAPER.
!
WHAT ?!
STRONG KIDS LIKE YOU...
...NEED TO LEARN HOW TO CONTROL THEIR POWERS.
YOU MIGHT AS WELL KNOW.
IF YOU STAY HERE ...
...THAT POWER OF YOURS WILL EVENTUALLY KILL YOUR GRANDMA.
WHAT ARE YOU ...
TUP

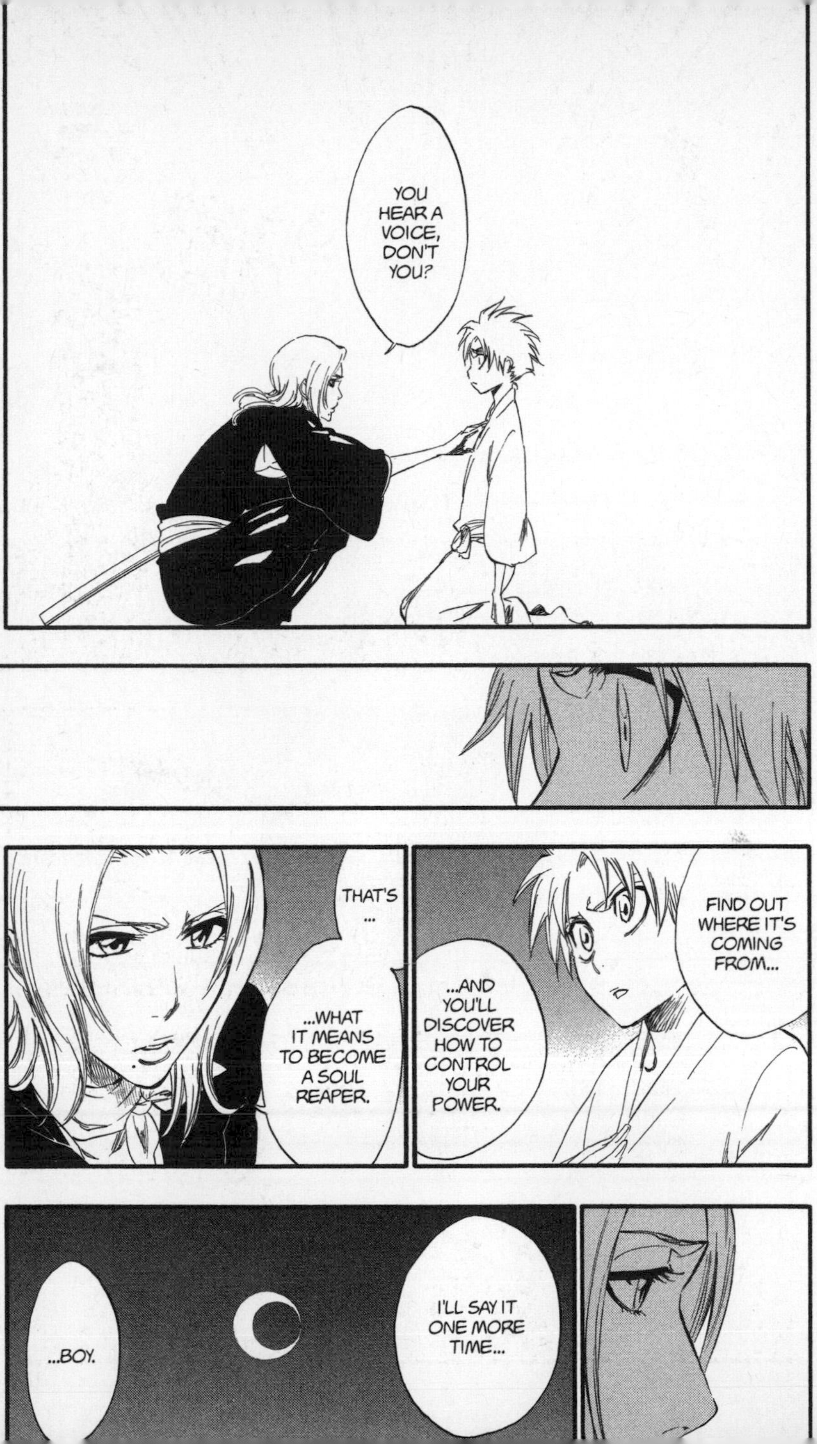
YOU HEAR A VOICE, DON'T YOU?
FIND OUT WHERE IT'S COMING FROM...
...AND YOU'LL DISCOVER HOW TO CONTROL YOUR POWER.
THAT'S ...
...WHAT IT MEANS TO BECOME A SOUL REAPER.
I'LL SAY IT ONE MORE TIME...
...BOY.

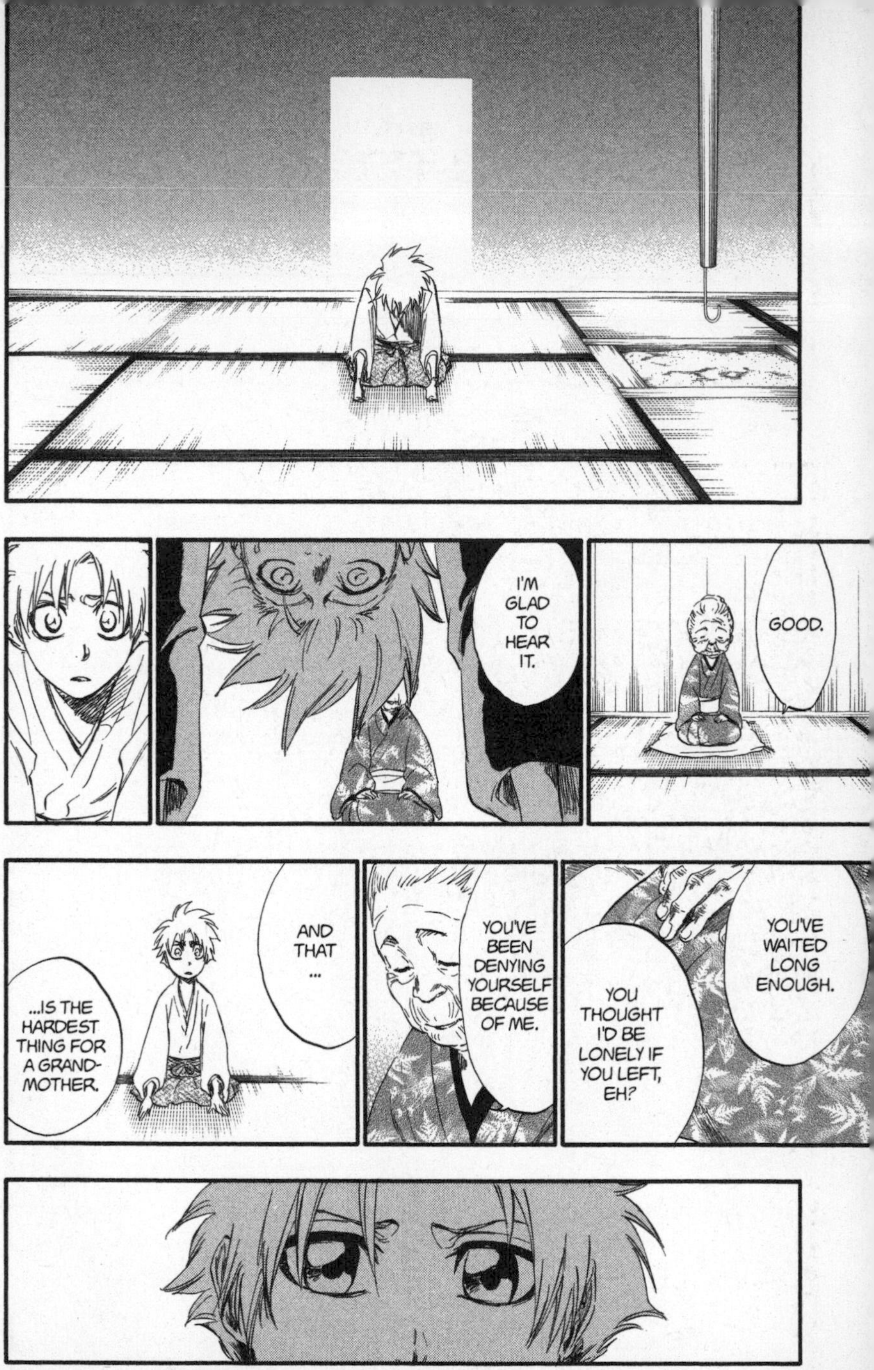
GOOD.
I'M GLAD TO HEAR IT.
YOU'VE WAITED LONG ENOUGH.
YOU THOUGHT I'D BE LONELY IF YOU LEFT, EH?
YOU'VE BEEN DENYING YOURSELF BECAUSE OF ME.
AND THAT...
...IS THE HARDEST THING FOR A GRAND-MOTHER.

I HEAR A VOICE.

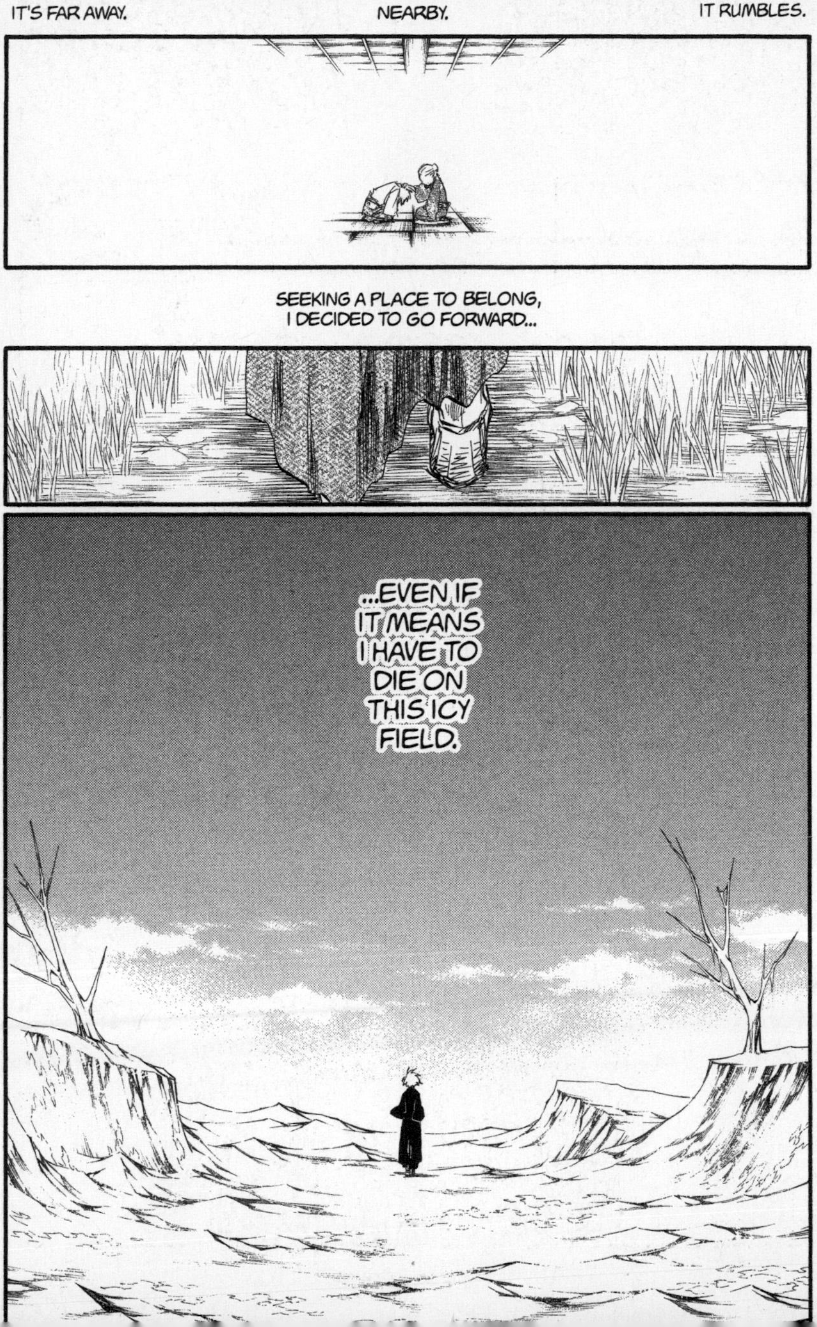
IT RUMBLES.
NEARBY.
IT'S FAR AWAY.
SEEKING A PLACE TO BELONG, I DECIDED TO GO FORWARD...
...EVEN IF IT MEANS I HAVE TO DIE ON THIS ICY FIELD.

Next Volume Preview

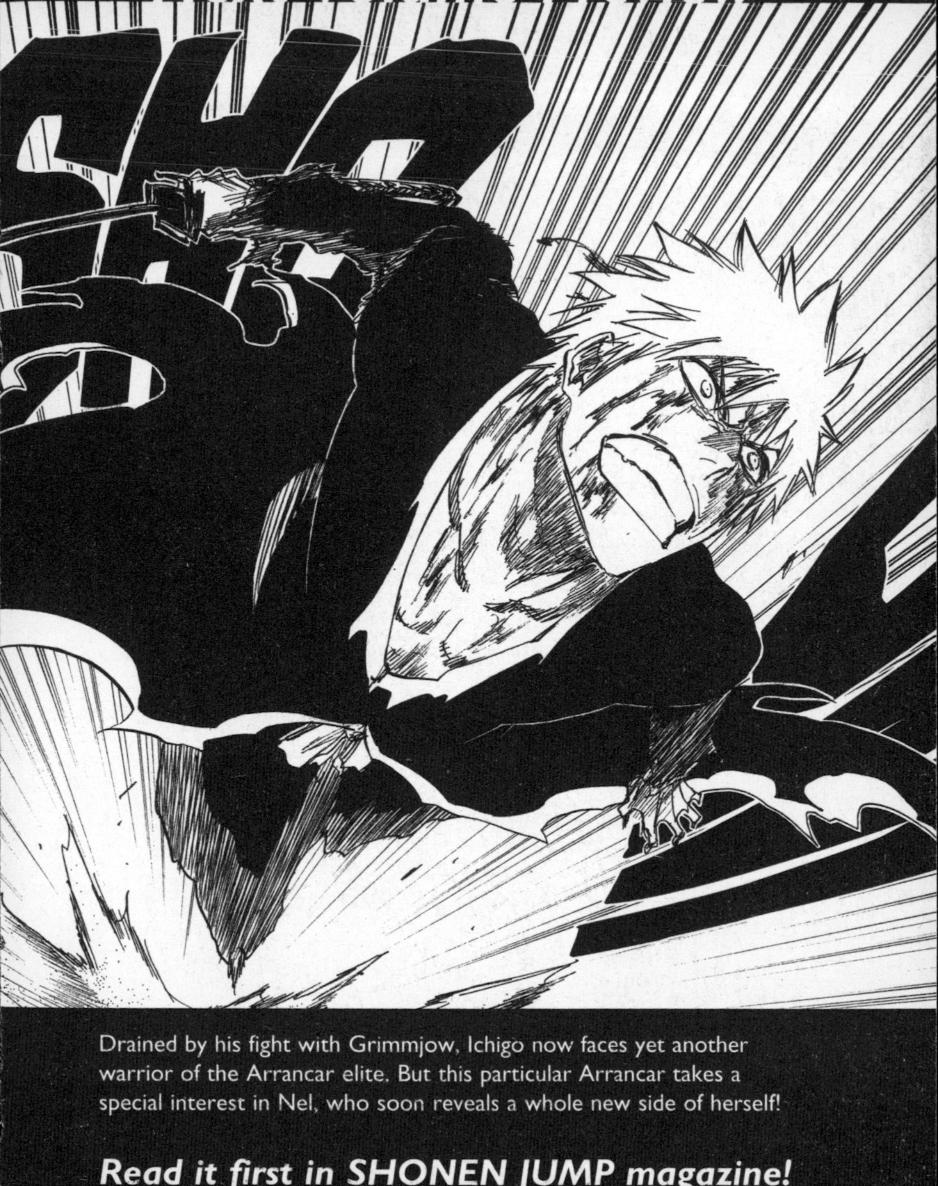

Drained by his fight with Grimmjow, Ichigo now faces yet another warrior of the Arrancar elite. But this particular Arrancar takes a special interest in Nel, who soon reveals a whole new side of herself!

Read it first in SHONEN JUMP magazine!

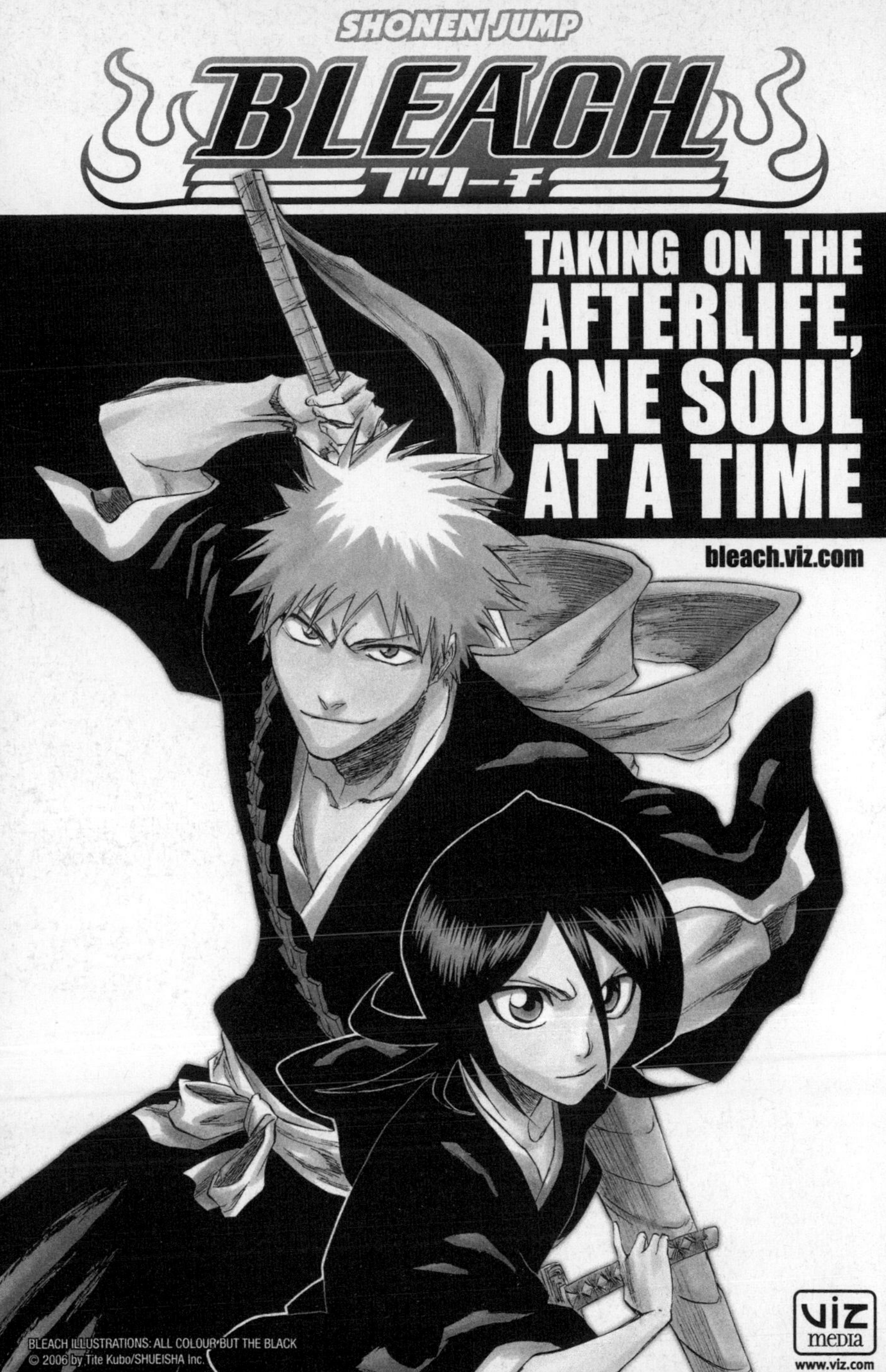
SHONEN JUMP
BLEACH
ブリーチ
TAKING ON THE AFTERLIFE, ONE SOUL AT A TIME
bleach.viz.com
BLEACH ILLUSTRATIONS: ALL COLOUR BUT THE BLACK
© 2006 by Tite Kubo/SHUEISHA Inc.
viz media
www.viz.com

SEE INTO THE SOUL
OF *BLEACH*
WITH THE MANGA,
PROFILES, AND ART BOOKS

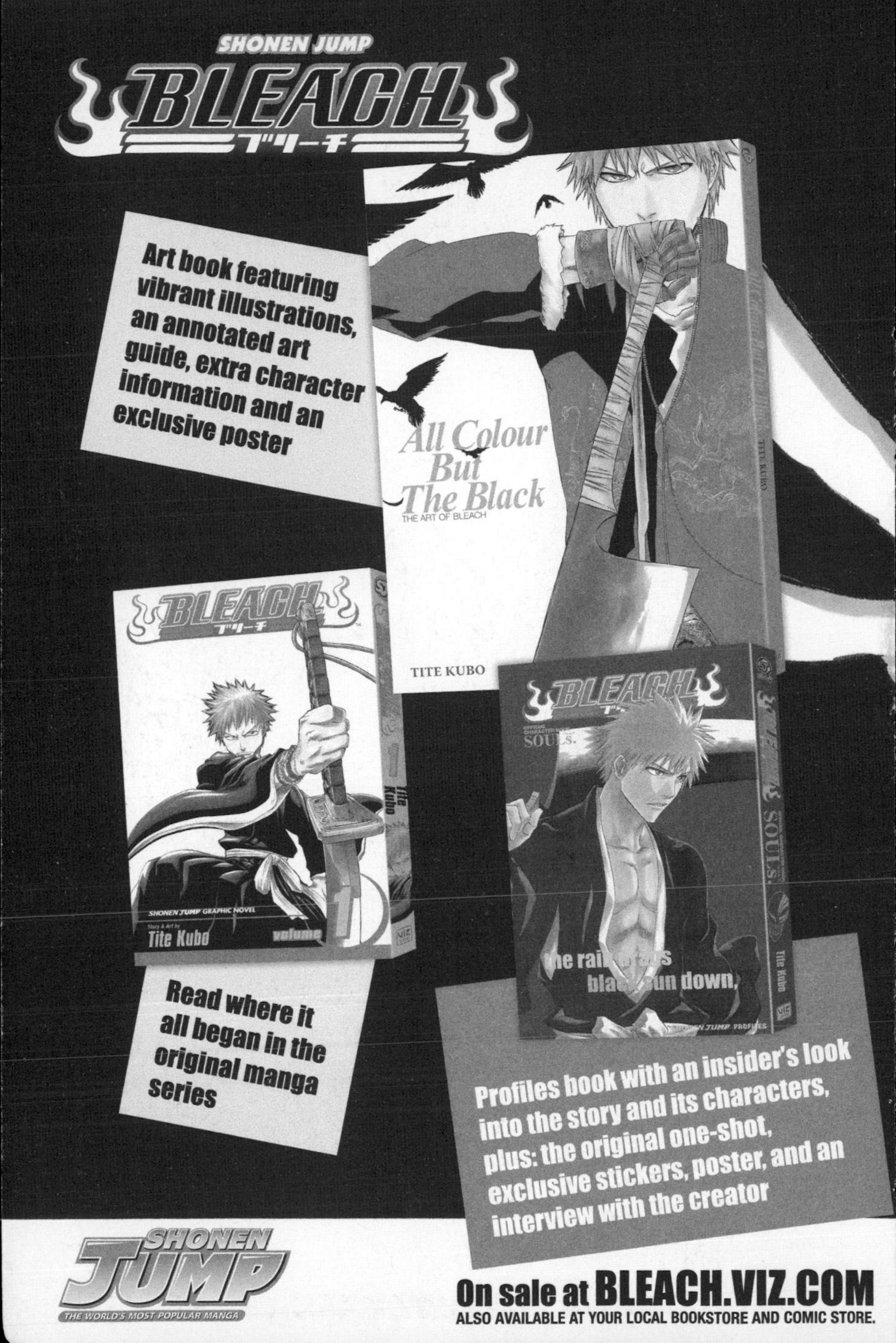
SHONEN JUMP
BLEACH
ブリーチ
Art book featuring vibrant illustrations, an annotated art guide, extra character information and an exclusive poster
All Colour But The Black
THE ART OF BLEACH
TITE KUBO
BLEACH
ブリーチ
SHONEN JUMP GRAPHIC NOVEL
Story & Art by
Tite Kubo
volume 1
Read where it all began in the original manga series
BLEACH
SOULS.
Profiles book with an insider's look into the story and its characters, plus: the original one-shot, exclusive stickers, poster, and an interview with the creator
SHONEN JUMP
THE WORLD'S MOST POPULAR MANGA
On sale at BLEACH.VIZ.COM
ALSO AVAILABLE AT YOUR LOCAL BOOKSTORE AND COMIC STORE.